A LITTLE ORIGINAL SIN

DISCARDED

From Nashville Public Library

D0108988

Property of
The Public Library of Nashville and Davidson County
225 Polk Ave., Nashville, Tn. 37203

Also by Millicent Dillon

A LITTLE ORIGINAL SIN

The Life and Work of

Jane Bowles

MILLICENT DILLON

UNIVERSITY OF CALIFORNIA PRESS

Berkeley   Los Angeles   London

University of California Press
Berkeley and Los Angeles, California

University of California Press, Ltd.
London, England

A Little Original Sin was originally published in hardcover by Holt,
Rinehart and Winston in 1981 and in paperback by Owl
Books in 1982 and Anchor Books in 1990.
The California edition is published by arrangement with the author.

First California Paperback Printing 1998

Grateful acknowledgment is made for the following:
Excerpts from Staying on Alone: Letters of Alice B. Toklas
© *1973 by Liveright Publishing Co.*
Excerpts from Dear Sammy: Letters from Gertrude Stein and Alice B. Toklas
© *1977 Houghton Mifflin.*
Excerpts from a hitherto unpublished letter of Alice B. Toklas to Paul Bowles
© *by William Naughton and Arthur Davies. By permission of Edward M. Burns*
for the estate of Alice B. Toklas.
Excerpts from Feminine Wiles © *1976 by Paul Bowles. This material was*
first printed by the Black Sparrow Press and is reprinted here with permission.
Excerpts from Without Stopping © *1976 by Paul Bowles. This material was first*
printed by G. P. Putnam's Sons and is reprinted here with permission.
Excerpts from The Collected Works of Jane Bowles, *copyright* © *1966*
by Jane Bowles, reprinted by permission of Farrar, Straus and Giroux, Inc.
Excerpts from "Going to Massachussetts," *copyright* © *1977 by Paul*
Bowles. First published in Antaeus. *From* My Sister's Hand in Mine,
an expanded edition of The Collected Works of Jane Bowles, *published*
by The Ecco Press and reprinted by permission.

10   9   8   7   6   5   4   3   2   1

Library of Congress Cataloging-in-Publication Data

Dillon, Millicent.
    A little original sin : the life and work of Jane Bowles /
Millicent Dillon.
        p.   cm.
    Originally published: New York : Holt, Rinehart and Winston, 1981.
    Includes bibliographical references and index.
    ISBN 0-520-21193-6 (pbk. : alk. paper)
    1. Bowles, Jane Auer, 1917–1973—Biography.   2. Women authors,
American—20th century—Biography.   3. Americans—Morocco—
Biography.   I. Title.
PS3503.0837Z63   1998
818'.5209—dc21
    [B]   97-33074
                                                                              CIP

ISBN 0-520-21193-6
Copyright © 1981 by Millicent Dillon

All rights reserved
Printed in the United States of America

TO MY MOTHER,
CLAIRE MILLMAN GERSON

CONTENTS

Illustrations appear after pages 64, 200, and 316.

ACKNOWLEDGMENTS

AMONG ALL THOSE WHO HAVE BEEN HELPFUL TO ME IN THE PREPARATION OF THIS book, I am particularly grateful to Karl Bissinger, Eleanor de Breceda, Ruth Fainlight, Isabelle Gerofi, Yvonne Gerofi, Katharine Hamill, David Herbert, Natasha von Hoershelman, Miriam Levy, Dione Lewis, Martha Ruspoli, Gordon Sager, Robert Saltzer, Lawrence Stewart, Virginia Sorensen Waugh, and Alec Waugh; and to the following: Judith Anderson, Joaquín Andreas, Carol Ardman, Jane Bavelas, Charles Beardsley, Roberta Bobba, Elizabeth Bohning, Abdelouahaid Boulaich, Andreas Brown, Xenia Cage, Sister María Candelas, Gilberte de Charanteney, Jack Clareman, Florence Codman, Edwin Denby, James Dewson, David Diamond, Frances Dixon, Andrew Drummond, Marjorie Eaton, Luis Egger, Robert Fizdale, Jack Frick, Leonore Gershwin, Arthur Gold, Morris Golde, Carla Grissmann, Maurice Grosser, Peggy Guggenheim, Daniel Halpern, Rex Henry, Robert Hines, Mike Kahn, Walter Kerr, Janice Kirkley, Bill Koshland, Larbi Layachi, Leo Lerman, Sylvia Marlowe, George McMillan, Jeffrey Miller, Mohammed Mrabet, Natalia Danesi Murray, John Bernard Myers, Elizabeth Ross Noyes, Mimi Orr, Montgomery Orr, Beatrix Pendar, Edouard Roditi, Ned Rorem, Dr. Yvonne Marillier-Roux, Rosamonde Russell, Oliver Smith, Roger Stevens, Pat Strachan, Mohammed Temsamany, Virgil Thomson, Colby Walworth, Christopher Wanklyn, Wendell Wilcox, Tennessee Williams, Audrey Wood, Ahmed Yacoubi, and Ira Yeager.

I have received invaluable help from the following institutions: the Humanities Research Center at the University of Texas at Austin (in particular from Ellen Dunlap), the American Music Center (from Frances B. Bishop), the Hedgerow Theater (from Gail Cohen), the Stoneleigh-Burnham School, The University of Michigan Bentley Historical Library, the Alumni Association of the University of Michigan, the Mugar Memorial Library at Boston University, and the Beinicke Library and the Music Library at Yale University.

I am grateful for assistance with medical material to Dr. Thomas Gonda and to Dr. C. B. T. Adams, Dr. Denis Baylor, Dr. Harold Edwards, Dr. I. E. J. McLauchlan, Dr. Antonio de Linares Pezzi, and Dr. P. D. Trevor-Roper.

I thank the following publishers for permission to quote from these works: Ecco Press, *My Sister's Hand in Mine* (reprinted by arrangement with Farrar, Straus and Giroux, publishers of *The Collected Works of Jane Bowles*); Black Sparrow Press, *Feminine*

Wiles; New Directions, *The Sheltering Sky*; Random House, *The Delicate Prey and Other Stories*; G. P. Putnam's Sons, *Without Stopping*.

I thank the estates of Libby Holman, Carson McCullers, Hal Vursell, and Alice B. Toklas for permission to quote from unpublished letters.

I am grateful to the National Endowment for the Humanities, who awarded me a fellowship for independent study and research in 1977.

I want to thank the following for their support and encouragement: William Abrahams, Bob Beyers, Freda and Martin Birnbaum, Joan Cooke, Donald Davie, Maxine Groffsky, Fran McCullough, Will Patterson, Peter Pesic, Bob Rosenzweig, Bernie and Edith Shoor, Judy Squier, Peter Stansky, Ayse Whitney, Alison Wilson, and my daughters, Janna Lesser and Wendy Lesser.

And to Paul Bowles, without whom there would have been no book—or certainly not this book—my affectionate gratitude.

A LITTLE ORIGINAL SIN

PROLOGUE .

THE NIGHT BEFORE I WENT TO TANGIER FOR THE FIRST time, I dreamed that I visited the grave of Jane Bowles. The stone that marked it was white under an intense sun in an unclouded sky. Awaking, I didn't know what the dream told me about Jane Bowles or myself. Such is the confusion in the mind of a biographer between one's subject and one's self in dreams.

When I did get to Jane Bowles's grave in Málaga, Spain, it was not as I had dreamed it. The San Miguel Cemetery is on a hill at the edge of the city. A cemetery official led me along a path between walls of graves down a slope to a large open space where the dead were buried in the ground. He hurried between the stones, checking numbers. Then he pointed to an unmarked space.

It was covered with rubble, old flowers from other graves, broken glass, pieces of plastic and paper. Surrounding Jane's plot were graves whose vertical stones were set upon a series of horizontal bases, white stone oblongs. The edges of the lowest pedestals were covered with white tiles.

Though the air was cool and there were some clouds in the sky, the sun was shining intensely. Real and plastic flowers, orange, red, and yellow, gleamed in niches in the walls and before the gravestones on the ground. Near Jane's grave were two cypresses. Around me women in black, relatives of the dead, scrubbed the gravestones with soap and water.

IT WAS JANE BOWLES'S WORK THAT LED ME TO HER LIFE. I HAD NEVER EVEN heard her name until May 1973 when, at the MacDowell Colony, the writer Virginia Sorensen Waugh told me about Jane's fiction. Virginia, who had known Jane in Morocco, told me that she was very ill in a convent hospital in Málaga, cared for by nuns.

As it happened, Jane Bowles was already dead. She died May 4, 1973, although the announcement of her death did not appear in the United States until May 31, when her obituary was published in *The New York Times*. Later that summer I began to read *Two Serious Ladies*, a work that Alan Sillitoe has called a "landmark in Twentieth Century American literature." From the first words, something of what she told, something of what she withheld, her style, and her language touched me as if I'd come upon a world I'd once known but had forgotten. The book is about sex, in some odd way, and about religion, in an even odder way. The notion of time in the work has as much to do with the evasion of time as with time passing. But, if there is a sense of dissolving and repeating, there is also a holding to daily life with great passion. Much later I realized that this narrative method was not only a method—it was the way Jane lived.

Early in 1976 I wrote to Virginia Waugh and through her to Paul Bowles of my interest in writing about Jane and her work. "To my knowledge no one has undertaken a biography. . . . If I can be of any practical use to you with regard to all this, please tell me," he answered.

I began my search for Jane with only a few published facts. I knew that she had been born in New York, that she had gone to a private girls' school for a brief time, that right after meeting Paul she had said to a friend, "He is my enemy." Yet she had married him and had followed him to Morocco. I knew that she had published only a small body of work. At age forty she had had a stroke. It was rumored in the underground press that she had been poisoned by her Arab lover.

Paul gave me the names of five people who had known Jane well in the United States. I met these five and they in turn led to others, who led to still others. Through a series of coincidences I found an unpublished notebook of Jane's, an autograph album that Jane had signed as a child, a portrait of her painted when she was thirty, and many photographs.

These are the kinds of coincidences that a biographer hopes for and welcomes. There were also, however, coincidences of another order that began to manifest themselves as I learned about Jane's early life: Jane's mother's name was Claire, as is mine. Her maternal grandfather's name was Louis, as was mine. She lived in Woodmere, Long Island, from 1927 to 1930. I lived in Woodmere, across the tracks, in 1929 and 1930. At thirteen, after her father's death, Jane and her mother moved to Manhattan to the very building where my family lived when I was born. Jane broke her right leg in 1931. I broke mine the same year.

But whether the identification with one's subject is imagined or based on coincidence, the biographer must cling to the ideas of separation and commonality—to see what is unique in this given life and to see what is shared, human, common. The writer's task mirrors the reader's. We seek to know another's life, knowing that at the same time, through that life we seek knowledge of our own. We look for the meaning of an individual life in a time when the meaning of an individual life has lost much of its force.

It was the grant of a fellowship for independent study and research from the National Endowment for the Humanities in 1977 that made it possible for me to begin work full-time on the biography. I went first to the Humanities Research Center at the University of Texas, where I studied Jane's notebooks and letters. The eighteen notebooks, like the letters—mainly to Paul—were undated. The notebooks were nearly indecipherable: paragraphs would begin, then would be crossed out; new paragraphs would begin, sometimes in almost identical words; these too would be crossed out. Each notebook contained fragments from what were obviously different works. Even within the fragments one character would suddenly dissolve into another. But as I went over the notebooks, I began to find connections within them and a tie to the life revealed in the letters.

In March 1977 I went to Tangier to talk with Paul Bowles. I went with some trepidation, with a fear of interfering, of stirring up old wounds. I knew from the letters that Paul and Jane had had an idiosyncratic marriage, with frequently separate sexual lives yet a deep devotion. On that first visit of six weeks, Paul and I talked each day for three to four hours. He wanted a book done that would do justice to Jane's complexity, not one that would show her in some pretended perfection. I think the first two times Paul saw me he became ill. He had to go back through years of anguish to give me the information I needed. He is a private man, yet to make certain things about Jane comprehensible to me, he had to speak of himself. My theoretical urgings, my attempt to find a continuity and theme in Jane's life and in her work must have gone against his grain. Like Jane he considered analysis of himself or his work "yenti" (a word Jane often used, derived from the Yiddish word *yenta*, a gossip or a woman of low origins). But still he worked with me each day, with humor and with patience, trying to tell me what he remembered.

I have tried to reconstruct with accuracy the life and the myth of Jane Bowles. To many who knew her well she was the most vital human being—and the most puzzling—they had ever met. To others she was irritating, even maddening, capricious as a child who never grew up. But though she was mysterious, she was also forthcoming, direct, and accessible —giving of herself, while at the same time intensely private.

Like any biographer of a contemporary figure I have had to face the serious and profoundly disturbing questions of privacy, the privacy of those living and even of those who are dead. A continual struggle is involved in balancing what is necessary in terms of the work and what is necessary in one's obligation to other people. More than curiosity drives one to knowing. More than curiosity must determine the telling. I have set certain boundaries for myself. I have changed names at the request of those who did not want to be identified, mainly in the case of Jane's lovers.

This biography is the record of the intricate interweaving between Jane Bowles's life and her work. I have placed side by side extended excerpts from Jane's letters and her notebooks; I have presented directly the memories of people who knew her well—all in the interest of capturing the many voices of Jane Bowles. For she had in her voice many voices, just as her photographs show the many aspects of her one image.

We do not like to speak of destiny anymore, but in Jane Bowles's life and work there is no avoiding it. From her earliest days as Jane Auer, in a family that does not seem very out of the ordinary, through her father's death and her own adolescent illness, through her marriage, through her move to Morocco, through love affairs that ended, through writing that could never be brought to an end, through an illness that she fought for sixteen years—she saw her own destiny. She kept trying to evade it. She knew her own evasions.

All biographers must believe in the value of the individual life. But there are some lives that are more than themselves. They show, as if they were transparent, the world of their time and place and another timeless world.

Jane Bowles had such a life.

PART ONE

1917 - 1947

To Mill —
~~You~~ asked me to write in
your book
  ~~I~~ ~~can~~ scarcely know how to
begin
    For theres nothing orriginal
abord me
      But a little orriginal ~~Air~~
        Loads of genuine love
          Youre best friend
            me

Overleaf: COURTESY MIRIAM LEVY

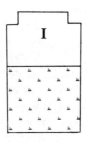

I

SHE WAS, FROM THE BEGINNING, AN ORIGINAL. YET she came to fear the power of her own originality, even as she made light of it. As a child she knew and felt and dreamed what other children did not. The knowledge made her separate and different and she carried it as if it were a burden of her own making. She became the Cassandra of her own existence, turning everything—the knowledge, the feeling, the dreaming —into play and story.

Only one thing remains out of all that play in Jane Bowles's childhood. It is an entry in a friend's autograph album, written in 1929 when Jane was twelve.

> To Mir—
> You asked me to write in youre book
> I scarcely know how to begin
> For there's nothing orriginal about me
> But a little orriginal Sin.
>
> > > Loads of *genuine* love
> > > Youre best friend
> > > Jane

Besides this entry there is left one photograph of Jane of uncertain date, perhaps 1927. She sits upon the steps of her house in Woodmere, Long Island, wearing a riding habit. She is not smiling.

All else is gone, all that one might expect from a middle-class family of the time: pictures of mother holding a child, pictures of mother and father and child together on the steps of the house or before the new Hupmobile, pictures of father and child in bathing suits at the beach; school reports, certificates, mementos of any kind. All personal physical evidence of the family's early life is lost or discarded, as if Jane herself had willed it so by secrecy. For she never spoke of her childhood except to Paul, a few words when they were first married, and in the last years, after she was ill, a phrase or two to others. It was as if in secrecy, like Sadie of her story "Camp Cataract," she sought absolution from the guilt of her origins and her originality.

Still there remains some official evidence of that life: a few facts in departments of records, a few listings in phone books. Then there are the memories of three people who knew Jane in her childhood: a cousin, her own age, who was her rival; a younger cousin; and the "Mir" of the autograph album. And finally there is the work, the fiction, to tell us of the early life. It is not a factual or sequential record, of course. Everything has been transmuted into story. But the felt life of that child who knew and dreamed what others did not is what shapes the work.

Those few facts and the three memories and the substantial shadows of the fiction, taken together, show that the words that survive in the autograph album came to be the theme of Jane's life—if one can speak of a life as having a theme. A little original sin: the story of the imagination as evil.

MARY JANE SHOUR WAS JANE'S FIRST COUSIN: HER MOTHER BIRDIE WAS THE sister of Jane's mother, Claire. Mary Jane was beautiful and popular as a child and was always held up to Jane as a model to imitate. They were rivals, Jane would later tell Paul.

Older than Jane by two weeks, Mary Jane was to marry four times, the first time at seventeen. In 1950, at the age of thirty-three, no longer close to Jane but still caught up in some rivalry with her, she began to write flippant articles on seduction, three pieces in *Esquire* in 1950 and 1951, "Blueprint for a Divorcee: How to Get a Husband," "The Care and Feeding of Millionaires," and "Brush Up on Your Brush-Off" (advice to men on how to get rid of women they're tired of). Sometime in the mid-fifties she committed suicide.

In her papers she left an unfinished fragment about Jane and herself as children in 1927:

> My cousin Jane was the bright one. When the aunts wanted to explain us to strangers, they always said, "Jane is smart and Mary Jane is pretty."
>
> Actually, we never really thought of it that way. I would have gladly changed my all-too-robust build, blue eyes, and wildly curling black hair for Jane's tiny, delicate frame, her slanted brown eyes, and that wonderful tip-tilted nose.
>
> I was even a bit envious of her limp. Jane had no patience with the leg that dragged slightly. She dismissed it with the derisive name of "Crippie" but I privately thought it lent zing to the picture I had made of

her. A sort of Camille–Elizabeth Browning portrait that I clung to absurdly through the years.

Actually, there was little of the romantic about Jane. It was in my breast that the fairy tales about princesses and evil godmothers and incredibly handsome young princes-in-disguise dwelt. Jane would have none of it.

The people in Jane's dreams were . . . earthy . . . and . . . had nothing to do with Jane. In them, there was always some wretched old man with a pipe and Troubles. Sometimes the Trouble took the form of a certain fish the W.O.M. had spent a lifetime trying to lure from its watery home. She wove fanciful tales about the old man and his fish, strange, primly outrageous tales, but never in one of them did he catch his prey.

I'm trying to make you see my cousin as I knew her. A wild, small creature with pixie's eyes and a determinedly unhealthy look; a fey sort of person who works just as hard at her lunacies as the rest of us do trying to keep on the mundane side.

The Jane who wrote that weird book [*Two Serious Ladies*] (the one the family whispers about) was very much in evidence some twenty years ago. When the book was published and people exclaimed "Goodness, what on earth is it all about?" I chortled. It made perfect sense to me. But then, I knew Jane.

The games we played as children had nothing to do with toys. The only props we ever needed were for the paper-doll games. The rest of the time we lived in a world of imagination peopled by a succession of beloved characters. . . .

Perhaps Freud could explain Jane and me. Maybe he'd have better words than "enchanted" to describe our childhood. What the hell, I never said we were nice little girls. I only said we had fun. . . . Jane moved to Woodmere, Long Island, when we were around eleven years old. I was very jealous as I wanted desperately to live in the country and own a dog. Jane had a dog—a Pekinese named Pa-o of whom I was in mortal fear.

Actually all animals have always terrified me . . . but, if Jane had a dog, then I wanted one.

That's the way it was with us. I was the big one, the elder by two weeks, and Jane was the ringleader. I think I loved her more than almost anyone I've ever loved since, and as Jane would say, "That's a strong statement!"

We come from a family of women. Our mothers were two of six sisters, all small and dark, peppery and efficient. Our maternal grandmother was born in Budapest and it was a source of great annoyance to us when The Aunts constantly made asides to each other in Hungarian. . . .

Jane and I are best remembered for the garage incident. The inhabitants of Woodmere and Cedarhurst still shudder when they hear our names.

I don't know to this day who started the thing. My mother blamed Jane and Aunt Claire blamed me. Jane and I swear the idea hit us simultaneously. . . .

It started with a clothesline. We were playing on a neighbor's lawn trying, in desultory fashion, to imagine that the tidy rows of shrubbery were a riotous mass of jungle underbrush. We had mentally tied Mr. Calvin Coolidge (for some reason Jane disliked the man) to a stake and were boredly frying that eminent gentleman when we saw the line hanging in back of the house.

Clothes pins dangled crazily from it and the family wash made grotesque forms against the bright, summer sun. We approached. On the ground was a can of paint. Blue paint. Like sleepwalkers we reached for the paintbrush, then, in a slow, ecstatic frenzy, we boldly painted clothes and clothes pins. They looked lovely.

The sight of these sky-blue shirts and sheets dancing in the breeze merely whetted our appetites. We headed for the garage. I swear that not a word was spoken. We were in luck. More cans of paint, a shiny sedan to decorate, bottles to break!

All that day we wandered over the countryside. No garage was safe. We pillaged and painted, smashed and destroyed property in the amount of $280.

We left a note in every garage. It read, "Repent your sins! The day of judgment is here!" and we signed it "Mrs. B. J. Harris," I don't know why. . . .

It is a curious document, this rough fragment, as if beneath the "smart" tone, Mary Jane were still struggling for an imaginative equality with Jane. It is also curious for its errors and omissions. The family were not Hungarians simply. They were Hungarian Jews. They were not entirely a family of women. There was a brother in addition to the six sisters. The color of the paint was apparently red, not blue. As to the inhabitants of Woodmere and Cedarhurst, they do not "shudder" when they hear the two girls' names. None of the neighbors who have lived there since the twenties remembers Jane Auer or Mary Jane or the red or blue paint.

MIRIAM FLIGELMAN LEVY MET JANE IN 1927, WHEN THE FLIGELMANS MOVED to Woodmere: "Lindbergh had just flown the Atlantic and the both of us were ecstatic. When I first started playing with Jane, the busy ladies on the block called my mother up and warned her, 'This is a terrible kid.' They spoke of dark and forbidden things in whispers. My dad, who was always a stickler for justice, insisted on evidence. He found out that Jane had painted some cars in neighbors' garages with bright red paint. I remember red, red paint. That it was red seemed to make it even worse. But my father also learned that the 'victims' had been paid for the damage, and he judged that Jane had learned her lesson. He trusted me, he said, so if I wanted to play with her, I could. Perhaps because of what had happened before I'd met her, there was an aura about Jane in my own mind, something that seemed deeper and more mysterious than childish pranks."

Miriam paid a price for that friendship. To be the best friend of this strange girl was to make of herself a kind of outcast. They would walk side by side, the tall long-legged Miriam taking giant strides and the tiny Jane, dragging her leg, taking a "funny little hop" to keep up. "She seemed to pay no attention to her leg, though I think I remember her wearing some kind of a corset because of it, to give her hip support.

"She looked like an elf with large luminous eyes and a ski-jump nose. Her imagination was so magical that I was swept up into it with her. We'd sneak into a neighbor's Chinese garden when it was dark and we'd imagine the pottery dragons coming to life and spitting fire at us.

"We also specialized in haunted houses, though we never actually found one in Woodmere, where most of the people were middle-class professional types or in 'wholesale.' We put on plays, sometimes for other children but mostly for ourselves—our own improvisational theater.

"There was a certain amount of mischief. We drank the brandy juice out of my mother's jars of preserved fruit in the basement. And we had one run-in with our black cook, Emma, a fierce lady, who was a Holy Roller and would sing Pentecostal songs while she was working. I knew she was bald and wore a wig and I told Jane. She said she had to have a look at Emma when she wasn't wearing a wig. So one night when Jane stayed over and my parents were out, we sneaked up to Emma's room after she'd gone to bed and opened the door. There was Emma in her four-poster bed with her wig hanging over one poster. She heard us and sat up in bed, her bald head gleaming. I was frozen with fright, but Jane let go a series of whoops and hollers. Emma chased us up one stairway and down the other, shouting the whole time in her deep voice. After that it was a long time before Emma would allow Jane to come around. But in the meantime Jane had picked up the way Emma sang those Pentecostal songs, and she'd mimic her perfectly. I felt guilty at the disrespect and was terrified that Emma would find out, but I couldn't help laughing at Jane's performance.

"At school we both loved Miss Foulke, who was a beautiful auburn-haired English teacher, and we'd talk about her endlessly. Jane was a good student, but school wasn't that important to her. What mattered was her life outside of school. Sometimes she'd read to me in French from dingy-looking novelettes. My French was just about nonexistent, so it was all mystifying to me.

"She herself was very mystifying and mercurial. She would go into a rage and right after that would come her wonderful wild laughter. She'd stamp her foot in petulance, the kind of thing you couldn't take seriously. I never understood the origin of her anger. She was moody as a child, with a moodiness that bordered on depression, but mostly for unaccountable reasons.

"Even so, the main thing I remember about her was her humor and how I'd get swept up into her fantasies. Only one thing I couldn't go along with her on. That was Elsie Dinsmore. I felt even at the time that Jane was obsessed by her.* Her favorite sport was to poke fun at Elsie's endless obedience. But I couldn't see the point. I thought Elsie was a terrible bore.

"Jane's house on Elm Street was a conventional house, but there she was, this very special child. You could sense that she was different. Everyone accommodated. I accommodated too. Her father was never around in the daytime. I remember him sitting quietly at night. I had the feeling Jane was very fond of him. He was very dependable looking. Jane's mother was tiny and she had olive skin and shiny black hair. The neighbors thought she was 'Frenchy-looking.' She always seemed to me to be very devoted to Jane, though she also seemed to have her own life.

"There was this odd incident about Jane's mother. I don't know quite what I thought of it when it happened. But something stayed in my mind afterward, something mysterious about Jane and her mother. One day a portly ruddy-faced man started driving Jane and me to school. The first day he picked us up at my house, where we had lunch. He opened the door for Jane to get into the car. As she climbed in she spit at him and then looked back at me as I got in, looking at me in such a way that I knew she expected me to do what she'd just done. I didn't know what was going on, but I did what was expected. I produced my token spit. The same thing happened for a couple of days, and then the man suddenly disappeared, as mysteriously as he'd come. That he was or hoped to be Jane's mother's lover was never said flat out, but that was the impression I had. I thought he was very unlover-looking. A lover was supposed to look like Ronald Colman or Gary Cooper or Fredric March. But mostly what I remember from that incident was Jane's rage. That I was sure of. I could feel it for her.

"But when I last saw Jane in 1953, I mentioned this incident to her and she was absolutely outraged. She denied that there was any spitting incident,

---

*Elsie Dinsmore was the heroine of a series of girls' books by Martha Finley, the first of which was published in 1868.

along with any suggestion that her mother had had a lover.

"It was hard to know why Jane behaved as she did. She was very private very early, as if there was a moat around her. She was my best friend and I loved her, but I never felt I could measure how close she felt to me. In a way I felt as though I was hanging on to reality for her. I was both conventional and unconventional, different from others, but in a way a lot like them. There were always things going on in my life, things out in the world. But for Jane, I felt most of her life was fantasy and imagination.

"Sometimes, I think she made a shadow out of me."

ROBERT SALTZER WAS JANE'S FIRST COUSIN, YOUNGER BY FOUR YEARS. HIS mother, born Florence Stajer, and Jane's mother were sisters. Of the Stajer family he says, "They were so close they breathed for each other.

"Jane's mother, Claire, was born in New York City. She was the second oldest of seven children. There were six girls and one boy, Stella, Claire, Violet—who died very young of diphtheria—Birdie, Constance, my mother Florence, and Sidney.

"Jane's father, Sidney Major Auer, was born in Cincinnati and was a graduate of the University of Michigan at Ann Arbor. He was a brilliant, gentle man.

"Mr. and Mrs. Auer met at a mutual friend's house in Arverne, Long Island. They were married in the Ansonia Hotel in Manhattan in 1913. They were living with my maternal grandmother, Mary, on West Eighty-ninth Street when Jane was born on February 22, 1917.*

"My grandmother ruled with an iron hand. She and my grandfather were both born in Austro-Hungary and came to the United States when they were very young. My grandfather was in the theatrical business. He died suddenly of pneumonia when my grandmother was thirty-nine years old and left her with seven children. It's a family joke that at the time he died he was negotiating for the property at Columbus Circle to build a theater there. I would tell my mother I could kill him for dying then, and she'd get hysterical. If he'd lived, we'd have all been zillionaires.

"The Auers were always comfortable. They were never really wealthy, but they never wanted for anything. But Mary Jane Shour's family—they were very wealthy. She and her brother Lawrence had everything they wanted.

"As a small child Jane was privately tutored. Then she went to Madame Tisnée's, a French school for children in Manhattan. She started going to public school after they moved to Woodmere.

*The birth certificate gives the name of the child as Jane Stajer Auer.

13

"My mother and I would often go out there to visit and spend weeks. In the summer we all rented a house together in Far Rockaway, on Jarvis Lane. Jane was zany and crazy and lots of fun. She wrote stories when she was a child; she always had a wild imagination. I loved being with her. She'd allow me to be with her for a while and then she'd tell me that she wanted to be by herself and I'd have to go away. Mary Jane and I were jealous of each other. We vied for Jane's time.

"You know Jane had a bad knee. It was my mother who discovered it. One day she was looking at her and she said, 'You know, dear, you seem to have something wrong with your knee. One is larger than the other.' There was a myth in our family that Jane had been dropped by a nurse when she was a child and that was why her knee was bad."

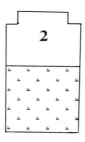

2

WOODMERE, LONG ISLAND, WAS A QUIET PLACE IN THE late twenties, with streets named Oak and Maple and Pine, a green haven less than an hour's ride by train from New York City. The Auers lived at 141 Elm Street, the corner house, next to the railroad tracks. It has two stories and an attic, a side and front entrance, a garage, a lawn with trees. It is a pleasant, unpretentious house, very much as it was in the late twenties and early thirties, though now, even from inside the house, one can hear the planes from Kennedy landing or taking off at frequent intervals, the end of a long progression that began with Lindbergh crossing the ocean, the event that Jane and Miriam had shared so ecstatically.

Theirs was a world mainly of middle-class Jews, first- or second-generation Americans, some practicing, most not practicing their religion. But even for those who were nonpracticing, says Miriam, "there was a great range of alternatives. Some became Christian Scientists, some were involved in Ethical Culture." In Miriam's family the ethical aspect of Judaism was carried on through a sense of service to the community and an emphasis on good works and on the democratic tradition.

Jane's family—and this included her mother's sisters and their families —were nonpracticing and separate, turned in upon themselves like a tribe. The sisters argued and reconciled and argued again. They shared family jokes and family sayings. They believed in getting on, in doing well, in the pleasures and necessities of the material world. While Mary Stajer, the matriarchal grandmother, was alive, the family would go to temple on Yom Kippur to please her. That was the limit of their observance. But when she died July 3, 1928, in Woodmere, where she had been staying with the Auers, even that practice ended. From then on the holidays were occasions for the family to get together for dinners. Jane herself never even seemed to know she was a Jew, says Miriam.

The Auer family lived as many families live, with the past put aside. But how does one put aside a past that permeates life in thousands of small ways, in words and attitudes, recognized or not, in leftover beliefs acted out half consciously? In a notebook from the early forties Jane wrote of a woman character: "She was disgusting in the way that anyone is disgusting who practices carelessly the ideology of a defunct group of people without feeling the need out of which such an ideology arises."

There are children for whom the past cannot be put aside so easily. If they are not given a past, then they must create one for themselves. There were a lot of things that would have to be reconciled for Jane in that past: her own sense of separateness so pervasive it seemed inborn, her "wild" imagination, the leg that made her "Crippie," her sense of sin. The puzzle is what that sense of sin meant to her; certainly it was not as in the original sin of Christianity: the sin shared by all human beings as a consequence of the Fall. Nor was it the fundamental sin in Judaism: the transgression against fellow human beings and the Law. It was a separating sin; separateness itself becoming sin. She had to find a past to circumvent and contain it, and as a child, she found it in the story of Elsie Dinsmore.

Elsie Dinsmore, by Martha Finley, had been an enormously popular classic for girls in the late nineteenth century. A moral tract in the form of a novel, it is a strange mixture of sentimentality and religion, of the dangers of sin, of the rewards for obedience. By the 1920s *Elsie Dinsmore* was going out of fashion, though there was something seductive in its almost sensual manipulation of feelings about sin and obedience.

Elsie, a beautiful eight-year-old girl with brown curls and soft hazel eyes and a sweet smile, is an heiress to an immense fortune. Her mother died when Elsie was born and she grows up on an estate in the South with relatives of her father's. Though not precisely an outcast, Elsie is not an accepted member of the family. When she is mistreated by her cousins and maligned by the cruel governess, she determines to accept her trials patiently. She seeks only to obey the dictates of Jesus. She wears a locket with a picture of her dead mother and dreams of meeting her in Heaven; she also dreams of meeting her dear father on earth someday.

Suddenly Horace Dinsmore, Elsie's father, returns to the plantation from Europe. Will he love me? Elsie wonders when she hears of his coming. When he arrives, Horace turns out to be stern and unforgiving, with a secret dislike for the daughter whose birth "caused" his wife's death. He is very cold to Elsie, and demands absolute obedience from her.

Elsie's struggle to gain her father's love is a test of her own love. She renounces her will in favor of his. "I don't want my own way," she says. "I know it wouldn't always be a good way."

"All you ever have to do is obey and you need never ask me why, when I give you an order," her father says to her. He forbids her ordinary pleasures and is only interested in what will develop her character.

Ultimately Elsie wins her father over by her obedience and devotion to moral principle. She earns her dearest hope, to sit on his lap and be cuddled by him. Horace becomes devoted to her. Looking at her sleeping, he says to himself, "The darling, she is lovely as an angel, and she is mine, mine only, mine own precious one. . . ."

But a conflict arises between Elsie's obedience to her father and to Jesus. Her father orders her to sing before company. She refuses because it is the Sabbath. Enraged at her disobedience, Horace insists. A friend of her father's, a Mr. Travilla, tries to persuade Elsie: "It's a very little thing. God wouldn't be angry."

" 'O Mr. Travilla!' she said, looking up at him in great surprise, 'surely you know that there is no such thing as a *little sin*. . . .' "

In later years, in a group of friends, Jane would suddenly say, "Most of all I would like to be a religious leader." Then they would laugh and she would say, "But of course, I'm not," and she would laugh as though she had meant it as a joke from the first. But in 1928, at eleven years of age, through her obsessive concern with Elsie, Jane kept many things in precarious balance: sin and obedience, dream father and real father, the power of the imagination and her own vulnerability.

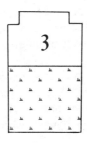

3

O N THE EVENING OF JULY 2, 1930, SIDNEY MAJOR Auer sat in the living room of his house on Elm Street with Claire and Claire's sister Constance and her husband Luis Eggers. For several days Sidney Auer had not been feeling quite right. On June 30 he had gone to a doctor, who had advised him to take things easy. In the middle of a conversation between the sisters, Sidney became ill. By 10:30 P.M. he was dead. The death certificate shows "hypertension" as the cause of death.

Jane was away at camp. "How odd," says Miriam Levy, "that she would agree to go to camp. I was much more conventional than she was, but I absolutely refused to submit to that regimentation." Jane, however, had wanted to go. She liked the notion of dormitories, she said in later life, of many people sleeping together in one room, of row upon row of beds. It was like a large family.

On the morning of July 3 the camp officials put Jane on the train to return to Woodmere. Jane's mother called Miriam and asked her to go to the train station with her to meet Jane. "I do not remember if I went, but I do remember that for days afterward Jane was in a terrible state. She was very, very upset."

Easy enough to understand that, a girl of thirteen grieving over her father's death. And there had been no warning. Sidney Auer had never been ill. Surely that made it harder for Jane. Whatever his death meant to her, she was so affected by it that she would almost never speak of him again. To Paul she once said, "He was a gentle man." "But it was as though she never had a flesh-and-blood father," Paul says.

There are few facts known about Jane's flesh-and-blood father. He was born Isaiah, July 5, 1885, at 27 Chestnut Street in Cincinnati, Ohio. His father, Emmanuel Auer, was born in Austria in 1854 and emigrated to the United States in 1870. His mother was Selma Ring, born in Germany in 1860. She also emigrated to the United States in 1870. Isaiah was the second of their five children. He had one brother, Jesse, and three sisters, Estelle, Mildred, and Florence.

The census of 1900 shows "Manuel" Auer and his family living at 709 Glenwood Avenue in Cincinnati. In the house besides his wife and five children are his mother-in-law, Rosalind Ring, and a servant, Carrie Fusell. Manuel Auer can read and write English, though he is listed as having had no schooling. He owns his home free and clear of a mortgage. He is an insurance agent.

By 1905 Isaiah has become Sidney and is a graduate of the University of Michigan at Ann Arbor. "Quite something for those days," says Robert Saltzer, for the son of Jewish immigrants to graduate from a university. A picture of him in the 1905 *Michiganensian*, the college yearbook, shows him as a bland, rather soft-looking though serious young man wearing pince-nez. He is a graduate of the Department of Literature, Science, and Art. Next to his name are listed his activities: glee, mandolin, and banjo clubs, class football team.

By 1911 or 1912, when he met Claire Stajer, he was living in New York and was owner of the Geisha Blouse Company, a romantic name for a shirtwaist business. He and Claire lived with her mother, Mary, until Jane's birth. The Michigan alumni records show him living at several addresses, on Fort Washington Avenue in 1919, and on West Eighty-first Street in 1925. He had a boat, which he also called the *Geisha*. He loved to go sailing and fishing and often took Jane with him. He used to call her by boys' names.

In the early twenties his business began to fail and he became a jobber, working free-lance for other manufacturers. By the mid-twenties he had become an insurance agent, working out of other people's offices. By 1928 he had his own office in Manhattan.

He was the one who wanted to move to Woodmere. He hated New York and the life of the city. Claire preferred to be in Manhattan, close to her mother and her sisters, close to the shopping and to the fashionable Madame Tisnée's school. But Sidney, for once, prevailed. And every weekday and often on Saturdays he went in on the train to his office and came home at night and sat quietly in his chair. Then that evening of July 2, at the age of forty-five, this quiet man who had never been ill a day in his life dropped dead.

One can speculate about the thoughts of a son who has not only to equal his father but to go beyond him. There was Manuel Auer, an immigrant, unschooled, at forty-five the owner of his own home, supporting a large family, a successful insurance agent. And there was Sidney, a graduate of the University of Michigan, at age forty-five with a wife and one child, living in a home he did not own, having failed at his own business and having ended as an insurance agent. From a brilliant beginning he had ended in poor imitation of his father.

It was 1930, the year after the Crash, the easiest of times for a man to judge himself or for his family to judge him. Many men were failing, but to most men it was not the economic system that was at fault: they themselves were to blame. In 1929 Louis Shour, Mary Jane's father, fearing failure on the stock market, had committed suicide. By his timing the family fortune was kept intact. As he sat quietly at night, Sidney Auer must have thought about that suicide.

He was a gentle man, but he was also a man who judged—himself as well as others. In 1954, in one of the few directly autobiographical notes Jane ever made, she wrote, "Nothing has changed. My father predicted everything when he said I would procrastinate until I died. . . . In America it was terribly painful to know this as a child. Now that I am nearly forty and in North Africa it is still painful. . . ."

And in 1967, when Jane was struggling with a terrible depression, Claire wrote to her, "Darling, there is nothing wrong with you. Your own father would have told you to 'stop dramatizing your troubles.'"

Perhaps it is not at all odd that a Jew of that time, though not a practicing Jew, should have an antagonism toward the imagination, toward "dramatizing." Though he had changed his name from Isaiah to Sidney, surely he carried with him some sense of obedience to the Law as it is worked out in daily life. In that context imagination can only be a sin, a threat to what has been handed down and should be obeyed.

In Jane's story "A Stick of Green Candy," a young girl sneaks off to a clay pit to play and imagines herself to be the head of a regiment of soldiers, her "men." When her father finds out that she's been playing in the pit instead of with other children, he reprimands her sharply. And in the unpublished *Out in the World*, the father declares: "Escapism is the big danger in our country . . . I want you to go out in the world looking at it, looking it in the face."

The voice of these two fathers, almost like one father, stands out in Jane's fiction because hers is essentially a work without fathers. From this voice and from the words of her mother and even from her own words, it is clear that though Sidney Major Auer was a loving man, he judged her for procrastinating and for dramatizing. He urged acceptance of the given order. He believed in going out into the world and facing it, not evading it in the imagination.

In play Jane had mocked Elsie Dinsmore for her unquestioning obedience to father and to God. Now her father was dead: games, after all, have consequences. Her imagination and her defiance were set once and for all as sin. No, there are no little sins, only large ones that must be paid for.

Jane was thirteen years old and puberty was beginning. Now all that needed to be worked out with a real father—the separation from him, the choice of others—could no longer be resolved in "real" life. It would all have to be pursued in imagination, the very imagination that her father had condemned.

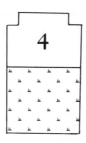

4

IT WAS THE WORST THING THAT COULD HAVE HAP-
pened to her, Jane once told Paul, that at her father's death she was left alone
with her mother. It was a horror that had to do with hate and love, a
complexity that Jane would spend her creative lifetime trying to unravel in
fictions of mothers and surrogate mothers, of daughters, and of sisters.

Through the screen of Jane's fiction, it is hard to see the woman who
was her mother. Miriam remembers her as tiny and olive-skinned, with
black hair. Virgil Thomson and Maurice Grosser, who knew her in the
thirties, remember her as blond, busy, attractive, likable, a woman of the
world. Others recall her as "a middle-class Jewish mother." One man
remembers her as "brassy." Most women remember her as "chic." She had a
passion for clothes.

Only one picture remains of Claire Auer, taken when she was in her
sixties. She is with her second husband, Julian Fuhs. Her expression is
active, watching. She reminds us of Mrs. Copperfield in Jane's novel, *Two
Serious Ladies,* who has "a sharp little face and very dark hair" and, like Claire
Auer, "is unusually small and thin."

Of Claire Stajer Auer we know that she was born on January 23, 1891,
in New York. She was twelve when her father died. Trained as a teacher, she
gave up her job upon her marriage to Sidney Auer in August 1913. Jane was
born three and a half years later.

Very early Claire was ambitious for Jane. She wanted her to have every
advantage she had not had, to be cultured and cultivated. She hired a French
governess, who took charge of Jane's early education.

When Paul and Jane were married, she told him that the governess had
had a lover. Jane knew about the lover and the governess knew that she
knew. The governess would pinch her arm, would slap her, and would say,
"If you tell that you saw him going out of the kitchen, I'll kill you." "But I
never would have mentioned it," Jane told Paul. "Children don't tell those
things to their parents. I'd have kept it a secret no matter how I hated her."

Years later, in the early sixties, when Jane made some accusation against her, Claire cried out, "Didn't I always do everything for you?" "You gave me a governess I hated," Jane replied.

Indeed, in her own view, Claire always did "everything" for Jane. Everyone who saw Jane and her mother together agrees that Claire was doting and possessive, adoring and ambitious for her. "Whenever she was with Jane, even when Jane was an adult, she couldn't keep her hands off of her. She was always touching her. And Jane just withstood it," Paul says. Claire would say to Paul, "We believe in showing our feelings. We're Hungarian, and we've got gypsy blood in us."

Jane hated her mother's effusiveness. She preferred the restraint of her father, Paul says. "German Jews are more civilized," she told him. Undoubtedly while he lived Sidney was a buffer between Jane and her mother, a buffer against the feeling that was so intensely expressed that even in her seventies Claire would write to Jane, "You are my life."

While there is no question about Claire's passionate devotion to Jane, it's also true that Claire avoided her at times, even feared her closeness. As we have seen, when Sidney died, Claire asked Miriam to go to the train with her to meet Jane, as if, two years after her own mother's death, she could not bear to see Jane—with her grief—alone. And even the hateful governess— whom Jane saw herself entrusted to so her mother could lead her own life—was a buffer, someone to take this child off her hands, to let her be free. To be a mother was apparently not easy for Claire, and especially to be the mother of this imaginative and difficult girl.

When mothers and daughters appear in Jane's writing the mothers usually berate the daughters for their perversity. In her play *In the Summer House*, Gertrude, the mother, scolds Molly, the daughter, for sitting in the summer house and reading comic books when she should be out with others, swimming and talking. Gertrude is also afraid of something in Molly, "something heavy and dangerous inside . . . , like some terrible rock that's ready to explode."

As a small child abandoned by her own father, at the mercy of her domineering mother, Claire had had to adapt to "real" life. The answers she found were in the "real" world. She was an ambitious woman. Once she had been ambitious for herself; now for her child she wanted a special, elegant life. She called Jane her "million-dollar baby."

There was in the Stajer family, as in many very close families, an intense rivalry. To win that rivalry was, in part, the obligation that Jane, as an only child, was expected to fulfill for her mother. While Claire acted out her indulgence and her sudden harsh angers, as she overwhelmed Jane with closeness and then, suddenly, feared to be too close, Jane constructed, as all daughters do, other very different mothers. She created them with the power of her imagination, and through her imagination they became powerful. In later years, when she wrote of mothers and daughters, she would struggle with the powerful mothers she herself had created as much as with the "real" Claire.

SOON AFTER SIDNEY AUER'S FUNERAL, CLAIRE AND JANE MOVED FROM Woodmere back to the city. At first they lived at the Croydon Hotel, 12 East Eighty-sixth Street, where the Saltzers, Carl and Florence and "Bobby," were staying. Robert Saltzer remembers Jane as being herself again, "charming and pixie. She had her moods, of course, and that upset me. She'd say, 'Now I'm going to read,' or she'd want to be by herself to listen to her records, a vast collection that included everything Lucienne Boyer and Mistinguett and Dietrich ever did."

Jane began to have "crushes" on women, particularly torch singers. Frances Williams was a singer who lived at the Croydon, and Jane told Bobby she had to meet her; somehow she was going to get into her apartment and talk to her.

"If you want to meet her, meet her in the lobby," practical Bobby said.

Jane ignored him. "I've got an idea how to get into her apartment. I'm going to dress up as a hotel maid. I'll get a broom and a pail."

"You'll never get in," Bobby said.

"Her mother's always there. She'll let me in."

And Jane did get in, dressed as a maid with her broom and her pail. "I'm sure the mother caught on," Robert Saltzer says, "but she let Jane stay there 'cleaning' until Frances Williams came back. So she met her. It was that kind of a schoolgirl 'crush.' She wanted to meet her and that was all."

Jane had another "crush" on Helen Morgan. She would listen to her records by the hour and learned to imitate her perfectly. Miriam Levy remembers that Jane once saw Helen Morgan perform, and was upset because the singer was drunk, but that did not seem to dim her obsession.

Miriam often came to visit Jane in the city. They'd walk in the park and have lunch at Alice Foote McDougall's restaurant, and go to the theater, "dressed in beige coats with little capes. We both loved Eva le Gallienne and our big treat was to go to the Fourteenth Street Repertory Theater and see her."

At the Croydon, Aunt Sallie, Mary Stajer's half sister, would often baby-sit for Jane and Bobby. "Sometimes Jane and I would drag her to the movies," he recalls. "At that time the Croydon had a marvelous delicatessen and after the movies we'd go to the delicatessen and Jane and I would each get a turkey sandwich, which we loved. We'd ask Aunt Sallie if she wanted one and she'd say, 'No, darling, I don't want anything, I'm not a bit hungry.' Then Jane and I would take our turkey sandwiches upstairs. And—it would kill us—it would end up that after all Aunt Sallie would like a turkey sandwich. Jane would give up half of her sandwich and I would give up half of mine. So Aunt Sallie had a whole turkey sandwich and Jane and I each had a half. Jane was livid. Then the next time it would happen all over again. We'd say, 'Aunt Sallie, do you want one?' and she'd say, 'No, darling, I'm not a bit hungry,' and she'd end up with the whole sandwich again. Somehow or other, we never caught on."

Soon the Saltzers and Jane and her mother moved to the Hyde Park Hotel at Seventy-seventh and Madison Avenue. There they shared a maid and ate dinner together almost every night. They even thought of buying a brownstone together. Claire had been left a considerable amount of money from Sidney Auer's insurance, and brownstones were relatively cheap at the time. Robert Saltzer remembers both families going to see the house on Seventy-eighth near Park six times. Jane and he had each picked out a room. But at the last minute, Florence Saltzer became nervous at the thought of such an investment, so they all stayed on at the Hyde Park Hotel.

The Saltzers and Jane and her mother were often joined by other members of the Stajer family, Stella and Harry Hornstein, Constance and Luis Eggers, Birdie Shour and her children, Mary Jane and Lawrence. There was also Uncle Sid, a gambling man, the "Gaylord Ravenal of the family," says Robert Saltzer. The one brother in a family of women, he was much indulged by his sisters. Jane was very intrigued by her Uncle Sid. In later years, she told Paul that Uncle Sid used opium and was associated with Arnold Rothstein, the gambler who was murdered in the Park Central Hotel. But even Uncle Sid was a loving family man in this family that was like a tribe, arguing, laughing, fighting, making up, the voices of the women usually dominating, the men quiet.

In the fall of 1930 Jane entered a public high school, Julia Richman, where she was encouraged in her writing by her English teacher. Jane stayed there only one semester. Claire decided that it would be better for her "million-dollar baby" to go away to a private school. She selected Stoneleigh, an exclusive girls' school in Greenfield, Massachusetts, and mother and daughter went together for an interview with the headmistress.

Paul remembers Jane describing the scene: "Her mother was wearing fox furs. The headmistress sat behind a desk asking questions. Suddenly Claire said, 'Jane is a very special girl. You see,' she added, 'she is a Jewess.' The headmistress leaned back in her chair. From that moment on everything seemed different to Jane. She went to Stoneleigh, but it was agony to her."

From Claire's viewpoint, it was not after all such a strange thing to say. She was sending her child away to an environment so different from her own family, so different from anything she had ever known, she could well have been fearful: that it would separate Jane from her past, from *her*, that it would make Jane forget what had been. Often in later years, Claire would say to Jane, "Remember you're a Jew," as if she were afraid Jane might forget.

Jane arrived at Stoneleigh at the beginning of the winter term in 1931. A former student, Elizabeth E. Bohning, describes Stoneleigh at that time as "a fairly small, close-knit school with very small classes and much emphasis upon supervised extracurricular activities. After breakfast we all attended a nondenominational chapel service. Classes were held in the mornings, and afternoons were devoted to sports: tennis, golf, hockey, basketball, hiking, or riding. . . . We wore uniforms at all times while at school."

Later Jane told Paul and a few friends how unhappy she had been at Stoneleigh. She felt she was treated as a special case because she was a Jew. On a tour of the dormitory the headmistress had shown Jane and Claire a room at the end of a corridor, which with three others formed an L. "We have three very nice Jewish girls living here and she'll feel at home," the headmistress said to Claire.

Elizabeth Bohning says, "I'm afraid I can't prove anything, but the idea of Stoneleigh's housing four Jewish girls separately seems absolutely fantastic. . . . I was aware of absolutely no special treatment for any group. . . . My impression is that there were *far* more than four Jewish girls and I am sure that they were scattered throughout the one dormitory that the school had in those days. I remember a number of them very well. Some of them were school leaders whom all of us looked up to. My own father came to the school once a week to talk on the Bible and some of his most enthusiastic students were Jewish."

At Stoneleigh, whatever the actuality of the external circumstances, Jane felt even more separate than before. Of the students who were there when Jane was, none remembers her except Elizabeth Bohning, and she has only a very vague recollection of Jane as a "rather withdrawn young woman. I cannot remember any close friends of hers at school. . . . Jane seemed to keep pretty much to herself, rather than seeking the companionship of the other girls, and she did not take any active part in the extracurricular life of the school."

Before the end of the school year, after having been at Stoneleigh less than six months, Jane fell from a horse and broke her right leg, the leg that had troubled her since childhood. The bone was set but the leg did not heal. A series of operations was performed and she developed tuberculosis of the knee. Much later, in an autobiographical fragment, she would write, "When I was little I had to imagine that there was some limit to physical pain in order to enjoy the day."

Wanting the best possible care for Jane, as she had always wanted the best of everything for her, Claire took her to a Dr. Rollier's clinic in Leysin, Switzerland, for treatment of the tuberculosis. Claire did not stay in Leysin, which is on the southern side of Lake Geneva, but went to live in Paris, returning frequently to visit. Jane remained in the sanatorium for two years, from 1932 to 1934, until she was seventeen. Much of the time she spent in traction, her leg in a cast.

It was at Leysin that Jane was to find her direction in life, her intellectual territory, and also her phobias. While there she was tutored by a Frenchman she greatly admired, though later she would say of him that he was "well versed in Greek mythology and venereal diseases." With him she studied Gide, Proust, Céline, Montherlant, and Louise de Vilmorin.

She spent her days reading and studying in a language not her own, but one that felt like her first language. She dreamed of imitating the clever style of Louise de Vilmorin. At Leysin, Woodmere and Stoneleigh were far behind. She was finding her own special direction. She was reclaiming the power of her imagination. But as it returned, she also developed a series of phobias, a fear of dogs, of sharks, of mountains, of elevators, of being burned alive.

A sense of her own history began to coalesce. First there had been the legendary fall as a baby, caused by the nurse who had dropped her and injured her leg. Then her father had died. Then had come the fall from the horse, and she'd been left with a wound that would not heal. But with that tubercular wound came a sense of heightened experience, as she felt it herself and as she read of it in the work of other writers.

The traction to which she was subjected day after day, the pulling in her own flesh and bones from one direction and from its opposite, was the crude symbol of all that pulled her: to her father, away from her father, to her mother, away from her mother, to imagination and away, to sensual pleasure and away, to her own power and away. Her only escape was an escape of her own devising, by whatever wiles of the spirit and imagination she could call upon. If there was an exchange, a kind of bargain struck with herself, it was for the reassumption of her power, for the reassertion of her own imaginative capability, though ever after she would pay with terror.

A remarkable release took place in her at Leysin. She was no longer the shy, withdrawn girl of Stoneleigh. Her imaginative wildness surfaced as extraordinary and fey charm. But she was on a knife edge, in precarious balance between opposing forces within herself. It was as if the external traction to which she had submitted was to remain within her forever.

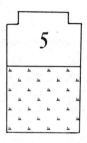

5

JANE WAS RELEASED FROM THE SANATORIUM, THE TB cured, but her leg still painful. She and Claire spent some time in Paris and then in the spring of 1934 returned to the United States on the liner *Champlain*.

On the boat Jane was reading *Voyage au Bout de la Nuit*. A stranger came up to her and said, "I see you're reading Céline." "He is one of the greatest writers in the world," she told him. "Céline, c'est moi," he replied. It seemed like a sign. The author and the girl spent a good part of the trip together. When she arrived in New York she said to her mother, "I am a writer, and I want to write."

In New York the Saltzers were now living at the Hotel Meurice on West Fifty-eighth Street. Jane and Claire moved there to be close to them.

Another operation was performed on Jane's knee. It was unsuccessful. Finally the decision was made to ankylose the leg. She would never be able to bend her knee again, but at least she would be spared the continual pain of a knee joint that would never heal. After the operation her leg was in a cast for seven or eight months.

From then on her leg would be stiff, though the rest of her musculature was remarkably flexible. ("I have never seen anyone so double-jointed as Jane," Paul says.) To walk with one leg yielding, the other unyielding, could be seen as the bodily proof of the disparity between the two sides of herself, as if fate had set in physical form the duality she lived in mind and feeling.

At home in the hotel Claire tried to indulge Jane's every wish. They had a maid named Ada who picked up after her, who washed her clothes, who even changed her pocketbook for her. Claire, focused on appearance as always, had a beautician come in twice a week to do their hair and their nails.

There was the question, of course, of schooling. At first Claire sent her to Reginald Goode's acting school, but as Jane later wrote, "I was neither talented nor determined and soon failed." It was hardly likely, talent or no talent, that she would surrender her own imaginings to either the words or direction of another.

"I am a writer and I want to write," she had told her mother. She began a novel in French, *Le Phaéton Hypocrite* (The Hypocritical Phaëthon). Practical Claire sent her to a typing school, so she could learn to type it. But though she made herself write, there was something about writing that she hated. She wanted to be out in the world doing, with her wildness, finding her own new way.

The writer George McMillan remembers meeting Jane in 1935 when she was eighteen: "I met Jane Auer in the Village in a little club near the southwest corner of Washington Square. It was six or eight steps down from the street, in the basement. For a time, maybe fifteen or twenty nights, I worked there as a doorman, bouncer, and cashier. I was perfectly aware that it was a place where lesbians gathered. When I first saw Jane she was with two other women, Charlotte Cohan and Lupe Levy. I don't know if I went home with them that night, but I saw them all afterwards."

McMillan was twenty-two, tall, good-looking in a "black Irish" way. He seemed not to give a damn what other people would think. There was a certain courtliness in his manner and also a provocative roughness.

He had grown up in Knoxville, Tennessee, a bright boy who hated school but loved to read. The son of a middle-class family struggling to keep up appearances, at a very early age he'd taken on the role of father, helping his mother and younger brother. At sixteen he came to New York, hoping to become a writer. He had lived as a bum on the Bowery, had worked at odd jobs, and had gone to sea.

"When I first met Jane, she had a cast on. She seemed very European. She wore little black velvet dresses with white lace collars. Charlotte was tall and black-haired, not pretty, but pleasant. Lupe was severe in the way she dressed and wore her hair. She was heavy and not attractive.

"I think I was snowed by how much money they had. I enjoyed them and got a kick out of them. For me it wasn't a matter of sex only. I was getting a lot of sex elsewhere at the time. It was, I thought, a matter of mutual liking.

"I saw all three girls. They trusted me and talked about their love for each other and their jealousies. I think I was a mediator between the three women."

He'd visit each of them at her family's home, wearing his one good gray flannel suit. "Lupe lived in the Hotel Carlysle, in a penthouse apartment. Her mother was very wealthy and her father was an investment broker. I had the impression that they were Jews who hated Jews. I remember visiting Lupe, going into the bedroom with her while her parents were there and having sex with her.

"I remember Jane's apartment at the Hotel Meurice. It was small and not luxurious. I met Marcus Loew there several times. He was a sober, courteous man. I met him going in and out. I thought he was Mrs. Auer's boyfriend.* I think Jane communicated that to me. Mrs. Auer was very nice to me, though I don't remember her as a warm person at all. I remember her as brittle, even brassy.

"I do remember that Jane and I used to go into her bedroom together. We'd lie on the bed and read Lawrence to each other." He remembers a good deal of "noodling around" and petting, but not the act of sex with Jane.

"I liked Jane a lot. We shared a common literary interest. I remember there was one poem of D. H. Lawrence that she would read to me. She typed it out and gave it to me and it was kind of a talisman between us. I kept it for many years, but then it disappeared.

"Jane was very adventurous. She'd do anything crazy. We'd walk down Broadway and play the pinball machines. I have a photograph of her that was taken in one of those arcades. We went on the Staten Island ferry several times. I didn't have any money to take her out but she didn't give a shit about money. She was wild and funny and we laughed a lot. I saw her only for a few months. I don't even remember how it ended."

By chance, McMillan kept a letter from Jane. He remembers nothing about receiving the letter or about the circumstances it referred to, but Robert Saltzer (who did not know McMillan) recalls the fight between Jane and her mother that preceded the letter:

"Jane stormed out of the house in a rage. She said she couldn't stand it anymore. She was gone for the whole day. That night my father and my Aunt Constance went down to the Village to look for her. Jane had talked some about her adventures in the Village, so they knew where to look and they found her."

In the letter to McMillan Jane tells of what followed:

Dear George—

Here's what happened when I arrived home. (Connie was lying about taking me to her place—but I didn't raise a kick—I knew I'd be with Mother—sooner or later anyway.)

Mother was potting around the kitchen (anticlimax) and Aunt Flo was wrapped up in Uncle Carl's bathrobe—Whenever there's grief around women always accumulate blankets, men's overcoats, hot water bottles, woolen scarves.

They whisked me into the bedroom while Mother finished gnawing at her roast-beef bone. Connie said, "Get undressed, dear." She was at

---

*Robert Saltzer remembers Marcus Loew as a family friend.

the burping stage and felt very ill as she had told us once or twice in the car.

I remained dressed—they were 4 against 1 anyway—Then Mother came in, in the awful black kimono she had on the night you were here. She said, "What's this?"

I took an arrogant stand. I had a 'Who are these people' look on my face, and 'I must get back down to the party.'

Then Connie started in: Now Claire, you know I don't feel well and I've been looking for Jane for 4 hours and I was cold and—

Mother: Well, what has Jane to say for herself?
Jane: Nothing. I don't know why I'm here.
Connie: Now Jane, you know that's not true! You wanted to come back. She told me she couldn't hurt you, Claire!

Hysterics on my part here—I don't quite know what I said but—I know I almost killed the poor woman—and started cursing myself because I couldn't hurt her.

Then she kissed me and they all sat down and said what a wonderful girl I was—and what a fine young man you were—and that if I still wanted to marry you 25 years from now I could—that Mother wouldn't think of standing in the way of my happiness—and that I was a grand normal girl and that this Lesbian business was just an adolescent phase (adolescence being from 7 to 33 in our family) and that if only I didn't have such an analytic mind I certainly would throw it off—and if I really were a Lesbian they'd get up a fund for me and send me down to the village in my own private bus. (I suggested that they might organize picnics for all us girls every 2 weeks.) But I really wasn't one, so they couldn't let me go to my ruin!

Aunt Flo suggested 130 more men—to straighten me out—Aunt Connie 135—The same remedy seems to go for you and the Les's—like 3 in 1 oil, or bleeding in the Middle Ages. . . .

I have been writing this letter for 3 days. Mother always comes in when I get started. George, pardon the tone of all this but I'm trying to counterbalance all the emotion—and drama that's been hanging between us so that we could hardly see each other.

You may come to see me! And tell Lupe anything you like. She hasn't called me since the night you were here.

Love to you—
Jane

The question of marriage to George McMillan, alluded to in the letter, is puzzling. Whether Jane's family merely thought she wanted to marry McMillan, or whether she herself had ever said anything about it, or indeed whether if she said it, she meant it, is not clear. As for McMillan, he says, "I wouldn't have asked her to marry me. I had no interest in getting married at the time. I didn't have a job or any money. It wouldn't be like me to ask a woman to marry me unless I meant it."

IN DECEMBER 1935 MIRIAM FLIGELMAN WAS MARRIED AND WITH HER HUSBAND Irving Levy came to New York on their way to Latin America. They went to see Jane and her mother at the Hotel Meurice and spent a long cocktail hour talking. Jane spoke of her time in Europe and hinted of many affairs and a mad Parisian life. "She seemed very flossy, very chic, a middle-twenties flapper almost. She was very affectionate and warm. It was all very pleasant but it seemed oddly conventional. It did not seem quite real to me then, and seems even less so in retrospect.

"It must have been the impression left by that occasion that led me to typecast Janie as a kind of Marjorie Morningstar. So later, when two good friends of ours, attractive young bachelors from Minneapolis, were on their way to New York and wanted suggestions for dinner and theater dates, I gave them Jane's telephone number. They called her up and invited her out for the evening; their other date was a young beautiful rich blond Cleveland woman named Sue. The four of them went to a fashionable supper club, but the evening ended abruptly. It seems the lovely, proper, beautiful young Sue went to the ladies' room with Jane. Five minutes later Sue came out in tears, on the verge of hysterics. Later they learned that Jane had told her, 'Now I'm going to count ten and if you're not a lesbian, get the hell out of here.' Our friends thought it was uproariously funny. It didn't appreciate my stock much as a matchmaker, but I thought at the time that Jane was being funny, defying custom, trying to shock the Minnesota 'hayseeds.'"

BY 1936, WITH HER CAST OFF, JANE WAS EXPANDING HER EXPLORATIONS IN Greenwich Village, going to new bars and new places. Claire, after the fight that resulted in Jane's running away, decided not to oppose her directly, though she still clung to the thought that Jane would marry a nice Jewish boy. Mary Jane Shour had already married at seventeen, and married well. To anyone in the family who criticized Jane's behavior, Claire said, "It's because of her leg."

Claire tried to give Jane everything she wanted, and even some things she didn't want. She wanted Jane to have a coming-out party, but Jane would have none of it. Well then, at least she should be as chic as possible. Claire dragged her to Bergdorf Goodman and Henri Bendel to get her a proper wardrobe. When Jane would object in the store, Claire would pinch her on the arm, a signal not to make a fuss in front of the salesgirls.

In the Village Jane met Dione Lewis, like Jane from a middle-class Jewish family, like Jane an only child. Her father was dead and her mother too was ambitious for her. Dione had been sent to the Ethical Culture School and was, at the time, attending the American Academy of Dramatic Arts. Jane and Dione met at first in a bar and then, by chance, at a respectable uptown party. They were amused by their double lives and became close friends.

"We both did and didn't do what our mothers wanted us to do. Sometimes we'd go out with these nice Jewish boys that our mothers had picked out for us. They'd bring us home and then as soon as they were gone, we'd go out again to Spivy's or maybe to see Gypsy Rose Lee in the Great Northern Hotel.

"Whenever Jane was going out, anywhere, her mother spent an hour getting her dressed. 'Wear this dress, this hat, take those gloves.' We'd go out the door," Dione says, "and off would come the hat and off would come the gloves and Jane was on her way."

Jane led the way from one bar to another in the Village. "When Jane wanted something or wanted to do something, she had to do it. There was no stopping her."

Dione, who was very ebullient, was nevertheless more cautious than Jane. "I followed her everywhere, but I was nervous. I kept making her wash her hands because I was afraid she'd get syphilis."

Claire kept hoping that Jane would bring home a marriageable young man, but the man she brought home was John LaTouche, whom she and Dione had met in a bar in the Village. "Instead of a belt, he wore a necktie to hold up his trousers," Jane wrote of the talented and budding lyricist, who was a perfect match for her own wild imagination and wit. At fifteen, living in Richmond, Virginia, he had won the James Branch Cabell Prize for poetry. Now a student at the Riverside Boarding School, he was sneaking out to Greenwich Village to find a world more to his liking.*

Dione's mother and Jane's mother decided that both girls should go to a milk farm. There one was supposed to have a healthy diet and exercise and lose weight. "They thought it would be a good change from the unhealthy New York atmosphere," says Dione. "But we sneaked out to the Village and brought back food to eat at the milk farm. When the people who ran it found out, they made us leave."

Back Jane and Dione went to New York and to their rounds in Greenwich Village. "Jane did everything with such innocence. You'd roll in the gutter with her and it was funny, never sordid."

---

*He was presently to write the lyrics for *Cabin in the Sky* (music: Vernon Duke), *Beggar's Holiday* (Duke Ellington), and *The Golden Apple* (Jerome Moross).

In a bar Jane met a woman named Cecil and fell in love with her. "She had straight red hair and white white skin, and she was always plastered. She slept in doorways. Jane decided she was going to reform her. She got the idea that she would bring Cecil home for a week to dry her out since her mother was going to be away."

Jane needed money for this reforming process. One day she appeared with some money and she told Dione that she had earned it typing for an author. With the money she bought Cecil some clothes. Cecil accepted the clothes, but as for the cure, she told Dione that she never drank so much in her life as when she was with Jane. After the week of "drying out" she went back to Greenwich Village and to sleeping in doorways. She died a few years later of acute alcoholism.

Later that year Jane wrote to Miriam:

I find myself staring at my writing materials from the couch as though they were "Nazis."

I get nauseous at the thought of putting a pen to paper—for any purpose, literary or otherwise. This incapability of mine to "act" is spreading. I stare at my corset for hours now before I put it on.

I am perfectly serious and solemn about the whole thing.

I feel particularly badly about not having written you because I remember the emphatic way in which I agreed that we must not —absolutely must not—lose contact this time and that I would certainly write. Either I don't know myself—or I'm a confounded skillful liar.

I thought about you for such a long time after you left—your face that looks just like little Miriam's in a magnifying glass—now—your subdued voice and the Russian toque which you were somehow destined to wear—

The silliness of you being married first—you with your inky hands and your ten thousand books—and your skinniness—you were so thin you looked like a drawing instead of a person.

To think you would deceive me too—and develop into a real human being.

I'm sitting in my living room with an old purple cover over me—the sun is in the room and the walls (remember they are yellow) glow—little strips of sky shine thru the Venetian blinds like blue birds' wings—and the mirror that stretches between the two windows takes on a green reflection like a pond.

All this is very soothing to a convalescent. I am recovering from a carefully nurtured grippe. It seems as though it just won't linger any longer—too bad—

Soon I shall be back in bed reading. As I look down my life I see one picture—"me in bed reading"—the only difference is that the heap under the bedclothes grew larger.

As you see you will get no news from me today. I prefer irrelevant detail. I never will write you any news probably—unless I marry—and then I shall probably insert a sentence or two about it between a description of a rice pudding and a thumb-nail sketch of Miss Foulke. I depend on you for facts Walter Winchell and plenty of them because I love reading them.

You have noticed my slipshod sentences and my repetition of words and my hundreds of prepositional phrases and my bad handwriting. It is because I am still nothing but a precocious child—and am I even precocious?

You have my sincerest love Miriam dearest—write me. . . .

Nevertheless, though she felt "nauseous at the thought of putting a pen to paper," Jane did finish writing her novel, *Le Phaéton Hypocrite*. Her mother was very pleased and had a professional typist make copies of it for the family. All copies of the manuscript disappeared years ago. Virgil Thomson, who read it, remembers only that it was a "brilliant literary conceit."

Written in French in a mock naïve style, the novel was a burlesque on the Greek myth of Phaëthon. In that myth Phaëthon, the son of the god Helios, asked his father to let him drive the chariot of the sun. At first Helios refused because he was afraid Phaëthon couldn't control the horses. Phaëthon insisted and, as Helios feared, the horses got out of control and charged all over the heavens. They went so high the earth grew cold and then they came so close to the earth that parts of Africa were turned into desert. To protect the earth and Olympus, Zeus hurled a thunderbolt and Phaëthon, on fire, plunged into a river.

After all, it had not been forgotten, all that had happened when Jane was a smaller heap under the bedclothes. She was still contending with her own individual myth, the fear of the uncontrolled power of her imagination, her "little original sin."

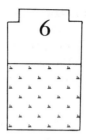

6

THE ART-LITERARY-MUSIC WORLD OF NEW YORK OF THE mid-thirties was small and private. There was one established salon, that of the art dealer Kirk Askew and his wife, Constance. To this salon came writers, musicians, painters, patrons, theater people, and many associated with the Museum of Modern Art. Among the habitués were Virgil Thomson, Maurice Grosser, Ettie and Florine Stettheimer, Charles Demuth, Charles Henri Ford, Parker Tyler, Alfred Barr, and E. E. Cummings.

It was John LaTouche who introduced Jane to the Askew salon. Into that world she came from the Meurice "beautifully dressed, prim and outrageous, limping with one knee stiff, carrying one shoulder higher than the other." She had a "wonderful, alluring voice." Saying whatever came to her mind, she was the "hit of the occasion." "All her observations were weird and screamingly funny."

Maurice Grosser painted a portrait of her, just after she'd come to the salon for the first time. She sits rather primly, unsmiling, elegantly dressed. She is wearing only one glove. She had lost the other in a taxi. Her expression is puzzling and mysterious. "People loved her," says Virgil Thomson, "but what she cared about no one knew."

In that small and private world Jane began to discover her own power. Through her wit and charm, her sophisticated and yet childlike quality, she drew other people to her. "She was in tune with basic primitive things," says Dione Lewis.

Soon there was a group of young people—LaTouche, Dione Lewis, Erika and Klaus Mann, and Genevieve Phillips among others—who gathered in the evening at Jane's mother's apartment at the Meurice before they went on to Spivy's, a nightclub then on West Fifty-second Street. "Sometimes we had dinner at Jane's," remembers Dione. Jane wanted to be called Sidney, her father's name. Her mother wanted her to be called Jane. People would ask her, "What do you do?" and she'd say, "I'm a writer." But none of her friends ever saw anything she wrote. Dione and another young woman rented a hotel room for Jane and insisted she stay in it an entire weekend. "So if you're a writer, write," they told her.

But combined with Jane's new sense of power was an old sense of humiliation. "If I said to her, 'Do you know what so-and-so said about you?' " Dione remembers, "she'd say, 'If it's about my leg, don't tell me.' She was sure that that was the first thing anyone noticed about her."

FROM DEAL BEACH, NEW JERSEY, ON JANUARY 29, 1937, JANE WROTE TO Spivy (who by then had moved her club to the top floor of an office building at Lexington Avenue and Fifty-ninth Street). It is a puzzling letter, puzzling first because Jane was in Deal Beach, a summer resort, in the winter. From the context of the letter, Jane seems to be alone in a rented room. The tone is also puzzling—fey, even arch—strange for Jane. It is as if away from home alone, for the first time since Leysin, she were uncertain and uneasy, trying too hard to be sophisticated. There is an edge of hysteria in the archness.

> Dear Spivy—
> I am all alone in a great big bed, twenty feet wide. Send me homeless Italian family at once. Man and wife retired at ten thirty. She sat all day twirling a long strand of hair round and round her second finger. Had a glassy look in her eye. At dinner they played foot games underneath the table. Neither of them seems to know who I am.
> The "apartment-by-the-sea" is very cold, very quiet, and very sad. I know that the janitor has been lying dead in the basement for weeks—under ten feet of water. In the field at our left are the corpses of twenty million crickets. They died on Labor Day. . . .
> I am distressed because Mother is taking me to Havana in three weeks—almost definitely. I'll either be eaten by sharks on the way—or I'll marry a Latin—and all my children will be born with earrings. I don't want to go to Havana, Spivy. . . .
> Drop me a note and I'll have them forward it to New York if I suddenly get weak or hungry and come home. I'll try my best not to because Genevieve would be furious—why—I don't know. I won't come home—really.
>
> Love to you—Miss Spivy
> Jane
>
> Note for LaTouche:
> How do you do—LaTouche.

Apparently Jane never did go to Havana with her mother. From New York—probably in early February—she wrote to Miriam, responding to a letter in which Miriam had said that she was pregnant with her first child, and if it was a girl, she wanted to name her Jane. The tone of the letter is, recognizably, Jane.

> For Heaven's sake don't name any babies Jane—ever—unless you're a sadist. I'm very jittery about this. I simply can't connect you with a baby. Why only a minute ago we were going to school. Life suddenly seems as short as a pistol shot. After this will you please address me as a "Maiden Aunt"—or something—my God—I'm not anywhere near getting married. . . .
>
> I am having a very lovely time here with many mad people—artists and Pseudo-artists but very night-clubby. As usual I am surrounded by musical people, I who dislike everything but "Swing."
>
> I am very very blue at the moment. I wasn't when I started this letter—my moods are getting almost pathological.
>
> It's so cold and the winter's so long and there seems nothing to experience that I haven't experienced before. I'm tired of loving and being loved. I'm sick of my own voice and I hate books. I'm not even hungry.
>
> I hope you have the most beautiful baby in the world and I wish you lots of luck.
>
> I shall now go and drink myself to death for a few hours—and what is more I shall have no hangover for which all my friends loathe me.

FOR WEEKS IN THE WINTER OF 1937 JOHN LATOUCHE HAD BEEN TELLING PAUL Bowles, "There's this fantastic girl I want you to meet. I'll bring her around." But LaTouche never did. Then one day in late February, he said to Paul, "I'm going up to Harlem with Erika Mann. I want you to meet her." LaTouche was translating Mann's anti-Fascist revue, *The Peppermill*, for production at the New School for Social Research. "And I'm bringing this girl," he added. The girl was Jane Auer.

They all met outside the Plaza. Jane had a great mop of bright red hair. (She was now touching up her dark hair with henna.) The four of them got into a cab and went up to Harlem to a dimly lit apartment where everyone bought joints for fifty cents and sat on the floor and smoked. Paul and Jane hardly spoke. She didn't seem to want to talk to him. He'd say something to her and then she'd respond briefly and turn away to talk to Erika Mann. He didn't find her endearing.

He was twenty-six years old, blond, handsome, a gifted composer, and a published poet. He had traveled extensively, including several trips to Morocco. He was impeccably dressed, formal, polite, reserved, witty, and charming, with a certain quality of detachment in that charm. This much others saw. Jane saw something different. Many years later she wrote two sentences about that first meeting: "He wrote music and was mysterious and sinister. The first time I saw him I said to a friend: He's my enemy."

Paul was an only child born in Jamaica, Long Island, in 1911. Brought up by a doting mother, Rena Winnewisser from Bellows Falls, Vermont, and a tyrannical father, Claude, from Elmira, New York, he had a strange separate childhood. He never played with another child when he was young, had never even spoken to one until he was five. By the age of five he had already filled several notebooks with stories. At eight he was composing an opera.

From his earliest years he considered that his father was his enemy, "that he wanted to be my enemy, that he wanted me to be unhappy. For there was no way of being happy if he was around." His grandmother told him that his father had tried to kill him when he was six weeks old. As Paul reported her story in his autobiography, *Without Stopping:*

> He came home one terrible night when the wind was roaring and the snow was coming down—a real blizzard—and marched straight into your room, opened the window wide, walked over to your crib and yanked you out from under your warm blankets, stripped you naked, and carried you over to the window where the snow was sailing in. And that devil just left you there in a wicker basket on the windowsill for the snow to fall on. . . .

Whatever the truth of that story, Claude Bowles had a violent temper when Paul was a child. As a young man Claude had wanted to be a concert violinist. When his family had objected, he suffered a nervous breakdown. On his recovery he went on to become the dentist they wanted him to be. He hated any evidence of softness, of impracticality, of unworldliness in his son.

"My father's philosophy was that you force the child to do what it doesn't want to do. Only through frustration and fear does the child learn what the world is like. Whatever I liked, I must not get near. Whatever I hated, I must be thrown into. So I had to begin to pretend to hate what I liked and to like what I hated in order to confuse him, naturally. That is very hard for a child. In the end you finish by kidding yourself; you no longer know what you want."

Paul managed to guard his creative capability by a ruse of the mind. "I became an expert in the practice of deceit, at least insofar as general mien and facial expressions were concerned. I could not make myself lie, inasmuch as for me the word and its literal meaning had supreme importance, but I could feign enthusiasm for what I disliked, and even more essential, hide whatever enjoyment I felt. . . ."

He saw early that the world of grownups was one of distrust and intrigue. He saw that his mother was afraid of his father, but she too found ways to adapt, ways to save herself. "Nothing's so much fun as games you play with your own mind," she told him. "You think you're running your mind, but then you find out that unless you're careful, your mind is running you. . . ." Very early he learned from her how to put his mind into a blank state, as if he were clearing a well of water and letting the water come up fresh.

As he grew older, he found other techniques to guard himself. He thought of himself as "a registering consciousness and no more. My nonexistence was a *sine qua non* for the validity of the invented cosmos . . . I received and recorded . . . ; others were people and had lives."

But he paid for his solutions:

One evening just after sunset I decided to go down the hill to where the nearest shops were and have something cold at Roth's soda fountain. The shop was on a corner, with a swinging screen door giving on to each street. As I pushed open the screen door, something happened to me. The best way of describing it is to say that the connection between me and my body was instantaneously severed. The soda fountain was there in front of me, but I could not go to it. Instead, I turned right, walked to the other door, and went out into the street. But then I had to turn to the right again, go around the corner, and back to the first door. I repeated the operation and saw Mrs. Roth look up at me with surprise as I went out for the second time. I was caught in something that I could not break out of, and I tried desperately not to go into the shop a third time. However, I did go in and marched straight through and out the other door. . . .

Only by chance as he came out this time did he see his parents' blue Buick coming down the hill, and the sight of it released him from his compulsion.

At school Paul did very well and was complimented on his intelligence, but he valued it little. He felt he was without a more important intelligence, the street wisdom other children had. He continued to write stories and at the age of fifteen published "The Waterfall" in *The Oracle*, the Jamaica High School literary magazine.

For his setting of "The Waterfall" he used a place he loved in a hemlock forest in Glenora, New York. In the story a young man has jumped to his death from a rocky point into a pool at the base of a waterfall. The boy's father comes to the rock. He is bitter at his son's death. The boy, he judges, was either a fool or a coward. He regrets all the money he has spent on his son's education. But standing on the point from which the boy has thrown himself, the father feels pulled by some magical power.

Far down below he saw the semi-vaporized cataract pounding and foaming on the rocks. The pool was green, with a circle of foam which radiated from the place where the tremendous force struck it. Outward, toward the slimy, pebbly shores, it moved always outward; diminishing until it merely rippled at the edge.

He tried to look straight down, and cried out, so distant did the earth seem. . . . He reclined against the rocks, panting. He believed he understood the power. He scarcely blamed his son, now.

The father tries to reason himself back to safety, but the power of the waterfall is greater than reason. He slips or is drawn into the abyss, "into utter oblivion and peace."

Paul remembers writing the story and remembers too that it upset him. "My heart beat much too fast. I thought I was committing some crime by writing it." Nevertheless, he finished it and published it.

At sixteen he was deeply influenced by Gide's *The Counterfeiters*. Reviewing it for *The Oracle*, he wrote: "It evokes more material for deep thought than any other book we have ever read. . . . A boy of sixteen leaves his home clandestinely to wander in the streets of Paris. . . . The book cannot become popular in America because of its Gallic viewpoint. . . ."

That same year Paul's poetry was published in the European avant-garde magazine *transition*. In his high school yearbook, next to his picture, was printed the quotation "This strange disease of modern life."

After several months at an art school, he went on to the University of Virginia.

It was a pleasant life in Charlottesville. I felt well physically. I think this was because it was the first time in my life that I had consistently had all I wanted to eat. The lack of nourishment at home was not due to poverty, but to an excessive preoccupation on my father's part with regard to my diet. If I said I was hungry, he would reply, "That's your indigestion. Wait two hours and you'll see that the pangs will go away." If I asked for a second helping, he often refused it to me on the grounds that I hadn't chewed the first properly. "Fletcherize," he used to say. [To "Fletcherize" was to chew each mouthful of food forty times, as recommended by a Dr. Horace Fletcher for health.]

It isn't surprising that in Virginia, away from these restraints, I soon put on twenty-five pounds. However, this unaccustomed physical well-being was unfortunately more than offset by a steadily increasing sensation of guilt. All this pleasure and freedom will have to be paid for. . . .

"There will come a day of reckoning," I told myself. . . .

The freedom included drinking with his fellow students, sniffing ether, and wandering in the countryside. But one afternoon at dusk he got back to his room and

> knew at once, although I had no idea of what it was going to be, that I was about to do something explosive and irrevocable. It occurred to me that this meant that I was not the I I thought I was or, rather, that there was a second I in me who had suddenly assumed command. I shut the door and gave a running leap onto the bed, where I stood, my heart pounding. I took out a quarter and tossed it spinning into the air, so that it landed on my palm. Heads. I cried out with relief and jumped up and down on the mattress several times before landing on the floor. Tails would have meant that I would have had to take a bottle of Allonal that night and leave no note. But heads meant that I would leave for Europe as soon as possible. . . .

So he went to Paris, running off clandestinely, as Bernard had done in *The Counterfeiters*. He left literature behind and turned to music. He became a protégé of Aaron Copland's. He met Gertrude Stein, who told him he was not a poet and who encouraged him to work on his music. "If you don't work, by the time you're thirty, no one will love you," Aaron Copland said to him.

This was the young man Jane met in February 1937, the cool, amusing, charming man, of whom she said, "He is my enemy." What did she mean? Paul himself never knew. "Once I asked her later and she said, 'I meant that I had never met anyone so inimical to me as you.' It wasn't true," he says, "I wasn't."

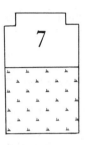

7

PAUL AND JANE MET AGAIN A FEW DAYS LATER, AT A
Sunday afternoon gathering at E. E. Cummings's on Patchin Place in the
Village. Paul had come with Kristians Tonny, a Dutch painter he had met
through Gertrude Stein, and Tonny's wife, Marie Claire. The three of them
were preparing to go to Mexico on an extended trip. Neither of the Tonnys
could speak English well. Jane was speaking French with them when
suddenly she said, "I'm going to Mexico with you."

She went into the next room and telephoned her mother. Then she came
back into the living room and said to Paul, "My mother wants to talk to you."

When Paul picked up the phone, Claire said flirtatiously, "I think if my
daughter is going to Mexico with a man, I should meet him, don't you?" He
agreed and they set a time for him to come round with Jane for a drink—but
he thought it odd that she didn't object to the idea of her daughter going off
to Mexico with a man she had just met.

Now Paul began to look at this young woman in a different way, this
odd girl who had hardly responded to him when they first met and who had
then announced to her friend, "He is my enemy." And suddenly she had
invited herself on the trip to Mexico. He was puzzled by her and continued
to be so: in the days before their departure he did not get to know her any
better. When he saw her, it was always with other people. Several times the
two of them went with E. E. Cummings to the Bowery to see a burlesque
show. Cummings called it pure poetry. Jane enjoyed herself hugely. She had
cut her hair very short and was smoking little Cuban cigars. Cummings was
delighted with her.

In mid-March Jane and Paul and the Tonnys boarded a Greyhound bus
for New Orleans. Claire had equipped her for the journey with a complete
new wardrobe, including evening dresses and matching shoes. She'd also
given Jane a letter of introduction from a friend to some people in Mexico
City. And she said to her, "You'll stay at the Ritz, of course."

Paul, who was thinking of joining the Communist party, was carrying with him fifteen thousand stickers calling for the death of Trotsky. He planned to find appropriate places for them in Mexico, where Trotsky was then living.

They spent two weeks getting to New Orleans, stopping en route in many towns. All the time on the bus, Paul and Jane sat together, talking and talking. They talked in French, of books they cared for and of people. They talked of their affairs. He had had affairs with men and women, she only with women. They talked of marriage, of their ideal of a marriage, and agreed that no marriage was any good unless the partners were free.

Jane made it clear that there was to be no sex between them. Though she was wearing Paul's fedora on the bus and smoking her little Cuban cigars, she was a true daughter of the middle class: she was determined to be a virgin until she was married.

Later Jane told Paul that it was on the bus to New Orleans that she began to fall in love with him. She must have seen in him both her own image and its opposite, or rather one of her opposites. They were alike in many ways: to begin with, in their having been so different from other children so early. Both he and she agreed that children understood everything, and that it was an insult to treat them as if they didn't.

They appreciated the wit and liveliness in each other. She, like he, didn't always know when she was being funny, but quickly discovered it from the laughter of others, and went on as if she'd intended to be funny from the first. Out of their naïveté they both had learned to fashion a way of being.

They both knew a good deal about humiliation. His experiences with his father had left that mark on him. She knew humiliation early, from some indefinable thing, something in her being—her sense of her body—her imagination—her food "sweet and natural" to her, but shameful to others. She had a deep sense of her physical flaws, of herself as "Crippie." And Paul, despite his impeccable, handsome exterior, felt a sense of physical ungainliness, some fundamental lack of coordination, which he associated with his father, who had hit him on the left hand until he became right-handed as everyone "should" be.

Paul had learned to disguise his wanting, learned not to want to want. Jane, once she wanted something, would accept no limit on getting it. Much that she had been given by her indulgent mother she had never wanted. Now, she felt, she knew what she wanted.

In their originality they shared an antagonism to imposed systems of thought, to academia, to intellectual and literary snobs. He put a value on the unconscious, on setting the mind aside and letting other parts of the self lead. He was able to make separations within himself that she would never be able to make. He came to regard work as a separate thing from life. For her, life and work would become the same thing.

To both of them the question of choice was crucial. When he had the decision before him whether to go to Europe or to kill himself, he had relinquished choice to chance. Choice had to do with knowing what you wanted. "If you don't know, it's better to have the choice made for you by the tossing of a coin." That was his way out of dilemmas. But she had no capability of relinquishing choice. She had to choose and to accept the consequences of her choice. It was to become a moral question so relentless, the matter of choice in all small and large things in life, that eventually she would be almost paralyzed by it. But now, when she was young, she was still able to choose, making trade-offs with herself, or so she was persuaded.

She judged herself unsparingly. Her way of evading the judgment of others was through her feminine wiles. Whereas from the time Paul set out for Europe—and even before—he refused to be judged. In giving up the responsibility for choice, he gave up his vulnerability to the judgment of others.

He could take models from the outside world to imitate—for example, Lafcadio in Gide's *Lafcadio's Adventures*, who would stick himself with a pin if he did not meet the standards of behavior he set himself. Jane never could do that; she had to create the model for her own behavior out of something in herself. If she took a model, it was only to mock it and herself. In this way Paul was much closer to the outside world than she was. Yet it was she who cared more for other people, whose whole life was lived through and with other people. For him what mattered finally was work, preserving and using his own talent: "Relationships with other people are at best nebulous; their presences keep us from being aware of the problems of giving form to our life." To be with others, she squandered her talent, a talent she both feared and hated. That talent made demands on her and yet she felt judged if she acceded to them.

She was a Jew who hardly even knew she was a Jew, who had found a mock past in Elsie Dinsmore's piety. He grew up in a household as intolerant of religious belief as of sensuality. In his family there was also a never quite acknowledged suspicion of Jewish ancestry. It was betrayed by a strange and brutal tradition. In his maternal grandfather's family, the father would shatter the bones of the nose of each son with a hammer.

"It was insane. They broke the bridge of the nose, smashed it flat. No one said why. I knew about it when I was a child. Later, much later, I thought about my great-grandfather emigrating from Germany to America. And I remembered what my mother's cousin had said after a visit to Germany, that the name Winnewisser was Jewish, and it occurred to me that perhaps it was because the nose was Semitic that they broke it. Perhaps that was why they were all atheists and so violently against any religion.

"When Lenny Bernstein first met my mother, he said, 'She's a nice Jewish lady.' And I said, 'Jewish? She's not Jewish.' And he said, 'Get off it.

Are you pretending, don't you know she is or what?' And then he wanted to see pictures of her brother and I showed him a picture of my uncle Paul and he said, 'Yeshiva bucher.'

"And Janie once made the mistake of looking at my mother's picture and saying to her, 'You look like Fanny Kaplan.' You know who Fanny Kaplan was. She was the Jewish woman who tried to assassinate Lenin."

JANE AND PAUL AND THE TONNYS SPENT THREE DAYS IN NEW ORLEANS AND then took a bus for Laredo, going through Houston. Paul wrote to Virgil Thomson from Houston:

> Wish that you could be with us. We stayed in New Orleans three nights. Superb city. Janie has lost her makeup case, her sandals, her disorder and that's all.

In Houston Jane was as high-spirited as she had been on the journey from New York. But once they left Houston and crossed the border into Mexico, everything changed for her. The buses were more primitive, and the landscape was unfamiliar, even savage. Suddenly she was terrified. All the fears that had arisen in Leysin when she was in the hospital bed now surfaced on that bus ride. She was terrified of the mountains and the precipices. She was terrified because the bus driver was drunk. She was terrified of the dogs that ran free in the villages, so she wouldn't stir out of the bus. She spent two days cowering on the floor in the back of the bus among the Indian women with their babies and their bundles. She wouldn't even look out of the window. She was terrified and she was also suffering from dysentery.

Tonny, who had been trying to get Jane to go to bed with him, was furious at her behavior. When the bus stopped, she wouldn't do anything that the rest wanted to do. She'd say, "You go ahead, I don't want to go." Tonny called her a "dirty little bourgeoise." He told her she should have stayed home with her mother. At first Marie Claire sided with Jane, but then she too said she was spoiled and difficult.

The night they arrived in Mexico City, Jane jumped out of the bus, hired a porter to carry her luggage, and announced she was going to the Ritz. Paul tried to stop her, but Tonny and Marie Claire told him to let her go. They found a cheap hotel and the next day the three of them went to get her at the Ritz—but she wasn't there. Three days later, having searched through the city, they discovered her at the Hotel Guardiola.

The night she had arrived she had awakened with a high fever and terrible pains from dysentery, had tried to crawl to the bathroom, and had lost consciousness. The hotel maids found her on the floor in the morning and called a doctor, who for three days gave her shots every hour. When Paul and the Tonnys came, she was lying in bed, surrounded by flowers she herself had ordered.

The three of them were apologetic about having let her go off by herself. They stayed several hours with her and joked with her, trying to cheer her up. When they left, they said, "Tomorrow you'll be better. You must come with us," and it was agreed that they'd come back the next day at lunch and get her. But when they arrived at the hotel, precisely on time, she was gone. The desk clerk said she had checked out and flown to Tucson.

"Thank God," Tonny exclaimed. Marie Claire said, "It's all your fault, you were so nasty to her. You were mean and sadistic and she's just a little girl." She kept arguing with him, and Tonny, feeling that his wife knew that he'd been after Jane to go to bed with him, said, "I said I was glad she's gone. What more do you want?"

Paul himself felt relieved that she had left. It would be easier traveling without her. That she had gone off so suddenly without a word—well, after all, he reasoned, there had been nothing between them. He thought he had come to know her during those days on the bus when they had talked so constantly, but he did not know her, after all. It was better that she go back. It would be easier without her.

FOR YEARS JANE NEVER TOLD ANYONE WHAT SHE DID WHEN SHE WAS IN Arizona. But in 1960, in Tangier, she told a story to her friend Ira Yeager. "She said she was once in Arizona and went to a carnival. There she saw a 'freak,' a half-man, half-woman. She said she flirted with the man-woman and they went out to dinner together. She told the story as if it were a great joke."

In 1943, in an early version of "Camp Cataract," Jane wrote a scene about a man who is like a woman—not a physical hermaphrodite as in the carnival, but a man who had accepted the place and feeling then ascribed to a woman. In the scene Sadie tells of a visit she had made to the house of an aunt and uncle when she was a child:

It was nearing evening and the kitchen was not on the side of the setting sun, like the parlor was where we'd been sitting—so it was dark in the kitchen. The lamps weren't lit yet and it took me awhile to get my eyes used to the darker light, when I did see my uncle in a corner doing something near the stove. I looked and looked all around the kitchen— for a woman. I thought it was the darkness that was hiding the woman but no matter how hard I looked I could not find her. I had never seen a man alone in a kitchen before and it gave me a funny feeling. "Where's the woman?" I asked him. "Where's the woman?" He turned round right away and came over to me.

"What woman, child?" he said.

"The woman—the woman for the kitchen."

"There is no woman for this kitchen, child," he told me, and then he stroked my hair.

"Who makes the food?"

"I make the food, child. I boil the potatoes and I roast the meat and I bake the bread and I bake the pie." He didn't sound unhappy, but my heart was heavy like stone, listening to him. We were almost in darkness. He went away to a place outside the kitchen, the cold pantry I should say it was, where they store some of their food in the fall of the year, and he came back to me with two cabbages, one in each hand.

"These I planted." He placed them side by side. "I boil them with a ham butt or with stew. They were only just picked a little while ago." He pressed a cabbage to my cheek. "Nice and cold?" That's what he asked me. "Nice and cold?" But I couldn't answer him. I was afraid because I was sorry over him. He listened—I remember how he listened—and waited for me to say something about the cabbage, but I couldn't. "I'd better get some light in here," he said finally. Then I wanted to run away. But I couldn't. I couldn't move my legs any more than I could talk.

The lamp shade was a big red globe with flowers painted on it. I stared at those painted flowers. They were pink with long narrow petals. Then I looked up at him. I could see his beard now and his dark eyes in this better light. They were the sweetest eyes I'd ever seen in my whole life, but that did not prevent his face from being very manly. He was big too and heavy set—dark hair like his dark eyes.

Jane may have spoken of the flirtation with the half-man half-woman in Arizona as great joke. But there is no trace of laughter or irony in this scene of a child seeing a man as sweet and caring as a woman. And even as she flirted with the hermaphrodite, there must have been in that joke an intimation of her own uncertainty about her own sexuality and about what choice she would make of that sexuality, assuming she had a choice.

From Arizona Jane went to southern California, where Genevieve Phillips was staying at the time. There, Jane later told Dione, she and Genevieve had an affair. From southern California Jane went on to New York, where once again she returned to her life "with artists and Pseudo-artists," going to Spivy's Roof and the Askew salon.

When she received a letter from Miriam saying that her baby had been born in April and inviting her to come to Minnesota to visit, Jane replied:

My darling darling friend

I have been in Mexico I have been in Arizona I have been in California. I did not know you had a baby—it's beautiful. I am in the middle of a novel—and Big dramas all around me. I'm not sure I'll come out on top there are so many things against me. Believe me Miriam I would have written you if I had known—I was very ill in Mexico. I can't write you now. I was on my way out when I got your letter and I was so horrified at what you must think was carelessness on my part that I had to sit down and write. . . . I am so glad you were persistent and wrote me. I lost all my addresses in the desert somewhere. I should love to visit you. Will you write me and tell me whether you are really serious or not? . . .

Please believe me I appreciate your loyalty.

Love

Jane—your vagrant friend

One of the "Big dramas" around Jane concerned her mother, who had met Julian Fuhs, a musician and a refugee from Germany. Claire wanted to marry Julian, but she would not do so as long as Jane was single.

Many years later Jane wrote about this period in an autobiographical fragment:

My mother was very nervous about me because I was not looking for a husband. She would try to frighten me with threats of being taken to live at the poor farm. My father had died . . . and my mother had spent what money he had left. Like all mothers she hoped I would marry a man who would take care of me. By the time I was twenty she had become extremely nervous, because she wanted to get married herself.

Claire kept pressing Jane to marry one of the eligible young Jewish men they knew, but Jane wasn't interested. She said she wanted her mother to marry and she wanted to be free herself. But her effort at freedom in going to Mexico had almost ended in disaster. Though by now she knew the power of her wit and her charm and her intelligence, still at the same time she felt a sense of helplessness. As she had written Miriam, "I'm not sure I'll come out on top there are so many things against me."

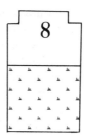

8

IN AUGUST, AFTER A FOUR-MONTH TRIP WITH THE
Tonnys in Mexico and Guatemala, Paul returned to New York and stopped
at the Hotel Chelsea. He was working on the orchestration of a ballet, *Yankee
Clipper*, one afternoon when the phone rang. It was a woman calling. Paul
didn't know who it was, and said very brusquely that he was working. The
woman became hesitant and suddenly Paul realized it was Jane Auer. She
was calling to ask him to spend the weekend at Deal Beach, New Jersey,
where her mother had rented a big house for the summer. Virgil Thomson
was also coming that weekend, Jane told him.

Paul had not heard from Jane since she had left Mexico. From the way
she had gone off, without a word, he was convinced that she didn't want to
see him. He himself would never have called her, but when she called him,
he accepted the invitation immediately.

There were many people at the house in Deal Beach that weekend.
Claire liked to have Jane's friends around. She saw to it that there was plenty
of food and she was not critical of their behavior. On Saturday evening Paul
and Jane went to the black section of Asbury Park and bought reefers. They
returned to Deal Beach and stayed up all night with the others, talking and
playing charades.

Soon after, Paul's parents went away on vacation. He invited Jane out to
their house for the weekend. He tried to get her to go to bed with him, but
she wouldn't have it. As usual she spoke French. "Je ne suis pas en train de
faire l'amour avec toi." He was disappointed, but accepted what she said. He
had come to understand that for all her outrageous behavior, Jane was a strict
moralist. To her, marriage was a commitment of a special kind.

They kept seeing each other all that fall and early winter. When *Yankee
Clipper* was performed in Philadelphia, Paul and his mother and Jane went
there by train along with John LaTouche and his friend Marion Chase. "We
must have ordered drinks as we rode, for I remember great laughing all the
way. That was when Mother decided that Jane was wild."

As Paul recalls it, "Jane and I used to spin fantasies about how amusing it would be to get married and horrify everyone, above all, our respective families." They talked about where they'd go on their honeymoon. Jane was to get some money when she married, and they could use it to travel. They'd spin the fantasies and then they'd say to each other, "But of course we won't get married. It's terrible to be tied." Then somehow that changed into, "Why don't we? Let's."

"From fantasy to actuality is often a much shorter distance than one imagines. . . ."

If some people were amazed at the announcement of the marriage, others concluded that it was just a marriage of convenience. The composer David Diamond recalls that he had "quite a talk" with Jane. "I can still hear that soft purr of a voice saying, 'But honey, I'm so lonely.' And she limped off to get a cigarette."

Still other friends decided that Jane was marrying Paul because her mother was pressing her to get married, because she wanted to get away from her mother, or because as the wife of Paul Bowles, the successful composer, she would have a status in the art and music world she had not had before.

And Paul? He was attracted to Jane and intrigued by her. He had never known anyone like her. One gets married, he said to himself, as if that were an answer or a reason.

ESTELLE LEWIS, DIONE LEWIS'S MOTHER, REMEMBERS THAT JANE RAN INTO her apartment to tell her the news of the engagement. " 'I'm getting married,' Jane said to me. She was full of excitement. 'I'm eloping.' 'Why do you have to elope?' I asked her. 'Your mother will be glad to see you married.' Anything to annoy her mother."

But Jane did not elope. The marriage was to be a conventional one. And first there had to be the proper preparations. Paul recalls that "all the women in Jane's family made such a fuss. Boxes of clothing kept coming in for weeks from Henri Bendel and Jay Thorpe and Bergdorf Goodman. I had to go around every night and see all these clothes which she was to take on our honeymoon." Jane's mother and her aunts were delighted at the turn of events. As for Paul's parents, his mother accepted the decision, though she said, "Her leg is going to be a handicap for her." Paul's father said something about marrying a cripple. They were careful, however, not to say anything about Jane being a Jew, though later when they met Jane's relatives, there would be many asides about furs and jewels.

Paul and Jane were married February 21, 1938, the day before Jane's twenty-first birthday. The marriage was performed in a small Dutch Reformed church in Manhattan, in the presence of Paul's parents and Jane's mother. Jane sent Dione a telegram: "MARRIED PAUL TODAY. OFF TO PANAMA TOMORROW. LOVE TO GENEVIEVE."

ON FEBRUARY 22 PAUL AND JANE SET OUT FOR PANAMA ON THE FREIGHTER *Kano Maru*. They traveled as if they were going to Central Africa in the 1890s. With them they had two wardrobe trunks, twenty-seven suitcases, a typewriter, and a record player.

The *Kano Maru* was a small freighter, with one room set aside for baths. In it were two wooden tubs, one eight feet deep, the other, a smaller well. The room had no lock. One morning Jane was taking her bath in the smaller tub. As she was bathing, the captain entered, undressed, and with perfect composure got into the other tub. Jane, who was always excessively modest about her body, kept saying, "I beg your pardon." The captain in clipped English discussed the good weather they were having.

Jane was in wonderful spirits. It was as if she'd been released from prison. She was amusing and funny and full of mischief. Paul found, more than he had expected, that she was an absolute delight to be with. He felt closer to her than to anyone he had ever known.

In Panama City they went to an American bookshop and bought a complete set of Lewis Carroll's works. While they were in the shop Jane caught sight of *The Young and the Evil*, a novel by Charles Henri Ford and Parker Tyler, friends of theirs from New York, and she stole it. "It was the only time she ever did anything like that," Paul says. "She was even more mischievous when I was around because I doted on her mischievousness, on her uniquely amusing quality that no one else could ever come near, on her wonderful elliptical way of seeing things."

With that "elliptical way of seeing" Jane would show, in *Two Serious Ladies*, Mr. and Mrs. Copperfield arriving in Panama. It is a caricature of Paul and Jane's own arrival:

> They got into a taxicab and Mr. Copperfield insisted on going to a hotel right in the center of town. Normally all tourists with even a small amount of money stayed at the Hotel Washington, overlooking the sea, a few miles out of Colón.
>
> "I don't believe," Mr. Copperfield said to his wife, "I don't believe in spending money on a luxury that can only be mine for a week at the most. . . ."
>
> "The room in which I sleep is so important to me," Mrs. Copperfield said. She was nearly moaning.
>
> "My dear, a room is really only a place in which to sleep and dress. If it is quiet and the bed is comfortable, nothing more is necessary. Don't you agree with me?"

"You know very well I don't agree with you."

. . . They found one [a hotel] right in the heart of the red-light district and agreed to look at some rooms on the fifth floor. The manager had told them that these were sure to be the least noisy. Mrs. Copperfield, who was afraid of lifts, decided to go up the stairs on foot and wait for her husband to arrive with the luggage. Having climbed to the fifth floor, she was surprised to find that the main hall contained at least a hundred straight-backed dining-room chairs and nothing more. As she looked around, her anger mounted and she could barely wait for Mr. Copperfield to arrive on the lift in order to tell him what she thought of him. "I must get to the Hotel Washington," she said to herself.

Mr. Copperfield finally arrived, walking beside a boy with the luggage. She ran up to him.

"It's the ugliest thing I've ever seen," she said.

"Wait a second, please, and let me count the luggage; I want to make sure it's all here."

"As far as I'm concerned, it could be at the bottom of the sea—all of it."

"Where's my typewriter?" asked Mr. Copperfield.

"Talk to me this minute," said his wife, beside herself with anger.

"Do you care whether or not you have a private bath?" asked Mr. Copperfield.

"No, no. I don't care about that. It's not a question of comfort at all. It's something much more than that. . . ."

They followed the bellhop to one of the rooms, and no sooner had they arrived there than Mrs. Copperfield began pushing the door backwards and forwards. It opened both ways and could only be locked by means of a little hook.

"Anyone could break into this room," said Mrs. Copperfield.

"I dare say they could, but I don't think they would be very likely to, do you?" Mr. Copperfield made a point of never reassuring his wife. He gave her fears their just due. However, he did not insist, and they decided upon another room, with a stronger door.

But this is fiction, life transformed and selected. Then, when they were in Panama City, she wanted to talk to everyone, to shopkeepers, to servants, to people she met on the streets. Paul, who was not inclined to talk to strangers, stood around waiting for her.

From Panama City they went to Costa Rica, going now toward the more exotic, the less populated places that always intrigued Paul. "We got in touch with people who had a cattle ranch in the province of Guanacaste and accompanied them there. The trip lasted two days. We had to go back down to Puntarenas and take a ferryboat that threaded through the inland lagoons and eventually pushed up a narrow, tortuous river. The vegetation hanging above us as we went inland was exciting, and the crocodiles sunning themselves along the banks not fifty feet away did not even bother to shut their monstrous jaws."

On the ranch they would get up at five each morning and ride horseback most of the day. Jane even agreed to go with Paul into the jungle on horseback, though he had to persuade her. At first she said, "Why don't you go? I'm not sure I'm up to it." But then she thought of a way that would work for her. Instead of Paul and Jane going alone with a guide, they went with fifteen cowboys and the manager of the estate. In the jungle, Paul remembers, "we passed by trees with great monkeys in them. On the lower branches were fathers beating their chests and way up were the mothers and babies looking down at us."

Both Paul and Jane were intrigued with the animals and the birds. In Guanacaste they were offered one of seven baby parrots, but Jane refused to take it because, she said, she couldn't bear to think of breaking up the family. At their next stop, Bebedero, however, the proprietor of their hotel appeared in the doorway with a full-grown parrot perched on his finger. This bird spoke its own language. "Its favorite word, which it pronounced with the utmost tenderness, was Budupple. When it had said that several times with increasing feeling, it would turn its head downward at an eighty-degree angle, add wistfully, 'Budupple mah?' and then be quiet for a while.

"Of course we bought it; the proprietor put it into a burlap sugar sack, and we set out downstream with it. The bend of the river just below Bebedero was still visible when it cut its way out of the bag and clambered triumphantly onto my lap. During the rest of the two-day trip to San Jose the bird was amenable enough if allowed to have its own way unconditionally."

In their hotel in San Jose, Budupple ate a tube of toothpaste, a contemporary Russian novel titled I Love, and a tortoiseshell lorgnette which Jane's mother had given her as a present. (Jane was very nearsighted and her mother had thought the lorgnette would be more fashionable than glasses.) Jane was delighted that the lorgnette had been eaten, but both she and Paul were afraid the glass would kill the parrot and for several days they carefully examined its excrement.

In Puerto Limón they had a tin cage built for the parrot, but he ate through the cage and perched on top of it. Hurrying through the streets of Puerto Barrios to catch a train—with six porters in tow with the twenty-seven suitcases, two trunks, typewriter, and record player—Paul, who was carrying Budupple on top of the cage, set it down for a moment. Budupple slid to the ground and waddled off toward a mango tree. Paul threw the cage after him and they hurried on to where the train was waiting. But a bystander ran after Budupple, caught him, and thrust him through the open window of the train just as it was leaving. Eventually they left Budupple in Antigua, in an avocado tree in the back patio of the *pensión* of a Señora Espinoza.

Out of their adventures with Budupple came a game that Paul and Jane played with each other for years after. In this game Paul was Bupple Hergesheimer, a parrot in the shape of a man. He was monstrous in his behavior, both disapproving and disobedient. He had a limited repertory of words, including "rop" to signify disapproval and "bupple" for the few occasions he showed approval. Jane was Teresa Brawn, the mother, the aunt, and the governess of this young man who knew he was a parrot. She'd say, "Come on, come on," and he'd light on her hand with one claw and she'd pull him toward the cage. "Now, aren't you happy? You see how pretty your cage is," she'd say to him. "Don't you love what your aunt has done? All that side has been done in plastic and if you bang your head on it, you won't hurt it." Paul would say, "Bupple," but then suddenly he'd say, "Rop."

They'd usually play this game when they were alone, though sometimes, when they were with other people, Jane would suddenly become Teresa and say to Paul, "Get back in your cage."

On the honeymoon Jane seemed to revel in the freedom of being away from her mother. Yet it was no simple freedom, young as she was, day after day in strange places with a man she had once called her enemy and then had chosen (and been chosen by). But that was only the first of the choices; there were all the others that would have to be made together in the marriage, made with another as complex as she. And there were all the puzzles of the likenesses and the differences, thrown into sharper relief by being alone with him over an extended time in places where none of her usual evasions were available to her. What she had seen in Paul as "sinister," she could see more clearly now as his need for the primitive.

Once Jane insisted on going her own way. They were in Guatemala City and had met a group of men students in the Hotel Astoria with whom they spent the afternoon talking about literature. The young men had just started to read Proust and Valéry and were astonished that Jane, "only a girl," knew so much more about both than they did.

In the evening they all went to a café together. Finally, at ten-thirty, Paul said, "I think we should go back to the hotel."

"Certainly not," said Jane.

"I'm going," said Paul. "If you want to stay, stay. You know where the hotel is. I'm going home to bed."

Back in the hotel, he couldn't sleep. He kept waiting for her, but she didn't come in and she didn't come in. Finally he fell asleep. When she came in hours later, he woke up and he saw immediately that she was very upset.

"I almost never got back at all," she said, but she wouldn't tell him anything more.

Only several years later did she tell what had happened to her. Somehow or other, she and the students got to talking about brothels. She told them that she'd never seen one, but had always wanted to. The students agreed to take her, and they went to a house at the edge of the city.

After their arrival, a large man in uniform entered with a pistol in his holster. He was the chief bodyguard of the dictator of Guatemala, and was surrounded by his own bodyguard of men. Looking around the room he saw Jane and said, "That's the one I want."

Jane was terrified. The students tried to protest. "This is a tourist," they said. The proprietor offered him one of the other women. "No," he said, "I want that one."

The prostitutes sneaked Jane into a back room, locked the door, and got her out of a window into an empty lot behind the brothel. When the chief bodyguard realized that the women had played a trick on him, he became enraged. He and his bodyguards went out into the street, got into their Cadillac, and began driving up and down, looking for Jane with a huge spotlight. All the time she was crouched behind a pile of refuse, terrified that they would find her.

Fortunately they did not and when she got back to the hotel, she would say nothing to Paul about what had happened to her. In secrecy she was still finding her absolution.

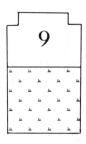

9

At the end of April, en route to Paris, Paul and Jane sailed from Puerto Barrios to Le Havre on the German liner *Cordillera*. It was not a pleasant voyage. They were surrounded by ardent Nazis, who objected to the "degenerate" calypso music Paul played on his phonograph. From Le Havre the Bowleses went on to Paris. Now they were in a civilization that they both knew, not in a world where he guided her to primitive places, but back where she had been before, in a place where she felt at home, with a language she knew well.

> In Central America [Paul writes] life had gone smoothly; Jane and I never argued, never grew tired of being together. In Paris she had friends, and I was suspicious of them. It was painful for me to go back to the hotel room at dinner time and find that she had not yet come in, finally to have dinner alone and rush back to find the room still empty. And Jane was not one to change as a result of my suggestions.

Though they had had an agreement that each was to be free in the marriage, Paul found it painful now that Jane had begun to act out the terms of that agreement. He had let himself feel closer to her than he had ever felt to anyone, and now things were not as he had anticipated. The two of them went to Max Ernst's, where they met a number of surrealists, but Jane was not comfortable with them. She wanted to be with friends of her own. So she would go out to bars by herself, especially to a lesbian bar, the Monocle.

He wanted to spend time with her, to be alone with her, but she was always with other people. He tried to get her to leave Paris, to go to North Africa with him, but she refused, and kept going to the bars. In a café near the Panthéon she met a man who kept after her to go to his hotel room with him. She told Paul about him; she said she found him absolutely revolting, he was so obscene and lecherous. Yet he fascinated her somehow. Each night she'd see him, he'd ask her again to go to his room with him, and each night she'd put him off, making an appointment to see him the next night. Only some years later did she see a picture of Henry Miller and say to Paul, "But that was the man in the café in Paris."

In the daytime she would also go off by herself, to a café on the Left Bank, near the rue Bonaparte. She went there to write. She would not discuss with Paul what she was working on; she told him only that she had begun writing in French, but had soon switched to English. Paul didn't know what to think of Jane's work. She had given him *Le Phaéton Hypocrite* the summer before, but he had read only about thirty pages of it, and then put it aside. At that time he had been too preoccupied with his own work to pay much attention to her novel. He had no idea what she was working on now since she would not discuss it. In any case, he was more concerned with what was happening to the marriage.

Several times Paul became so upset that he went to the café near the Panthéon and tried to get her to come back to the hotel. He insisted that she go to the south of France with him and she refused.

Jane and I had disagreements about her coming in at three o'clock every morning, but with the result that she was annoyed with me rather than repentant. . . . After a scene which was more heated than usual, I took off for St. Tropez by myself. . . .

Paul may have been the one who left—that is, the act of leaving was his—but by this time their relationship was already so complex that it was not clear to either one who had abandoned whom. Further, every action and every gesture between them was always more than itself. It was also an action and a gesture in their creative imaginations, part of their separate fictional worlds that were coming into being.

So one day Jane would write of a wife leaving a husband. Her setting is Panama, shortly after Mr. and Mrs. Copperfield have arrived there. Mrs. Copperfield leaves the hotel to spend most of her time with a woman she has met, Pacifica, a prostitute. Still, with a certain guilt, she thinks of Mr. Copperfield back at the hotel, and returns to him. Mr. Copperfield presses her to go off to the jungle with him, but she does not want to.

"Please let's not discuss it."

"All right," said Mr. Copperfield. He looked sad and lonely. He enjoyed so much showing other people the things he liked best. He started to walk away towards the edge of the water and stared out across the river at the opposite shore. . . .

"Oh, please don't be sad!" said Mrs. Copperfield, hurrying over to him. "I refuse to allow you to be sad. I feel like an ox. Like a murderer. But I would be such a nuisance over on the other side of the river in the jungle. You'll love it once you're over there and you will be able to go much farther in without me."

Mrs. Copperfield gets on the bus and goes back to Pacifica, while Mr. Copperfield goes ahead into the jungle.

"I hope his day has not been spoiled," she said to herself. The tenderness that she was feeling for him now was almost overwhelming. She got back on the bus and stared fixedly out the window because she did not want anyone to see that she was crying.

Paul, for his part, would one day write of a husband leaving a wife. In "Call at Corazón" a young couple are on their honeymoon on a boat in Central America. The husband is a young man who is detached yet unforgiving. He carries a notebook in which he records his observations:

> More than anything else, woman requires strict ritualistic observance of the traditions of sexual behavior. That is her definition of love. . . . Modern, that is intellectual education, having been devised by males for males, inhibits and confuses her. She avenges. . . .

Just as the boat is about to leave port the husband purchases a monkey. Angered by his purchase and upset by a storm that rocks the boat, the wife begins to drink. He reproaches her:

> "You realize what you're doing, of course."
> She glared at him. "What am I doing?"
> He shrugged his shoulders. "Nothing, except just giving in to a passing emotional state. You could read, or lie down and doze."

They argue about the monkey who has made a mess of the cabin. "I like monkeys because I see them as little model men," he says to her. "You think men are something else, something spiritual or God knows what." Nevertheless, to please her, he gives the monkey away.

The next day they board another boat, which goes through a waterway so narrow that branches from the trees on the bank scrape the walls of the cabins and lash the deck. Once again the wife goes on a drinking bout and now he becomes angry and leaves the cabin. When he returns she is gone and he is very disturbed: "It was always very hard to sleep when she was not there in the room. The comfort of her presence was lacking, and there was also the fear of being awakened by her return."

He searches the boat for her and finds her lying drunk and unclothed beside another man. Without saying anything to her, he packs their things and leaves the boat with them at the next stop.

The story ends with the husband feeling a sense of vengeance:

On the crowded, waiting train, with the luggage finally in the rack, his heart beat harder than ever, and he kept his eyes painfully on the long dusty street that led back to the dock. At the far end, as the whistle blew, he thought he saw a figure in white running among the dogs and the children toward the station, but the train started up as he watched, and the street was lost to view. He took out his notebook, and sat with it in his lap, smiling at the shining landscape that moved with increasing speed past his window.

These were fictions yet to come, translations by their imaginations of what had happened between them. The actuality of what had happened, as Paul reconstructed it, after the fight in Paris and his flight to the south of France is: "Once I got there, I found that I was completely miserable. I wired and urged Jane to come to Cannes, where I met her."

He was still upset, he who had always prided himself on being cool. When she arrived, she began to talk about what she had been doing, about the Monocle, about the people she had met. He became sullen and dismissed the life she had been leading as worthless. She upbraided him for being a killjoy and in a sudden rage he struck her. He was stunned at his loss of self-control and his violence toward her. Weeping on the bed, she said to him, "I love you just the same." He felt a terrible remorse and they reconciled.

Still, something had changed between them. He had learned how vulnerable he was to her. Only one other person in his adult life had caused him to become violent, his father:

> . . . at the age of nineteen I was astonished one night to discover that I had just thrown a meat knife at my father. I rushed out of the house, shattering the panes of glass in the front door, and began to run down the hill in the rain . . . the throwing of the knife, which was now a fact rather than a fantasy, worried me with its implications of future danger. If it were so easy to lose control in this situation, it would be just as possible to lose it in one where the results might be tragic. As usual I reminded myself that since nothing was real, it did not matter too much.

But with Jane, when he lost control and struck her, it was not possible to say that "nothing was real, it did not matter too much." For it was with Jane and through Jane that things had become "real."

FROM CANNES, PAUL AND JANE WENT TO ÈZE-VILLAGE, ON THE GRANDE Corniche, where they rented a house on the top of a mountain overlooking the Mediterranean. Without the distractions of Paris, Paul was able to begin work on his music again. In their daily life he tried to correct what he felt was Jane's sloppiness. Jane had never learned to dress herself, let alone wash her clothes or iron them. And she was in the habit of just dropping things on the floor when she undressed. Paul would pick up after her and would say, "Jane, you're so messy, so untidy." That didn't interest her at all. "If you don't want to see it on the floor," she'd say, "you take care of it." But though she hadn't the slightest interest in housekeeping, in Èze-Village she began to work in the kitchen with their cook, a peasant woman named Jacqueline. Jane learned to love cooking, and in time proved an excellent cook herself.

At Èze the Bowleses met S. L. M. Barlow, an American composer, whose wife invited Paul to dinner without Jane. It was not uncommon for women in the musical world at that time to invite husbands without their wives, but this incident enraged and upset Jane.

For the most part, however, Paul and Jane got on very well in Èze. They continued to talk of things they had never spoken of to others. She tried to convey to him something of her ideas about men and women. She'd say to him, "Men are all on the outside, not interesting. They have no mystery. Women are profound and mysterious—and obscene." She told him of having fallen in love with Cecil, and of going out to earn money to buy clothes for her. She said she made some money when she was paid for an act of oral sex with a man she picked up. "It didn't mean a thing," she said to Paul. She was just glad when it was over. "There's nothing disgusting about men," he remembers her saying to him, but then she added "in an almost religious way, 'There *is* something disgusting about women.'"

What Jane meant by that Paul did not understand, though in her fiction, working laboriously, a few words at a time, then scratching them out, she was always trying to explore in fictional form what was mysterious in women. In an unpublished version of "A Guatemalan Idyll," Jane uses the word *disgusting* about a woman character, for the one and only time.

She describes Señora Ramirez as middle-aged and fat, with a deep voice like a man's. Her chin is heavy and her skin is dark and coarse, but she has beautiful blue eyes. Staying at a *pensión* (modeled on the *pensión* where Paul and Jane stayed in Antigua), Señora Ramirez seduces a young American traveling salesman. He is astonished and even terrified by her passion. When they have completed the act of sex, she says to him, "That is all I want to do ever." In the morning she goes for a walk to dream of her lover, but is distracted by the sight of a volcano in the distance.

> She had started on this walk in order to dream joyously about her lover, but the thought of this volcano which had erupted centuries before chased all the dreams of pleasure from her mind. "God doesn't send such big trials any more—like floods over the whole world—and

plagues." She thanked her stars that she was living now and not before. She was always quite weak at the thought of any woman who had been forced to live before she was born. The future too, she had heard, was to be very stormy, because of wars. "Aye," she said, "precipices on all sides of me." It had not been such a good idea to go on this walk. It was better to do always what you were used to doing and not take a chance. She thought again of the traveler, shutting her eyes for a moment. "Lover—my darling lover—" she whispered and she thought of all the little books lettered in gold which concerned love and which she had read as a young girl, without the burden of a family. These little books had made the ability to read seem like the most worthwhile and delightful talent in the world to her. Never of course had they touched on the grosser aspects of sex but it did not occur to her to find it strange that it was for this physical culmination that these tender lovers pined. For to her it all seemed part of the same beauty, the nosegays and the thrashing about and groaning with pleasure at night. But then she was a woman who did not find it embarrassing to pull her pants down and make pipi in the fields in front of other ladies—and who had never averted her eyes from a pregnant woman's stomach even as a child—so connecting the traveler with the poplars and the red flowers that grew out of the walls along the road, seemed to her quite natural after the night before. She was disgusting in the way that anyone is disgusting who practices carelessly the ideology of a defunct group of people without feeling the need out of which such an ideology arises.

And immediately Señora Ramirez finds a young boy on the road and seduces him.

Señora Ramirez is disgusting in her too easy reconciliation of tenderness with the "grosser aspects of sex," in her naturalness that exists side by side with a sentimentality she has accepted unquestioningly. What is disgusting in her is that she "practices carelessly." Except for fear, she has finally no imagination. She is without a sense of sin.

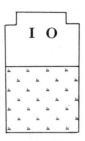

I O

IN SEPTEMBER 1938 PAUL RECEIVED A TELEGRAM THAT Orson Welles wanted him in New York to work on the music for William Gillette's farce *Too Much Johnson* for the Mercury Theatre. With their twenty-seven suitcases and two wardrobe trunks and record player and typewriter Paul and Jane sailed on the German liner *Europa* to the United States. In New York Paul set to work on the score, but when he finished, Welles decided to postpone the production. Paul felt that he had been "taken":

> We were now very poor, having spent what was left of our wedding money, after the Central American honeymoon, in getting settled in our house at Èze. The fact that we had then given it all up and returned to America on the strength of a promise which failed to materialize rankled considerably with me. I felt that I should have had some compensation for my work and my trouble, something more than the $100 I was given. But there was nothing to do about it.

They found a cheap place to live in a 150-year-old house without heat on the corner of Seventh Avenue and Eighteenth Street, run by an elderly woman, "Lady" Saunders. Lady would stand outside her door and ask passersby to come in off the street and have a drink with her. She also liked to tear things out of one room, then use the wood or bricks to build a bookcase or a fireplace in another room. Never one to worry about the building codes, Lady improvised, drunk and sober, so the building was in a continuous state of change.

Once Paul and Jane had a fire in the fireplace Lady had built in their room. The entire floor ignited. Lady laughed and said she'd rebuild everything. Then she went out on the street and invited someone in for a drink. On cold days, when the wind blew through their room, Paul and Jane stayed with a friend on Sutton Place.

But if their housing was not all it might have been, to comfort them they still had that world within a world they had known when they first met. They spent a lot of time with John LaTouche and Teddy Griffis and Harry Dunham and Marion Chase. Virgil Thomson referred to these four and Paul and Jane as "The Little Friends." He was their unofficial guru.

The Little Friends faithfully attended the Askews' weekly salon. Certain composers were always present: Virgil Thomson, Aaron Copland, Elliott Carter, and Marc Blitzstein. Lincoln Kirstein and George Balanchine would appear with their dancers. Others who came were connected with the Museum of Modern Art: Tchelitchew, Eugene Berman, Philip Johnson, Russell Hitchcock, Alfred Barr, and Iris Barry.

At the Askews' Paul often sat at the piano and played and sang his own songs. Meanwhile, Jane sat first in one man's lap and then in another's.

"She wasn't really flirting," says Paul. "She might touch the man's ear while she was talking to him. She was making contact, I guess. I never understood what it was all about. I think it was for her own pleasure and also to test her powers. She was always having to be sure of how strong she was. The men enjoyed it. I don't think the wives always did. As soon as she sat in one man's lap another one from across the room would say 'Come on over here and see me.' And she'd say, 'Just a minute until I finish with Bob.' And when she was done with Bob, she'd go on to the next one."

She combined in herself the gestures and behavior of a small child, an apparent innocence, along with an extreme sophistication in her conversation. Often she said things that people didn't understand. The lightning-quick connections she made were never obvious. She didn't disclose the intermediate steps. What she said was often puzzling and at the same time hilarious. If asked, "What did she say that was so funny?" no one can give an exact answer. Her wit was in her words, of course, but was also in her timing, in her play of voice against gesture.

Aaron Copland remembers her as mysterious. "I never knew what went on in her head. She was far more mysterious to me than Paul was. He was reserved, but open with those he knew well. She had a curious childlike quality. She was very sensitive and easily upset, but only at certain things, and you never knew why. You only knew that whatever her response would be, it would be original.

"When I knew them then, Paul and Jane seemed inseparable, though they were rarely together. I had the impression that she needed him more than he needed her."

Jane, as far as anyone observed, was not writing. People thought of her as too self-indulgent to be a writer, as someone who was only interested in her own pleasure. She was spending a lot of time with LaTouche and with a singer named Marianne Oswald, who called herself "The Voice of France," at Spivy's and at other nightclubs.

With his usual self-discipline Paul kept working hard at his music. He was offered a job as a composer for the Federal Music Project at $23.86 a week. But in order to qualify he had to be on relief. He went through a complicated procedure, establishing residence at a room on Water Street in Brooklyn.

> The investigator came sooner than I had dared hope and was more than sympathetic. She was an intelligent and attractive girl named Kaminsky, very much interested in culture. I explained that I was in the midst of writing an opera and played her some of the second act of *Denmark Vesey*, which I was working on there. I told her how I had given up my home in France and come to New York to work for the Mercury Theatre, only to be let down and left stranded. She was indignant and thought I had a case against the theatre, but I insisted I was not thinking of lawsuits—only of getting on relief. She said she would do everything to help me and hoped to be able to bring me my card on Friday. I suggested that she come to dinner Friday night at John Becker's on Sutton Place, where Jane and I were actually living. The guests, the champagne, and the works of art pleased Miss Kaminsky very much. She did have my relief card ready for me, and she went home at two in the morning as happy as I was.

As a result of the events in Europe—the downfall of Republican Spain, the takeover of Austria by Hitler, the appeasement by Chamberlain at Munich, and the surrender to Hitler of Czechoslovakia, Paul decided to join the Communist party. The year before he had attended a CP meeting on Republican Spain, but he had been regarded with suspicion by members of the party. One of the women said to him, "I may as well confess to you that when you first came in we all said to each other, 'A typical fascist head.' " But now Paul joined and was accepted without question.

Jane, who had almost no interest in politics on her own, accepted Paul's political opinions and joined the party with him. They were sent to a beginning class on Marxism-Leninism at the Workers' School. "I don't know what I'm reading," she complained to Paul as she went over the textbook. "I knew what I was reading," Paul later wrote, "but that made it worse. We tried to compensate for our lack of devotion to Marxism-Leninism by seeing every Russian film that came to New York."

Looking back now, Paul says, "My interest in the party was strictly personal and neurotic. I thought it was a nice slap at my family. I liked the ideology because it was destructive of the given order. That fit in with my nineteenth-century romanticism."

But whatever the reasons that moved him, once he joined he was to find it very painful to accept that the party betrayed his hopes as fully as his

Sidney Majer Auer, Jane's Father, 1905.
COURTESY ALUMNI ASSOCIATION, UNIVERSITY OF MICHIGAN

Jane, Woodmere, late 1920s.

*Jane, taken in a penny arcade
booth, June, 1935.*
COURTESY GEORGE MCMILLAN

Honeymooning At Sea

—Ella Barnett photo.

MR. AND MRS. IRVING LEVY, 420 N. Mississippi River blvd., aboard the liner Santa Paula, off for a wedding trip through the Panama canal to the Pacific coast. Mrs. Levy is the former Miriam Fligelman, daughter of Sol Fligelman, Hotel Lowry.

COURTESY MIRIAM LEVY

Paul's family and Jane, 1938. Front row, from
left: *Pauline Winnewisser Sackett; Jane; Rena Bowles, Paul's mother;
Aunt Dorothy Winnewisser.* Back row, from left: *Claude Bowles,
Paul's father; Uncle Paul Winnewisser; Paul; Uncle Fred Winnewisser.*

Helvetia Perkins, 1940.

Jane in Mexico.

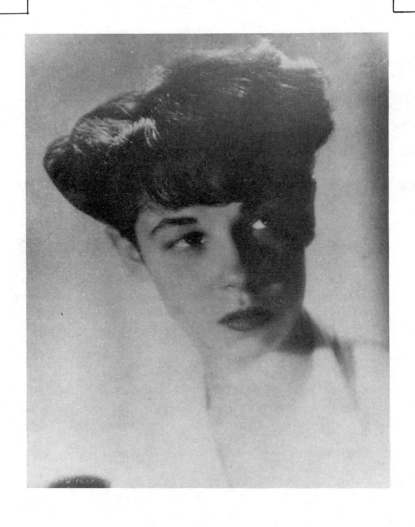

Jane, early 1940s.
COURTESY HEDGEROW THEATER COLLECTION

family had ever done. In that disillusion, for him as for many other artists who joined the party then, some permanent fracture was to take place, some final loss of hope of reconciling their inner creative life and the outer "real" world.

ON HER RETURN FROM EUROPE, JANE WAS NO LONGER THE ELEGANTLY DRESSED young woman whose mother had taken her from Henri Bendel to Bergdorf Goodman, pinching her if she made a fuss before the salesgirls. Now Jane had taken to wearing boys' shirts, to dressing in what was then a shockingly casual fashion. Estelle Lewis, Dione's mother, said to her when she saw her, "Don't you care how you look? Are you trying to get back at your mother?"

In fact Jane saw her mother infrequently. Claire had married Julian Fuhs in March 1938, the month after Jane was married. According to Dione, Julian did not care for Jane. He was "very Germanic and a real stickler for discipline," and he thought Jane was self-indulgent and spoiled. Though Claire was now his wife, her feelings about Jane, her focus on Jane, had not diminished. She still called Jane her "million-dollar baby." She still could not resist touching her, patting her, picking at her when she was present, a situation Jane tried to avoid. When Claire saw Paul, she talked to him of her worries about Jane's complexion and hair and health. She kept asking Paul to take care of her.

That spring Miriam Levy came to New York again with her husband. The Levys were both intensely involved in refugee work, trying frantically to get as many Jews out of Germany as they could; they knew they had little time left.

The Levys visited Jane at Patchin Place, where she and Paul were now living. "I found that whole environment completely incomprehensible. While I was there, people kept coming in and out, making announcements. Jane would say, 'Mir is my best friend,' and they'd nod and go on with whatever they were saying. I remember that there was a delicate screen in a corner—maybe it was a Chinese screen. You could see that behind it laundry was collected in a big pile, so high it was falling over the screen.

"I had the feeling that in some way Jane was unfit for the practicalities of daily living. She'd always been protected from having to do things for herself. There had always been lots of money and people to pick up after her and do things for her. But now that wasn't so.

"When I spoke to her about the refugee problem, she sat there with a half-surprised look on her face—it's a look many nearsighted people have—and I remember her chin was cupped in her hand. I spoke very seriously because it was of great importance to me, but I had the feeling the whole thing didn't exist for Jane—either the war that was coming or the thing with the Jews. In her response to me there was a sense that she had no interest in Jewish things, as if being a Jew was only an accident of her birth. With anyone else I would have been very angry, but with Jane I didn't feel that way. I don't know how to say it, but she was a being apart, and I didn't use the same standards with her as I did with other people."

At the time Paul was working on the music for *My Heart's in the Highlands* by William Saroyan, and Miriam went with Jane to a rehearsal. She remembers that Jane was very proud of Paul and excited about his work. Later that day they went to Spivy's for a drink. There for the first time, "it began to dawn on me—something in the way others treated her and the way she responded—that Jane was a lesbian. Perhaps I should have known before. I'd been told that story by the two men who had gone out on a date with her and that other girl. But I'd just thought that was Jane being funny. Now I realized that it wasn't quite that."

When Miriam left Jane she felt strangely sad. It wasn't Jane herself, wearing her boys' clothes, mimicking and laughing, as bright and impish as she'd always been. Nor was it the bohemian life as such, nor the lesbianism. "It was more the way the people were with whom she was spending her time. Maybe it was me, but I had the feeling that there was no way of getting under their skins—as though the only contact you could make with them would be of the shallowest kind. And that bothered me for Jane. I didn't think that life was good for her."

ONCE AGAIN, AS SHE HAD DONE IN PARIS, JANE WAS STAYING OUT LATE AT night, at parties or at Spivy's or other nightclubs. Paul had given up trying to change her. He had decided that "if you want to be with someone, you accept what she does." They spent a lot of time apart, he with his work and his friends, she with her friends. Still he often waited up for her at night, sometimes all night long. "She would be out and she wouldn't come back all night and then she might come back in the morning without her shoes. More than once she did that. And it was the middle of winter."

"Where did you leave your shoes?" he'd ask her. "Where have you been?"

She'd answer that she'd been wandering around the docks all by herself at four or five in the morning.

"Why?"

"Because that was the one place I didn't want to be. I'm terrified of it."

"Then, Jane, why did you go?"

"Don't ask me. You ought to know why. I had to or I couldn't face myself in the mirror tomorrow if I hadn't gone because that was the one thing I was afraid of."

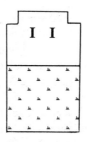

I I

IN THE SPRING OF 1939 WITH THE MONEY PAUL MADE
from *My Heart's in the Highlands*, he rented an old farmhouse on Woodrow
Road in Staten Island. At that time southern Staten Island was a landscape of
small woods and open fields, with here and there a farmhouse. 1116
Woodrow Road—long since bulldozed by developers—was surrounded by
trees. Across the road, several hundred yards east, were a church, the
parsonage, and a cemetery.

The Staten Island farmhouse became the model for Miss Goering's little
house in the country in *Two Serious Ladies*.

Paul and Jane painted the inside of the farmhouse and furnished it with
basic necessities. He was working hard on his own music and on his
assignments from the Music Project. She was working sporadically on her
novel. He'd speak to her about working, but she was more interested in
cooking. Sometimes when she had done some work, she would come and
show Paul a small section of it, but he couldn't understand it. "I'd never seen
anything like it before. So many things were left out. And then Jane's
spelling and punctuation were terrible."

Many visitors would come out to the farmhouse on weekends, John
LaTouche, Colin McPhee, Leonard Bernstein, the Brazilian singer Elsie
Houston, and Judy Tuvim (Judy Holliday) among others. But Paul and Jane
were often alone, and Jane felt isolated. She would, like Miss Goering, be
frightened by noises in the silence.

There was a sudden scrambling in the bushes below the window. Miss
Goering jumped.

"What's that?" Her face was very white and she put her hand to her
forehead. "My heart hurts so for such a long time afterwards whenever
I'm frightened," she said in a small voice.

And Jane, just as Miss Goering would do in the novel, began to make

journeys to the mainland. She would walk to the train that would take her to
Tottenville, at the end of Staten Island, and from there would take the ferry
to Perth Amboy, New Jersey. It was Paul who first introduced Jane to Perth
Amboy. He pointed out the surrealist and the Kafka-esque quality of the
city. "We both pretended we were in a foreign country. It seemed very
exotic."

In *Two Serious Ladies* Miss Goering takes her trips to the mainland out of
a compulsive need. Her friends reproach her for going alone. One of them
suggests that he accompany her. " 'Not this time,' she said. 'I must go
alone. . . . It is not for fun that I am going, but because it is necessary to
do so.' "

What defines the necessity for Miss Goering is never clear. She only
knows that she has a moral obligation, something to do with "salvation," and
she makes her journeys out of that obligation. "She even felt a kind of elation,
which is common in certain unbalanced but sanguine persons when they
begin to approach the thing they fear."

As Paul remembers, Jane did not go on her journeys to Perth Amboy
alone. She took someone else with her to see the little brick buildings with
neon lights and the seedy bars. "Jane loved the bars. She thought there was
something sinister in them."

If Miss Goering is only partly Jane, Jane was only partly Miss Goering,
the character who so resolutely goes on her journeys. Jane was cooking, she
was writing now and then, she was living her daily life, she was being "Jane."
Paul remembers an incident from that time, which he feels is "completely
Jane."

"We were all sitting out on the porch, LaTouche and Teddy Griffis, and
Harry Dunham and Marion Chase, and Jane and I. It was a Sunday evening
and suddenly we heard piercing screams of agony coming from the
parsonage down the road, next to the little church. The screams were so
terrible that we all jumped up and Jane ran to the phone and called the
police. Five squad cars arrived at the parsonage almost at once. One of
them later came to tell us what had happened. The pastor had caught his
twelve-year-old daughter trying to get out of the house. He was a very
restrictive man and she wasn't allowed out in the evenings. He caught her
just as she was going out the door, and he closed the door on her arm and was
squeezing it. That was what the screaming was. 'That guy's nuts,' the police
said, but there wasn't anything they could do but warn him. When they left,
this terrible fear began in Jane. It went on for days, the belief that the pastor
was going to come and wreak vengeance on her for having called the police.
Weeks later she was in New York, in the Murray Hill Hotel on Park Avenue
and Fortieth Street, and I went to see her. She had a room on the top floor.
The ceiling had a double pitch—the hotel had a mansard roof—and the walls
and the ceilings were covered with very bright wallpaper. Jane was supposed

to be working, but on her desk were eight or ten letters which all began the same way, 'Dear Pastor Dowe.' Some of them said, 'I'm so sorry to have bothered you.' Some began, 'I feel I should apologize for interfering.' The last one, on the top, said, 'Dear Pastor Dowe, I hate the wallpaper in this room.' "

Everyone found the story preeminently "Jane" and laughed. She herself laughed. Perhaps she recalled—though she said nothing to anyone—Elsie Dinsmore and her father, who was so angered by his daughter's disobedience. Whatever Jane remembered, the laughter she evoked from Paul and the others over the letters was a triumph of sorts, a temporary settling of past anxieties, from a childhood that would never be killed.

LATE THAT SUMMER, AS THE WAR WAS ABOUT TO BEGIN IN EUROPE, PAUL received a letter from Mary Oliver, a woman who had helped him when he first arrived in Paris, penniless. Mary was a flamboyant woman who claimed to be an illegitimate daughter of Gurdjieff and who also practiced levitation. She loved to eat and drink and was skilled at running up huge bills in department stores and grocery stores without ever paying for them. Now she asked Paul if she and her German maid could stay with him, adding that she had enough money for beer and champagne if he could provide the food. Since it was Mary Oliver's mother who had gotten Paul an illegal passport for the trip to Paris, he felt under great obligation. "I suspected that her arrival would bring trouble, but I could scarcely do otherwise than tell her to come whenever she felt like it." Jane also wrote to Mary, but apparently her letter was never mailed. Instead Paul sent it to a friend, Kay Cowen, saying, "I hope Mary Oliver never will see it." He was obviously amused by it.

Dear Mary Oliver,

I would be so delighted to have you and your German maid come to Staten Island (S.I.). First I shall explain about money and then I shall go on. Paul earns at the moment twenty two dollars a week on WPA (music project) and that is what we live on. I'm perfectly willing to take a chance on our all eating on that if you are. There are many exceedingly cheap foods such as rice, potatoes and faroja—faroja is a strange Brazilian flour which you brown in butter and salt. You receive it by mail from a Mr. Silver in Brooklyn. There are also the excellent Brazilian black beans which when cooked with a lump or two of fatty meat and a great deal of garlic make an exceedingly tasty dish. Two people or rather four people are not twice as expensive to feed as two strangely enough. And if you ever do get a little extra money while you are here I might tell you that around eight dollars will feed two people for a week. Paul will probably stop getting his checks suddenly anyway and then we will all be in the soup which doesn't frighten me. The only people who must eat are Paul and the cats. Paul is extremely desperate and neurotic if he doesn't. I have explained all this to you because I want you to know what you are getting in to. We would all have a place to live as the rent has been paid until November the fifteenth. I daresay we might get some friends such as Harry Dunham who has paid half of the rent to keep it with us another month or two. As for room during the week there are two extra beds. On many weekends Harry Dunham comes down with his fiancée, therefore one bed is occupied. I have two very fine mattresses which we bought in Nice and three thick sofa cushions all of which could be made into an adequate bed which I would be glad to sleep on when there were extras. A German man slept on them last summer on the roof for weeks so it would be no hardship for whoever gets them. I myself have a huge innerspring mattress on a straw mat which sleeps at least three and many extra ladies have slept with me on weekends. Paul has one too but he refuses to share it with anyone. You can see that there is enough room presenting no problem at all during the week and really none on the weekend as weekends are always very complicated or terribly simple and rainy and lonely.

We have now dispensed with the purely physical aspects of your visit if there is to be one. Paul is terribly worried that you might not like the house. He wants you to know it is like a little cottage in Glenora. We have no servant and very few rugs. At any rate you can see no other house from our grounds. We are surrounded by fields rather dry. I do not think it's depressing. There are fruit trees and a rotten vegetable garden. Harry Dunham just arrived, and he is a wonderful person to have around. We go into New York City once a week. One can get there for around forty-five cents so you could if you liked see your friends when you wanted to. And for people with cars it is no effort at all to drive out here nor does it take much time at all. The only thing that worries me is that you might be bored as Paul is working on his opera [*Denmark Vesey*] and I on my book, but he says you love to read. In the evenings we can play games and drink champagne. I am not working every minute of the time but I must finish it while we still have a roof over our heads and I am always tempted to chat and lazy around. If you do not think it will be too awful we would really love to have you. I myself am always completely happy when there are three people in the house and four people will be a real *nest*. . . .

When Mary Oliver arrived, Paul later wrote, the "quantity of alcohol consumed at the farmhouse increased by the week. Mary would call the nearest liquor store, which was several miles away, and get the manager to promise to drive out with some bottles after he closed. Once there, he would begin to drink and would stay on interminably. Then she would find a pretext for not paying him. When I left the establishment, she owed him more than $200. I kept urging Jane to leave with me (for there was no way of getting Mary to do anything quickly) but Jane said she was enjoying herself and saw no reason to cut the enjoyment short in such an arbitrary fashion. If she did not come with me, I warned, I would not answer for bills that came after my departure. But Jane intended to leave the farm on Woodrow Road when she was ready and not before; she advised me to relax. I suddenly had become a teetotaler, from long watching of what happens to people when they drink too much. Also, abstention naturally gave an edge to the voicing of my complaints. But from the drinker's point of view there is nothing so unpleasant as having a nagging ex-drinker at his side. . . ."

Still Paul stayed on, trying to work despite what was going on around him. Jane by now was enjoying herself so much she found it hard to work at all. In response to a letter from Charles Henri Ford inviting her to a party, she wrote:

> . . . I am asking your permission for Mary to come although it is hardly necessary as she is the nicest lady in the whole world. . . . I was rather upset about what you wrote concerning Robeson. . . . I shall take matters into my own hands and phone Juanita Hall immediately because Paul is a slow person. Juanita said earlier in the summer that she would introduce Paul to him as she thought Paul Robeson would be excited about the opera. He was then abroad. I am going to call Juanita this evening. Of course the opera isn't finished. Paul hasn't worked this week because we got into debt. Since the arrival of Mrs. Oliver our life has been quite exciting and there are a lot of changes in the house. I hope Paul will work next week. . . . I will let you know if anything happens as a result of my call to Juanita. . . . I hope you will like my book. I hope to get it finished this month if too many upsetting things don't happen.

Jane did not finish her book that month. Furious at the disorder and the drinking and the extravagance, Paul left the farmhouse and moved to a room in Brooklyn Heights. Jane stayed on in Staten Island with Mary, who continued to pile up enormous bills which no one could pay. Shortly after Paul left, without money but with her usual persuasive powers, Mary rented an apartment on Thirteenth Street in Manhattan. She moved there and Jane accompanied her.

"Jane came several times to spend the night with me in Brooklyn," Paul has written, "but claimed she did not want to live there, and anyway Mary was ill, and she had grown very fond of her and felt that Mary needed her to help her land on her feet. 'You'll ruin your health,' I declared. 'Nobody can drink that much.'"

Jane stayed with Mary for several months until things began to deteriorate. Wanamaker's came to take away the houseful of furniture that Mary had obtained on credit. By now she was lying on a mattress on the floor, drinking gin, and occasionally eating Broadcast hash, which sold for nine cents a can. She was also practicing levitation. "I'm leaving my body," she would say. "Uh, I'm against the ceiling."

By the spring of 1940 Jane and Paul were living together at the Chelsea Hotel. Paul was working on the music for William Saroyan's *Love's Old Sweet Song*. He had been out one evening and came back late to find their room full of people drinking and smoking. Jane had been telling Paul for years about a man called "Dick the Shit," and she introduced him to Paul that night. Paul wanted to go to bed, as he had to get up early the next morning to work on the show. He went into the bathroom and found a woman with bright red hair lying in the empty tub, wearing Jane's peignoir, a gift from Claire, of gray moiré silk with mauve satin stripes. Paul went back into the room and said, "Get these people out of here and get that woman out of the bathtub." Jane said, "These are my friends. They'll leave eventually."

There was a heated argument and finally Jane's guests left. But when she and Paul were alone, the argument began again. Paul kept saying that he would not be able to work if he didn't get some sleep. Once again, as in Cannes, Jane reproached him for his gloominess, for being a "killjoy." Once again Paul struck her and was horrified at what he had done. Once again she forgave him and said she still loved him. But after this the marriage broke apart sexually.

Paul tried to persuade her to renew their sexual relationship, but she said she did not want to. She did not want to discuss it. Eventually he gave up trying. In a way it was a relief to him. At least, he felt, it would be the end of having to wait up night after night, wondering what she was doing, whom she was with, whether she'd been hurt.

Changed, the marriage would go on. Their sexual life together was ended, but the devotion between them would now be sealed through their creative lives.

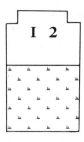

I 2

THE WAR IN EUROPE HAD BEGUN IN THE FALL OF 1939.
For months those Americans who were members of the Communist party, or
sympathizers, kept trying to account for the Molotov-Ribbentrop pact in
ways that would leave intact their own belief in the party. Paul recalls a
discussion of the pact with musicians who were party members or
sympathetic to the party line:

> . . . they were a very gloomy lot. Said one of them bitterly: "Well,
> where do we go from here?" I replied that we went straight ahead as
> though nothing had happened, because we would see it later as a Soviet
> ploy to crush the Nazis, and I argued that to falter in one's convictions
> at this point merely because of a detail like the pact would be proof that
> one's faith in the Soviet government had never been profound.

But despite Paul's emotional involvement with the party and the war,
the war was after all a continent away. What finally preoccupied him was the
immediate question in his daily life, how to be able to write his music, how
to earn a living so he would be able to keep on composing. In the spring of
1940 he was dropped from the Music Project, because he was judged
ineligible for relief when his case came up for review before the relief board:

> I had hoped to keep from the board the fact of my father's existence, but
> they got wind of it finally and sent an investigator to his house. The man
> they sent was black; he was asked to use the service entrance rather than
> the front door, where he originally presented himself. His report read:
> "Not in present need," and I was swiftly dropped from the relief rolls
> and thus from the Federal Music Project. "Damned good thing, too,"
> said Daddy.

Just at that time, however, the Department of Agriculture asked Paul to write music for a film being made by the Soil Erosion Service about the Rio Grande Valley. He told Jane he had accepted. His plan was that they would go to New Mexico for six weeks and then they would cross the border and go into Mexico, where they would stay as long as they could.

Jane wanted to go, but she didn't want to go with Paul alone. She had told him before how his gloominess depressed her. She called him "Gloompot" as a joke, but in fact she also admitted that being alone with him for long periods of time away from New York frightened her. She was unable to throw off the sense of despair which, she said, he created, especially when he made pronouncements about the coming end of modern civilization.

So when Paul suggested that they go to New Mexico and then Mexico, Jane went to Robert "Boo" Faulkner and asked him if he'd care to come along with them. At the time Boo was working for *The New Yorker*. Since he had a small independent income, he said he'd be delighted to quit his job and join them. He had found Jane to be a wonderful drinking companion. "She was rough and gentle and liberating, all at the same time. She would go into people's lives and make some dormant thing inside them come to life."

He was also charmed by her playfulness. On Halloween night the year before, Jane had telephoned him. " 'We're having a party,' she said. 'Come on over.' When I went into the house I saw that there was a Communist party meeting going on in the front room. Paul was there. I breezed right through. In the back were Mary Oliver, Ivy Troutman, and a Georgian princess named Nina Mdvani. The princess and Jane were bouncing rubber balls and drinking champagne.

"At the end of the evening Jane said to us, 'It's time to go home.' Then she went into the front room and announced to the CP meeting, 'It's time to go home.' "

After Boo agreed to go to New Mexico, Jane asked Paul if it would be all right. Paul wasn't pleased. He knew that with Boo along Jane would drink even more. But he finally agreed, knowing Jane didn't want to be alone with him away from New York and her familiar surroundings. He thought too that he could watch her and see that she didn't drink too much.

In April 1940 Paul, Jane, and Boo boarded the train to Chicago and from there took the Santa Fe to New Mexico. Paul was elated by the trip. "As we sped southwestward . . . , and I saw the sky growing clearer and brighter, I felt that life was opening up once again and taking on meaning, an ill-defined sensation which inexplicably comes upon me when I move toward unfamiliar regions."

As for Jane, she was drinking in the club car with Boo, counteracting in herself what made every journey a torment. As Mrs. Copperfield expresses it to Mr. Copperfield, "I don't have wingèd feet like you. . . . You must forgive me. I can't move about so easily. . . ."

After the long train journey Jane and Boo arrived in Albuquerque with a scenario worked out between them. To explain Boo's presence on the trip, they decided to say that Boo was Jane's brother. However, at a formal dinner at the home of filmmaker Richard Boke and his wife, the scenario, Boo remembers, got out of hand. "Jane was down at one end of the table and I was way at the other end. One of the women turned to Jane and commented on how nice it was that her brother could come along. 'Except for Boo,' she asked Jane, 'do you have any brothers or sisters?' Jane suddenly yelled down the whole length of the table, 'Do we have any brothers or sisters?' "

Paul's version of the disintegration of the scenario, as he writes it in *Without Stopping*, is somewhat different:

> I was for keeping the Bokes away from our apartment, but Jane felt that courtesy demanded we invite them, since she and I had so often been their guests. I suspect, too, that the idea of having them see Bob living there with us intrigued her. It was one of those setups that appealed to her dramatic imagination. And so, typically, she invited Desert Rose [a woman Jane had met in the local bar], too, for the same hour. The effect on the Bokes was interesting to watch. At first they took for granted, because she had a certain flair, that she was an eccentric drunk from their own milieu, but they did not remain under this impression for more than a minute or so, I should imagine. When they understood that they had a primitive in front of them, they were disconcerted. I glared at Jane for having called into existence this uncomfortable situation. I had asked her: "Who is Bob supposed to be?" "We're brother and sister," she had said, and this is how he had been presented. What with the nervousness caused by Desert Rose's presence, for she continued to talk, both Jane and Bob forgot their roles, and each began to refer respectively to "My mother" and "*My* mother." The Bokes looked confused, but again not for long, even when Bob tried to make it all into fantasy, saying "*My* mother's on tour with Barnum and Bailey. She's got two heads." As all nightmares do, the scene eventually came to an end.

After six weeks Paul finished the music for *Roots in the Soil* and he and Jane and Boo Faulkner took the train to Mexico. They crossed the border at Juárez and stopped at Zacatecas for a week.

"It was very cold in Zacatecas, so while Paul went around the town exploring, Jane and I stayed in the hotel and drank and played paper dolls," says Boo. "When I was in New York I'd bought a cut-up paper doll set of *Gone with the Wind*. In Zacatecas Jane and I reconstructed the entire plot. We changed sexes and ages. Jane rather fancied the mother.

"After Zacatecas we went on to Mexico City, where we stayed at the Hotel Buen Tono. But Paul wanted to be out in the country. He found a hacienda at Jajalpa, about fifty miles out from the city, near Toluca, complete with monastery. Jane said she wanted the room next to mine. At night, when she got nervous, she'd come in to see me. She wouldn't intrude on Paul. The two of us would sit and drink. She would talk in a dreary way about whatever was bugging her and then she'd tell funny stories."

Paul, who had chosen the hacienda, found it melancholy and sinister, though beautiful:

> It was a huge place with many rooms around a great courtyard. The mountaintops were on all sides, and the volcano of Toluca was there in all its detail, across a wide valley. I used to sit in an abandoned upstairs room and look at it. The vastness of the landscape had a paralyzing effect on me. . . . It was a melancholy place; the fact that it was so beautiful made the melancholy more insidious, more corrosive. The maidservants insisted that evil spirits wandered around at night in the rooms. . . .
>
> I went down to party headquarters in the capital and offered my services. They wanted to know where I lived. When I told them, they decided to run Sunday bus excursions to Jajalpa for tourists who wanted to visit a real, old-fashioned hacienda. This happened on only two Sundays. The sightseers were largely American, although there were a few Europeans among them. They looked at the livestock (we had eighty-five cows and hundreds of sheep) and the chapel and the immense courtyard, and wished they were back in Mexico City. But they had to have lunch first, for they had paid the agency for that before starting out. Jane was stoical about the situation.

Soon Paul began to feel ill. He couldn't eat and the sight of food made him sick. He decided to go to Acapulco to visit Lou and Rosamonde "Peggy" Reille, who had rented a beach house there. In Acapulco he quickly recovered.

"Then Paul sent us a telegram to come to Acapulco," says Boo. "We took a taxi for seven hundred miles, Janie and myself, two maids, and Janie's animals, a cat and a duck—maybe it was a hen."

Jane and Boo told Paul that when they moved out of the hacienda, the landlady had presented them with an enormous bill for lost objects, none of which they'd ever seen. Since neither Jane nor Boo was any good at business matters, they paid most of the bill. Paul was indignant, but recognizing that he'd left them to settle things, he didn't say anything.

While Boo went off to San Miguel de Allende, Paul and Jane stayed with the Reilles in Acapulco, then a very small town with a wooden pier, almost no electricity, and many mosquitoes. Rosamonde Reille, now Rosamonde Russell, had met Jane and Paul through Aaron Copland in New York. She remembers being delighted at first at the thought of having the charming Bowleses as houseguests. But there were unexpected complications.

"Both Paul and Jane were very hypersensitive and very vulnerable. They were afraid of Indians, of insects, and of being murdered. If a cock would crow in the middle of the night, they would be afraid. In the daytime they thought people in the plaza looked at them in a strange way, that they were conspiring against them. The whole world was hostile to them and everything was proof of danger. We ourselves began to absorb those fears the way blotting paper absorbs moisture.

"Then there were practical difficulties. Paul had certain compulsive requirements. He had to have hot soup in the middle of the day. He worked with earplugs in his ears and a bandanna on to shade his eyes."

The Reilles found it difficult to have the Bowleses living with them, yet they recognized that Paul and Jane were in Acapulco at their invitation. Their solution was to rent another house for them nearby. It was an exotic house with a patio 150 feet long, shaded by avocado and lemon trees. Between the rooms and the garden was a wide covered corridor, strung with hammocks.

With the Bowleses at a greater social distance, the Reilles could now enjoy their charm. "Paul could be very funny. He'd talk about his father, who had perfect occlusion. One of the family dramas he related had to do with his father's finding a tiny grain of sand in the spinach and going into a rage. Paul also had a great identification with parrots. I remember him as someone who did not show emotion.

"Jane was extremely devoted to Paul and very protective of him. She was also very funny. She'd make up songs. I remember there was one about a friend of ours named Schönborn. It had in it a line about his teeth being like piano keys."

Paul and Jane found the new house ideal for collecting animals. In addition to the cat and duck, they acquired a parrot, a macaw, a parakeet, a kitten, an armadillo, and two coatimundis. One of the coatimundis would sleep only in Jane's hair, Paul later wrote. "If she slept late, so did the coatimundi. I learned not to try to remove it; its resistance was expressed in two phases, the first of which consisted of covering its eyes tightly with its two paws and chattering rapidly, and the second of suddenly sinking its terrible little teeth into my hand."

Jane called the armadillo Mary Shuster. When Rosamonde would come to visit, Jane would say to her, "I'm giving Mary Shuster French lessons and she's learning quite rapidly."

"Jane didn't laugh—perhaps a little giggle. Once I went over there and she said to me, 'I've sent Paul to do the shopping. The list was pumpkin seeds for the parrot and Tampax for me.'"

Rosamonde remembers only one serious conversation with Jane. "Jane always wore a little piece of adhesive on her stiff knee, as if it were covering a wound. We did discuss TB, since I too had had it as a child."

Tennessee Williams met Paul and Jane in Acapulco that summer. Lawrence Langner of the Theater Guild had suggested he look them up.

> They were staying at a pension in town and Paul was, as ever, upset about the diet and his stomach. The one evening that we spent together was given over almost entirely to the question of what he could eat in Acapulco that he could digest, and poor little Jane kept saying, "Oh, Bubbles, if you'd just stick to cornflakes and fresh fruit!" and so on and so on. None of her suggestions relieved his dyspeptic humor.
>
> I thought them a very odd and charming couple.

Morris Golde, a young New Yorker, was in Acapulco that summer with his friend, the writer Gordon Sager. They had never met the Bowleses before but knew many people in New York that the Bowleses knew, including Marc Blitzstein and Leonard Bernstein.

"When we first met Paul and Jane, I had the impression that they were surrounded by an entourage. They both spoke Spanish very well. Jane was always concerned about others. I had the feeling that other women weren't concerned about me the way she was—about what I wanted to eat or what I wanted to do. I was a young kid who had just come out of the ghetto and it was extraordinary for me to meet someone with such wonderful manners, who was at the same time so concerned about me.

"We often went to the beach together. Before we went Jane would often have some confusion about making up her mind—whether we should go to the beach, and if we did go, what we should take. Paul would stay out of it and let us have our little discussion with Jane.

"Paul was an elegant, an exotic. He was elegant in the best sense, the most human sense. He'd let you know if he liked something or didn't. I do remember being astonished by one thing he said to me about his work. He told me that he would only write music on commission. In a way that was shocking to me. That wasn't the way other composers I knew worked. But then I thought about it and I decided it made sense that he would only compose what he was paid for."

To Rosamonde Paul and Jane were hypersensitive and vulnerable. To Tennessee Williams, Paul was petulant and Jane was "poor little Jane," trying to humor him. To Morris Golde, Paul was exotic and elegant and Jane was beautifully mannered and concerned. The differences were not imagined. Of course, we are all different with different people, changing according to place or circumstance. But with Paul and Jane that difference was extreme. People meeting them would be struck by particular aspects of their complex personalities and respond to those aspects intensely. And Paul and Jane responded to that response, intensifying it.

To each other, though, they were not paradoxical, or rather they saw and needed each other's paradoxes. If she complained that he made her feel gloomy, it was also true that she needed his gloom at times to keep her own at bay. If at one time he was fearless and she fearful, at another time this would reverse itself and she would become the courageous one.

He was fearless in going to strange, even threatening places, but he was always worried about his health. She was fearless in taking risks in terms of her health. She acted as if her body were invulnerable, yet she was terrified of almost any new landscape. He had learned how to deal with his own fears, but the fears of others—out of his control—he turned away from resolutely. She could not deal with her own fears, but for others she could take decisive action.

Once in the mid-forties, when Paul and Jane were living on Tenth Street in New York, they were on the roof and the wind blew a page of Paul's score to an overhanging edge. It was Jane, with her stiff leg, who crawled out and retrieved the paper, while he was paralyzed with terror for her. And one day when they were at dinner in the Acapulco house two peasants appeared, carrying a rattlesnake between two notched sticks. Suddenly the snake slipped out from between the sticks and darted to the floor. Jane's kitten, on the floor nearby, prepared to pounce on the snake. While everyone sat motionless, it was Jane who jumped up and got the kitten out of the way.

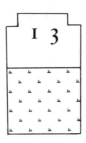

13

ΑFTER SEVERAL MONTHS JANE BEGAN TO TIRE OF Acapulco. She was trying to write, but was unable to. There wasn't enough diversion, there weren't enough people, she complained to Paul. When Morris Golde and Gordon Sager told her they were driving to Taxco for a weekend, she decided to go with them.

She found Taxco much more to her liking. It is a hill town, not far from Mexico City, known for its silver workshops. Americans who at another time would have gone to Europe, but couldn't because of the war, had discovered it. In Taxco there were some serious artists, some not so serious, some people there for pleasure, some to escape the war. At the center of town, just off the main square, was a bar where all the expatriates gathered. At once Jane felt at home. She stayed in Taxco a few extra days and then sent Paul a wire that she had rented a house there.

Paul was annoyed because Taxco was the one place in Mexico where he didn't want to live. He found its "carefully nurtured bohemian atmosphere" very depressing. Nevertheless, he agreed to the move if it would make Jane happier. With their accumulated birds and animals and belongings they moved to Taxco late that summer.

Boo Faulkner arrived from San Miguel to share the house with them. At once Boo and Jane got into the habit of spending a good part of the day at the local bar. They were on their way there one day, crossing the town square, when three women, obviously expatriates, walked by. "Do you see those women?" Jane said to Boo. "I'm going to change their lives." In fact it was her own life that was to be changed. One of the three women was Helvetia Perkins.

HELVETIA ORR PERKINS WAS FORTY-FIVE YEARS OLD WHEN JANE MET HER IN Taxco that late summer of 1940. She was divorced and had a twenty-one-year-old daughter. She was short and sturdy, with beautiful blue eyes. She looked like a conventional matron, but she was not what she seemed to be.

Helvetia, the youngest of six children, was born in Switzerland while the Orrs were traveling. The family home was in Evanston, Illinois, a large Victorian house near the lake. Helvetia's father was a self-made business-man, her mother a gentle quiet woman of "good" family. From an early age Helvetia was considered a rebel. She adored her father, whom the other family members considered a tyrant. When she was nine years old, her father died. Her mother fell into a state of melancholia, from which she never recovered. At first Helvetia was cared for by a governess and then by a brother.

In her teens she was sent to an exclusive girls' school, Miss Porter's in Farmington, Connecticut. In 1912 she went to Bryn Mawr. She never graduated. She was asked to leave, she later said, because of a funeral ceremony she held for her dog, whom she buried in a cap and gown.

Helvetia had strong political feelings and considered herself a radical. As a young woman she marched in a protest in Chicago. Her picture was in the paper and her family was horrified. In 1916 she married Frank Perkins and they moved to New Mexico. Their daughter, Nora, was born in 1919. Two years later Helvetia divorced Frank Perkins and moved to New York with Nora. She tried to find a job writing for a New York newspaper. She was even willing to take a job without pay, as she had an income from a trust fund. But she had no luck finding work, so she decided to go to Europe instead. She and Nora went to live in Paris, but traveled a good part of the time. In 1934 they went to Russia. It was another disgrace as far as Helvetia's family was concerned.

In the mid-thirties Helvetia and Nora returned to Chicago for a time and rented a house on the South Side, where, according to her family, "Nobody who was anybody lived." Nora went to public school and Helvetia attended classes in dialectical materialism. In Europe she had dressed elegantly, in the height of fashion. In Chicago she wore trousers and low-heeled shoes and bought her clothes at Penney's or at Marshall Field's basement.

She was a rebel who, away from Chicago, dressed as the genteel lady she was brought up to be. She was a very strict disciplinarian with her daughter. She wanted her to have an important career and became very angry when Nora later chose marriage and a family instead. Helvetia was a perfectionist who demanded perfection of herself as well as others. She was interested in writers and in writing. As a young woman, she had correspond-ed with Theodore Dreiser. Each day, with her usual discipline, she sat herself down to write. She was determined to write a book.

In 1940, with the war on in Europe, Helvetia and Nora came to Mexico. They had planned to go to Cuernavaca but somehow ended up in Taxco, which Nora disliked because of the "pseudo-artistic atmosphere. Everyone was writing or composing music or painting, or so they said. A lot of fakes, draft dodgers, and remittance men were staying there then," says Nora, who particularly objected to the fact that the Americans kept to themselves, separate from the Mexican society they lived in.

Nora remembers meeting Jane in Taxco that year. "Jane was terribly witty and amusing—though often witty at other people's expense."

IN *RUN SHEEP RUN* GORDON SAGER WROTE A FICTIONAL ACCOUNT OF WHAT happened in Taxco that late summer and fall of 1940. The novel is set in the village of San Pedro on the mythical island of Nunca-Nunca in the Caribbean. Three young people arrive in town, a husband and wife, Andrew and Gillian (Gill) Greenfeather, and their traveling companion, Kevin. Gill is a painter and Andrew is a writer. Gill has asked Kevin to accompany them on their travels since she is terrified of being alone with Andrew.

Kevin observes the "strange, very tender relationship that existed between Gill and Andrew. They loved each other very deeply (that fact was inescapable), although there could be no question of a conventional marriage. . . .

"Both Gill and Andrew were witty, imaginative, highly—perhaps excessively?—civilized. They were perceptive, they were articulate; they had odd theories on a number of exotic subjects. Beside them Kevin felt occasionally gauche, like a St. Bernard with two exquisite, thoroughly confident Persian cats."

Living in San Pedro, a refugee from Philadelphia, is a Mrs. Amelia Macy, who has come with her twenty-five-year-old daughter Janet. Mrs. Macy is forty-three years old. "Her life had been lonely and her face wore a fretful look it should not have had, for she was otherwise quite handsome. . . . Her blue eyes were as pale in tone as her hair, cold yet simple, trusting, rather impassive: often one did not know, when Mrs. Macy spoke, what was going on in her head."

When Mrs. Macy first meets Gill, she cannot account for

the feeling of excitement, of distilled vitality that surrounded her. There was also a faint tinge of lunacy in the air.

It was very peculiar, for Mrs. Greenfeather was not outwardly unusual at all. She was not tall, she was small-boned and slender. Taken apart, piece by piece, she was a feminine woman . . . and yet the general impression she gave was gamin more than anything else. She looked like an extremely alert newsboy, such as one might see on Third Avenue in New York, hitching up his pants, already aware that life was vagarious and not taken in by it. She looked as though she had long ago determined not to be stable in a world where all else gyrated.

Yet of course she doesn't look like that at all, Mrs. Macy thought; I'm reading all kinds of odd, romantic notions into her as I always do with new people who interest me. She is a pleasant girl of twenty-four or -five with a piquant sort of face. Her nose is impudent, her lips full and sensual, and her eyes are brilliantly sympathetic and remote at the same time—which of course is only another conceit, for her eyes are large and dark brown and nothing more.

Gill is also described as having certain morbid fears, of elevators, of high balconies, of large animals, and yet in spite of "all her morbid cowardice, her terror at so many aspects of contemporary living, Gill nonetheless had certain areas where she resided with a magnificent bravado."

She is very witty and playful and makes jokes that only Andrew can understand. Speaking to the real-estate agent Miss James, Gill says:

"I think the house sounds marvelous, don't you Andrew?" She turned to Miss James: "Is it called the Casa Simmons because it has Simmons beds?"

Miss James saw only the first level of the joke; but it was more complicated than that, for it was not a joke that Gill would make. Therefore she was imitating someone, but Kevin was not sure whom. It was not always easy to tell. Sometimes Gill herself was not sure, although Andrew generally knew. Kevin looked at him now, but he was talking confidentially to the other parrot.

It seemed likely that Gill was imitating Miss James. These little games were more than mere imitation; they were serious, in a way, as though Gill could no longer bear to be Gillian Greenfeather but had for a moment or two to be someone else, someone less tiring to be. That someone else was almost always a middle-aged or elderly lady. . . .

In this fictional version of that first season in Taxco, Gill Greenfeather and Amelia Macy have a love affair and Amelia is liberated by her new passion. (The novel ends in an act of murder and necrophilia at a masquerade party with Gill, cowering in fear, seeking comfort from Amelia.) Actually the love affair between Jane and Helvetia began as little more than a flirtation, one of many for Jane. Jane was always telling Paul about her flirtations. "What did you say?" he would ask her. And she would laugh and answer, "We talked about Paris."

The pursuit and seduction of Helvetia was a great challenge to Jane. Helvetia appeared to be so conventional—but was she? She appeared to be so in command of herself—but was she?

"Even as a young woman," says Gordon Sager, "Jane was powerful and she knew she was powerful." And she always had to be testing those powers. But with Helvetia, Jane was to find those powers tested in a way she had never anticipated. She was, perhaps unknown to herself, preparing for the words of Mrs. Copperfield: "I once was in love with an older woman. . . . She was no longer beautiful, but in her face I found fragments of beauty which were much more exciting to me than any beauty that I have known at its height. But who hasn't loved an older person? Good Lord!"

IN SEPTEMBER PAUL WAS CALLED BACK TO NEW YORK TO WRITE THE SCORE FOR the Theater Guild's production of *Twelfth Night* with Helen Hayes and Maurice Evans. Once there he decided it was time to quit the Communist party.

Jane stayed on in Taxco while Paul went to New York, expecting that he'd return in six weeks. But when he'd finished *Twelfth Night* Theresa Helburn of the Theater Guild asked him to start work on *Liberty Jones* by Philip Barry, a play that would require a complex musical score. Paul wired Jane and told her to come to New York, since he had no idea how long his work for the new show would take.

Jane and Boo Faulkner left Taxco for Mexico City en route to New York. In Mexico City Boo noticed that Jane was wearing sandals. "We'll go out and buy you shoes," he said. "But I don't have any stockings," she told him. They went out and bought Jane shoes and stockings and "somehow or other, I don't remember how, we got on the train to New York. I remember it was Christmas Eve when the train stopped in Pittsburgh for a short layover. It was snowing. By that time Jane had lost her shoes and her stockings and was back in sandals. Jane got off the train and I went with her. She walked up to a policeman and said, 'Can you please direct me to the nearest cocktail center?' "

In New York Jane went to live at the Chelsea, where Paul was staying. Now she resumed her old social life, seeing friends and going to Spivy's. She was again working on her novel. Now and then she would read a section of it to a small group of friends including LaTouche and Virgil Thomson and Edwin Denby, the dance critic and poet. They found the novel outrageously funny, particularly the way she read it. Jane would read, "When the traveler arrived at the pension the wind was blowing hard." (Then it was the beginning of the novel. Later it was to be the beginning of "A Guatemalan Idyll.") LaTouche would dissolve in laughter. "Stop it, Touche," Jane would say, though the laughter encouraged her.

She went to the Askews' salon, as she had before, but a change had taken place in it. What had only begun the year before—the takeover of the New York intellectual world by the French surrealists—was now accomplished fact. It was people like Marcel Duchamp, Yves Tanguy, and Dali who set the intellectual tone at the Askews.

Jane was uneasy with the surrealists. "She was very aware of them and felt left out," says Paul. She spoke French, as they did, but the language didn't seem to be the same language. "She thought they didn't want to know her because she didn't have any good surrealist ideas."

Jane may have said she didn't have any "good surrealist ideas," but in fact in her hesitancy about herself was hidden a profound disagreement with the ideas of the surrealists. They were interested in theory, in codifying the attack on society that had begun with the Dada movement. Their intention was to show the disarray and failure of existing society through distortion, through placing things side by side that contradict logic. They were committed as a group to the purposeful dredging up of things from the unconscious as a tool to show the disorder of the society they hated. It was a political as well as a literary and artistic movement.

Paul's early life and inclinations were such as to make this a technique fitting for him. When he was a child his mother had taught him how to let his mind go blank, and he had used that technique to discover what existed below the mind's surface. He had always been intrigued with bringing things back across the border. But the assumption of a definite border existing between the conscious and the unconscious and the deliberate intention to crossover were at odds with Jane's own vision.

For her there was no need to dredge up from the unconscious: its terrors existed side by side and interwoven with ordinary events. The distortions the surrealists deliberately created were those she experienced in daily life. If anything, her energies and her wit and wiles had to be used to keep in precarious balance what they deliberately tried to undo. No wonder she had no "good surrealist ideas." And then, unlike many of the surrealists, Jane did not think of herself as a political revolutionary.

THAT WINTER HELVETIA PERKINS ARRIVED FROM TAXCO AND STAYED WITH Jane at the Chelsea for a few weeks. When Helvetia returned to Mexico, Jane went with Paul on tour with *Liberty Jones*. In their hotel they shared the same room and, as always, played their invented games. Once they were staying at the Princeton Inn, which in those days had transoms above each door. Paul and Jane began to play their "seduction" game. In the game there was a great deal of shouting and this time, at one point, Jane suddenly yelled, "I'll get you for this. You've ruined my uterus." They both suddenly became silent and looked at each other. They had forgotten the open transoms. Across the hall, within easy hearing distance were Lawrence Langner and his wife Armina Marshall of the Theater

Guild. In the morning Paul was sure they looked at him suspiciously.

After *Liberty Jones* opened in New York, Paul and Jane moved to Middagh Street in Brooklyn at the suggestion of Lincoln Kirstein, for whom Paul was writing a ballet.

> Lincoln had made it possible for George Davis, who at that time was fiction editor of *Harper's Bazaar*, to sign a lease on an old brownstone house on Middagh Street in Brooklyn Heights. The purpose of his gesture was to provide reasonably priced living quarters for a group of people working in the arts. Gypsy Rose Lee had taken up residence in the house while writing a mystery called *The G-String Murders* (which George Davis always claimed he wrote), and having finished the book, she had moved out. Jane and I occupied the two empty rooms.
>
> . . . It was well heated, and it was quiet, save when Benjamin Britten was working in the first-floor parlor, where he had installed a big black Steinway. George lived on the first floor, Oliver Smith, Jane and I on the second, Britten, Auden and Peter Pears, the British tenor, on the third, and Thomas Mann's younger son Golo lived in the attic.

Paul was working on his ballet *Pastorela* and he kept urging Jane to write. But Jane was entranced by Auden and spent her mornings doing his typing and secretarial work for him. She would get up at six and go down to the dining room in the basement of the house and there she'd do his typing while he dictated to her. She also talked with Auden about literature.

"She was reading Kafka at the time and she discussed him with Auden," Paul remembers. "Auden knew quite a lot about Kafka's work. We had a terrible argument about it, Auden and I. I objected to his taking Kafka's work as religious writing. He considered it strictly religious. I said, 'But that's nonsense.' Now I don't feel that way, but that was 1941. Fundamentally Auden considered that each novel of Kafka's was a philosophical quest, fleshed out in allegorical terms. I said, 'Why can't they just be marvelous inventions, great novels?' And Jane said, 'Oh get back in your cage, Bupple.'"

Auden set and enforced the rules of the house. At the dinner table he insisted that there be no religious or political discussions. He also came around each week collecting money from the other boarders for food and rent and the servants. At that time Paul was still renting the small unheated room in Brooklyn Heights, where he occasionally went to work. One day Auden came to Paul at the Middagh Street house and said, "I'll be requiring your room for a time. A friend is coming." Paul, who was just getting over the measles, was incensed. He said he had no intention of leaving, to go and stay in an unheated room. Thereafter he and Auden did not speak.

With Jane, however, Auden was very indulgent. One day he came down the hall and found her playing one of her games, supervising a whole line of invisible girls. "Adelaide, tenez-vous droit," she was saying. Auden found it very amusing.

Boo Faulkner mentioned to Jane that he'd like to move into the Middagh Street house. He remembers that he was very hurt when Jane said to him, "You're not important enough." If Jane ever wondered just how important *she* was, there were those at Middagh Street to reassure her. Not only was Paul always after Jane to write, but Oliver Smith also recognized her talent. Oliver, who was a distant cousin of Paul's, kept telling Jane that he thought she had great potential as a dramatist. He admired her skill with dialogue, her lack of pretense, and her originality. He said to her, "Someday I'll give you money to start writing a play." Beginning in 1943, after he'd produced the successful *On the Town*, Oliver did give her money. And he kept giving her money over a period of ten years. Jane finally did write that play. It was *In the Summer House*.

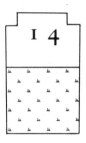

1 4

WITH THE MONEY FROM PAUL'S GUGGENHEIM FELLOW-
ship and with the royalties from his music for *Liberty Jones* and *Watch on the
Rhine*, Paul and Jane returned to Mexico in the summer of 1941. They sailed
to Veracruz and then went on to Fortín for a few days. Paul recalls the entire
valley there reeking of gardenias.

> The surface of the swimming pool at the Hotel Ruiz Galindo was
> strewn freshly each morning with hundreds of the flowers, which gave
> me the idea of buying enough gardenias to cover our bed. We got them
> at intervals throughout the day rather than all at once, so as not to be
> seen lugging a great quantity of them past the reception desk. When we
> had what seemed a sufficient amount of the blossoms, we dumped them
> all onto the sheeted surface of the bed, undressed, and lay on top of
> them. I have a hyperactive olfactory nerve, so the experience was
> unforgettable.

Back in Taxco, Jane began to work seriously on her novel while Paul
started a new score. In the morning he would leave the house to work in a
small hut, about an hour away on horseback. The hut was near the top of a
cliff, "overlooking an abyss where, from far below, there rose the faint roar of
a waterfall," a tropical version of the scene of his adolescent story, "The
Waterfall." Each day, when he left, Jane would set to work. It was hard
going for her, as it always was. Sometimes she would show Paul the work
when he returned at night. Other times she would say she had done nothing.
On the few mornings that he stayed home, he remembers, she would stand
by the window a great deal. Then she'd sit and write a few lines, scratch
them out, and go and stand by the window again.

When she wasn't working, she was drinking. Paul tried to get her to cut
down, but she paid no attention to him. Gordon Sager recalls that one
morning he and Boo Faulkner were out on the terrace drinking. "Jane, who

liked her booze as well as anyone, came out. She'd been working and she said, 'What's the matter with you two? Don't you have any inner resources?'"

To make the work go faster Jane took Benzedrine. But everything written under the influence of the drug was no good, Jane decided, so she threw it all out.

As during the previous fall, Jane was caught up in the social life of the town, in the drinking at the bar on the square, in the many masquerade parties. She went to one masquerade party as the "Spirit of Purim," to another in a white sheet which said "Ward Number Six" on her back, to another as "Flower." Each costume was equally inappropriate, each part of some little game Jane was playing.

She was seeing Helvetia Perkins every day and that relationship was becoming more and more intense. Yet between Paul and Jane and Helvetia everything was conducted in a polite and pleasant fashion. Helvetia had a station wagon and would take both Paul and Jane to market in nearby Iguala, where they bought fruit and vegetables and great quantities of the native pottery.

In a letter to Virgil Thomson that July, Paul wrote:

The old, accustomed paralysis takes hold of one's consciousness here. The place in itself is nonexistent, and some days are so completely empty, the hours of events and the air of any suggestion of an idea, that one is tempted to look down at one's toes and think of life and death. Which is a very bad sign, as you know. At any rate, I can always truthfully say that nothing has happened, because no matter what did happen, nothing would really have happened at all.

That summer the composer Ned Rorem, then sixteen, arrived in Taxco with his father. He had an introduction to two foreign residents in the town, Magda Marquez and Gilberte de Charanteney. Rorem called them and they invited him to come to tea. When he arrived, Paul and Jane were there.

"I was intimidated because I had never met anyone I'd heard of before and Paul was already a recognized composer. He was very blond then, somewhat like a blond angel.

"I said to Paul, 'I'm a composer.' He invited me to come and visit them at their house. I do remember at that first meeting watching the two of them. Jane wasn't paying much attention to me. I remember her rubbing her hand up and down his spine and he turned to her and said, 'Really, such intimacy.'

"Later I did go to see Paul. He was very interested in my musical work. I didn't see Jane to speak to again, though I remember seeing her with Helvetia Perkins at a big party given by a man called 'The Major.' Jane was very attractive."

In early August, Paul and Oliver Smith and Oliver's mother and stepfather and a young Mexican painter, Antonio Alvárez, went to Acapulco while Jane stayed in Taxco. After three weeks the others left Acapulco, but Paul decided to stay on, living in a tent on the grounds of the Hotel Costa Verde at Caleta.

In Taxco again Paul became ill. He kept taking enterovioform and could barely make himself eat. When he did eat, he felt even worse. Finally he became so ill that he had to be taken to Mexico City to the British Hospital, where he was diagnosed as having a severe case of hepatitis. "The hatred of Taxco which I had conceived during the days I lay ill there was so intense that I told Jane to get rid of the furnishings and the house."

Jane joined Paul in Mexico City, but he had not recovered from the hepatitis and had to go into a sanatorium in Cuernavaca for treatment. In November, while he was still there, Jane brought him the manuscript of *Two Serious Ladies*. He had seen sections of it before, and had in fact made many suggestions that Jane incorporated into the manuscript, but this was the first time he had seen it as a whole. He read it and told her that he thought it was wonderful. She said that it was no good. But then he shouted at her because it was such a messy manuscript. "You can't let anyone see such an abject manuscript. The spelling and punctuation are terrible." She said, "If there's a publisher, he'll take care of those things. They don't publish a book because it has perfect spelling, Gloompot."

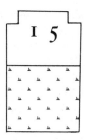

*T*WO SERIOUS LADIES IS AN AUTOBIOGRAPHICAL NOVEL, but not in the confessional sense. It is autobiographical, rather, in that in every moment of the novel Jane is present in each of her characters. She uses the fears she has known, the confusions she has had, and her own small meannesses. She uses the arguments she has heard and the tendernesses she has felt. The characters are not Jane, but she is in the characters, creating them and herself.

It seems, at first reading, to be a funny, eccentric novel and maybe not even a novel at that. It begins with a five-page section about thirteen-year-old Christina Goering, the daughter of a very wealthy family, who is despised by other children. Christina, who has the look of a fanatic and is in the habit of "going through many mental struggles—generally of a religious nature," persuades Mary, her sister's friend, to play a game called "I Forgive You for All Your Sins." She wraps Mary in a black burlap sack, packs her with mud, and submerges her in a stream to wash away her sins. When the game is over, Christina, troubled, tells Mary to go home.

This introduction was an extraordinary conjunction and rearrangement of autobiographical elements. It is a return to the age of thirteen, when Jane's father died, a return to the Holy Roller she had imitated, a return to her old and mocked friend Elsie Dinsmore.

Elsie Dinsmore's favorite book, after the Bible, was *Pilgrim's Progress*. Often Elsie talks to her father about Christian and his travels, how he tries to rid himself of the sins on his back. It is a very curious *Pilgrim's Progress* Jane is writing, with a very curious heroine—one of two—Christina Goering. (As for the name Goering, Paul says: "Jane used the name Goering purposefully, when she began writing the book in 1938. He was a ridiculous man at the time. We didn't know what monsters the Nazis were then. She wouldn't have joked about it, had she known.")

After this abrupt beginning, we see Christina Goering as an adult, "no better liked than she had been as a child." She still has the look of a fanatic and offends people by the way she talks. She has a code by which she judges everything, though she has not yet applied it to her own actions.

Miss Goering goes to a party where she meets her old friend Mrs. Copperfield. Mrs. Copperfield is about to go on a trip to Panama with her husband, though she hates travel and is very fearful of going. The narrative follows Mr. and Mrs. Copperfield on their journey to Panama, where Mrs. Copperfield feels lost and alone, while her husband is elated at all that is strange and exotic.

She says to herself that "when people believed in God they carried Him from one place to another. . . . Now there is nothing to carry with you from one place to another. . . ." And she determines that she will "find a nest in this outlandish place." She is interested in pleasure—the pleasure that Elsie's father was always so quick to forbid—and in happiness, though exactly what she means by happiness is almost as mysterious as what Christina Goering means by salvation. She finds her happiness in Panama by attaching herself to the prostitute Pacifica and by choosing to stay with her rather than going on with her husband.

The narrative shifts back to Miss Goering, who has sold her family estate and now lives in a run-down house in the country with a companion, Miss Gamelon, and a hanger-on, Arnold. Miss Goering likes property and comfort, she admits, but she has felt it necessary to live in a tawdry place to work out her own "little idea of salvation." Once settled in the house, she makes trips, by train and ferry, to the even more tawdry mainland. There, in a bar, she finds the unappetizing and menacing Andy. But after eight days of living with him she finds he is no longer menacing. She then attaches herself to an even more threatening man she has found in the bar, the gangster Ben, this too in pursuit of her own "little idea of salvation."

In the last scene of the novel Miss Goering sits in a restaurant in the city, while Ben confers at another table with his brutal associates. Feeling lonely, Miss Goering telephones Mrs. Copperfield, who has just returned from Panama with Pacifica. When the two women meet in the restaurant, they scrutinize each other after their "journeys." Miss Goering observes that Mrs. Copperfield seems to be going to pieces.

"True enough," said Mrs. Copperfield, bringing her fist down on the table and looking very mean. "I *have* gone to pieces, which is a thing I've wanted to do for years. I know I am as guilty as I can be, but I have my happiness, which I guard like a wolf, and I have authority now and a certain amount of daring, which, if you remember correctly, I never had before."

For her part Mrs. Copperfield finds that Miss Goering has changed, has lost her charm, and become stodgy and less comforting. "You used to be so gracious and understanding; everyone thought you were light in the head, but I thought you were extremely instinctive and gifted with magic powers."

When Mrs. Copperfield leaves, Miss Goering is alone, for the gangster Ben has also deserted her. Standing on the sidewalk, Miss Goering confronts her own sin:

"Certainly I am nearer to becoming a saint," reflected Miss Goering, "but is it possible that a part of me hidden from my sight is piling sin upon sin as fast as Mrs. Copperfield?"

And the novel ends with the words:

This latter possibility Miss Goering thought to be of considerable interest but of no great importance.

It is a puzzling novel to read, this complex parable of religion and sensuality, of salvation and sin, continually defused of terror. Many things seem to make no sense. Why do the two women behave as they do? The narrator's comments on their actions are even more bewildering. Instead of being offered explanation, we are given further complication.

The two serious ladies never stay still. One can't say they are this or that, for in the next instant they'll change. Sometimes the two women are very much alike. Sometimes they are absolute opposites. Within themselves they seem in a perpetual traction of the emotions.

Miss Goering appears high-sounding and moral—if vague. Though she is always at the mercy of her fears, she forces herself to make journeys to find her salvation. Yet she is the one who must come to the moment of submission. Agreeing to go to bed with Andy, whom she's just picked up in the bar, she says to herself, "One must allow that a certain amount of carelessness in one's nature often accomplishes what the will is incapable of doing." Her true moral test seems to be in the submission to what is menacing. Yet she is terrified by that menace and keeps hoping she will be exempted from her trial.

Mrs. Copperfield is fearful in her own way. To her, God is dead, and the only answer to that is to be found in security and in immediate happiness:

"Now," she said, jumping off the bed, "now for a little spot of gin to chase my troubles away. There just isn't any other way that's as good. At a certain point gin takes everything off your hands and you flop around like a little baby. . . ."

Mrs. Copperfield put her hand over her heart. "*Le bonheur,*" she whispered, "*le bonheur* . . . what an angel a happy moment is. . . ."

Miss Goering, to obtain salvation, must dismiss the past and obey her own inner promptings. Mrs. Copperfield, obeying her inner promptings, must duplicate "an old dream." What matters to her is the memory of "things I have loved since I was a child." She, who is so passive and always leaning on others, is the one who decides the course of her life. Miss Goering, who is always striking out on her own, ends up flopping about in her fate like a little baby.

ONE REVIEWER SAID ABOUT *TWO SERIOUS LADIES* THAT TO TRY TO TELL ITS plot was to risk one's sanity. Obviously it's not plot that seams the novel together. The novel is a series of repetitions, variations on a theme or themes. It is as though the work proceeds by a series of analogies, all tied to that original scene with Christina as a thirteen-year-old. In that scene Christina, about to baptize Mary, says, "It's not for fun that we play it, but because it's necessary to play it." Christina as an adult, embarking on her trips to the mainland, says, "It is not for fun that I am going, but because it is necessary to do so." Ben the gangster says to Christina, "I can't stand what people call fun." And Christina answers, "Oh, I love all that. Fundamentally I am a light-hearted person. That is, I enjoy all the things that light-hearted people enjoy."

In that original scene thirteen-year-old Christina leads Mary to the water and immerses her in it as part of the game of getting rid of sin. In Panama the prostitute Pacifica leads Mrs. Copperfield into the water to teach her to swim. She holds her just as Christina once held Mary. This baptism leaves Mrs. Copperfield with the sense of having taken part in a sexual experience.

These and many other repetitions—in phrasing and in gesture and in scene—connect the separate sections and the two serious ladies as if they were each an old dream of the other. There is, however, one character in the novel that seems to stand outside this interweaving. It is Mr. Copperfield. In a letter to Mrs. Copperfield, after she has left him for Pacifica, he writes the words that come closest to revealing what Mrs. Copperfield—and Miss Goering—are at the mercy of:

I do not mean to be cruel but I shall write to you exactly what I consider to be your faults and I hope sincerely that what I have written will influence you. Like most people, you are not able to face more than one fear during your lifetime. You also spend your life fleeing from your first fear towards your first hope. Be careful that you do not, through your own wiliness, end up always in the same position in which you began. I do not advise you to spend your life surrounding yourself with those things which you term necessary to your existence, regardless of whether or not they are objectively interesting in themselves or even to your own particular intellect. I believe sincerely that only those men who reach the stage where it is possible for them to combat a second tragedy within themselves, and not the first over again, are worthy of being called mature. When you think someone is going ahead, make sure that he is not really standing still. In order to go ahead, you must leave things behind which most people are unwilling to do. Your first pain, you carry it with you like a lodestone in your breast because all tenderness will come from there. You must carry it with you through your whole life but you must not circle around it. You must give up the search for those symbols which only serve to hide its face from you. You will have the illusion that they are disparate and manifold but they are always the same. If you are only interested in a bearable life, perhaps this letter does not concern you. For God's sake, a ship leaving port is still a wonderful thing to see.

J.C.

(In the initials of that signature—we never do find out Mr. Copperfield's first name—is another of Jane's jokes that was more than a joke.)

The question of decision permeates the novel, decisions about food, about trips, about things small and large. All decisions, no matter how small, have a moral dimension that makes them weigh heavily. The novel asks questions about decisions: how do we make them and how much do we make them ourselves, even when we think we're making them? Miss Goering, for example, wanted to change of her own volition and according to her own inner promptings before they imposed "completely arbitrary changes" upon her. Yet later she "felt for one desolate moment that the whole thing had been prearranged and that although she had forced herself to take this little trip to the mainland, she had somehow at the same time been tricked into taking it by the powers above." We think there are alternatives, but are there really alternatives—in the self or without? And yet it is clear that choices have to be made and much hinges on the choices taken. The characters inhabit a world in which they always tremble on an edge of choice. Some choices are surrendered to, some are fallen into, some seem to be—are—deliberately taken.

The style of Jane's language is strikingly original, but there are overtones now and then that are familiar. It is as if certain of the cadences, of the archaic rhythms of Martha Finley's *Elsie Dinsmore*, have become mixed with the cadences of Kafka. But this is not the locale of Kafka. There are no law courts or government buildings or cathedrals or castles. The locales are bars and dingy houses and apartments. And the surface is never one of terror. Often there is talk of terror, but then something interferes to cause a distraction. The prose slips and glides in unexpected associations. Something is said and before it can be elaborated something else is said that completely contradicts the previous dialogue or feeling. There are ellipses of thought and feeling but before we can catch them something else preoccupies the characters. Feelings come and go and overlie each other like polyphonic music. And yet the final effect is very funny.

The characters of this complex world inhabit places that Jane herself knew well physically. Pacifica's hotel, the Hotel de las Palmas, was in fact an old hotel in the Old Quarter of Cristóbal in 1938. There were bird cages in the hall and wooden partitions seven feet high between the rooms, just as in the novel. The house on Woodrow Road in Staten Island was the model for Miss Goering's house. The ferry ride from Tottenville to Perth Amboy was the ferry ride that Miss Goering takes. The street going uphill from the ferry and the red brick buildings and seedy bars that Miss Goering found were the things Jane saw in Perth Amboy in 1938.

Jane also modeled the physical form of her characters on people that she knew. Arnold, the hanger-on, was modeled physically on John LaTouche, though Jane never admitted it to him. Arnold's father was based on Paul's father, whom Jane thought to be very eccentric. Ben the gangster was modeled on threatening men she had met in bars, with perhaps a little of Uncle Sid mixed in, or the man she had sex with to get money for Cecil. Jane is Mrs. Copperfield and she is Miss Goering, and yet she is outside of them in the narrative voice, shaping dialogue and transitions, finding in her gift for language what must be said and not said about sin and salvation, about sensuality and hope and fear. At twenty-four, she was writing of the tractions that existed so insidiously and continuously within her: the pull toward men and the pull toward women, the pull to pursue her own destiny and the pull to accede to the needs of others, the pull to assert her own power and the pull to succumb to the power of others, the pull toward a belief in some kind of salvation and the pull toward the absolute denial of such a belief.

Her narrative method is to locate and identify the feeling of conflict in all its intensity and then suddenly to deride it, to make it less "important," funny, and thereby more terribly human. When Ben suggests to Miss Goering that she come into the bedroom with him, she makes the excuse that she is tired.

"All right," said Ben. "I'm going to my room and stretch out till the steaks are cooked. I like them overdone."

While he was gone, Miss Goering sat on the couch pulling at her sweating fingers. She was torn between an almost overwhelming desire to bolt out of the room and a sickening compulsion to remain where she was.

"I do hope," she said to herself, "that the steaks will be ready before I have a chance to decide."

In the middle of thoughts of profound conflict about sex or love comes a thought about food—which to Jane was not unimportant. In the letter to Miriam Levy in 1937 she had written: "I'm tired of loving and being loved. I'm sick of my own voice and I hate books. I'm not even hungry."

Thus, small things acquire great weight: small shifts in dialogue, small decisions. In the last sentence of the novel Miss Goering makes a distinction between what is of considerable interest to her and what is important. The microscopic world of small shifts of feeling and their attendant discoveries was of "considerable interest" to Jane. Yet she also incorporated in herself the judgment that what mattered to her was not of great importance to others. One hears the echo of her father saying to her, "Stop dramatizing your troubles."

AS JANE ORIGINALLY CONCEIVED THE NOVEL, IT WAS CALLED *THREE SERIOUS Ladies*. In addition to the sections with Miss Goering and Mrs. Copperfield, there was a third set in Guatemala. This section included the story of Señora Ramirez, who thinks of nothing but sex, and also the story of Julia, a prostitute who is afraid that she is dying and who can think of nothing but how she will escape punishment for her sins.

Julia lies in her bed in the whorehouse—modeled after the one Jane visited—and moans with pain and fear. She goes out for a day in the country with Señor Ramirez. He gets drunk and insists on carrying Julia into a nearby stream, close to a waterfall. His taking her into the water is yet another repetition of the original scene with thirteen-year-old Christina. But as he carries her, Julia can only think of the hellfires that await her. She clings to him all the more tightly. He falls and she strikes her head against a stone and bleeds profusely.

There is one other important character in the unpublished Guatemalan section, a Señorita Córdoba, who was apparently originally destined to be the third serious lady of the novel. (She survives only as a minor character in "A Guatemalan Idyll.") Señorita Córdoba has but one goal in life: to own a dress shop in Paris. Intending to seduce Señor Ramirez and to get money from him to set up a shop, she goes to his hotel room:

"I have always been interested to know a man like you," she said, "with such a wonderful way of knowing how to live."

"There are no disappointments in my life," said Señor Ramirez. "And I love it. I can show you some wonderful things."

"My life is a terrible disappointment to me," said Señorita Córdoba and her heart beat very quickly as she felt she was approaching her goal.

The room was badly lighted and she searched his eyes avidly to see what effect her words had made on him. It seemed to her that they had a slightly blank look, like the eyes of anyone who is gazing at a particular object without really seeing it.

"You have not had the right kind of love," he said.

"That is not the only reason," said Señorita Córdoba, shaking her head vigorously. Señor Ramirez was feeling suddenly very drunk and he threw himself down on the bed.

"You must not go to sleep," she said nervously, rising to her feet.

"Who in the devil is going to sleep?" Señor Ramirez leaned on his elbow and looked at her like an angry bull.

"I want to go away to Paris, where I have friends and start a dress shop."

"Sure," said Señor Ramirez.

"But I have not got any money."

"I have so much money."

"I need five thousand quetzales."

He started to unbutton his pants. Señorita Córdoba remembered that many men were not interested in ladies nearly as much after they had made love to them as they were beforehand, so she decided that she had better make sure that she received a check first. She did not know how to do this tactfully but her own greed and the fact that he was drunk and that she thought him a coarse person anyway, made her believe that she would be successful. She walked quickly to the window and stood with her back to him. "What are you looking at outside of the window?" asked Señor Ramirez in a thick voice, smelling trouble.

"I am not looking at anything. On the contrary I am just thinking about you and how little you are really interested in whether or not I open a dress shop."

"You can open a thousand dress shops, my beautiful woman. What is the matter with you?"

"You lie. I cannot even open one dress shop." She turned around and faced him.

"Wildcat," he said to her. She tried to look more touching. "You will not help me to open a dress shop? Must it be someone else that will help me?"

"I am going to help you to open fifty dress shops—tomorrow."

"I would not ask for fifty. Only for one. Would you make me happy and give me a check tonight so that I know when I go to sleep I will have my dress shop? . . . "

It was at Paul's suggestion that the entire Guatemalan section was deleted from the novel. Then *Three Serious Ladies* became *Two Serious Ladies*. Señorita Ramirez's story was later published as "A Guatemalan Idyll," Julia's story as "A Day in the Open." The Señorita Córdoba section was left unfinished and was never published.

From a literary viewpoint the decision to take out the Guatemalan section was undoubtedly correct. The work has a unity and tightness it would not have had otherwise. But when Jane acted on Paul's suggestion, she was doing more than cutting a character or characters out of a book. Each of the three women who were excised from the novel is single-minded in a way that neither Miss Goering nor Mrs. Copperfield can ever be. Not for any of them is there the traction of feeling that besets Miss Goering, "torn between an almost overwhelming desire to bolt out of the room and a sickening compulsion to remain where she was."

For the two serious ladies neither a simple goal nor a reconciliation is possible—there is only deadlock and equivalency. The actions of Miss Goering and Mrs. Copperfield are not true alternatives, or rather the alternatives always lead to the same end. Jane was not simply creating characters as she wrote; she was also creating herself and her life to come. When she took out the third serious lady, she committed herself to the deadlock she created. Mrs. Copperfield and Miss Goering are two, yet they are one. Within each of them there is an ever-shifting ambiguity. They are deadlocked together in sin.

The ending of the novel is the discovery of a choice that has been made. The book can be looked upon as the splitting of Christina Goering, from the time she was thirteen, into the two characters of Mrs. Copperfield and Miss Goering. It is the confirmation of a bargain, a decision once made. And as Jane wrote of the past, she also predicted her future.

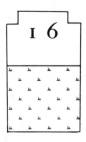

16

IN APRIL 1942 JANE LEFT PAUL IN MEXICO CITY AND returned to the United States with Helvetia Perkins, driving with her in her station wagon. In New York they first stayed at the Chelsea Hotel. While she was there, Jane gave John LaTouche the manuscript of *Two Serious Ladies*. LaTouche passed it on to Ivan van Auw, an agent in the firm of Harold Ober. Then Jane and Helvetia went on to Holden Hall, a century-old house belonging to Paul's family, in Watkins Glen, at the southern end of Lake Seneca.

One day in that late spring of 1942 Jane slit her wrists. Only Jane and Helvetia knew about it at the time. Much later Jane was to tell Paul: "It didn't mean anything. I was angry at Helvetia. It wasn't serious."

What specific incident set off the suicide attempt (serious or not) no one knows. It is clear, however, that by this time difficulties had developed between the two women. Though Jane had begun the relationship as a game, it had soon become far more than that for her.

In *Two Serious Ladies* Pacifica takes Mrs. Copperfield into the ocean to teach her how to swim:

"Now lie on your back. I will hold you under your head," said Pacifica.

Mrs. Copperfield looked around wildly, but she obeyed, and floated on her back with only the support of Pacifica's open hand under her head to keep her from sinking. She could see her own narrow feet floating on top of the water. Pacifica started to swim, dragging Mrs. Copperfield along with her. As she had only the use of one arm, her task was an arduous one and she was soon breathing like a bull. The touch of her hand underneath the head of Mrs. Copperfield was very light—in fact, so light that Mrs. Copperfield feared that she would be left alone from one minute to the next. She looked up. The sky was packed with gray clouds. She wanted to say something to Pacifica, but she did not dare to turn her head.

Pacifica swam a little farther inland. Suddenly she stood up and placed both her hands firmly in the small of Mrs. Copperfield's back. Mrs. Copperfield felt happy and sick at once. She turned her face and in so doing she brushed Pacifica's heavy stomach with her cheek. She held on hard to Pacifica's thigh with the strength of years of sorrow and frustration in her hand.

"Don't leave me," she called out.

At this moment Mrs. Copperfield was strongly reminded of a dream that had recurred often during her life. She was being chased up a short hill by a dog. At the top of the hill there stood a few pine trees and a mannequin about eight feet high. She approached the mannequin and discovered her to be fashioned out of flesh, but without life. Her dress was of black velvet, and tapered to a very narrow width at the hem. Mrs. Copperfield wrapped one of the mannequin's arms tightly around her own waist. She was startled by the thickness of the arm and very pleased. The mannequin's other arm she bent upward from the elbow with her free hand. Then the mannequin began to sway backwards and forwards. Mrs. Copperfield clung all the more tightly to the mannequin and together they fell off the top of the hill and continued rolling for quite a distance until they landed on a little walk, where they remained locked in each other's arms. Mrs. Copperfield loved this part of the dream best; and the fact that all the way down the hill the mannequin acted as a buffer between herself and the broken bottles and little stones over which they fell gave her particular satisfaction.

This is the imaginative life that Jane brought with her to Helvetia, some tie between passion and "an old dream," some tie to a sense of baptism, a hope of release from what she meant by sin—a hope that she would be buffered, that she would not drown.

But the hard fact was that Helvetia was not, nor could ever be, a Pacifica. Helvetia was a stern and unforgiving woman, to herself and to others. She was proud and a perfectionist. (She was not an accomplished chess player, yet she would sit and plan each move for a half-hour.) She was harsh in her standards as to how people should behave. They should accomplish things; they should not be self-indulgent. She continually judged and she continually made her judgments clear.

And Jane was not one to take comments on her behavior with good grace. Like Mrs. Copperfield, she was only seemingly compliant. She would try to charm Helvetia, to beguile her, to "bamboozle" her. She was drinking heavily. Her inability to make decisions was getting worse all the time. Helvetia could not understand the complexity of Jane, that the fears were all part of her creative life, that the drinking and indulgence were the other side of her search for salvation. If Helvetia wanted to write, she made herself sit down each day at her desk and she wrote. But there was Jane, who was so talented, and what was she doing but squandering her talent in her drinking and self-indulgence?

Yet Jane saw an equivalent weakness in Helvetia. Jane felt that she had seduced Helvetia, that Helvetia had been the innocent one. And she probably saw too—though she could not accept it with equanimity—that Helvetia felt a great sense of guilt about the affair with her. Helvetia could not permit herself to be wholeheartedly in the affair. She returned Jane's affection physically, but she withheld tenderness from her, being as severe with Jane as she was with herself.

And of course there was in Jane that darker part of herself, despite her enormous vitality and will to live. That darkness is expressed simply, almost naïvely, though purposely so, in "Farther from the Heart," a lyric she wrote for Paul in Taxco earlier in the year:

> *Oh I'm sad for never knowing courage,*
> *And I'm sad for the stilling of fear.*
> *Closer to the sun now, and farther from the heart.*
> *I think that my end must be near. . . .*

Jane was always evading this darker self through wit and wiles, but in the relationship with Helvetia, the darker self was often drawn to the surface. Jane might say of the suicide attempt, "It didn't mean anything. . . . It wasn't serious." But she was serious enough to have made the gesture.

IN MEXICO PAUL WAS STILL FEELING ILL. AFTER JANE LEFT, HE WROTE TO Virgil Thomson:

I have been ill so often lately that I am completely fed-up with this republic. . . . This is a charming country if one is full of vigor. Otherwise it turns easily into an almost perpetual nightmare. If I hadn't had previous years of Morocco and other hostile spots to prepare me more or less, by this time I think I should be completely mad. The way of staying sane is simply that of accepting, accepting, one horror after another, and being thankful to be still alive. I suppose war is like that, but perhaps not, since one doesn't undergo it alone. Here there are no horrors unless one is alone. But I generally am alone. Anyway, I am escaping. I have been working as hard as I could to forget my miserable insides; a one-act opera which is not finished, but it will be.

I don't know where we shall be this summer. Probably somewhere near N.Y. Janie wants my Aunt Mary's house, in Watkins Glen. I don't care where I am as long as I can eat a full meal with appetite.

In the early summer of 1942 Paul arrived at Holden Hall with Antonio Álvarez. He found Jane in the best of spirits. He immediately set to work on his opera *The Wind Remains*. In the afternoons Paul and Jane and Helvetia and Álvarez often went for a walk in the country. The local residents became suspicious of the four of them; they were convinced that Álvarez was a Japanese spy. Paul was arrested twice and held for questioning. (Jane had already been interrogated by the FBI about a telegram Paul had sent her from Mexico concerning a missing drum.)

In Mexico Paul and Jane had felt separated, physically and emotionally, from the war. Now that they had returned, they found themselves suspected. It was clear—once again—that they were outsiders, just as they had always been—though finally they would be no more immune from the war's effects than those others from whom they thought themselves separated.

IN THE FALL HELVETIA SET OUT WITH JANE ON A TRIP THROUGH VERMONT AND New Hampshire, looking for a place to buy. She found what she wanted, an operating farm, in East Montpelier, Vermont. Paul and Antonio returned to New York. At first Paul stayed at the Hotel Chelsea. From there he moved into a penthouse belonging to the architect Friedrich Kiesler. Jane and Helvetia moved into the city for the winter and took an apartment on Waverly Place. Every day Jane would come to see Paul and have lunch or dinner with him.

In the spring of 1943 *Two Serious Ladies* was published by Knopf. The reviews were generally disheartening. Most critics found it incomprehensible. Of course there were those who recognized Jane's talent, who called her work brilliant, but these were often people she knew from the salon world of art and literature and music. She did not get the popular success she had hoped for.

"What upset her most," says Paul, "was that the reviews were so beside the point. They depressed her and made her sad, of course."

The book was dedicated to "Paul, Mother, and Helvetia." But Helvetia didn't approve of the book, Paul remembers. She thought it was too obviously lesbian. So did Jane's family and Paul's family. "It was very much looked down on by both of our families."

Claire was very disappointed, both with the book and with the poor reviews. After she read the book, she said to Paul, "I'm not proud of my little daughter. But maybe she'll do better next time." Jane's aunts were more straightforward in their criticism. One of them said to Jane, "There's only one bit of decent writing in the whole book and that's the letter from the husband, Mr. Copperfield." Jane's Aunt Birdie added, "And Paul probably wrote that."

Paul, who admired the book enormously, did once say to Jane, "You make me out to be a complete idiot in it." In answer she only giggled, as if she'd been caught in one of her jokes.

Jane's response to her family's disappointment and to her lack of popular success was to say what she had said before, that *Two Serious Ladies* wasn't any good anyway. Yet she went on working in her own fashion in New York and in Vermont, though seeming to most people to be indulging herself most of the time, drinking and partying.

Paul, leading his own separate life, was working hard, writing music and music criticism. His Flute Sonata was issued as one of a series of records, *Art of This Century Recordings*, produced by Peggy Guggenheim. His one-act opera, *The Wind Remains*, was performed at the Museum of Modern Art. Leonard Bernstein directed, Merce Cunningham did the choreography, and Oliver Smith did the sets. Paul was also reviewing concerts daily for the *Herald Tribune* and writing jazz criticism for the *Tribune* and for *View*, a surrealist magazine edited by Charles Henri Ford.

Ned Rorem remembers seeing Jane and Paul in New York that year. "I was at the Curtis Institute in Philadelphia. I used to come to New York to get drunk. Paul was my friend. Jane was peripheral. Paul was with his milieu, Jane with hers. I remember meeting her with people from the music world and people from the Museum of Modern Art. I would see her drunk at parties. She always had a magical quality.

"In his milieu, Paul always seemed on the outside looking in. The relationship between the two of them was very unusual. They were very dependent on each other. I remember at the time Paul was continuously giving out Jane's book to people."

That summer Paul was called for examination by Selective Service. He describes the interview in *Without Stopping*:

Very early one morning I had to be at an armory on the East Side. Women had set up little counters and were handing out rather good doughnuts and coffee. Then a large parade of us straggled up Fourth Avenue to Park, and on to the Grand Central Palace. It seemed grotesque to have to walk into the psychiatrist's office stark naked and sit before him while he put his questions and cocked his head to one side. "How do you feel about the Army? Think you're going to like it?" I said I was worried about one thing: I doubted that I'd be able to sleep. I explained that I was a composer and lived day and night trying to escape noise, to such an extent that I wore wax stoppers in my ears to reduce its volume. The doctor looked at me with a suddenly aroused interest. He reached out quietly and pulled a pair of scissors toward him across the surface of the desk—out of my reach, I noted. Then he said something very strange, with an inflection which made him sound as though he were reasoning with a small child: "No one's going to hurt you." I did not reply. I thought of saying: "I know," or "Aren't they?" But he had got started on a whole train of thought that interested him, and he went ahead questioning me, finally getting me to admit that I felt hostility toward him. Cheered by this confession, he went on from there. In the end he wrote: *Not Acceptable. Psychoneurotic Personality.*

In October, Paul decided to take a vacation in Canada and went to pick up Jane in Vermont.

We had never been to Canada and were curious about what lay across the border. We got on a train for Montreal. As we read and looked out of the windows, Jane did not seem unduly nervous; only after some time had passed did I realize she was ordering one whiskey after another. By then it was too late to undo the mischief. In Montreal we got off the train and onto an escalator that took us up into the main waiting room of the station. As we reached the end of the escalator, Jane lost consciousness. People helped me lay her out on a bench and found a cab for me. At the hotel she came around, but with no idea of what had happened.

The anxieties which Jane had managed to keep within bounds earlier were now breaking through her control more and more. Paul dates the beginning of this change from the time when their sexual life together ended. "We used to take elevators all the time earlier and then one day—it seemed suddenly—she had this terrible fear of them. She'd always had many fears. But she would laugh at them and be able to push through them, often by making fun of herself. Or she'd bring other people into her anxieties, involve them somehow with her. John LaTouche always said, when he saw her coming, 'Here comes Complications Janie.' "

But on that trip to Montreal neither being Complications Janie nor making fun of herself worked. She was away from Helvetia and alone with Paul away from the city. Further, she had another dread which she did not reveal to Paul. Some months earlier Jane and Helvetia had gone to Mexico by train. They were in the dining car when the train crossed a bridge over a river. Suddenly the train left the tracks and fell from the bridge into the river. Jane lost consciousness, and when she came to, she was lying beside a dead man. Her arm was over him. This much she said to Paul many years later, adding, "Please don't ask me to tell you about it. It was terrible." Now on the trip to Montreal, she said nothing to Paul, she only drank herself into a stupor.

However, once they were in Montreal Jane seemed to become her usual self. They spent some time in the city and then went on to Quebec. To Paul the foreignness of the city was a great reassurance. "Absurdly, when I returned to New York the city seemed a little less sinister and virulent, because I knew Quebec was nearby."

JANE RETURNED TO VERMONT AND TO HELVETIA AND TO TRYING TO WORK, TO A life that was a series of repetitions of alternating tendernesses and arguments, like a series of cycles that went on and on, that seemed to signal change and no change at the same time.

The painter Maurice Grosser spent the summers of 1944 and 1945 with Helvetia and Jane in Vermont. "Jane was writing and I was painting. She was awfully good company, charming, perverse, quarrelsome, and insistent, yet with an enormous warmth—like a sister.

"In the morning she'd come down to a rather late breakfast. She was often in a bad temper in the morning. She'd have her breakfast, which consisted of two eggs, fried so they were burned on the outside. She loved to have the whites crinkled and scorched. Then she took a canteen of water and a notebook and a pillow and she went out under a distant tree and she'd stay there all morning. But if it rained, she'd come back, leaving the notebook and the pillow lying under the tree.

"Helvetia had beautiful manners and looked very much like a tabby cat. She was always reading the most advanced intellectual books, like Kierke-gaard and I. A. Richards's *The Meaning of Meaning*. I think she was a little in awe of Jane. I thought Jane was rather outrageous with her.

"Helvetia was a woman of extraordinarily good taste. She had a marvelous collection of French furniture. She did the Vermont house over and did it perfectly beautifully. The barn had burned, so she had it torn down, and had a wonderful room made out of the burned and blackened wood. She loved things and she loved food. I think she was very gener-ous and easy to get along with. She had a passion for exploring Vermont. There wasn't a corner of the state that we missed in that old Ford station wagon.

"Jane and I shared the cooking. I remember one funny story about Jane and food. There was meat-rationing on at the time. We used to go to the meat market in Montpelier and one day we saw that pigs' feet weren't rationed. Jane and Helvetia asked me if I knew how to cook them. I'd eaten them often in Paris and I said, 'Well, I think I do.' So we bought them and when we got back to the house I rolled them in bread crumbs and dipped them in egg and put them in the oven. I didn't know that they had to be boiled for hours. When they came out, I looked at them and said, 'We can't eat these.' Jane said, 'Yes, we can.' No one else would eat them, but she ate three of them. In the middle of the night she got acute indigestion and

Helvetia took her to the hospital in town. They got the surgeon down, but Jane refused to get undressed to let the surgeon examine her.

"Jane drank a lot but she was never really an alcoholic. There was no drinking early in the day, but the cocktail hour was sacred. Whatever was cooked had to be something that could be kept indefinitely while the cocktail hour stretched on and on. Often Jane had so much to drink that she wasn't capable of eating at all."

Virgil Thomson also remembers that prolonged cocktail hour. When he visited Jane and Helvetia in Vermont, Helvetia would have a cocktail or two, but Jane would start drinking and continue to drink and would not eat. Then "no matter what Helvetia said, they'd fight. Then they'd both cry. Often they ended up going to sleep without eating."

David Diamond recalls seeing Jane at many parties in New York during 1943 and 1944. "I hated the affectation of the queens in the group. Jane adored it. My conversations with Jane were only about human relationships. She would ask me why I was so unhappy, why I was fighting with everybody. I would do things at parties that would upset her. Sometimes at a party where everybody else was drinking red wine, Touche would come in with a bottle of cognac and he'd sit there drinking it, while the rest of us just had the red wine. I'd ask him for some and in his childish voice with his childish charm he'd say, 'No.' And Jane would say, 'Touche, you give David a drink. Stop being such a pig.'

"I remember Helvetia as a prig. I used to say 'fuck' and 'shit' and she'd get very upset.

"Jane was feminine and cuddly. She would wear men's shirts. She used to touch up her hair with henna. Earlier she'd been the cuddler of all times, especially, I remember, in Aaron Copland's arms. She had a way of finding just the right position. She wouldn't cuddle in Oliver's arms. She said he was too bony, like a crane.

"After 1940 Jane was often emotionally overwrought. There were often tears in her eyes. I remember seeing her at a party at the Askews'. I would date this about 1943 or 1944. I was with Reeves McCullers. As I came out, Jane was leaving. One of her wrists was crudely bandaged. I asked Touche, and he said Jane had slashed her wrist in a fit of depression, and I think he said something vaguely about Helvetia."

The editor Leo Lerman had met Jane at a party before *Two Serious Ladies* was published. "At first, I was afraid of her. She told me a frightening story about a snake and I thought she was teasing me. I thought she knew I was afraid of snakes. I later learned that it wasn't me she was teasing, that she was really afraid of snakes herself.

"Several months after I'd reviewed *Two Serious Ladies* [Lerman praised it highly], I went to a party at Boo Faulkner's. Jane was arriving just before me and she was going in the door when she turned to me and said, 'Don't come in, Leo, there's something you won't like here.' There was a huge rubber snake sitting in the living room and Jane went in and threw the snake out the window. Then she told me I could come in.

"Jane was vulnerable and strong. She was always testing herself and she kept on testing to see how it would come out if she put herself in danger.

"I remember Helvetia as a strong-looking woman, someone with a frieze of bangs, looking as though she were from the 1880s. Jane, I felt, was pathologically in love with Helvetia."

Edwin Denby remembers: "Jane used to like to hang on to her girl friends, to ask them for some favor, not naggingly. Say it was a question of going out to get a bottle of liquor: Jane would ask Helvetia. Helvetia would just as likely say no. Then Jane would ask somebody else in a giggly way. With me Jane was always cheerful and sweet and kind. With others I saw her sharp-tongued, but just for fun.

"I have an image in my mind of being at a party with Jane and Helvetia and someone coming to call for Helvetia, and Jane's eyes filling with tears at her leaving and then the tears going away.

"I wasn't very fond of Helvetia. She was perfectly nice and attractive. But we were all very vague in what we said and she was authoritative."

Yet the writer Florence Codman remembers: "Helvetia was diffident in her manner. She was apt to hesitate and say, 'Well . . . ,' before she committed herself or made a statement. I don't remember her smiling or laughing. Mostly I remember her listening, and now and then remarking."

Paul remembers hearing of one incident—he did not personally witness it—that suggests Helvetia was capable of sudden unpredictable behavior. One evening when Jane and Helvetia were living on Waverly Place, Helvetia went out while Jane stayed in and entertained some of her friends. Helvetia returned quite late. She went up to one of the men present, said, "Hello," and hit him in the face so hard he almost fell over. Everyone was astonished, including Jane, although Jane, says Paul, rather admired Helvetia's action.

When Paul and Helvetia met, they were very polite to each other. There was never any active falling-out between them. Paul's way of handling the situation was to try to avoid seeing her. Yet he often had arguments with Jane over Helvetia. He felt that Helvetia had a very bad effect upon Jane, that with her she was drinking more, that her health was being affected. He felt too that there was some terrible rivalry between them. "Helvetia was a very bright woman, very intelligent. If you mentioned archaeology, she'd been digging. History, yes, she'd studied that at the Sorbonne for years. She really knew what she was talking about, there's no doubt about it, except that she didn't really understand the phenomenon of creation. She didn't understand Jane. But then the person who would have understood Jane wouldn't have interested her."

He saw Helvetia being very hard on Jane, quoting from books to her, being argumentative, challenging her judgment. Helvetia was also very critical of Jane's friends. She called them *cabotins*, ham actors or strolling players in the pejorative sense.

Still, there was never any quarreling when the three of them were together. Sometimes Paul would go to Jane and Helvetia's for lunch and dinner. More often Jane would come alone to have lunch with Paul. Alone, they would have their arguments about Helvetia. "She's bad for you," Paul would say. And Jane would say, "I know what I'm doing."

Helvetia, moreover, was trying to force Jane to choose between Paul and herself. Jane would tell Paul this, but would say that of course she would do no such thing. She did tell Paul that Helvetia hated the idea of her coming so often to see him. Yet Jane would not choose. She would not break with Paul, but she could not break with Helvetia. Just as Mrs. Copperfield had chosen to live with Pacifica, so Jane had chosen to be with Helvetia. But unlike Mrs. Copperfield, who left Mr. Copperfield, Jane could not leave Paul. "Paul was her rock," Dione Lewis says.

Jane herself gave fictional form to the world she and Helvetia created in the puppet play, *A Quarreling Pair*. In this short play two sisters in their early fifties sit in adjacent rooms. Harriet, the old puppet, is "stronger-looking and wears brighter colors." She is practical, insistent, and active. She berates Rhoda, the second puppet, for having no knack for making a home, for not minding her own business, for being preoccupied by the world "and its sufferers."

HARRIET: . . . You're not smart enough to be of any use to the outside . . . you have no self-sufficiency. . . . You're a lost soul, when I'm not around. . . .

RHODA: You're right. But I swear that my heart is big.

HARRIET: . . . You can breed considerable discontent around you with a big heart, and considerable harmony with a small one. . . . And my heart is small like Papa's was.

RHODA: You chill me to the marrow when you tell me that your heart is small. You do love me though, don't you?

HARRIET: You're my sister, aren't you? . . .

RHODA: Even though you have a small heart, I wish there were no one but you and me in the world. Then I would never feel that I had to go among the others.

After a heated argument, Harriet leaves, then returns carrying two glasses of milk:

HARRIET: I'm coming with your milk, and I hope the excitement is over for today. . . . Oh, why do I bring milk to a person who is dead-set on making my life a real hell?

RHODA: Yes, why? Why? Why? Why? Oh, what a hideous riddle!

HARRIET: You love to pretend that everything is a riddle. You think that's the way to be intellectual. There is no riddle. I am simply keeping up my end of the bargain.

Harriet offers Rhoda her milk, but Rhoda hits the glass and it flies out of Harriet's hand. Then Harriet hits Rhoda on the face and runs back to her own room. Each puppet has a song she sings, alone, mysterious, and sad. The play ends in a standoff between the two sisters:

HARRIET: Rhoda?

RHODA: What do you want?

HARRIET: Go away if you like.

RHODA: The moment hasn't come yet, and it won't come today because the day is finished and the evening is here. Thank God!

Between the two puppets, as between Helvetia and Jane, there is a battle of will and need. They are caught in this contest, unable—and unwilling—to escape. The resolution of the contest can only come through a violent outburst. It is an exchange that brings an equilibrium for the moment. But there is also a sense of interchangeability between the two puppets. In a song Harriet sings:

> *I dreamed I climbed upon a cliff,*
> *My sister's hand in mine. . . .*
> *A girl ran down the mountainside*
> *With bluebells in her hat.*
> *I asked the valley for her name. . . .*
> *But wakened not yet knowing*
> *If the name she bore was my sister's name*
> *Or if it was my own.*

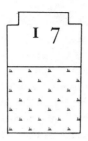

1 7

FOR JANE AS FOR RHODA, THE WORLD "AND ITS sufferers" were on her mind. The effect of the war upon her was to summon up the fear of vast inhuman forces overwhelming individual choice. Further, the reality of the suffering in Europe and in Asia was not part of daily life in the United States: it remained, to a large extent, distant, impersonal, and abstract. And that suffering which Jane could not experience directly, she experienced as sin.

In a notebook from the early fifties for the unpublished novel *Out in the World*, Emmy Moore, one of Jane's fictional selves, writes to her husband Paul:

> I will write to you soon about the effect the war has had upon me. I have spoken to you about it. You never seemed to take it very seriously. Perhaps seeing what I feel in black and white will effect your opinion of me. Perhaps you will leave me? . . .

Though during the war years Jane lived out her daily life of pleasure, of drinking, of writing, of partying, often she would say to Paul that she had no right to live while others were dying. In answer he would say to her, "Jane, don't be foolish. You have to go on living."

She would speak of sin and he would say to her, "But I don't know what you mean." And she'd say with asperity, "Oh, you have no depth."

Then she'd add a little later, "I am at the mercy," just as Miss Goering had said in *Two Serious Ladies*. But these discussions would take place in the middle of other discussions having to do with the most trivial details of daily life. So how could they be taken seriously?

"She was always worried about choice," says Paul. "I would say, 'Just let things happen naturally.' But Jane's worry was that a choice had to be made and every choice was a moral judgment and monumental, even fatal. And that was so even if the choice was between string beans and peas."

Though she said she didn't believe in God, she insisted that she was very religious. It was as if she had absorbed early in life a religion without substance, but one that she was obliged to obey, even though she would never be able to discover its rules.

She does not seem to have identified more with the Jews suffering in the Holocaust than with others suffering in the world. Her sense of what it was to be a Jew was established early and seems never to have changed. Her Jewishness manifested itself overtly in the daily use of Yiddish words—like *yenti*, *schmoozing*, and *shlepping*. Associated with her mother's family, they were used humorously and self-mockingly—in the way that she had worn the "Spirit of Purim" costume to the masquerade party in Taxco. She rejected the Jewish God. She said that she didn't believe in Him because He was a vengeful God. To Paul she said, "I always hated the idea of God because He said He was a jealous God, because He'd smite you down if you didn't believe in this or that."

In the prewar salon world of New York many Jews tried to leave their Jewishness behind. That was part of the heritage they were seeking to escape in their world within a world. Their abandonment was, in some cases, a response to the anti-Semitism of the times. Some Jews never mentioned publicly that they were Jews. John LaTouche, for example, never told anyone that his mother was a Jew. Jane never denied that she was Jewish, but perhaps she proclaimed it more openly after the war. Then in her most bitter self-derision, which was at the same time self-mocking humor, she called herself, "Crippie, the Kike Dyke."

There is a parallel between some of Jane's beliefs and those of Simone Weil. Of course, the two lived lives that couldn't have been more different. Simone Weil was never even told she was a Jew until she was almost an adolescent. Jane did not have to be told. Through her family—in particular, her mother's family—her Jewishness was inescapable. Yet Jane's best friend, Miriam, could say that she was a Jew who "hardly seemed to know she was a Jew." Both Jane and Simone Weil from childhood were beset by a sense of sin and driven by a need for salvation. Both could not bear the thought of a jealous and vengeful God.

When Jane discovered Simone Weil's writings in the early fifties, she recognized an affinity between Weil's words and what she herself felt. She would carry *Waiting for God* around with her and would read it every night before she went to sleep. If anyone commented on it, she would deflect it from seriousness by saying, "But I have a sensual side too."

IN EARLY 1945, OLIVER SMITH AND JANE AND PAUL AND HELVETIA MOVED into a house on West Tenth Street. As Paul later told it, Oliver got hold of the top three stories of a large old house on West Tenth Street, had the landlord pull out some walls and remove the plaster from others, leaving only the brick surface, and induced Jane and me, as well as Helvetia, to join in the venture. Helvetia signed the lease for the second floor, he for the third, and I for the top.

There, for the next two years, Jane worked on *In the Summer House*, a play she had begun in Vermont. Oliver Smith kept giving Jane money to work on the play. He loved Jane and he admired her writing. He felt it had a kind of "prim barbaric strength with its sense of the ridiculous and the horrible, but yet had a beautiful style." He remembers Jane as fascinating, mercurial, and brilliant.

"She was like an adorable child who loves you but will get her own way. She deliberately used her charms to get what she wanted.

"Her life was in terror, but disguised terror. She had a dark, murky inner life. She was afraid to go to sleep. She took endless amounts of coffee and booze, enough to knock herself out, and a great many barbiturates. She had heart palpitations and high blood pressure, but that didn't stop her. She had a great self-destructiveness and at the same time an enormous will to live.

"She was one of the most important people in my life. Despite her selfishness, beyond the fun and games, she was a great kind sister who would cook for you, advise you, and always encourage your creativity. In that way she was very unselfish. She never had children. I think she was afraid of the pain of having children. Yet she herself was a mother figure, a kind of child-mother. She was mysterious, with a marvelous sense of humor and wit and an adorable playfulness; but behind it all was a strict moralist.

"She had been extremely spoiled by her mother. She rebelled against her mother and her stepfather. Her creative friends and her lovers became her family.

"She had a tortured emotional life. She loved Paul, yet at the same time she was emotionally involved with other women. I think she felt her emotional life was a mess.

"In her life she could never do anything easily. If she was catching a boat, she'd manage to misplace the tickets. She loathed traveling, but she spent a lot of time doing it. She was terrified of elevators and would walk thirty flights not to have to take one. Everything was a *gontzeh megillah* to her, and her friends indulged her in this.

"I think her Jewishness was very important to her. She had a Hebraic morality, though I think she was probably an agnostic."

Other close friends, the family she had created for herself, remember her from this time, each in his or her own way. The harpsichordist Sylvia

Marlowe had known Jane since the late thirties and had "a kind of family relationship with Jane, a closeness but with arguments."

"She would do completely outlandish things. My sister had a house on Long Island and belonged to a beach club there. Janie went out on the train with me once to visit her. She didn't have a bathing suit. I gave her one. It was far too big and had to be held up with pins. She enjoyed that enormously.

"Later, coming back, she and I were on the train crossing the bay, on a trestle, and suddenly the train stopped. She started screaming, 'I can't stand it.' I said, 'Stop it, Janie.' Everybody around was trying to comfort her, but she kept on screaming. Finally I slapped her and she stopped. But she insisted that we get off at the next stop. So we got off. It was some godforsaken place. We walked around and finally she found a bar she wanted to go into. We ended up getting on another train hours later.

"She was often difficult. She was a prima donna who had to have things her own way. On the other hand she was easygoing and lovable. She could be divinely charming and funny, and then suddenly she'd be difficult. I said to her, 'It's a dangerous game you're playing. Someday you'll really go nuts.'

"She fussed a lot about her work, but she really didn't spend the kind of time working that most artists have to spend. She was self-indulgent and spoiled. She had no routine, and she got almost no sleep.

"She adored Paul. If he looked sideways at another woman she was jealous. She treated him like hell, though she loved him. She would get into hysterics when she was jealous.

"She was a flirt and she loved older women. She had a little coterie that did things for her. She had to have her own way. Once Jane, Helvetia, my husband Leonid, and I went to Montauk Point together. Even there she found a horrible dive that we all ended up in. Why did we go along with her? There was no way to stop her. She had in mind a particular kind of a bar. She got her way because it mattered so much to her. And then too, Helvetia spoiled her."

Xenia Cage remembers a party given by Jane and Helvetia: "They were living in the house on Tenth Street. I remember there was the skin of a python on the wall. I think it was Paul's.

"I can see Jane with a frown on her face, getting up in the middle of the party and bringing out the carpet sweeper and starting to use it right then and there.

" 'For God's sakes, Jane, what are you doing?' I asked her.

" 'Somebody dropped a crumb on the floor,' she said.

"Jane projected the way an actress does, even when she was very quiet. She would frown and then suddenly smile. She was very straightforward and direct, not bitchy.

"It amazed me that she had no self-consciousness about her leg. She would sit on the floor or on a couch with her leg sticking straight out into the room. My leg had also been stiffened when I was an adolescent, for the same reason as hers, but I always tried to disguise the fact. It was something that I was always conscious of. It made certain kinds of situations very difficult—for example, getting on a bus.

"I remember Helvetia as very conservative and ladylike, as someone who would wear fur stoles. She was like one of those ladies who eats at Schrafft's and has a Manhattan first. I remember too that Jane would sit on Helvetia's lap at parties."

Duopianists Robert Fizdale and Arthur Gold met Jane and Paul in the mid-forties. They remember her as "a miracle of charm, yet her indecision was such as to almost make one say, 'Jane is mad.'

"Once we were supposed to go out to dinner with Oliver and Paul and Jane. We arrived early for a drink. At midnight we still hadn't decided whether to go out to a Chinese restaurant or whether to go out at all. Finally Oliver said, 'I'm taking you.'

"The delaying was a great joke. She would go over the menu, what we should have when and if we went to the Chinese restaurant. Should we have won ton soup? But then if we have won ton soup, we can't have spareribs. Then she'd say, 'I'm tired of spareribs, I had spareribs yesterday.' It was all hilariously funny. And all the time, during all of this, there was cuddling and kissing and embracing. She'd put her head on your shoulder, as if she wanted protection. She looked at you from under her bangs as if to say, 'Are you going to be angry or love me?'

"Her whole life was a delaying action. Her compulsion was to act out what was going to happen next. When Jane would act this way, Paul would say, 'Janie, you're mad,' but actually he was rather pleased. When all of this delaying was going on, he might disappear, but he was never impatient with her.

"Jane and Paul were very different. Paul liked an American dinner with nothing to drink. Jane liked to drink from six until twelve and then eat. Once we had dinner at Cavanaugh's, an old New York steak house at Eighth and Twenty-third Street. Jane got there late. She wouldn't make up her mind what she wanted. She had a Scotch and then finally decided on something, but by that time it was very late. At the end of the meal, Paul got the check and he divided it into four equal parts. That was his mania. By this time we were in an island. The waiters were piling chairs on tables around us. Then Jane said to Paul—in a Yiddish accent—as he was going over each item of the bill, 'I didn't have that.' Paul was very embarrassed, but she was making perfect sense. It wasn't just a quiet dinner at Cavanaugh's. It was a drama.

"The way she said things had the implication that we were all just like real people, but we weren't actually. She even saw our piano-playing as a theater outside of our lives. After our concert once she said to us, 'You look so glamorous, so dressed up.' The implication was that we usually looked like slobs.

"She came to our concerts because we played Paul's music. She never gave any indication of being interested in things outside of her own games. She was always playing the role of helpless child in a world of adults, and yet everybody knew that she ran the show.

"She loved to tell stories about her mother's 'yenti' qualities in the jewelry store that she and her husband ran in Ohio.

"Once Jane went to Macy's to get a brassiere. It took about two weeks of planning. When she got it home, it was the wrong cup-size. This evoked a whole world of 'yenti' to her. She spent hours in bed writing a draft of a letter to Macy's. Finally the reply came from Macy's and she said, 'I think I'll have to write them again.' 'But why don't you just go down there?' we asked her. 'It's on the fifth floor,' she said, 'and you have to take an elevator.'

"Jane was very flirtatious and seductive with everyone. With Touche she had a special rapport. She and Paul and Touche did extraordinary imitations and improvised with each other. Paul gave the impression of being somewhat stiff and repressed, but it wasn't so.

"Jane would create instant disorder if she was in the room. Once Helvetia was sitting with Jane's Pekingese, Donald [which Paul had given to her in Mexico City], and Jane said, 'Don't you think Donald looks just like Helvetia? It's a darling little bunny and looks just like Helvetia.'

"Jane was cruel only in the way children are cruel. Oliver, who adored Jane, would sometimes say to her, 'Sit down, Cookie.'

"When we first met Paul and Jane, they seemed so worldly, so famous. It was a privilege for us to know them. Paul mixed his own perfumes, collected wristwatches and snakeskins, and spoke of Gertrude Stein. We admired both their talents.

"In 1947 we spent six months at the house on Tenth Street, renting Paul's apartment. There were three studio couches in the room and the first morning we were there, we woke up and there was Jane sitting on the third bed. 'I'm waiting for you to wake up,' she said. It was one of those miracles of charm.

"Since we were planning to go to Paris, we decided to have French lessons with Jane. That amused her terribly. She wrote out the exercises every week. It took her hours to get the sentences right. They were sentences meant to get us hysterical: 'Can you tell me where the nearest Jewish delicatessen is?' 'Do you know where I can find David Diamond?' All the sentences were about what we didn't want. She'd say them with a mock severe look.

"We paid her five dollars a lesson to make it more businesslike. She'd come to the door and ring the bell and say, 'Can I have the five dollars now?' And she'd telephone for a bottle of Scotch. She was always resisting work.

The French lessons were only an excuse not to work. At times she thought she was an extraordinary talent, and at times she didn't think so.

"She had cowboy evenings on Saturday night. She'd say, 'You can't come to my apartment as I'm having a cowboy party. No men are allowed.' The women wore cowboy hats and sang cowboy songs. The climax was Jane doing the Mexican hat dance."

Katharine Hamill and Natasha von Hoershelman were Jane's closest women friends at this time. Both of them worked for *Fortune*, Katharine as a writer and Natasha as head of the research department. Over the years they saw Jane's love for Paul and her intense dependence upon him, and her need and love for her women lovers.

"Jane was wonderfully affectionate with her friends," says Katharine. "She would throw her arms around you and hug you. At the same time she was a great worrier. Her worrying was not playacting. It was what she felt, though it might be about something that anyone else considered unimportant. One weekend we were in Vermont visiting Jane and Helvetia. Somebody was coming for dinner. Jane was obsessed. Would it be all right to serve spaghetti or wouldn't it? She was a very good cook and she would laugh at herself when she was worrying, but still that didn't stop her.

"She would come to our country house in Pennsylvania by train and when the train went through the tunnel, Jane was terrified," Natasha recalls.

"Yes, she drank a lot, but she wasn't a drunk. She would say, 'I sleep where I drink.' She would fall asleep on the couch after drinking. Once at Katharine's house in New Hampshire we were all drinking and Jane said, 'You can pick me up with a spatula.'

"We never talked about our work to Jane. She wouldn't have been interested. We often threatened as a joke to give her a subscription to *Standard Statistics*. When we were with Jane we spent our time eating and drinking and talking. She was a wonderful talker. She talked about the life around her and the people she knew, the life she was in, not about politics or the affairs of the world.

"Sometimes when we were together, sitting and talking, Jane would get up and improvise, sing and create a personality. She would do the 'zandunga,' a Mexican dance, and make up words to go with it. She was always saying 'Oy.' She never talked of her work. Only about Carson [McCullers], she once said, 'She's one year younger than I and has done much more.'

"We used to visit Jane and Helvetia in Vermont. We could see that Helvetia was jealous about Jane. Jane would say to us that Helvetia was very jealous. But she'd also say, 'Helvetia is very intelligent.'"

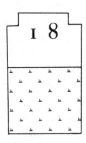

HELVETIA HAD REASON TO BE JEALOUS OF JANE. During the time that Jane was with Helvetia—as well as before and after—Jane apparently had many brief affairs with other women. "She never made any pretense about it. She would go to bed with almost anyone," a woman friend, who was not a lover, has said. "But it was more in the spirit of warmth and affection. She was like a playful, loving puppy dog."

She also appears to have had, during the time she was with Helvetia, an extended affair with an older woman from Boston, married, with children, well-to-do, described by several people as "a large woman with a large bosom." Many people thought of this woman as one of Jane's jokes. But in fact there were two crucial requirements that Jane seemed to have for her more extended affairs: that she herself be the aggressor and that the choice seem ludicrous or outrageous to others.

Whatever the actuality of Jane's sexual life was, about her there grew a mystique of sexual promiscuity. The power of her personality captured and heightened other people's hidden fantasies. In her, many people saw a being of unlimited sexual expression. Almost any woman that she knew and a great many she did not know were identified in terms of this mystique as one of her lovers. And the mystique itself has served to hide the actuality of her sexuality.

To Jane sex was indistinguishable from the imagination. "Sex is all in the mind," she would say to Paul. And in an interview in the early sixties she spoke of herself as being lusty, not sexy. Even those words had a particular meaning to Jane.

She was certainly always interested in pursuit as a game, though the game might, as with Helvetia, become serious. In one letter she speaks with a certain wryness of having pursued one woman for over eleven years, apparently unsuccessfully. Another woman, who was an object of Jane's pursuit during this time, says, "When I first met her, she seemed to take a terrific attachment to me. It was unnerving. I admired her, but she would sit and gape at me. It was not embarrassing, but I found it difficult. I wanted to know more about her, but she was very private. She would hold back about herself; she would ask me a few questions, very direct ones, but then she'd let it go. She wouldn't ask any more.

"I don't think Jane was as much in love with people physically as emotionally. She wanted me to return affection to her, but she didn't press me physically. She was aggressive in saying, 'You must say you'll see me. Oh, forget what you were going to do,' she'd insist, and I'd give in. She was persistent, not aggressive.

"Was her adoration a game? I felt it might be, that the pursuit was a game. I think she was manipulative in that she would move things around, though it never seemed so."

In an early notebook for "Camp Cataract" Harriet speaks of her sexual compulsion:

The dangerous thing about me is that I get behaving too quickly for my reasoning powers—during certain periods. It is because I am too highly strung I believe—and I try to allow myself sexual gratification whenever I am attracted to someone who I know is trustworthy because I feel that it calms me down. It's supposed to at any rate.

And in a notebook of the fifties for the never-completed *Going to Massachusetts*, Bozoe Flanner describes herself to her lover Janet Murphy:

There is a Bozoe Flanner who goes forth to seek for happiness and glory with a wild uncontrollable greed, with the appetite of a gorilla—an appetite which is even more embarrassing since she has declared to herself the urgency of cultivating her spirit—however much like a bad flower it might be. To seek its shape is what she has declared she would do—declared not only to herself but to her friends. I have always been seeking my spirit, Janet, and yet the more urgently I seek it, the more like a gorilla I seem to behave—an earthbound gross woman, content to gratify base instincts.

The fact that I seldom do seem to gratify those instincts doesn't matter at all. . . .

Here the "base instincts" seem to be cast in opposition to "cultivating her spirit." Yet in her last book of notes (from the early sixties), for a play she never completed, these gross and spiritual instincts become indistinguishable as love:

Tommy falls in love and associates or confuses love with a spiritual experience. He has love completely confused with God if it is a confusion. . . .

That Jane had one or two passing affairs with men is also part of the sexual mystique about her. It is true, of course, that many men found Jane sexually attractive and she knew it. However, Jane told Dione Lewis that because of Paul she would not have an affair with a man. She said that she knew he did not mind if she had affairs with women, but that he would be very hurt if she had an affair with a man.

Mike Kahn, Libby Holman's nephew, met Jane when he was in his early twenties. "With her," he says, "I was an adoring audience." He fell in love with her and tried to get her to go to bed with him. She would giggle and treat it all as a joke. But once he pressed her more energetically and she said to him, "Oh Mike, I'm not there with you at all," and she put her arms around him and held him close.

In "Plain Pleasures," a short story published in February 1946 in *Harper's Bazaar*, Jane wrote of an affair between a man and a woman, an affair that begins and ends in the imagination. Mrs. Perry, a widow in her early forties, whose eyes are "of an extraordinary clarity and beauty," lives alone in a tenement apartment house in a New England town. One day she goes out into the backyard to bake potatoes on an open fire. John Drake, an "equally reserved" man who occupies the tenement below her, offers to help. As they share the potato bake, Mrs. Perry asks him, "Don't you think that plain pleasures are closer to the heart of God?"

Mr. Drake invites Mrs. Perry to have dinner at a restaurant with him. She gets there earlier than he does and sits in a booth waiting for him. After fifteen minutes she is afraid that he is not going to come at all and she feels very hurt. However, when Mr. Drake arrives she acts very resentfully toward him. The more tender he becomes, the more inimical she is to him. Finally, having drunk too much, she stumbles up the stairs to try to find a place to be alone. She finds a room with a bed in it—the proprietor's bedroom. She sits at the window, tries to get back to her sense of her own life, weeps, and falls asleep on the bed. In the morning she awakes, unclothed, dresses and goes down to the restaurant. She is unable to remember which booth she shared with John Drake.

> The tables were all identical. In a moment this anonymity served only to heighten her tenderness.
> "John Drake," she whispered. "My sweet John Drake."

In fact what has happened, but is not explicitly stated in the story, is that in the night she has been raped by the proprietor. Only after this violation is she able to feel tenderness for John Drake. Just as Miss Goering sought salvation through the gangster Ben, whom she found repellent, so Mrs. Perry can only find tenderness through violation, and violation while she is unconscious, at that. The pleasures that are involved here are hardly plain.

Sitting in the proprietor's room, alone and drunk, just after she has left John Drake, Mrs. Perry tries to persuade herself that she has kept the pathway to her life open—that she can get back to it, that she has not left it starving by the wayside. In the original manuscript, but omitted from the published version, is a strange dark image that comes to Mrs. Perry's mind at that moment:

> While she sat there half in a dream and half awake, she felt distinctly that it would be possible for her to get from the room in which she was now sitting to her own room without going downstairs again and out through the restaurant. A clear image of both rooms riveted together in space by a thick bar took shape in her mind and filled her with delight. She straightened her back in malevolent triumph. "Hoist along—that bar," she murmured in a thick drunkard's voice and then the dark area revealed by the open closet door caught her eye. . . . She sat upright for a little while, still gripped by her fantasy—but gradually the image dissolved and faded into a faint and meaningless apparition of an ape hanging onto a pair of dumbbells.

The triumphant sense that she can keep the two worlds apart—yet connected—deteriorates. What is left is only the image of "an ape hanging onto a pair of dumbbells." Although Jane discarded this image in the published version of the story, it remains an apt reflection of a darkening that was overtaking her at the end of the war.

KARL BISSINGER REMEMBERS PHOTOGRAPHING JANE IN 1946 ON ASSIGNMENT from *Harper's Bazaar*. "She was living on Tenth Street. Jane met me at the door. 'Well, clearly we can't take the picture,' she said, 'I've been in a cat fight.' She had some scratches on her face. 'You don't mean a cat,' I said, and she laughed."

He liked her immediately and said that he would go ahead and take the pictures anyhow and airbrush out the scratches, something he would ordinarily not have done. "We had a good time," he remembers. "She was funny and charming."

Bissinger took two sets of photographs that day, one of Jane in shadow, sitting on a table holding her Pekingese. Her right leg is stiffly in front of her. Her left leg is bent; she holds on to her knee. In the second set, she is standing in a well-lit corner against some white shutters. The images in the two sets seem so unrelated, they could be of two different women.

After this Bissinger saw Jane often. He admired her enormously and told her so. Yet he felt she was "in the position of the kid on the block who has done something marvelous and had better come up with something even more marvelous next time, with everyone watching and waiting for her to fall on her face. She was, during the time I knew her, constantly in the process of giving up and you felt as if you'd have to fill in the pieces. I think she was on the edge of hysteria every minute of her life. She was unforgettable. She was powerful and knew that she was. Though she had all that anxiety, she had a very powerful effect on other people.

"I think most women didn't like her. She was incredibly sharp and direct. Though she herself might hide behind ten different screens with you, you couldn't with her. She was interested in people leveling with her. She could be cutting with them if they weren't.

"When she was drunk, she would say to me, 'Don't put me on a pedestal. I'll tell you what I'm really like.' And then out would come this terrible self-hatred."

To others she might speak of herself as "Crippie, the Kike Dyke," but when she'd laugh, they would think of it as a great joke.

Jane's mother saw the darkening and was in anguish over it. She would come to New York and she would try to talk to Jane about taking care of herself, about her clothes.

"Once Jane's mother came when I was at Tenth Street," says Florence Codman. "Jane kept avoiding her. When Jane went to the bathroom, her mother said to me, 'Please tell me you'll take care of her.'"

Yet if there was growing darkness in Jane at this time, it would be wrong to say that this was the reality behind the more frequent appearance of charm and humor. The very qualities that make Jane's fictions so puzzling—the continuous turnings, the contradictions that are so enmeshed—are the expression of her being. It was not a matter of superficial style. She was, in her life as in her work, a being continuously revolving and twisting, as she slipped from one alternative into and through another.

We all have many selves that we defend "ourselves" against, that we keep well in place. But Jane was someone who seemed either not to have the usual defenses or not to need to avail herself of them. The alternate selves were present continuously to her.

There was a Jane who, in despair at what was happening in her life, could write:

I waited where the water was falling but no water fell after awhile. Flat land seems flat forever—and the pain of my beloved reaches as far as the road reaches. There is always a point where the coaches stop passing —passing again with fat arms and waving hands flung out of windows, clutching treasures of ribbon and jewels. But there is a time when the coaches stop passing—when each pain is rooted like a tree—where it was in the beginning when only the coaches were passing. There is not a coach in sight. Pain is the stone statue behind the soft eyes—and the heartbreaking skin—not to be married not to be loved—

And there was the Jane whom everyone found so amusing, whose actions were so playful that no one knew if she was acting or not. "If she did something cuckoo," says Dione Lewis, "people would say, 'Oh well, that's Jane.'" And there would be another story to tell like the one Boo Faulkner remembers:

"Claire had been after Jane trying to get her to dress better. She kept urging her to go and buy some clothes, telling her to use her charge account at Saks Fifth Avenue. So one day Jane went to Saks and bought a lot of things and put them on Claire's account. But the next day she decided she didn't want the clothes after all. So she picked up the package and took it to the store. She went up to the woman at the counter and said, 'I want to return all of this.' And she dumped everything out on the counter. Only she had picked up the wrong bag. There on the counter was a big mess: eggshells, coffee grounds, and other garbage. Jane limped out the door up Fifth Avenue and went into Saint Patrick's Cathedral, laughing and laughing."

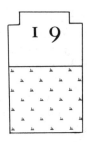

I 9

Despite Jane's intimate life with Helvetia and with other women, her devotion to Paul and her dependence upon him did not change. During the years they lived on Tenth Street, 1945 to 1947, she still sought to preserve certain forms in the marriage.

Florence Codman, who lived in the Tenth Street house for some months, remembers that "Jane was working on *In the Summer House* at the time. She would get up at eight-thirty. I'd already be up and we'd have breakfast and sit and talk. Then I'd go into my room and work. Jane would walk up and down the hall outside waiting for Paul and Oliver to get up so that she could get them breakfast. She would be walking there until twelve or one o'clock. Sometimes I'd go out in the hall and I'd say to her, 'For heaven's sakes, forget about feeding them,' and she'd say, 'Oy,' but she didn't stop."

It was not form for form's sake that impelled Jane to wait in the hallway. She had a sense that it was necessary to fulfill certain obligations within the marriage. That she was Paul's wife remained enormously important to her, and she was jealous of anything that might threaten the marriage as it was. She was, in fact, very jealous of the composer Peggy Glanville-Hicks (Mrs. Stanley Bate), with whom Paul was spending a lot of time. But if Paul recognized Jane's jealousy, he disregarded it.

Though Paul and Jane lived their separate lives, they continued to make crucial decisions together. "If Jane knew what she wanted," says Paul, "it was taken for granted that she'd do it and she generally did. But when she didn't know, then it became terrible, no matter how small the decision was. Often then it came down to what did I want. We'd have a great long discussion. I'd say, 'Why must it depend on what I want? It should depend on what you want.' She was often asking me what did I really want and I was asking her what did she really want. She'd say, 'Don't ask me that. You know I can never say. Are you trying to torture me or what?' I'd say, 'You must know what you want. Everybody knows what he wants.' 'If I did,' she'd say,

'I wouldn't be like this.' Then I'd say, 'Let's do so-and-so.' Then she'd say, 'But—' and she'd have a million reasons for not doing it."

So these discussions went on as they always had gone on between them, as if nothing were changing. But in fact a crucial change was taking place: Paul found his way back to writing fiction, "a territory I had considered forever shut to me."

In a fragment from a notebook of Jane's from the early fifties, Emmy Moore writes to her husband, Paul:

". . . Then you would look grave and dreamy the way you do always look when you think of what you admire. Your eyes become starry and you don't actually mention what you're thinking of. It makes me feel so lost." She put down her pen for a moment. There was a lump in her throat, but she shook her head and went on. "I must now say what I feel. When your eyes become starry and I know you are dreaming of forces which have to do essentially with neither you nor myself—There is no reason on earth why I should not call these forces the forces of nature—it is as if you were listening to some river with a strong current whose swift and steady flow was irresistible to your ear. Always when I recognize this starry look in your eyes I feel that I am [being compared] unfavorably with that river. . . . I myself, needless to admit, can hear no such river, nor do I have any equivalent communications with what I shall continue to call the 'forces of nature,' for want of a better term. Naturally I mean the forces that work inside us but seem to be part of [Here the manuscript breaks off.]

Some of Jane's greatest fears were reflected in the forces of nature. "She was afraid of anything unknown, of the jungle or the mountains," says Paul. "Nature in general horrified her. Her idea of a beautiful landscape was a meadow with cows grazing, no mountains in the distance, nothing else. The sea or storms frightened her. She'd say, 'Yes, yes, they're beautiful, but it's terrible. I don't want to look at it, thank you. Let's go inside. It's almost the cocktail hour.' What was unknown, overpowering, not within human measure, geysers, tornadoes, thunderstorms, she hated."

It was, in fact, through these dark forces of nature that Paul found his way back to fiction. In early 1945 while he was writing music and music criticism, Charles Henri Ford, the editor of *View*, asked him to edit the May issue of the magazine, which focused on tropical America. The issue, when published, contained translations by Paul, photographs he had taken on his trips, and factual accounts of terrible violence: a story of a woman who killed her children and ate their hearts; a story of a man who beat his paralyzed mother to death.

Paul had long ago decided that "the world was too complex for me ever to be able to write fiction; since I failed to understand life, I would not be able to find points of reference which the hypothetical reader might have in common with me." But the day-by-day reading of the myths from the Arapesh and from the Tarahumara began to work upon his imagination.

> Little by little the desire came to me to invent my own myths, adopting the point of view of the primitive mind. The only way I could devise for simulating that state was the old Surrealist method of abandoning conscious control and writing whatever words came from the pen. First, animal legends resulted from the experiments and then tales of animals disguised as "basic human" beings. One rainy Sunday I awoke late, put a thermos of coffee by my bedside, and began to write another of these myths. No one disturbed me, and I wrote on until I had finished it. I read it over, called it "The Scorpion," and decided that it could be shown to others. When *View* published it, I received compliments and went on inventing myths.

But myths or no myths, Paul admits that he would never have gone back to writing had it not been for *Two Serious Ladies*. It was the experience of helping Jane with the novel, of taking part in its creation as teacher and adviser, of seeing it take on shape, that had made him begin to think of writing again. *Two Serious Ladies* had made him wish he were writing a novel—were in fact writing that novel. But the style of the primitive myths, unadorned and basic, and the identity of human and animal motivation in them gave him the key to another kind of writing.

In "The Scorpion" an old woman lives alone in a cave infested by scorpions. Her sons have left her to live in town. One day one of them returns to take her with him, but she does not want to go. Finally she agrees, but says she must sleep first. She sleeps and dreams that she goes to town and searches for her sons. In the town she is thrust into a room and the door is shut behind her. She is a little girl alone, not in a cave, but in a room, weeping. A single scorpion comes crawling down from the ceiling toward her. She tries to brush the scorpion away, but the scorpion grabs her fingers with its pincers.

> Then she realized that he was not going to sting her. A great feeling of happiness went through her. She raised her finger to her lips to kiss the scorpion. . . . Slowly in the peace which was beginning, the scorpion moved into her mouth. She felt his hard shell and his little clinging legs going across her lips and her tongue. He crawled slowly down her throat and was hers. She woke up and called out.

With the old woman swallowing the scorpion, Paul was released into a new life. What had been impossible for him for years was now not only possible but necessary. With his usual self-discipline he set about working, and produced a series of stories of degradation, violence, and vengeance.

The question arises as to why it was not possible for him to deal with these dark forces of nature in his music. Aaron Copland says: "The charm of Paul's music was that it was so natural and open and flowing. There was a directness in it. While other people were using a twelve-tone system and calculating things out according to a preconceived theory, he kept composing and working in the way Satie did. Paul's music had interest because of its spontaneity and because of the personality that showed through, one of great charm and with a lively imagination.

"He never, even as a very young student, wanted to be a Beethoven. He was interested in only certain kinds of music and he knew from the beginning what they were. Satie didn't write monumental or great long works, but he remains important. Given Paul's gift, I could have imagined him being of that importance, if he had continued."

But it was also true that something in the music itself had become terribly burdensome for Paul. "When you're composing, the mind is in use, but only with musical ideas. Those ideas become obsessive, but you are completely confined to musical terms in solving them. You become hypersensitive then to any sound at all. A rooster crowing a half-mile away will startle you. You're hearing a combination of instruments in your head and the phrase you're writing at the moment, and you have to have silence because you can't hear that phrase against a real sound."

Even other music became terrible because he found he could not escape it. "When I heard music I did not want to hear, I knew what key it was in and where it was going and that drove me mad, that I couldn't not listen to it. I had to listen to it, every note." In a sense he had become a prisoner of his own ear.

He needed silence, but he was living in a world in which there was little real silence to be had. In *View*, in a column of jazz criticism, he wrote of the invasion of sound in the city and of a phrase he had brought back from a dream: "Poets have ears, but the world of sound is unkempt, chaotic, and barbarous." And while working on the *Herald Tribune*, he began to experience spells of deafness.

Writing was a great release for him. From the confinements of musical terms he was released into silence and into the dictates of his own unconscious. Writing, he thought of himself as surrendering to his unconscious in the surrender to the characters he created. He knew the words they said, he could see their attitudes, but he didn't have to hear their voices.

In the first paragraph of his autobiography, Paul speaks of his relation to

sounds and to words when he was a child four years old. He had been
puzzling over the word *mug*, repeating it over and over again to himself until
it had no meaning.

> The room was very quiet. . . . Suddenly the gold clock chimed four
> times. As soon as the last stroke was stilled, I realized that something
> important was happening. I was four years old, the clock had struck
> four, and "mug" meant mug. Therefore I was I, I was there, and it was
> that precise moment and no other.

In late 1946 Paul wrote "A Distant Episode," a story about meaningless
sounds and words. In the story an American professor of linguistics is
traveling in North Africa. He is condescending to the natives, though he
counsels himself, "These people are not primitives." In search of a
camel-udder box he covets, he goes out alone into a strange territory. He is
savagely beaten by the natives and his tongue is cut out. He is reduced to the
most primitive stage of existence, dressed in a costume of metal that makes
ringing sounds as he moves, miming obscene gestures taught to him by the
natives.

"A Distant Episode" is a story of vengeance taken against the civilized
world by the primitive, of vengeance by the emotions against the false
intellect. At the end the professor is left alone in a native house. When he
runs out into the desert, a soldier shoots at him:

> The soldier watched a while, smiling, as the cavorting figure grew
> smaller in the oncoming evening darkness, and the rattling of the tin
> became a part of the great silence out there beyond the gate.

When *Partisan Review* accepted "A Distant Episode" for publication in
early 1947, Paul felt triumphant. Now, he knew, he would be able to go on
writing fiction. Then two things happened, virtually simultaneously.
Doubleday offered him a contract to write a novel, and he decided to go to
Morocco.

Perhaps "decided" is the wrong word; he had a dream that "decided" him:

> This dream was distinctive because although short and with no
> anecdotal content beyond that of a changing succession of streets, after I
> awoke, it had left its essence with me in a state of enameled precision: a
> residue of ineffable sweetness and calm. In the late afternoon sunlight I
> walked slowly through complex and tunneled streets. As I reviewed it,
> lying there, sorry to have left the place behind, I realized with a jolt that

the magic city really existed. It was Tangier. My heart accelerated, and memories of other courtyards and stairways flooded in, still fresh from sixteen years before. For the Tangier in which I had wandered had been the Tangier of 1931.

On July 1 Paul sailed on the S.S. *Ferncape* for Casablanca. With him was Gordon Sager, then working on the manuscript of *Run Sheep Run*.

The morning of the day we were to leave, Gordon came to Tenth Street early, several hours before we needed to be aboard. In view of the amount of luggage I was taking along, I called the Cadillac rental agency and asked for a car to take us to South Brooklyn. We had lunch, and I began to collect my things. Soon I realized that my passport was seriously missing. It had been lying on a bookcase shelf earlier that morning. Now it was nowhere to be seen. We searched feverishly; the car was due to arrive in a half hour. Gordon was for going through all my valises; he thought it likely that at some point I had unthinkingly slipped it inside one of them. We continued to look for it everywhere. Just before the car came, I unearthed it, buried beneath a neat pile of Jane's underwear in the back of a bureau drawer. It was a mystery; Jane earnestly claimed to know nothing about it. Yet no one else had come into the apartment. We looked at her accusingly. She laughed. "You *know* I don't want you to go," she said. "So I must have."

If Paul left America feeling that he was impelled by the dream, it is also true that external forces contributed to his going. For most Americans the period immediately after the war was a hopeful one. The threat of nazism and fascism was ended; democracy had triumphed. Hiroshima and Nagasaki had "happened," but at least the war was over and the United States had emerged physically unscathed and ordinary life could be taken up again. There was a euphoric hope for the future.

But for those like Paul who always felt themselves separate from society in their work and in their vision, there was no such feeling. He felt the dread and guilt of the atomic bombing as if it were the final proof on a societal scale of the blackness he saw existing but never acknowledged in individuals.

Politics was a vain hope, and the war itself—though he hated nazism and fascism—was not his war, finally no more than a political struggle whose outcome, even when the Allies won, was tainted. Had not the United States with all its pretense of nobility and high ideals dropped the bomb on Hiroshima and Nagasaki?

If World War I had made expatriates out of many artists, and had left them with a sense of a "loss of innocence," the effects of this war on

Paul—and many other artists—was even more fundamental. Dropping the atomic bomb did not simply confirm the evil in society; it confirmed too that there had never been any innocence to be lost.

Before the war artists, writers, and musicians had been able to separate themselves from the larger world by their mode of living, often by their sexual preference, and by their disregard for the conventions of the established society. But now, as a result of the war, all those ways by which the bohemian élite had distinguished themselves were to be preempted or at least tolerated by a substantial part of the larger society. It is a paradox that those who lived at odds with the society, as Paul and many other artists did, were at the same time most vulnerable to the changes within it. If one creates oneself in opposition to the larger society, one's very self is at stake in its disintegration. When modes of conduct used as the evidence and proof of one's transgression come to be more generally accepted, the very notion of transgression loses its force. And the notion of the artist as a citizen of special vision, transgressing against society, yet finally responsible to it, becomes an anachronism.

In his choice of Morocco as a place of voluntary exile Paul was unlike American artists of an earlier generation who fled from the United States to Western Europe. He chose rather to go to a world that he had long identified with the unconscious—though he did not think of it then as making a choice.

"You don't make a choice. You follow a scent," he says. "If you stop to make a choice, you lose track of the scent and then you're lost. You can see how that can be. The unconscious is the only thing there is to trust in. What else do you have contact with except your idea of your own identity?

"When I had that dream, I realized that happiness could be bought, but only at the expense of the mind. And the choice was made by the dream."

On the boat to Morocco, Paul wrote a story, "Pages from Cold Point." It is, in a curious way, a rewriting of "The Waterfall."

In "Pages from Cold Point" the narrator, Norton, tells of taking his sixteen-year-old son, Racky, to live on an island in the Caribbean, in an isolated house on a cliff, high above the ocean below. (Hope, Norton's wife, has died, and it is with her money that he is able to make the trip.) Norton views Racky as a boy of extraordinary innocence of vision. He does not expect him to be an intellectual. "That is no affair of mine, nor do I have any particular interest in whether he turns out to be a thinking man or not. I know he will always have a certain boldness of manner and a great purity of spirit in judging values."

However, their idyllic existence together is interrupted when a native policeman tells Norton that Racky is seducing the native boys and paying them to keep quiet about it. The policeman warns Norton to keep the boy at home or send him away to school. On hearing of what Racky has done,

Norton says, "It was as if I wanted to believe it, almost as if I had already known it, and he had merely confirmed it."

Norton cannot think of the right words with which to approach Racky to tell him of his discovery, but it is Racky who approaches Norton: he appears, passive, in his father's bed. Now, after the act of incest, it is the boy who has the power over the father; Racky leaves Norton to live his own life, taking most of the money with him.

Of the days spent with Racky in sexual intimacy, Norton writes, "I think that this period was what I had always been waiting for life to offer, the recompense I had unconsciously but firmly expected, in return for having been held so closely in the grip of existence all these years."

Yet the beginning of the story is really its ending:

Our civilization is doomed to a short life; its component parts are too heterogeneous. I personally am content to see everything in the process of decay. The bigger the bombs, the quicker it will be done. Life is visually too hideous for one to make the attempt to preserve it. Let it go. Perhaps some day another form of life will come along. Either way, it is of no consequence. At the same time, I am still a part of life, and I am bound by this to protect myself to whatever extent I am able. And so I am here. . . .

Of Paul's work, and in particular of this story, Norman Mailer later wrote:

Paul Bowles opened the world of Hip. He let in the murder, the drugs, the incest, the death of the Square . . . , the call of the orgy, the end of civilization. . . .

In the act of escaping Paul became a forerunner. In going to Morocco, which he identified with the unconscious, he was going to find that which men and women of the next generation would find and call their own vision, twenty years later.

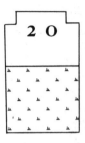

2 0

JANE HAD DECIDED—IF AGAIN "DECIDED" IS THE right word—to stay in the United States while Paul went to North Africa. When he left, she briefly sublet her apartment on Tenth Street and went to stay with her friend Libby Holman at Libby's estate, Treetops, in Stamford, Connecticut. Paul and Jane had met Libby in 1945 and had become very close friends with her. Libby, famous as the original "torch singer"—the star of several musical revues in the late 1920s and early 1930s—was a zesty, highly intelligent woman, whose singing voice rendered directly her emotional range and complexity. Her first husband, an heir to the Reynolds tobacco fortune, had been killed under mysterious circumstances and she had suffered a series of further tragedies in her life.

A group of letters that Jane wrote to Paul from Treetops has survived to tell of her life there, of her writing, of the ending of her affair with Helvetia, of her flirtations with other women, and of her money problems.

Her letters are "agonizers." As she herself says, ". . . unless I present a problem in a letter I have not really written one." She agonizes about her own work, about not being published, about going to Africa to join Paul: when will she go, if she does go? A fortune-teller in Morocco has told Paul that something is going to happen to someone coming on a journey to see him, and Jane is sure the fortune-teller is talking about her.

These are extraordinary letters in the exactness with which they reveal Jane's thoughts and feelings. The exactness is not chance—she describes one letter as an exercise in precision. The agonizing over Paul's apartment, for example, is a drama of her world in microscopic detail. If she does this, then what about that? She speaks of what she has tried and will try. She rages at Paul, then suddenly laughs at herself. She says, "I've talked about this enough," only to resume the subject once again a few pages later. The alternatives have now shifted slightly. It is not possible for her to dismiss either the subject or any of its complexities. What is to be done involves what has happened, what could happen, the real, the imaginary, the necessary, the probable, money, time, urgency, judgment, and error. She reports on how others want the apartment and make demands on her. It is all only one drama among the many dramas—the drama of going to Africa, the drama of the fortune-teller, the drama of her flirtations—but that makes it none the less pressing.

Each letter is a complete document in itself, as if it were an artistic whole. Her comic asides reveal that though she knows what she is doing, she cannot help herself. Once when Paul says something to her about the length of the letters and the agonizing repetitions, she says, "You know I'm a fanatic."

However, in the discussion of her work, even in the agonizing, there is a lucidity and a precise self-knowledge:

. . . It has been hard enough for me to get on with my novel *here* because of four or five tremendous stumbling blocks—none of them however due to the circumstance of my environment. (My novel is entirely in this laborious style.)

The more I get in to it, which isn't very far in pages but quite a bit further in thinking and consecutive work the more frightened I become at the isolated position I feel myself in vis-à-vis of all the writers whom I consider to be of any serious mind. Because I think there is no point in using the word talent any longer. Certainly Carson McCullers is as *talented* as Sartre or Simone de Beauvoir but she is not really a serious writer. I am serious but I am isolated and my experience is probably of no interest at this point to anyone; . . . you have always been a truly isolated person so that whatever you write will be good because it will be true which is not so in my case because my kind of isolation I think is an accident, and not inevitable. I could go on and on with this and explain to you better what I mean but there is not space for such a discussion. Not only is your isolation a positive and true one but when you do write from it you immediately receive recognition because what you write is in true relation to yourself which is always recognizable to the world outside. With me who knows? When you are capable only of a serious and ponderous approach to writing as I am—I should say solemn perhaps—it is almost more than one can bear to be continually doubting one's sincerity. . . . As I move along into this writing I think the part I mind the most is this doubt about my entire experience. This is far more important than feeling "out" of it and "isolated," I suppose, but it also accentuates that guilt a thousand times. It is hard to explain this to you and in a sense it is probably really at bottom what this novel will be about if I can ever get it done! Another souris [*tsuris*: Yiddish for "troubles"]: (or is that spelled Tzoris?) I realize now . . . that really "Two Serious Ladies" never *was* a novel, so we are both facing the same doubt exactly, although I cannot imagine your not being able to write one. Helvetia is making her way into this novel which is inevitable since I have thought so much about her for the past seven years. I am also in it in the person of her son, Edgar. This is good because I am usually trying to be too removed from my own experience in writing which can be tricked in a short story very well but not in a novel. It is *bad* because it is simply not much fun. It is upsetting and I get confused. You know what a state of confusion Helvetia has put me into anyway so that I am a far more uncertain person today than I was at twenty-three, so you can imagine how difficult it is for me to hammer a novel out of anything she has prompted me to think. Because it is really not Helvetia whom I mind writing about; I have transformed the situation sufficiently so that I am not too certain every second that she is this character but it is difficult, very difficult to put into words all the things she has caused me to brood about which are I think foreign to my nature but which now obsess me. There are *other* elements in the novel, natch!

Jane's uncertainty about choice now turned backward upon herself and her life. When she was younger, before she knew Helvetia, the future was danger, but her talent and her wit were the weapons she used to subdue it. Now, after the years of contest with Helvetia and after the failure of others to understand *Two Serious Ladies*, her past and the meaning she had given her past were called into question.

In the few fragments that remain of the novel in which Helvetia is the mother and Jane her son Edgar, that disabling doubt has taken hold of Edgar:

His head ached as a result of knowing so much about himself—and he felt that by this knowledge he had somehow trammeled his source of what he termed "Live Feelings" for want of a more accurate term . . . like so many unfortunates who despise themselves he had periods of elation when he felt himself to be his own opposite. . . . [He had] a vision of himself jumping up and down on his own face.

She had lost the sense of her own "Live Feelings" in the face of the continual intellectual justification that Helvetia demanded of her. Her duality had become something she herself condemned.

She made herself sit in her room and work on the novel. Still, she had her techniques for evasion, as she admitted to Paul:

To give you an idea of my slow pace—I have done about thirty-three typewritten pages in the same number of days. One day I do *three* pages but then the next I do nothing—possibly—and this is working *all day* and after dinner! I mean going at it and stopping for a while and then going at it again. Of course I do a great deal of thinking which takes me forever—because my mind is apt to wander—every twenty minutes if I have reached an impasse or a complicated thought and then I am apt to dream the whole morning about some flirtation. It is always nice to slip out and escape into the pool at a bad moment but actually I have been conscientious about staying in my room almost all of the time. I don't write much and I don't read but I am at least in my room. And in a few months I will know once and for all whether I can write this novel or whether I have to give up writing anything. I have thus far been saved by an idea or a little run of dialogue at the last minute when I was about to despair.

And she continues her pursuit of pleasure as intently as Mrs. Copperfield ever did:

I flew down with Libby (for a weekend) to Louisa Carpenter's and Sister [Eugenia] Bankhead's. The plane—Louisa's mother's it is—was wonderful and I loved every minute of the flight. I drank heavily on the weekend, played poker and did no work.

Louisa C. is the most sexually attractive woman in the whole world, but I am alas not alone in thinking this.

But then immediately after the talk of Louisa and sexuality comes a sentence about piglets and Pekes—a very Jane-like juxtaposition:

We went crabbing and we saw two litters of baby pigs—11 little piglets in each—or maybe nineteen. Also Sister's two *black Pekes*!!* Naturally I was "aux anges" with them. They are really pitch black. Can you imagine it?

She also has her obligations. Her mother is coming to New York for ten days and Jane is going into the city to see her. She must see Helvetia sometime soon, to settle things. Meantime she keeps herself busy swimming and reading, and thinking and not thinking about coming to Africa.

My swimming stroke is improving. I am reading *Sons and Lovers* as well as Kierkegaard. I wish you were here. I am by myself more than I have ever been since childhood. I am worried about Helvetia getting me down but otherwise O.K. except when the work is stale. I suppose both you and G. [Gordon Sager] have *written* novels already. I still think that it was a good idea for me not to go to Africa, don't you? Because with

---

*Jane's Pekingese Donald had been killed by a car.

outer complications as well as inner ones I don't think I could have got anything done. But then perhaps you are so disgusted with my slow pace that you don't think what I do matters at this point. I do think I might come to Africa before I have entirely *finished* the book, but I shall not think of that until November . . . when you will have either returned or not. I shall not move before then unless something awful happens which would make it impossible for me to work here. I must document myself on hurricanes too before long. I hope to have better news on my progress the next time I write, but I want you should always know the worst so that you will have no false idea of me . . .

She ends by telling Paul about his passport that so mysteriously disappeared on the day he left for Morocco:

As for packing your passport away—I thought it was mine—I looked to see whose picture was in it—and I dimly remember my own face and not yours. As Libby said when I told her, "How psychosomatic can you get."

In her next letter, Jane writes that she has spent ten days in New York with her mother:

It was a terrible holocaust, worse than I expected, because I did not do one lick of work for ten days. I slept in a different bed every night, including I.B.'s (of film research fame). You know whom I mean; I.B. was pretty annoyed to find me in her place the next morning, I think, which upset me for a good three days. I spent one pleasant afternoon at the little zoo on 59th Street and thought of you all the time. There was a little baby monkey you would have loved. . . . I saw several lunatics sitting around waiting for night to fall and I was sure glad it was only four in the afternoon. I have got back on my work again with unbelievable difficulty and continue crawling along. I am so slow it is almost as though I were going backwards. In a sense I am a little less discouraged than in my last letter but I don't dare say that because by tomorrow I may be in despair. Tonight I read a story by Katherine Anne Porter called "Pale Horse, Pale Rider." It has completely ruined my evening because it [is] so sad and depressing and moving—and yet I am not sure I like it. If I feel terribly sad and terribly moved by something it is very puzzling not to be able to say I like it. I keep forgetting what writing is supposed to be anyway. I cannot however think of anything that I have really liked that has made me sad or depressed, no matter how depressing or sad it really was. Perhaps you can write me what I mean.

On the day after tomorrow I am taking a train to Pittsfield where Helvetia and Maurice [Grosser] (He is visiting her) are meeting me. I shall be with her about five days and then I'm coming back here. We have to see each other I suppose to settle certain things, but it is naturally, "inquiétant." I'll bet she's written more than I have this summer. I used to read Valéry when I was younger and I loved it but I'm sure I couldn't now. . . .

As for me, I can't stay here at Libby's forever but probably through the fall. I hope that after I do about twenty more pages of this novel, I shall have completed a section, at least psychologically, and then I will write a short story and try to sell it to [Mary Lou] Aswell [of *Harper's Bazaar*]. I shall need more money eventually, when I leave here, and although I know you would send me some I don't want to ask you because there is no reason why I shouldn't earn a little, since I am doing no housekeeping whatsoever. . . .

In your letters you sound as though it were *I* and not you who were disappearing into the wildernesses and the inaccessibles, which is typical of you. . . .

I am plump and in extremely good health though not at all satisfied. I miss you very much indeed and wonder how we are ever going to meet again with all these distances. I feel quite homeless and yet I think in spite of everything maybe it is better I didn't go to Africa. I am not too worried or sad as long as I keep hearing from you because I know that all at once you will be coming here or I shall simply be going there.

. . . Oliver says he's working on jobs for you, (ossir)* so I'm sure everything will be fine. (ossir): In any case you must do what you see fit to do. Maybe if you came back we could go down to our beloved Mexico. I am being vague and half cocked about plans because I'm trying to fool myself out of an "agonizer." I can feel this letter slipping into one.

. . . I am enjoying my *Sickness unto Death* throughout the summer. Please write to me. It is much easier for you to write than for me, because I always feel that unless I present a problem in a letter I have not really written one.

Much love
Teresa†

In September, Jane went to visit Helvetia. From Treetops, on her return, she wrote:

*Ossir—a word used frequently in Jane's mother's family (of Hungarian origin?). It implies the denial of what's just been said.
†Teresa was the role Jane played in their game about the parrot.

I was with her a little under two weeks and we got a great many things settled . . . about my apartment and other details. She offered to keep my room for me if someone else paid for the other half of the apartment but I refused because she said that she did not think she would be in New York very much and I saw no reason for her keeping a room all winter mainly for me. D'abord she would in no time feel that she was being used and the psychological dramas would begin all over again.

A great many things may have been settled, but some things had only ended. In another fragment from the unfinished novel, Jane describes Edgar and his mother arguing. Edgar asks:

"Don't my arguments even worry you?"
    This she could never answer, but she would look at him with a veiled and secret expression, one which almost broke his heart because in her eyes he could see that she could not speak even though she wanted to. . . .
    Was it that she refused to speak or that she could not? Certainly the expression that came into her eyes at such moments was not a calculating one. His worst fear was that she could not answer—which made him love her intensely and at the same time moved him to shake her very hard.

As the days passed, Jane could get no further into the novel. In her next letter to Paul she began her obsessive discussion about subletting his apartment. "I wish that you would tell me what you want me to do." Perhaps she should do this. But on the other hand . . . but then again. . . . Some pages later she says, "I am willing to do this as best I can but I will take no responsibility about doing it wrong."
    She returns to the question of her work, comparing his success with her failure:

I am desperate however at all this time passing and have done little more on my novel than you have. . . . I am terribly discouraged and of course the fact that you get these letters from publishers complimenting you on stories is no help to my morale as far as a *career* is concerned. I have never once received a letter from anyone about Plain Pleasures or the first Act of my play or my little *Cross Section* stories ["A Guatemalan Idyll" and "A Day in the Open"] and *Partisan Review* would laugh and probably does at my work. This does not concern me deeply but I realize that I have no [career] really whether I work or not and never have had one. You have more of a career after writing a few short stories than I have after writing an entire novel. All this while, I have been slap-happy, not realizing that publishers did write anybody but now I see how completely unnoticed my work has been professionally. Arthur Weinstein told Virgil that at Knopf's they pretend never to have heard of me so I'm sure they will not publish my next novel. I am quite discouraged about all that and must say that if it were not for you and Edwin Denby, I would feel utterly lost. However none of that bothers me except to make me frightened about never making any kind of reputation which means no money and I refuse to have my non-existent career referred to any longer. I feel silly about it. I don't feel like being in New York at all and would like to go and live somewhere in a small town. I am eager to get back on my novel in spite of all this but that is probably because I haven't been writing it for awhile and possibly when I begin again I will feel an inner discouragement and boredom compared to which any hurt pride is poppycock. I wish too that you would not refer to *your* work as your "little novel" [*The Sheltering Sky*] which you did in your letter as I'm sure it will be very powerful and twice as excellent as mine, as well as more successful, and so are Dostoievsky and Sartre. Oliver says your story is wonderful and I am certainly eager to see it. I don't mind how much better or worse you write than I do as long as you don't insist that I'm the writer and not you. We can both be, after all, and it's silly for you to go on this way just because you are afraid to discourage me. I suppose I was irritated and appalled because you referred to your work as your little novel just as Helvetia would do! She has written more than either of us this summer but also she has had more time. Well I hope all the novels will be good novels and published. I must now however write a short story in order to get some money. Perhaps I can.

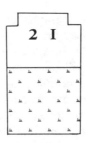

2 1

Bᵧ LATE SEPTEMBER JANE HAD STILL NOT MANAGED TO
get back to the novel. She wrote Paul that she felt beset by the heat and by
unpaid bills:

> I feel that I must make a little money. This is not an appeal for money,
> but an explanation of why I would veer off my novel which I'm sure you
> don't approve of. I want to be able to take care of those little things
> myself, because it is a terrible feeling not to be able to earn enough to
> pay for even the details of one's life at the age of thirty. I am not
> frightened because it is not as though I were out on the street or could
> not ask for money (even my mother would give it to me but I would
> never ask her!). It is simply a matter of humiliation.

She had started work on a short story—to make money, she said. And
she was slowly approaching the decision to go to Morocco to join Paul, who
was clearly not coming back to New York. She played with the thought of
what she might do in Morocco.

> Oliver says you can't wait to get me into the desert. Of course I'm sure
> that when I get there, if I do, all the part I would have liked will be
> over—like the wine and the nice hotels. I would like to stay in a hotel in
> Fez, I think, rather than Tangier, and I still refuse to cross the
> Atlas [es] in a bus. But if O. came maybe we'd take a cab. I wish to hell I
> could find some woman still so that I wouldn't always be alone at night.
> I'm sure Arab nightlife would interest me not in the slightest. As you
> know I don't consider those races voluptuous or exciting in any way, as I
> have said—being a part of them almost. . . . It is hard for me to think of
> going anywhere by myself of course, and I'm not even *going* to think
> about it yet. If my novel is not coming along at all by then it would be
> more painful than pleasant to go over there and see your manuscript

almost done or even half done. I don't think I could bear the sense of failure made so palpable, but I couldn't bear it either to have you in such a terrible state about yours as I am about mine. I really am very glad you are coming along with it and I don't believe any of the things you say about the value of it, but aside from that I also think it is very important that you have this extra source of income if you can really develop it substantially, because it will permit you to do much more work out of the country than your music does which is after all what you want, and in a sense a good way to keep alive with the prices here the way they are. None of this makes my life any simpler perhaps or maybe it will but that's beside the point. It will all work out, or it will never, I can't imagine. But certainly I don't like to see you miserable and bored, which you are in New York. I myself cannot get into New York at all. It is almost as difficult for me as getting on a boat to Africa.

Soon after, however, Jane did go into New York to get Paul's apartment ready for subletting. On her return to Treetops she wrote to him:

. . . I have waited to write because I have been in such a boiling rage with you having spent most of this week trying to make some order out of the havoc of your clothes and pure junk left around the apt. none of which I dare to throw away. The number of filthy articles that were simply stuffed into the closets is unbelievable. It was like cleaning out an old Vermont farmhouse—the dirt left by two generations of maniacs. . . . It is all very well and your business to keep hoarding things and collecting more—but then you should not expect to just go away and have it taken care of. You do not live in an apartment but in a *storeroom* with a little space in the middle! . . .

She goes on to say that she has discovered from Oliver Smith that Paul is planning to buy a house in Tangier for $500, and she is hurt that Paul has not told her anything about it*:

Everyone seems to know about your buying a house in Africa except myself—and why on earth you would suddenly have written about it to Bob Faulkner whom you don't ever see I can't understand. I just *happened* to be in town when Oliver got your wire and I of course advised him to send the $500. I knew you were getting a kick out of the house and I cannot help but want your pleasure. I was hurt though that you had written to Oliver and Bob Faulkner about it and yet no word to me. In your letter to Oliver you don't sound at all as though you expected us

---

*In fact, Paul was short of money, and he and Oliver Smith bought the house jointly.

both to come over but only he. He refuses however to go without me and perhaps you didn't expect that he would. I know that you asked me over . . . but that was before this house came on the scene, and possibly now you feel instinctively that it is all wrong for me. Of course you know how I feel about houses and living in quarters where I might be conspicuous. I don't of course know about the Arab town of Tangier (I *refuse* to use that Arabic word). It may be filled with European and American eccentrics in any case. That is all I would mind, being conspicuous. As for worrying about comforts—as you know, or should by now—that is not the kind of thing that concerns me. Have you forgotten Mrs. Copperfield? . . .

Sometimes I am in despair and sometimes very hilarious but I have a terrific urge now to go to Africa in spite of the house, although even the house I would like in the day time I imagine. The plans are to come in Feb. I hope maybe to have done enough writing by then so as not to be completely ashamed and jealous when confronted with your novel. At the moment I can't even think of it without feeling hot all over. And yet if you had *not* been able to do it I would have wrung my hands in grief—I say this sincerely. . . .

However little I have done I am pleased with, but shall probably throw it in the rubbish heap when I see yours. The story I am working on to get some money is nearly 60 pages long in my notebook already—and they are large pages—so I worked at a good rate but have not touched it in over a week. I flew down to Maryland for two days and when I returned I tended to your things at the studio for 3 or four days. I feel like getting back to it. It is utterly unsaleable but I like it thus far if I can only work it out! It's coming out much better than the unfinished novel did—and I know why—it's because I tried to put myself into the novel in the guise of a boy, which somehow throws the whole thing off. I shall go back to it eventually but with grave misgivings. Possibly I am meant to write plays, or short stories. . . .

P.S. . . . Perhaps you don't want me to come? I shall naturally not mind the house when there's more than you and me in it. And it does sound beautiful because you can see the water—yes I think I would have worked much better over there. I have had too much the burden of my entire life here, but in a sense I have learned far more by staying.

In December, from Helvetia's farm in Vermont, Jane once again scolds Paul. He has told her that from her letters he was expecting her to be in Tangier by this time:

Dearest Bupple:
Your letter from Tangier the one written on Thanksgiving day has

thrown me into a state. I think it is rather mean of you not to be more careful of what you say when you know how easily upset I am and how quickly guilty even when I know I'm not in the wrong. I don't know where on earth you got the idea that I would arrive suddenly in Tangier. Surely unless it is just wishful thinking—because you were bored and ready to have me arrive—it must have been Oliver who confused you.

The letter continues as an "agonizer" about when she will come to Tangier. She is now planning to come with Cory, a new lover, a middle-aged woman from New England. But M., Cory's business partner (not a lover, according to Jane, but still jealous), "has gone off to Honolulu in a semi-huff and it would be cruel of me to walk out on her . . . to get a month sooner to Tangier. About this I am morally certain . . . I have made no promises to her but I would not be cruel and I am fond of her. I have as usual precipitated a holocaust."

Paul had sent Jane the manuscript of his new story, "How Many Midnights":

I *loved* your story. . . . In fact I am convinced that you are a writer down to the marrow of your bone. . . . Perhaps writing *will* be a means to nomadic life for you, but I hope you won't slowly stop writing music, altogether. I think you will do both. You have always wanted to go back to writing anyway and I remember your discussing it very solemnly once at the Chelsea. You were standing against a bureau. . . .

Please be good and don't worry me about Africa. In other words don't be slipshod and get mixed up about what I tell you. Your letters can be very confusing too, but I do try to get the meaning out of them and not falsify. In the most recent one you don't mention your trip into the desert, only to Fez, and I understood from the other one you were starting out on a real Safari. I am so worried that I shan't hear from you for months. *Please* take care of yourself and don't for God's sake get sick down there. Also afraid I won't have any place to mail a carbon of my story when it's finished—for a long while—Is there any mail delivery in the desert? . . .

> Much much love, as ever
> Teresa

P.S. I miss you very much indeed and want to see you naturally. If ever you are troubled or puzzled about my inertia just imagine everything you feel about "setting out" in reverse!! Of course I vacillate but I have come a long way nonetheless. I can now actually imagine the trip alone without exactly shuddering, whereas this summer I feared it even with you along. I should hate truthfully at this point not to get to Africa at all.

P.S. I am going to walk to town and mail this before I throw it away. I
have as usual gotten too wound up about some remark which you
have by now forgotten. I suppose it was your saying you were now at
last "going to lead your own life"—as though you had been hanging
about Libby's kitchen all summer. In the next breath you told me
about the parrot's Thanksgiving dinner, so I know you realized that
you were being unnecessarily petulant. I have noticed that whenever
you are cross in a letter you atone for it quite automatically by
describing some gesture of the parrot's. He sounds like another
lunatic—thank God—how *will* you lug him all over Africa? Be sure
to get a strong cage so that he doesn't stick his head and shoulders
through the bars. Does he *say* anything? Is he pretty or just crazy?
Your hotel sounded charming but whenever I get to Morocco, I shall
insist on Fez. You must let me know if you think the Fortune Teller
infallible.

Love again,

J.

PART TWO

1948 - 1957

Overleaf: *Jane in Tangier marketplace.*
COURTESY KATHARINE HAMILL AND NATASHA VON HOERSHELMAN

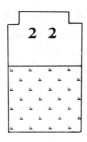

2 2

On JANUARY 31, 1948, JANE ARRIVED IN GIBRALTAR with Cory. They crossed over to Tangier by ferry. In the evening Jane went out walking alone.

The Tangier of that January night was a place of mystery, a city of arches. Veiled women in white robes and men in hoods and cloaks moved silently through dark by-streets. The trees everywhere were filled with birds. As Jane walked, she came across large wooden packing crates in the streets. Lights flickered inside them. She peeked in and saw people cooking and eating and sleeping. It was exotic and yet strangely familiar, as if, she later said, she had dreamed it long before.

Paul was in the Sahara working on the manuscript of *The Sheltering Sky* when he received a cable from Jane telling him she would arrive in Gibraltar. With the parrot he had acquired he hurried to meet her, traveling from Timimoun to Adrar, from Adrar to Béchar, and then from Béchar to Algiers. From Algiers he took three different trains to get to Fez. But once in Fez he was stranded because of sudden rains and could not get to Gibraltar in time to meet Jane.

He arrived in Tangier two days after she did, and at once took her to see the house he was buying with Oliver Smith in the medina, the native quarter, near the Place Amrah. It was a tiny house with no plumbing, with ceilings so low one had to crawl from one room to another. But from its roof was an extraordinary view of the city and of the bay.

She had not expected to be so intrigued by the medina, by the deviousness of its streets, by the small scale and the secrecy of its houses, closed off from the street. In the lives of the people she saw things that made this world of special interest to her, the separation of the lives of the women from the men, the slow pace of personal relationships—it might take hours for the sharing of a cup of tea, yet in that sharing were hundreds of nuances of behavior to be observed and wondered at.

Almost at once Paul and Jane and Cory and Edwin Denby, who had just arrived in Morocco, set out for Fez. Paul preferred Fez to Tangier. Jane loved the hybrid seedy quality of Tangier, he remembers, but he liked the "medieval formality of Fez, even in its state of decay."

At the Palais Jamai in Fez Paul introduced Jane and Cory and Edwin Denby to majoun, a thick paste made of hashish and dates and honey. It had been prepared by the mother of Ahmed Yacoubi, a young Moslem boy Paul had met in Fez. The majoun was one more new experience that Jane was eager to try in this world of new experiences. She was throwing herself into this world, casting off the sense of paralysis she had about her work and the doubt about her own experience that had overtaken her since the affair with Helvetia.

Paul warned her not to take much majoun at first, but to eat only a small amount and then wait for the effect before trying any more. Jane said, "Ah, this stuff is nothing," and finished off a large piece. Paul became angry. "Now you've taken too much," he told her. But she simply shrugged it off and went to bed.

The next morning, Paul recalls, she was very upset:

> She had not yet been able to sleep, she claimed, and her night had been ten nights long and totally horrible. First she had begun to worry that something was happening to me; then as the drug came on more powerfully, she had become convinced that I was about to steal in and murder her. Finally she had noticed her hands and had not understood what they were. When she saw her fingers move, she became paralyzed with terror. Illogically enough, from that day on she remained an implacable enemy of all forms of cannabis. The fact that her experience had been due solely to an overdose seemed to her beside the point. "Anything that can do awful things like that is dangerous," she contended.

While Paul stayed on in Fez with Edwin Denby, Jane and Cory set off on a tour of Morocco. Paul recounts with amusement their lack of preparation for what they would see. Thus, while they were in Marrakech, someone suggested they go to the *amara* of Moulay Brahim. Not knowing that it was a particular kind of religious ceremony, Jane and Cory assumed it would be like going to a county fair, and packed a picnic to take with them. A taxi brought them to the base of a hill, where they began to climb to the site of the tomb, carrying their picnic basket with them.

> After a half hour they began to hear sounds up ahead and assumed that they were about to arrive at the fair. A minute later some thirty men were suddenly running full tilt down the mountain toward them, their

eyes staring like marbles, their mouths wide, screaming, their faces and garments red and wet with blood. . . . Jane said nothing at all, merely stood waiting for the onslaught. The men ran by, still screaming, and disappeared down the mountainside. After resting for a while on a rock beside the path, the picnickers decided to start back to the car rather than continue upward. The men were Aissaoua who had just gone through the ceremony of eating a live bull. . . .

After the Moroccan tour Jane went with Cory to Spain for several weeks. She saw her off to the United States and then, toward the end of March, returned to Tangier, where she and Paul moved into the Hotel Farhar on the Old Mountain.

On April 20 Paul wrote to Peggy Glanville-Hicks:

I have been working intensively on my novel for the past fortnight here at the Farhar on the mountain. . . . Jane and I have communicating rooms, and as soon as I type she types. I imagine that she has got a good deal of work done too these past two weeks. . . .

Jane and I have been attending native weddings and parties, and she is about decided to remain here forever. She says, "You'll never get me out of here now, I can tell you."

As the days passed Jane began to see similarities between the life among the Moroccan women and her own early life with her mother and her mother's sisters. She saw how the Moroccan women would wrangle with each other, how they would shout and make sardonic jokes. In the focus on their daily life, in the repetitions, in their bitter humor she found what seemed entirely natural to her.

AND THEN PAUL INTRODUCED JANE TO CHERIFA. HE HAD MET HER THE SUMMER before when an Algerian named Boussif had said to him, "There's a wonderful savage girl in the souk and you must come to meet her." Paul had gone to Cherifa's stall in the grain market with Boussif and there was presented to her.

"She was sitting in her hanootz, a booth not high enough even to crouch in, just high enough to clear the top of her hat if she sat on the ground. It was like a little box. Outside were mountains of wheat and barley and oats that she was selling. She was dressed as a country woman with a great big hat and a red-and-white-striped blanket around her. At that time she was very extraordinary looking, with beautiful shining black hair that fell around her head. She had a laugh like a savage. She was like a public monument, one of those beings you took a visitor to see—like the woman who sold coal under a certain tree in the Grand Socco, or the man who sold spells and potions in the church courtyard."

Paul could not talk to Cherifa since she spoke only Mohgrebi and he was just beginning to learn the Fez dialect. But he took Jane to see this wild creature, this illiterate but powerful peasant girl nineteen or twenty years old, a descendant of the patron saint of Tangier, a woman different from the other Moroccan peasant women in her wildness and in her drinking. She was known as a lesbian.

After Paul introduced them, Cherifa asked Jane to have a bowl of soup with her. Jane fell immediately and passionately in love with Cherifa. It was as if Cherifa were a realization of her own most fertile imaginings. In the first act of Jane's play *In the Summer House*, Gertrude says to Molly, "Whenever I think of a woman going wild, I always picture her with black hair . . ." Molly says, "I don't guess I've ever pictured women going wild." And Gertrude answers, "And why not? They do all the time. They break the bonds . . . Sometimes I picture little scenes where they turn evil like wolves. . . ." And here, in life, in a hanootz selling grain, was a wild girl-woman.

ON MAY 10 FROM FEZ, WHERE PAUL AND JANE WERE AT THE BELVEDERE HOTEL, Paul wrote to Peggy Glanville-Hicks that he had finished *The Sheltering Sky*.

My novel is just a novel like any other: a triangle laid in the Sahara. Jane is busy farding her eyes with kohl at the moment. She bought the stuff from a crazy woman in the Grand Socco. She has almost decided to be tattooed like a friend of hers, the daughter of the patron saint of Tangier. The friend has blue designs on her chin and on the end of her nose. Yesterday at Sidi Abdeslam ben Moulay Ali Ktiri's house we sat through the most ridiculous tea I've ever witnessed. One member crawled in on all fours, with a tablecloth over her head. She looked and sounded like Touche when he does Lester O'Toole or Queen Victoria on her deathbed. We were choking back the laughter and it was painful. There was a madwoman who looked like Ethel Barrymore in a new part; she came in done up in bustles and hoods, and leaned on a very thick clublike cane. They all kept wanting to know why Jane wasn't with child, and they repeatedly pressed their abdomens and breasts and smiled at her. Then they all tried to feed her up because they think she's terribly thin; of course she weighs more than she ever has before. . . . Jane's conversation with the daughter ran: "How do you do?" Reply from daughter: "Merci." A cat walked through the patio. Jane: "Do you like cats?" Daughter: "Not very much. There are many cats."

It was also in Fez, with Paul's help and advice, that Jane finished her long short story, "Camp Cataract."

At the end of May, Oliver Smith came to Morocco to join Paul and Jane for a vacation. Soon after he arrived he fell ill and for some weeks lay in bed with a high fever. During this time Jane also became ill. Paul has no memory of that illness; whatever it was, it terrified her. She went to a local doctor, who indicated to her that there was something organically wrong with her heart, and that terrified her even more.

In mid-June Libby Holman and her son Christopher (Topper) arrived in Tangier. Paul and Oliver and Jane went to meet them. Paul had planned that they would all take a long trip south, through the desert and across the mountains, but Jane refused to go: she did not want to go over the High Atlas, she said. Instead she remained in Tangier.

Soon after they came back from the trip, Paul received a telegram asking him to return to New York to write the score for Tennessee Williams's *Summer and Smoke*. He left for the United States on July 18, but Jane stayed on in Tangier at the Hotel Villa de France. In her first letter to him after his departure she wrote:

Dearest Bup

It is stupid of me to take so long to get down to writing you. There seems too much really to write about—I mean Fez and money and Africa altogether and my failure to like in it what you do and to like what you do at all anywhere. I love Tangier—the market and the Arab language, the Casbah etc. And I long to go now to Marrakech and Taroudant. It's a pity and since reading your novel I take it very much to heart. I hope you will not complain about me to Peggy Bate. I know you love to talk behind someone's back, just as I do, but oddly enough I don't get any pleasure complaining about you. On the contrary I am horrified and scared when people attack you because you are difficult to defend at times. Now that I've seen you waiting for O. to arrive and witnessed the subsequent disappointment I shudder to think of my own failure to react properly. I have reason to hope that you simply could not have been that excited about my coming or at least that your excitement was of a different nature. I can't believe that after ten years you would have secretly been expecting someone like yourself (or Edwin Denby) to arrive from Gibraltar. . . . At the Farhar I was peculiarly disturbed by the fact that you lingered on in Fez with Edwin instead of rushing to the Farhar to see me. I felt very jealous and left out; I sensed that you were really better off with Edwin and that there would be an unfortunate comparison made at some future date. Alas! it came much sooner than I had expected it would and I have not ceased brooding about it yet; also I have never tried harder to be in your world—to see it the way you did which probably is why I was in such a foul temper the whole time. I wanted to be companionable and pleasant—a source of mild pleasure at meal times and otherwise calm and self-effacing. I am really and truly sorry that it turned out so differently. I don't quite know yet what happened but I do know I have never been so near to a crack-up before. It was not pleasant and I prefer not to think about it ever again. I daresay I won't want to be in Fez ever again, either, unless by next year I've forgotten it all. You are happier there without me anyway, but perhaps the Palais Jamai?—Also before I go on to new subjects, I hope that you did not really *think* I would "*pull* a heart attack" on the trip, as you said to Libby and Topper. It's the only thing you've ever said that I've minded, that and your Fez remark about visualizing me in a wheelchair or dead. I was so frightened by my heart anyway. I can find only two explanations for such statements—either you never believed for a minute there was anything wrong at all or else you were really worried and therefore mean. I am at my meanest when I feel the greatest tenderness. Seeing you dead in the novel* brought out the spitfire in me at the Belvedere in Fez. Perhaps harpy would be a more suitable word. . . . Sometimes I find nice explanations like the above for your attitude and sometimes I feel that you saw the whole thing, I mean the state of my health, as nothing but a threat to your trip, which mattered to you more than anything. I wonder—It must be that you never believed there *was* anything wrong—but then you must have or you wouldn't have gotten so gloomy and had visions of me in a wheelchair. I thought I was *finished*, I assure you. . . . Cheroux should have never worded his diagnosis the way he did. I told him I was "pulling a heart attack," and he told me that on the contrary there was something organically wrong with my heart—that is why I was frightened. Much more frightened than I told you. I would so much rather have been the neurotic faker than someone really ill and I was still not sure whether I was really well when you mentioned my pulling an attack to Libby. Surely the English in this letter has gone to pieces long ago but I just can't worry about it. You can understand with a little effort what I've written.

I shouldn't mention all this perhaps but I can never write anything else if there is something that must come out and I'm sure you would not like to be without any letters from me at all. I hope that I'm a horror to even *think* of these remarks and that I should not invest them with too much importance but I cannot forget them, or some aspects of your behavior. I think a word from you would put my mind at rest on this subject. You have a way too of saying things easily so that it wouldn't

*Paul's novel, *The Sheltering Sky*.

take you much time. I am not attached to you simply because I'm married to you, as you certainly must know. If I were I could pass over these things conveniently. Oliver thinks that I'm "hanging on to you." I hope you don't think that or that it isn't the actual truth even without your thinking it. I shall approach the awful financial question some other time. Maybe not in a letter—I get upset because you say you have enough money for one but not for two etc. It's probably true, unless we lived in a house—it's surely true when one is traveling. It is also true that I could have stayed behind in America indefinitely and have cost you nothing. But now that I am here I am damned if I'll ruin it by worrying about these things. I am extremely grateful to you for letting me stay and use the money. I don't believe I have it coming to me because I'm your wife. I just can't bear that idea and yet I'm not sure either that atavistically I don't probably consider myself—partly —entitled to this sojourn because I am your wife? In other words I feel both things at once. That you are completely free and someone who will help me when he can, out of affection, and yet also that you are a husband. I don't think about the husband part very much but I am trying to be *very* honest. I am not sure either that being confined a bit by the social structure is altogether bad for either one of us. We will see.

The view of the Arab town from my window is a source of endless pleasure to me. I cannot stop looking and it is perhaps the first time in my life that I have felt joyous as a result of a purely visual experience. The noise in the Villa [deFrance] is something I must fight constantly but I cannot leave the *lieu*. Certainly it's the only place in Tangier I want to be. If I left it I would go to the states I think. The [Old] Mountain, I know, would be bad in summer—unless one found a tree to work under far away. I am just beginning to try to work now and the morning noises are very bad. It makes me frantic because I love it here, but I'm sure that I shall find some quiet spot or else reverse and work at night. Or say from five to nine A.M. I am going with Boussif today about the deed. Cherifa, I'm afraid, is never going to work out. I think she's very much in love with Boussif. She's in a rage because she expected that once his wife left he would marry her, and instead he's taken some woman to cook for him whom he also sleeps with. He brought her to the grain market and introduced her to Cherifa. . . . They all sat in the hanootz . . . (I was not there) and joked together. Boussif, however, said that his mistress told Cherifa that only *she*, Cherifa, could come to see Boussif while she lived there, because she was not afraid that Boussif would ever marry a woman who wore no veil and sold grain in the market. I asked Boussif if Cherifa were not insulted, and he said, "No, why?" They are definitely confusing people. I think Cherifa is afraid of me. I saw her sneak behind a stall yesterday when I appeared so that I wouldn't see her. Nonetheless I am determined now to learn Arabic. It is good exercise for the mind in any case and there are more chances that I will get pleasure out of it than not. Even if my evenings with Cherifa and Quinza [with whom Cherifa lived] turn out to be a pipe dream. I am so utterly dependent now on Boussif that it is foolish to even think about it. The pronounciation . . . is impossible to master—ever. One can just vaguely approach it—enough to be understood because it takes years to develop certain throat muscles. I said my first words yesterday—after Cherifa sneaked behind the stall—and I suppose I said them in desperation. The older dyke was there, thank God, (she comes to the market irregularly), so I walked over to her and somehow spoke. Just a few words actually, but immediately some old men gathered around me and everyone nodded happily. They said to each other that I spoke Arabic. I am slow and stupid but determined. I shall never of course be as clever as you are.

. . . I must know about your contract. I hope and pray that it is all settled. Oy! I hate to think of it. Also keep me posted as to news about your novel. I shall let you know of any progress or total lack of it on my part (in writing) within a month. It is a little soon yet for me to know whether or not this was a wise decision. (Staying here—I mean.) Of course the less I worry about whether it was or not the wiser it will have been and I am more and more pleased that I've stayed so far. I am trying to get Helvetia to come over here, and still think she might be persuaded to come with you if you do come back. I am not very worried about all that, but very eager to see whether I can work or not seriously. If I can't I think I'd better just plain give up writing. Conditions here should be ideal. Except for that awful war cloud, I should say I was very happy. Naturally, I am moody but I'm savoring more separate minutes than I have in many years. I love this spot geographically and I'm always pleased to have lots of blue around me. Here there's the water and the sky and the mountains in the distance and all the blue in the Casbah; even in the white, there's lots of blue. . . .

Please—Please write me—Much Love—J.

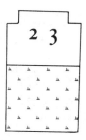

2 3

AND NOW FOLLOWS A SERIES OF LETTERS TO PAUL about Cherifa and two other Arab women Jane begins to pursue. There is clearly a compulsion here—both in her actions and in her writing about them to Paul. Though she knows what she is doing, she must go back and back to the women, follow after them, offer them things, and ask them to be with her. In one sense she must go again and again into a situation, waiting to be liberated from it. In another sense, she herself must do the liberation: she is the one who must press for changes, who must hurl herself into the Arab world, who must hold on with tenacity.

Desire—and something more than desire—drives her. What is being enacted here is the liberation from all that happened with Helvetia and from the dark images that were overtaking her. Jane is also, in trying to break into the world of the Arab women, going back to her earliest years, trying to break in there—to force a change there. The source of her own talent and power has become hidden from her and it is in the Arab world, through the Arab women, that she hopes to find it again.

Dearest Bup:

. . . I continue loving Tangier—maybe because I have the feeling of being on the edge of something that I will someday enter. This I don't think I could feel if I didn't know Cherifa and the "Mountain Dyke" and that yellow ugly one (!?) It is hard for me to separate the place from the romantic possibilities that I have found in it. I cannot separate the two for the first time in my life. Perhaps I shall be perpetually on the edge of this civilization of theirs. When I am in Cherifa's house I am still on the edge of it, and when I come out I can't believe I was really in it. Seeing her afterwards, neither more nor less friendly—like those tunes that go on and on or seem to—is enough to make me convinced that I was never there. . . .

Now that I've mastered a few words it's become an ordeal for me to go into the market. I am frightfully shy and embarrassed by the whole thing—my pronunciation, my inability to understand them most of the time. They each speak differently. All that is a terrible strain and I must steel myself before I plunge into it. I do not underestimate the importance of knowing Jay*—who is really sweet to me—because I would not be able to just struggle with Arabic all the time. Also there are days when they disappear entirely and it is nice to know someone here. I am terribly happy because the Mountain Dyke asked me to go for a walk with her either on the mountain or by the sea. I was amazed because I had just about given up getting anywhere with any Arab women ever. I was in a terrible state of despondency because Cherifa had just rushed past me leading a mule to the country. She wore a pink embroidered vest and a new red-and-white-striped blanket. She was on her way to visit her family in the country (Three feet out of Tangier). She was supposed to leave three or four days ago and be back yesterday which is precisely why I was hanging around there and instead she was leaving.

Yet after all the talk about the women, Jane goes back once again to how important Paul is to her:

I wonder too if I would bother with all this if you didn't exist. I don't know. Surely I would not have begun it—got the idea without you, I mean. It is the way I feel about my writing too. Would I bother if you didn't exist? It is awful not to know what one would do if one were utterly alone in the world. You would do just what you've always done and so would Helvetia but I don't exist independently. . . .

And Jane ends her letter with some "practical" advice to Paul about food:

Instead of complaining like a maniac why don't you try to solve some way of eating so that you will be stronger when you get to the next place you go. Even if it costs you a little more than the automat, and it needn't, you would be better nourished. Libby says that Willy May would cook lunch for you and she also said you should call up Scotty at any time and go out there to Treetops. You have no right in the world to complain so much when you've been away an entire year, and it's only the fact that you can be there and earn some money that will permit you to live over here. I don't mean this time but any time. You sound more spoiled than ever, ranting against civilization and the Americans and

---

*Jay Haselwood, who with Bill Chase owned the Parade Bar in Tangier.

their noise (after having lived among the Spanish—MY GOD!) and in spite of the fact that I see exactly what you mean and that New York must *really* look hideous after this part of the world, it frightens me to think that you have no part of yourself you can retire into, though that is what you advised *me* to do when the noise and confusion got me down in Fez. . . . I don't like to see you so helpless and so unable to take one minute of something you don't like, gracefully. Please do something about Treetops or your food. You can perfectly well and you will be stronger in the next primitive place you visit. If you think of it that way and not simply as spending money or any effort in New York, you might be able to do it. What do you mean by Peggy's ambivalence —about me? or you? I don't understand. Is she really worried about me? Does she think my coming back would keep you there longer? What's it all about? I have no plans. Do you think you'll come back here or do you prefer to go somewhere else. For God's sake go where *you* want to go and don't dare come to NORTH AFRICA just because of me if you'd rather go to West Africa. How can I say yet what I'll do? I refuse to. I am very happy—with moments of depression because I always have them, but very few. I am delighted I stayed. . . .

Much Love

J.

P.S. I take for granted that you don't mind my being over here—will come home if money matters make it advisable for me to live at H.'s [Helvetia's] or Libby's.

Dearest Bup—

I started a long letter to you the other day telling you all about my terrible afternoon with "Tetum" (the Mountain Dyke). We never did go to the mountain—in fact she never had any intention of going there. We went to a dry triangular square, right in Tangier surrounded by modern villas and near a bus stop. It was too long and sad and funny and involved to write about, so I gave up. All I can say is that I have never been so frustrated by anyone in my life as I am being right now—except by Iris Barry, and that lasted eleven years—so God knows I'll probably stick around here forever just for an occasional smile from Tetum or Cherifa. I wrote you how exciting it was to feel on the edge of something. Well—it's beginning to make me very nervous. I don't see any way of getting any further into it—since what I want is so particular (as usual)—and as for forgetting them altogether, it's too late for me. Africa right now is the grain market. . . . I am still learning Arabic, and I still love Tangier but I cannot tell how long it will take me to admit that I'm beaten. It is not any personal taste that I'm obliged to fight, but a whole social structure, so different from the one you know—for certainly there are two different worlds here (the men's world and the women's) as you've often said yourself. As for Cherifa, I am utterly dependent on Boussif as far as seeing her goes, and he's not around much lately.

I still have a dim hope that if I learned to speak Arabic she would be friendly *maybe*—and I could sit in the hanootz with her when I chose to. She *never* asks me in unless Boussif is there and then he does the asking. Either she is ashamed to be seen with me alone, or quite sensibly doesn't see the point—because I cannot really speak to her. I don't know. I am merely trying to know her better socially (having given up hope as far as anything else is concerned). I can't bear to be continually hurled *out* of the Arab world—the rest of Tangier really doesn't interest me *enough*—though I am very grateful to have Jay here and Bill. . . . I would be lonesome otherwise, though I wouldn't be if [the women] would let me sit with them in the market when I wanted to. Perhaps you have never been in this inferior position vis-à-vis the Arabs. I can understand how if one could get all one wanted here—and were admired—courted—and feted—that one would *never never* leave. Even so—without all that—and you've had it—I have never felt so strongly about a place in my life, and it is just maddening not to be able to get *more* of it. How I would love to have walked on the mountain with Tetum (I realize it's a ridiculous name). Naturally she couldn't and never will and I was a fool to believe her. She's a big liar, and each day she says just the *opposite* of what she said the day before. Do any of the men do that? I mean really the *exact* opposite? Whenever I suggest anything to her at all—even a glass of tea—she cuts her throat with an imaginary knife and says something about her family—at least she uses the imaginary knife one day, and on the next is prepared to do anything (verbally only). I am puzzled, vexed, and fascinated, but deep inside I have an awful feeling I shall never never find out any more than I know now. Still it is only August. We'll see—but I haven't much hope. I wept for two hours after my walk with Tetum. So you see, I am very different about these things than you are. I didn't realize how much I have hoped for, and how vividly I had pictured the walk on the mountain until I started to cry. After I had cried awhile I began to laugh. If *only* you had been here it wouldn't have mattered—because frustrating as it all was, it was certainly *ridiculous* and you would have loved hearing about it. I wish to hell I could have the same sort of adventures in Fez or that you liked Tangier. I cannot imagine a better time really than being in a place we both liked and each of us being free and having adventures. Even if mine were frustrating, they would be more amusing, naturally, if you were here. I wonder how I shall ever be able to leave the view of the Casbah. It means so much to me. Enfin—I do not have to leave yet.

She ends, almost as though in a postscript, by writing of "Camp Cataract," which has been accepted by *Harper's Bazaar:*

Pearl [Kazin] and Mary Lou [Aswell] have written me wonderful letters about Camp Cataract. I'm so happy about that. Now that it has been fixed up, I know that it's the best thing I've ever done—and always was latently. But I don't think it would ever have been if you hadn't helped. I wish though that you had liked it more. . . .

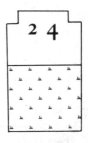

2 4

I

N FACT, THOUGH JANE WOULD NEVER HAVE BEEN able to finish "Camp Cataract" without Paul's help, he did not, when he first read the story, like it very much. "I said, 'Yes, I like it, but it's strange and mysterious. I don't understand it.'"

It is not an easy story to "understand" even after many readings. It has the same unsettled and unsettling tone Jane used before, the alternation of the compassionate and the sardonic, of the tragic and the comic, but this story comes to an ending in a new way.

"Camp Cataract" seems to be a story of two rather loony middle-aged sisters, Harriet and Sadie. The two women and their sister, Evelyn, and her husband, Bert, live together in an apartment in the city. Recently Harriet has had fits—real or pretended, it is not clear. She has decided it is time to escape from her family and has gone to Camp Cataract, a resort built around a waterfall. Her plan is to establish herself there, to "set roots there in imitation of the natural family roots of childhood," and from there to make her "sallies into the outside world unnoticed."

Sadie, left behind with Bert and Evelyn while Harriet pursues her plan, has only one focus in life, her passionate love for Harriet. She has never revealed her secret to anyone, not even Harriet. In her secrecy is her "absolution from guilt." Suddenly she decides, without telling anyone, that she will go to Camp Cataract to persuade Harriet to return home. Though the family agreement had been that Harriet was to be left alone without visitors, Sadie arrives at Camp Cataract one night without warning. Harriet is appalled to see her, and tries to keep her at a distance. She does agree to meet Sadie for lunch the next day.

In the strange atmosphere of the camp Sadie begins to recognize that:

all desire to . . . return to the apartment had miraculously shriveled away. . . . This did not in any way alter her intention of accomplishing her mission; on the contrary, it seemed to her all the more desperately important now that she was almost certain, in her innermost heart, that her trip was already a failure. Her attitude was not an astonishing one, since like many others she conceived of her life as separate from herself; the road was laid out always a little ahead of her by sacred hands, and she walked down it without a question. This road, which was her life, would go on existing after her death, even as her death existed now while she still lived.

Suddenly Harriet arrives, "wearing her black winter coat trimmed with red fur" and with her marceled hair "neatly arranged in spite of the strong wind." In desperation Sadie leads her along a narrow path to a small clearing. Here she notices a tree whose torn roots are "shockingly exposed" and surrounded by a dense swarm of flies. She tries to tell Harriet that she wants her to come home, but instead reveals the truer purpose in her coming: " 'Let's you and me go out in the world . . . just the two of us.' A second before covering her face to hide her shame Sadie glimpsed Harriet's eyes, impossibly close to her own, their pupils pointed with a hatred such as she had never seen before."

Harriet leaves, the sound of her footsteps not diminishing with distance. "Sadie knew then that this agony she was suffering was itself the dreaded voyage into the world. . . ."

Sadie returns to the souvenir booth near the waterfall, presided over by an Indian who is clearly not an Indian. Feeling shame at seeing the failure of his disguise, she takes him with her behind the waterfall to hide him.

But this is only the false ending of the story. The true ending comes with the revelation that the meeting with Harriet never took place, that Sadie, standing near the falls, imagined both the meeting and her agony. The true ending is her suicide in the falls, a final keeping of her secret, which is her only absolution from guilt.

Between the prison of childhood and the outer world—which others can get to but never Sadie—is an agony that must be traversed, the "dreaded voyage into the outer world." That Sadie's voyage has taken place in her own imagination makes it no less real or fateful. In its inception and pursuit it is very rational. It incorporates the way others view her, it allows for errors in her own judgment; it incorporates the greatest tenderness for and understanding of her sister.

If it is madness, it is madness only one step from reality, therefore so hard to distinguish even for the reader. Sadie had conceived of her life as separate from herself, the road laid out "by sacred hands," but in the agony of imagination the separation is ended. At the moment she and her life are merged, she falls into her own death.

Much in "Camp Cataract" is tied to Jane's own life. The death of Sadie occurs in a camp, just as in her own life at the age of thirteen she was in a camp when the news of her father's death locked her into a way of being that she never escaped. Further, the waterfall and surrounding landscape of Camp Cataract are taken from the landscape of Watkins Glen, near Holden Hall, where in 1942 Jane attempted suicide after a fight with Helvetia.

And there is one other tie, to a life that was not hers, but Paul's. Jane had never seen his adolescent story "The Waterfall." That story, rewritten as "Pages from Cold Point," had finally released Paul into fiction as he made his own journey to Morocco. Now the death of Sadie in the waterfall at Camp Cataract offered the possibility of the release into new and different fictions for Jane. At the same time, in Tangier, through Cherifa and Tetum, she believed she was being offered the possibility of entering a new and different world.

Dearest Buppie—

I am off to Cherifa's hanootz. Our relationship is completely static: just as I think that at least it is going backwards (on days when she sneaks behind a stall) I find that it is right back where it was the next day. Nothing seems to move. I have finally—by wasting hours and hours just hanging about and mentioning the L'Ayd Essgrir [a Moroccan feast day] about every five seconds—managed to get myself invited for tonight. So I shall go soon to the grain market from where we will leave for M'sallah—together. I don't know whether I shall walk behind her or in front of her or parallel to her on the other side of the street. I made my invitation secure by suggesting a chicken—I made wings of my arms and flapped them.

Later: It would take far too many pages to explain how the L'Ayd Essgrir came a day sooner than moon experts expected that it would, and how I therefore went to Cherifa's the very night after the carousing was over. Because in a normally arranged world the whole appointment would have evaporated. On the feast day they don't come to the market at all, and on that day we had fixed our rendezvous there which was in everyone's opinion the day *before* the feast. I was to give her the chicken then so that it could be plucked and put with the olives for the following day—it is all so ridiculous—because others said it wouldn't come for five days. Then I worried about the chicken rotting—well how can I even explain this?—but somehow in this peculiar world where nothing is arranged there is a sudden miraculous junctioning, a moment of unraveling when terribly complicated plans—at least what would be a complicated plan anywhere else—work out, somehow as if in a dream, where one has only to think of something for it actually to appear. . . .

Well in any case I wandered down there at 7:30 A.M. just thinking, well maybe she has thought of our appointment and come to wait for me at some point. She wasn't there but the old yellow-faced mountain dyke was and alas I had to eat quantities of perfectly terrible tortilla-like bread soaked in rancid oil, flies and honey!! Then I followed a parade thinking "Well it's such a funny country, maybe I'll meet her this way." The policeman said the parade was going to M'sallah but of course it stopped a little above the Villa de France, and the next policeman (also an Arab) said they were *not* going to M'sallah but turning 'round and going back down to the Mendoubia. By then I'd already waited around for it an hour, while it just remained in the square behind the Villa. I was planning to follow it to M'sallah. It was thus far the hottest day in the year and the Tangier flies in August are terrific—funnily enough I don't mind very much—because I am having fun. The men in the parade, some of those wonderful old men, were really beautiful in pink chiffon over white—some in pointed red Fez [hats] and others in the usual square ones. The horses were wildly spirited even in the heat and there were hundreds of women gathered all on one side of the road in beautiful djellabas. I went back to the market feeling that there was no chance of meeting her but somehow I went anyway. She *was* there—no glimmer of surprise or pleasure in her eye when she saw me—in spite of the arrangements having been completely bitched up because of the L'Ayd Essgrir coming a day sooner, probably because she'd forgotten there were any arrangements. I had to go through the whole thing again about the chicken . . . and she said I should meet her at 7:00 P.M. there in the grain market. At 10:30 we started for M'sallah with her cousin Mohammed (who is a good musulman), as our escort. He always steps in when she is on the outs with Boussif—which is now the case. I shall tell you the rest of the story some other time. I miss you and I wish that we could once be together in some place where we could both be having such foolish days and yet days that are so full of magic too. It would be fun to come back and talk about them.

I can see that I would *hate* to have someone waiting here at the hotel for me, with an eye on the watch and feeling very sad. How eleven women wandered in and out of Cherifa's house and all had tea out of the tiny pot in the morning is something I so wish I could make you see in *color*. But I'm afraid I never can. I was delighted to hear from my mother that you called her up and that you *are* doing the show [*Summer and Smoke*]. I would have felt so terribly responsible if you weren't because I half pushed you into it. I appreciate your calling her tremendously. I imagine you'd be bored to tears staying with her in Dayton, she mentioned a possibility. You needn't put yourself through *that*. If you see her for God's sake don't mention *anything* about my being nervous or thinking my heart was bad—*nothing* remotely connected with that or she'll be right over here. Of course you wouldn't. Perhaps I *am* the

"Dorothy Dix" of Tangier. But for the Arabs, the world's biggest "sucker"—I don't know. But I don't mean any "double entendre." I just realized with horror the pun, I have *no* occasion to make one. I am being extremely economical, so don't worry about that. I would always be completely scrupulous about your money because you earn it. I continue pleased that I've stayed on, but I'm in despair about Arabic. I can speak a little. But understanding them, when they speak to each other, is another cup of *tea*.

Much Love
Teresa

In a letter to Paul dated October 1 Jane writes pages about her financial difficulties: her check to the Villa de France has bounced. It has been more expensive to live in Tangier than she expected. She insists she is being very frugal, but she is not making ends meet. Once again she speaks of the possibility of returning to the United States, but it is the presence of Tetum, she says, that deters her.

I have done no work lately because I am in a very poor frame of mind, suffering from what you suffer from in New York—except that it does not seem to interfere with your work. I find I can think of nothing else—and yet I cannot *bring* myself to leave. I refuse to face the fact that there is no hope for me—other than a *slightly* increasing social life with Tetum and Cherifa. By offering a present at the right moment, I manage to keep my oar in. Perhaps if I were here long enough and I really learned the language thoroughly (I now speak I suppose about the way you did—or less—which is hardly conversation) I suppose I might get further, though I doubt it. Tetum has her friend Zodelia and Cherifa is mad about Boussif. That no longer bothers me since I am crazy mad about Tetum—a hopeless hopeless situation. I feel a kind of fever and I even wonder if she hasn't given me a gri-gri to eat—a gri-gri made for Europeans and which prompts them to give away everything they own. Fortunately I restrain myself. But it's the war situation that has been driving me frantic, mainly because I think at every second that I should go home before it's too late—if it isn't too late already. . . .

I suppose if I were dead sure I could never have Tetum I'd leave—but it is the nature of Cupid not to allow those who are stricken to see the truth so that I do see and I refuse to all at once. Still, socially I am making some headway—particularly in a new role that started last week—that is of a procurer for Cherifa. I procure Boussif for her when he disappears, which he does for days at a time. Tetum doesn't touch liquor by the way. If she did it would have made things easier. Still my being European makes everything almost impossible. Are you coming here or not? I know you'll go on to French Morocco, and I might go along for a while anyway, depending on where you were headed. It is all too mixed up for words. . . .

But though she has written that she has done no work lately because she is in a "poor frame of mind," she adds in a P.S., "I've started on my novel and as usual getting back into it is hell!"

She is "crazy mad" about Tetum, though it is hopeless. She knows that Cherifa wants nothing from her but money, that "there is no hope" for more than that. It is "all too mixed up for words." Yet it is to words Jane turned, as if they were the corollary of this obsessive pursuit of the women, as if through words—as well as through the women—she would regain some fundamental mystery lost in the years with Helvetia. And indeed *Out in the World*, the novel she was "getting back into," is about mystery regained, about the secrets hidden and revealed in the pursuit of love.

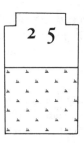

2 5

IN NEW YORK, WHERE HE WAS WRITING THE MUSIC FOR *Summer and Smoke*, Paul was looking for a publisher for his completed novel, *The Sheltering Sky*. Doubleday had turned it down, saying that it was not a novel. It was soon accepted by an English publisher and then by New Directions in America.

People have speculated that Jane was unable to go on writing because Paul had begun to write. It will be recalled that Jane had compared his career and hers, when she had written to him the year before from Treetops. But for Jane, beyond the question of rivalry—even of small envy—there was a much more fundamental problem. She had already been blocked trying to write her novel in the United States, as she had told Paul over and over again in her letters from Treetops. The more she worked, the less she was able to break through her own prohibitions. What she was grasping at now in Tangier was the hope that she would finally break through that block.

But if *The Sheltering Sky* did not cause her block—as many people have erroneously thought—it did present her with a prophecy about her own life to come, about her own "going out into the world." In his relationship to Jane as teacher and adviser, Paul had helped her and made it possible for her to finish *Two Serious Ladies* and "Camp Cataract." But now in his own work, writing of a couple who had a great resemblance to himself and Jane, he would inadvertently confirm her greatest fears.

The Sheltering Sky is the story of Port and Kit Moresby, a husband and wife, married for twelve years, who arrive in North Africa "fleeing the aftermath and memory of the war." Port is a traveler, not a tourist, "a man who moves slowly, over periods of years, from one part of the earth to another. . . . Before the war it had been Europe and the Near East, during the war the West Indies and South America. And [Kit] had accompanied him without reiterating her complaints too often or too bitterly."

With them on their trip is an astonishingly handsome young man, Tunner, whom Port has persuaded to accompany them. Tunner keeps trying to convince Kit to have an affair with him. Port and Kit have not had sexual relations for some time. Kit keeps hoping that Port will return to her. He, for his part, thinks of the possibility of returning, but tells himself that it is not yet the right time.

Shortly after the three arrive in Africa, Port goes for a walk alone in the medina. He thinks of Kit back at the hotel, seated at an open window, as the spectator, "while he is the protagonist of his existence." In the medina he sleeps with a beautiful young prostitute who tries to rob him.

The three of them set out for the desert, Port in a car with an incestuous mother and son he has met, and Kit and Tunner by train. On the train she is thrown into terror by the appearance and behavior of some of the natives, and for comfort she submits to Tunner's sexual advances.

When the three meet, Port and Kit continue into the desert by bus, without Tunner. In the desert Port becomes ill with typhoid. Kit cares for him, but feels repelled by him in his illness:

> "He's stopped being human," she said to herself. Illness reduces man to his basic state: a cloaca in which the chemical processes continue. The meaningless hegemony of the involuntary. It was the ultimate taboo stretched out there beside her, helpless and horrifying beyond reason. . . .

She leaves him and spends the night with Tunner, who has reappeared. In the morning she finds Port dead.

The last third of the book shows Kit going into the desert alone, running from Tunner and from the memory of Port. She goes deeper and deeper into a savage landscape where she is subjected to a series of rapes and brutalities. She even comes to love her degradation in a world that is sex and death and violence and nothing else. She finally falls into madness.

For the character of Kit, Paul drew upon many details of Jane's personality. Kit is described as terrified of trains, of tunnels, and of trestles. She is fearful of omens of any sort. In her there is a continuous struggle, "a war between reason and atavism." In Kit's feelings for Port, Paul echoed certain of Jane's feelings for him:

> In normal situations she felt that Port was inclined to lack understand-ing, but in extremities no one else could take his place; in really bad moments she relied on him utterly, not because he was an infallible guide under such circumstances, but because a section of her conscious-ness annexed him as a buttress, so that in part she identified herself with him.

Yet Kit also realizes that "in spite of their so often having the same reactions, the same feelings, they never would reach the same conclusions, because their respective aims in life were almost diametrically opposite."

But if Paul began with Jane as the model for Kit, he departed radically from that model, he felt, as the work progressed. Relying upon his unconscious, he did not permit himself to know ahead of time what the day-by-day course of the novel would be as he wrote it.

> The structure and character of the landscape would be supplied by imagination (that is, by memory). I would reinforce each such scene with details reported from life during the day of writing, regardless of whether the resulting juxtaposition was apposite or not. I never knew what I was going to write on the following day because I had not yet lived through that day.

In the novel a blind woman who is dancing conveys to her audience that "a dance is being done. I do not dance because I am not here. But it is my dance." It is in this way that Paul thought of himself as writing the novel.

But Jane read it differently. She had written to Paul that she took him to be Port: "Seeing you dead in the novel. . . ." And from what she had told Paul, we know she also took Kit to be herself.

"She thought that Kit was Jane Bowles. Well in a way she was of course—but she wasn't. You know how those things are; you use a living model to build your mythical character. I remember that she said to me that the end made her very sad, because she didn't know what I meant. She seemed so sad when she said it that I didn't want to go into it. I said, 'Oh, come on.' I was afraid that what she meant was that the end was a kind of conscious form of wishful thinking, which it was not. But I didn't want to hear what she meant. I don't know what she was going to say. I never found out why it made her sad. Did she think I felt she was going to have that kind of an end to her life? Well I didn't, naturally. By the time she got down to the desert, the character was no longer Jane; she was Kit."

In later years Jane would come back again and again to the sentences from Kafka—"From a certain point onward there is no longer any turning back. That is the point that must be reached"—which Paul had used as the epigraph for the third section. She would say that was the way he saw her life. He would deny to her that he had meant any such thing. "If you didn't believe it," she would say to him, "why did you use it?"

To Paul *The Sheltering Sky* was fiction, not life. To Jane it was prophecy. Years before in New York she had called him "Gloompot" when he began his discussions of the coming doom of modern civilization. Now that his "gloom" had turned into fiction, she could no longer make a joke of it.

Writing out of the deepest levels of his unconscious, Paul touched upon the very questions that preoccupied her most: sin and the relation of sexuality to the spirit. He himself had very little choice as to whether or not he should write. He would either write and make his sense of doom a palpable thing—and a fiction—or he would, he feared, go mad. The work, in effect, was his salvation.

But fiction for Jane—her fiction and his as well—carried some ultimate truth inseparable from her own destiny. And the destiny he portrayed in the novel was a terrible one. The two main characters betray each other and themselves and are punished, he by death, she by madness. Atavism triumphs over reason, but there is a final punishment for sin.

Two Serious Ladies had a profound influence on Paul when he read it. As he himself says, it was the generating force that brought him back to fiction. And there is, in fact, in *The Sheltering Sky* a curious resemblance to *Two Serious Ladies*. From the moment when Port becomes ill and insists on going farther into the desert with Kit, it becomes clear that the two are opposite sides of the same self. Port will suffer; Kit will run from the suffering. Yet like the two serious ladies, they will both be "piling sin upon sin." And like Miss Goering, who sought salvation through men she feared, Kit will find her answer in the fearful power of the men in the desert.

Two Serious Ladies and *The Sheltering Sky* are novels that deal with the same basic themes: choice, sin, sex, and the spirit. But, as Paul had Kit think about herself and Port, "in spite of their so often having the same reactions, the same feelings, they never would reach the same conclusions, because their respective aims in life were almost diametrically opposite."

In Paul's novel there is none of the indeterminate sin of *Two Serious Ladies*. Kit's sin is specific: she has gone to bed with Tunner, betraying Port. She has deserted Port in his final illness. Port's own sin is a failure of love; there is a "glacial deadness" at the core of his being. "Just as [Kit] was unable to shake off the dread that was always with her, he was unable to break out of the cage into which he had shut himself, the cage he had built long ago to save himself from love."

In *The Sheltering Sky* Paul wrote of a nihilistic universe, of what appears when the sky is no longer sheltering. It is a universe with no God or meaning, in which people act with bestiality. He condemns his characters. Though he is in his characters, he runs them down and offers them no final escape. His drive is toward ending. The suspense in his work is connected with this insistent drive to final destruction. The suspense for the reader arises out of the hope that things will not be so. But that hope is always shown to be illusory. The worst is what is.

Jane, on the other hand, for all her fears of fate, never finally condemns her characters. Even for Sadie in "Camp Cataract," the only character Jane created to die, death is a reaching out and an absolution. As for Miss Goering and Mrs. Copperfield, in their ending they go on as they were. The one punishment for sin that Miss Goering suffers is her momentary recognition of it. But even that could be dismissed by her as "of considerable interest but of no great importance."

That Paul wrote using the process of going into the unconscious, that he did not feel as if *he* judged, does not alter the fact that his work reads as a judgment. Jane's work was constructed laboriously, consciously, as much as possible. It creates surprise but not suspense. It is a delaying action against final condemnation.

In the character of Kit, Paul used Jane's vulnerability to omens and signs even though in conversation she would insist that she was very rational and logical. But finally, she would say to Paul, reality was to her what she felt in her heart. And in her heart she came to take *The Sheltering Sky* as an omen.

Still, being Jane, even while she accepted it as prophecy, she willed herself to doubt it. "Is the Fortune Teller infallible?" she had asked. Fearing what he had said, she still came to Tangier. And once there, seeing the possibility of a new life, she kept trying to make her way into the Arab world through Cherifa and Tetum, even as she tried to break through the writing block, the cage she herself had built.

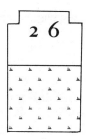

2 6

WHEN PAUL RETURNED TO AFRICA EARLY IN DECEMBER 1948, Tennessee Williams and Frank Merlo were with him. When they anchored at Gibraltar, Jane came aboard.

Tennessee remembers her as a lovely girl,

small, piquant, darting between humor, anxiety, love and distraction. I had met nervous girls before, but her quicksilver animation, her continual cries, to me and herself: "Shall we do this or shall we do that? What shall we do?" showed such an extreme kind of excited indecision that I was skeptical of its reality—intrigued, certainly, but still somewhat incredulous.

Used to it as Paul must have been, he stood there, simply smiling in a bemused sort of way. It seems to me that Frank Merlo took command of the chaotic situation, much to the relief of us all. (Of course, Paul may already have known how things would go, but was simply waiting for the accustomed flurry to subside.)

Frank saw that the car was put onto the European shore; we settled down for the night at the Rock Hotel in Gib.

"Is she for real?" I asked Frank, when we had retired.

"Are *you* for real?" he countered, a little grimly, perhaps.

I wasn't sure about that, but I soon came to see the reality of Jane. All the indecision was a true and dreadful concern that she might suggest a wrong move in a world that she had correctly surmised to be so inclined to turn wrongly.

There were many subsequent meetings, in Tangier, Paris and New York. What most impressed me about Jane, the person, was her concern for others, for their comfort and their entertainment. The important little things, especially such as providing meals, acquainting you with the right doctors in foreign places, conducting you through markets, introducing you to the interesting people, and somehow, in the midst of confusion, finding the precisely right words to reassure you in your own confusion—these were her particular gifts—ways to get agreeably through day and evening.

The Bowleses and Tennessee and Frank drove to Málaga, intending to go on to Granada, but Tennessee insisted on going directly to Tangier because of the bad weather. To Donald Windham, Tennessee wrote about his stay at Tangier: "We arrived at just the beginning of the rainy season and for reasons of economy (the Bowles') we put up at a perfectly ghastly hotel called the El Far-Har, (rhymes with horror) at the top of a very steep hill over the ocean. Spectacular view: every possible discomfort. . . ."

After two weeks in Tangier, Tennessee and Frank Merlo drove to Fez with Paul. There they had another rainy week and Tennessee and Frank left for Casablanca, en route to Marseilles. Still, said Tennessee, "Morocco is wildly beautiful: I want to go back in the Spring when it has stopped raining. One night in the Casbah of Tangier was really worth all the difficulties, when we were climbing up a steep, narrow street of mysterious white walls and arches and heard someone chanting the Koran.—I believe Paul was quite cross with us for leaving. . . ."

While Paul stayed on in Fez, Jane was in Tangier with Cory, who had arrived for a visit. In February Jane went with her to Marseilles and saw her off by train to Paris. Then she returned to Africa and she and Paul set off into the Sahara together. From Taghit in Algeria she wrote to Katharine Hamill and Natasha von Hoershelman:

Dearest Katharine and Natasha—:
    No one could have been happier than I was to receive your Xmas wire. It was wonderful to know you thought of me (I sound like a real cripple or "Public charge") certainly you were the only ones who did. Then I started many grateful letters and Cory was with me and it was all very complicated. Now I am in the Sahara desert. I got to Marseille in February, stayed four days and came back to Africa, scared to go to Paris because there is a very long tunnel outside of Marseilles. . . . Of course I'm not neurotic anymore, which is a good thing, but I do find it very hard to go *North*. This place we're in is an oasis, a very small one—we had to walk to it from a bus with donkey carriers for our luggage. The dunes are extremely high and I shall not attempt to climb them again—well maybe I will because it is so beautiful up there. Nothing but mountains and valleys of sand as far as the eye can see, and to know it stretches for literally hundreds of miles is a very strange feeling. The sand here is a wonderful beige color, it turns bright pink in the evening light. I am impressed, it is not like anything else anywhere

in the world, not the sand or the oasis. Anyway the rest is all rocks and rather terrifying. . . . We are going on to Beni Abbes (Paul and I) next Friday. The hotel here is kept up for the army since no tourists ever come—but occasionally army people stop by for lunch. There are just Paul and me, the Arab who runs the hotel, and the three soldiers in the fort, and the natives—but *they* are just a little too native and frightfully underfed. It is very very quiet, no electricity, no cars, just *Paul* and *me*. And many empty rooms. The great sand desert begins just outside my window—I might almost stroke the first dune with my hand. Friday we are going further "in" (oy!). But I am looking forward to the next place, though I doubt that it will be as beautiful as this oasis, nothing could be. The little inn there is run by a woman, a *Mademoiselle* Jury—Paul says she's a yenti old maid. Hoorah! I think there are 8 or nine "whites" there, a real mob. Paul thinks there will be too much traffic because the truck goes through twice a week. There is no road leading *here* at all, so he's gotten used to it. We plan to be in the desert about a month and then back to Fez, then to Tangier, where I can resume my "silly" life with the grain market group—Tetum, Zodelia, Cherifa and Quinza. You remember them. I have gotten nowhere but Cherifa calls me her "sister" and I eat with them several times a week. I bring the food and the two heavy quarts of thick sweet wine. I had Tetum X-rayed. She was determined to go to the doctor's because I'd taken Cherifa 10 times about her foot. I spent all morning in the Dr's waiting room among women wrapped in sheets. But I love to be with her—anywhere. She was happy because she had caught up with Cherifa: she felt the X-ray equalled the foot treatments Cherifa got out of me. It is all really about prestige—their life I mean—but I cannot tell them even that I know they are making an ass of me. I am always scared that they might find out I know. I'll tell you about it when I see you. Forgive this disjointed letter, please, I have had a fly after me—and then in the middle of it the Arab who runs the hotel asked me to write a letter for him (naturally he can't write) to a man living in a place called "Oil Pump number five." It's a famous hell-hole south of here. I hope we don't go there to live. . . .

Much Love—as ever—

Jane

P.S. Tennessee Williams got me a thousand dollars from the Author's League—100 a month for 10 months. He liked my play—I love him. . . .

Returning to Tangier, Paul and Jane went to stay at the Farhar again. They decided to add on to the little house in the medina, as Jane wrote to Katharine:

When the rooms are built I shall have Cherifa and Quinza over to sleep. Tetum won't come, I'm sure, but this time when the rooms are ready I shall offer her a present if she lives with me for a day, two days, or a week or more. One month—she gets a whole sheep. One night is going to be a toothbrush or a key ring. Two nights—socks. One week —pajamas. The addition to the house (it is unlivable now) will cost 350 dollars roughly. . . .

I had planned to come back sooner thinking that I would go to Paris and then on to New York, but it hasn't worked out that way —particularly since we're adding on to the house. I would like that done before I leave and then I will know it's there. I expect I'll come back here in summer—very often—In any case it is not a great investment! and it can be sold at any time so I do not feel tied to it either. I am trying to get on with my novel, and if it isn't reasonably far advanced by fall, I shall chuck writing forever—but I am working now—and did in the desert. But then I stopped again for 3 weeks in Fez and 1 week here, so I've decided no moving about for the moment.

That summer in Tangier Jane found herself more and more caught up in the social life of the expatriates. She wrote to Katharine:

Katharine dear—(and N. *if* she's there—but I doubt it)

What a Beast I am not writing. I've become very British by the way these last weeks. Our English summer crowd is here (2 people)—one of them Cecil Beaton—and the locals are all going to a masquerade very soon given by C. dressed as *events*. Isn't it awful? For me I mean. Because as usual I don't remember what's happened. We have a fifty-year range—I can think only of Lindbergh's return—but need New York City for my costume. . . . I have no plans—more mixed up than ever—writing off and on, mostly off when it's hot. Also have my drinking stomach back—God knows why—probably because I stayed off it for so long. Everything has changed since Truman Capote arrived. I wrote you about his staying here. Then all we needed was "Cecil" on the opposite hill for Africa to pick up its skirts and run. So I feel that though I have not gone to Paris, it has come here, which is perhaps a good thing. Happy to find myself as uncomfortable, shy and insecure as ever—I mean it almost makes me feel young again to know that I must still have 4 drinks to feel at ease. I am as indestructible as an armored truck—in that sense—and it is a kind of relief to know that it will never change.

Of that summer, Paul wrote:

There were some very good parties that summer, including an unforgettable one given by the Comtesse de la Faille, in which she cleared out the ballroom, leaving only the Aubussons on the walls, and then covered the floor with straw for the snake charmers and acrobats. The Moroccans built a fire in the middle of the room and made themselves completely at home. Another party held on the beach at the Cave of Hercules, with one grotto previously decorated by Cecil, served only champagne and hashish. Truman, who claimed to be afraid of scorpions, had to be carried by a group of Moroccans down the face of the cliff in order to get there. An Andaluz orchestra was partially visible, surrounded by rocks and lanterns; the guests lay in the moonlight among cushions on the sand, went swimming and sat around a big fire. . . . *

Though she was spending much of her time with the expatriate international group, Jane continued her "silly life" at the grain market. As she told Katharine and Natasha, she knew Cherifa and Tetum were "making an ass" of her. She recognized that the power she had in the situation came not from her person, but from her money. (What little she had was far more than what they had.) In this way she had become like Mrs. Copperfield. And yet, though they made an ass of her, they were also the key to some revelation, some secret necessary to her.

In the desert, in Taghit, alone with Paul, Jane had completed one more story, "A Stick of Green Candy." It was like a coda to all that she had done before, a story of the loss of belief in the imagination.

Mary, a girl of twelve or thirteen, plays every day in a clay pit outside of town, in defiance of her father's orders. There she imagines herself the head of a regiment. Her own belief in the truth of what she says to her men is crucial. "She never told them anything until she really believed what she was going to say."

When her father finds that she has disobeyed him by going to the clay pit again, he threatens her. Nonetheless she returns to the pit the next day fearful of only one thing, "that by looking into her eyes the soldiers might divine her father's existence. To each one of them she was like himself—a man without a family."

Her imaginative life in the clay pit is suddenly interrupted by the appearance of a strange boy, younger than herself. Angry at his invasion of her world, she follows him to the house where he is staying and pushes her way in the door. But once in the house, she is no longer angry at him. " 'If he

---

*Looking back in 1971 Paul could add: "The summer proved the apogee of postwar prosperity in the International Zone. Immediately afterward the cracks in the façade began to appear, and they constantly grew wider, until the entire edifice collapsed in the riots of 1952."

would tell me now where he comes from,' she said to herself, 'then I could go away before anybody else came.' "

But the boy's mother appears.

> . . . Mary shrank from her. She had never before been addressed so intimately by a grown person. She closed her eyes, seeking the dark gulf that had always separated her from the adult world.

During her conversation with his mother, the boy never speaks. Yet the next day, Mary goes to stand on the road above the pit, waiting for him to appear. It was unbelievable . . . "that he should be ignorant of her love for him. Surely he knew that all the while his mother was talking, she in secret had been claiming him for her own. He would come out soon to join her on the steps, and they would go away together."

The boy does not come. Mary goes down into the clay pit alone to summon her men, but she has lost her sense of immersion in her own imaginative world. She tries to get back to it by "seeking the dark gulf" again, the gulf that separates her from the adult world. She shouts orders to her men, but she has lost the capacity to believe in her own play. Her father has won. Though he could not stop her play by himself, it is ended by her own vulnerability to love. The clay pit that protected her and yet sullied her with its dirt is no longer her own territory.

In "A Stick of Green Candy" Jane was telling of the breakdown of her belief in her imaginative world. In the desert, as she wrote the story, her sense of its truth held her, and she could complete it. Like Mary, she had to believe in the truth of what she said in the clay pit, that place like a grave to play in. But when the story was done, when she returned to Tangier, she again began to disbelieve her own words, to mistrust her own imagination, as she had in New York and in Connecticut. She kept trying to get on with the novel: "if if isn't reasonably far advanced by fall—I shall chuck writing forever. . . ." she wrote to Katharine. She never would chuck writing forever, though she would never be able to finish the novel. "A Stick of Green Candy" was to be the last work of fiction she was ever to complete.

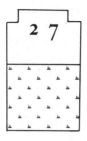

27

EARLY IN THE FALL OF 1949 PAUL AND JANE MOVED
from the Hotel Farhar into a villa rented by David Herbert. In his
autobiography, *Second Son*, David, who was to become Jane's closest friend in
Tangier, wrote of the Bowleses.

> They had been married quite some time but their enjoyment of each
> other's company was undiminished. It was touching and extraordinary
> to hear them talking and laughing in the next room as though they had
> just met and were being at their most scintillating in order to charm each
> other.

David described Jane as "an unpredictable marmoset, . . . small and
dark with enormous brown eyes and a shock of dark curly hair; her nose is
tiptilted and her mouth slightly negroid"; he saw Paul as "tallish, fair with
pale china-blue eyes and so delicately made that a breath of wind could blow
him away. He has the beauty of a fallow deer."

An exuberant, energetic man with a great zest for pleasure, David gave
innumerable dinner parties where Jane was the center of attention. He was
devoted to her, reveled in her wit, and wanted to show her off. He loved to
talk about people, as did Jane. He was intelligent, but made no pretensions to
being an intellectual. He came from a wealthy and titled English family—he
was the second son of the Earl of Pembroke—and was a devout Anglican. At
his home Jane met many wealthy people, whom she enjoyed in part for the
power their wealth gave them. (As Mrs. Copperfield in *Two Serious Ladies* had
said of the rich, "They want to be liked for their money too, and not only for
themselves.")

Something in David's dramatic quality complemented Jane: they
"played" to each other. "Go to your room, Janie," David would rebuke her
when she was being "completely impossible." He and Jane made a pact that
"if anything happened to Paul—and we survived him—we would marry."

She was sympathetic when he told her of his grief at the end of a long-term love affair. She in turn confided details of her pursuit of Cherifa.

Though in letters and in conversations Jane spoke of her infatuation with Cherifa as of crucial importance to her life, she was, in fact, already preparing to leave Tangier. *The Sheltering Sky* was doing so well on publication in England that Paul's publisher there, John Lehmann, had asked him to come to London; afterward he intended to go to the Far East to travel and to work. Jane had arranged to meet Cory in London and then to go with her to Paris, where they would spend the winter.

Late that fall Jane and Paul and David Herbert boarded the liner *Koutoubia* for Marseilles. From Marseilles they drove through the Rhone Valley, stopping at famous restaurants along the way. While Jane and David ate with pleasure, Paul suffered from "colonial liver."

> I was not surprised by the three days I spent in bed at Lyons with an attack. Jane and David would go out and try one great Lyonnais restaurant after another, and then return to the hotel to sit in my room going over each bout of gorging. The concept of eating was in itself repulsive; the lingering descriptions and discussion of the food's texture constituted a kind of torture.

They passed through Paris, where Paul introduced Jane to Alice Toklas. On meeting Jane, Toklas wrote to friends:

> Do you know her (Jane Bowles') novel called *Two Serious Ladies* which Knopf published at the beginning of the war—obviously not a propitious moment to present gaiety and insouciance. It is *the* most delightful novel (to) come my way in years and years. Unfortunately she doesn't produce much—since then only a play and short stories. . . . Mrs. Bowles is spending the winter here which will be nice—for she's—not surprisingly—like her novel. . . .

In England, Paul and Jane stayed at Wilton, the country estate belonging to David's family. While Jane remained there, Paul made frequent trips to London, where he was introduced by Lehmann to the British literary world. It was an ironic realization of one of the games Paul and Jane had played in the early forties. In that game Paul was Cecil, a famous English writer, and Jane was his secretary. Cecil was always about to go out to a literary reception. The secretary kept pleading that she would like to go along. "You wouldn't like it," Cecil would say in a high, thin, squeaky voice. "But I think I would," the secretary would say eagerly. "I would very much enjoy meeting so-and-so." "You wouldn't like him. He's very cold," Cecil would respond. "Couldn't I help in the cloakroom?" Jane, the secretary, would say, still trying, but never getting to go.

But Jane soon had other things to occupy her. Cory arrived, and shortly thereafter she and Jane went to Paris for the winter, taking rooms at the Hôtel de l'Université. Almost from the beginning their stay together was a disaster. As Jane wrote Paul, who by then was traveling in Ceylon and India, working on his new novel:

> I have never been through anything quite like this winter. How I ever got myself into it, I don't know. But by the time I reached England it seemed too late to wire her and too cruel. I was not *sure* either how really over it was. Perhaps even recently I thought something might be saved.

But Cory, realizing that they were "all washed up," became gloomy and began to drink. She made it clear to Jane that she couldn't endure Jane's friends, and none of Jane's friends, in turn, could understand her affair with Cory. Rosamonde Reille, who had known Paul and Jane in Acapulco, was now living in Paris as the European feature editor of *Vogue* and was married to Georges Bernier. She remembers that Jane "showed up in Paris with Cory, who ran a tea room. Cory wore steel-rim spectacles and sensible shoes. She had iron-gray hair and she wore a nice blouse with a bar pin. I think the tea room she ran was very successful."

Rosamonde was amused and puzzled by Jane's odd infatuation with Cory. "I could only think it was Jane's sense of the ludicrous. In that sophisticated milieu, Cory couldn't have been more out of place and more bored. I don't know if I said anything to Janie; perhaps I did. I think she said to me, 'She's a volcano in bed.'

"Once Cory came with Jane to dinner. I tried to make conversation with her. 'How are you enjoying your stay?' I asked her.

" 'Not much,' she said.

" 'Why not?'

" 'All those friends of Jane's do nothing but talk, talk, talk, and they don't talk about anything.'

" 'What do your friends talk about?' I asked her.

" 'Business and sports,' she said."

To Paul Jane wrote:

> I have miraculously avoided a real bust-up drama, and have kept the most severe check on myself. I think now that things are well adjusted, and I am clear in my mind about how to conduct the rest of the winter until she leaves: in solitary confinement as much as possible.

When Cory first arrived, the thought of being alone with her for what seemed like a lifetime—the whole winter—had thrown Jane into a panic. But now she decided that for the two of them to be alone was the only solution:

> . . . (the strain of wondering whether [Cory] was enjoying an evening or not gave me a headache) . . . getting into the habit of eating dinner in silence (unless I talk) . . . is, after all, not so bad. I don't know what I was afraid of. Despair, I guess, as usual. Now there seems to be not enough time left. I have grown used to her again, and fond of her, and we have moved into Frank Price's flat, which will be much better. I had taken my own room on the other floor because our room was not suitable for working; and because of a scene she made about my "walking out" on her, I felt guilty every time I was in my room and was not strictly working. She later explained how she felt, and tried to reassure me that she no longer felt that way about it, yet I could never be in my own room with any serenity. . . .

But being alone turned out to be a very limited solution. Jane wrote to Paul a few weeks later:

> I had counted somehow on routine and solitude hiding the absence of love or even inviting it again. I was quite wrong, but at least I think Cory can stand it better this way and there is less drinking. My close friends know the reason for my seclusion and others think I've become a hermit, I imagine. . . . I am not complaining really about my life, at the moment. I would not mind anything if only Cory did not look so sad. I am doing everything I can, but nothing will make up for one terrible lack. She is often pleasant but most of the time gloomy and if even slightly drunk, vindictive. If her partner were here it would be better to split it up quickly, but I would not dare to let her go off somewhere to wait for M. alone. I do not think she can take it, and is happier here with me despite the difficult and dismal situation. I put all the blame on myself naturally, and feel now that perhaps I should never start anything with the innocent again. I am not hard enough to take it, myself, not to speak of them. . . .

There was, too, the effect all of this was having on Jane's being able to write. Cory, she told Paul, was both a hindrance and a help. "A help because she gives a center to my day, and a hindrance because if I read, and wrote the letters I should write, and simply wandered around chewing my cud as one does when one's writing, I would have very little time left for her." Still, Jane recognized that part of her difficulty with her writing had nothing to do with Cory:

> My work went well last week. I had got into a routine, but this week it's all shot to hell again . . . not because of my life really, but because I have come to the male character again. I must change all that I wrote about him in Tangier. Not all, but it must become real to me, otherwise I can't write it. I have decided not to become hysterical, however. If I cannot write my book, then I shall give up writing, that's all. Then either suicide or another life. It is rather frightening to think of. I don't believe I would commit suicide, though intellectually it seems the only way out. I would never be brave enough, and it would upset everybody. But where would I go? I daresay the most courageous thing to do would be nothing. I mean, to continue as I am, but not as a writer. As the wife of a writer? I don't think you'd like that, and could I do it well? I think I'd nag and be mean, and then I would be ashamed. Oh, what a black future it could be! That is why I have to use some control, otherwise I get in a panic. I am trying to write.

She had now to think of herself as "the wife of a writer." But to Paul she writes of her pleasure in his success, the success that she has never had:

> The book, though second from the bottom, made the best-seller list, which I think is wonderful. Your literary success is a fact now, and it is not only distinguished but widespread. I think to have [Cyril] Connolly and Toklas and a host of other people, plus a public, is really remarkable and wonderful. . . .
>
> Much much love, Bupple dear. I miss you very much. Write me your plans and don't stay away forever. I hope you'll return sometime this spring. Will you?

A few days later she writes him:

> Yesterday the whole thing [the novel] dried up on me again and I had the terrible pain in my head that I get—not a pain exactly but a feeling of tightness in my scalp, as if it were drawn tight over an empty drum. (My head is the drum.) It happens too often really and I'm afraid that it is the physical expression of a sterility. . . . I do feel very strongly that I should give up writing if I can't get further into it than I have. I cannot keep losing it the way I do, much longer. This is hard to explain to you who work so differently. I may really have said all I have to say. Last night I felt so bad about it, I drank almost an entire bottle of gin. I had

gone back to my desk after very nearly throwing everything into the fire (mentally). It was an effort and after that I just started drinking. I felt better as a result and by eleven o'clock I was very cheery indeed. Nora [not her real name] who lives in the hotel, came by, and we all three of us went out to the Monocle. It has gone down terribly and the tough proprietress I was so crazy about whose name was Bobby and because of whom I hung around Paris for weeks [in 1938], (you remember), after you had left for the South, has gone. "Elle n'est plus dans le métier," the bartender told me; he had known her too. "Elle s'est mariée et elle est propriétaire de deux énormes châteaux." Why would she have *two* castles? She was the most masculine woman I had ever seen. I would have been depressed if I hadn't been drunk.

At the Monocle Jane meets an Algerian belly dancer:

I was wildly excited and spent the rest of the evening talking Arabic with her—though God knows how, because there is practically nothing left of mine. . . . I wanted so badly to rush somewhere and tell you about it. It was certainly not what I had expected of the Monocle. And to think twelve years ago I sat in that place night after night drunk as a lord and partly because I didn't want to go to Africa—in the beginning entirely for that reason—until I met Bobby "aux deux châteaux."

Jane ends by saying that she has had news from Tangier that Cherifa is planning to move from her old stall to the new market.

So that will be the real end of everything. I just can't bear to think of her empty stall. I am awfully upset and am writing Kouche Said about it. I shall enclose a letter to her which I'll ask him to translate, saying that I dreamed a terrible misfortune would befall her should she change her stall. Do you think it would be a sin to try and play Deus Ex Machina in this? You think I am joking probably, but I am not. I am terribly upset. If one by one all the things I loved about Tangier disappear even in a few months, how can I even look forward to going back. The terrible thing is that I love it still just as I did when I left. I am no less hysterical. What is it do you suppose? The fact that I do not rush back at once is no indication of how I feel.

A life alone with Cory—at least not attending dinners and parties —could be continued only so long. There came a night when Jane decided to take Cory and Nora to a party at Peggy Guggenheim's. "It was a disaster," she wrote Paul.

Peggy took me over to Marie-Laure de Noailles and introduced me. I kept glancing over my shoulder at Cory to see if she was all right (engaged in conversation) and she was. Madame de Noailles dragged me into a different room so that we could talk quietly. I was uneasy, but Cory was still in a group with Nora and some man when I left her. We talked mostly about Cecil and Truman, and then since we had no cigarettes, I went back into the big room to get them. I was horrified to see Cory standing quite alone, framed in the doorway. I rushed up to her: she was in a rage with Nora and me . . . a little drunk, too. I tried to calm her down, but alas, by the time I had, Marie-Laure had wandered back into the big room. I started running about like a maniac, looking for cigarettes. It was sort of like a Kafka. . . . It was all ridiculous, and I'm glad I haven't been out with Cory more. It's hopeless, and I told Peggy not to invite me. I don't care really. . . .

She may not have cared about losing out on the social life in Paris, but she was dismayed, she admitted to Paul in a postscript, that Alice Toklas had given her up: "A blow I scarcely need at the moment."

From the first time that she had met Alice Toklas Jane had felt that she was being judged by her and found wanting. She felt stiff and afraid with her, unable to talk in her presence:

This is not a result of my shyness alone, but of a definite absence of intellect, or should I say of ideas that can be expressed, ideas that I am in any way certain about. I have no opinions really. This is not just neurotic. It is very true. And Alice Toklas gives one plenty of opportunity to express an idea or an opinion. She is sitting there waiting to hear one. She admires your book tremendously . . . she talked of little else the last time I saw her. . . .

In fact, it was just about this time that Alice Toklas was writing to Paul of her great admiration for *The Sheltering Sky*: "No novel since *The Great Gatsby* has impressed me as having the force—precision—delicacy that the best of Fitzgerald has until yours. Limiting yourself as you have in the number of characters has not prevented you from completely portraying an epoch." And about Jane she added:

I haven't seen as much of Jane as I would have liked. She is very delightful—she says she is working regularly—but is she. Has she any intimate acquaintance with either work or regularity—can and should one introduce them to each other. . . .

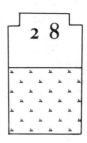

2 8

ALICE TOKLAS, LIKE MANY OTHERS, MAY HAVE WON-
dered if Jane was working, but there is the testimony of her notebooks to the
time and effort she spent in Paris writing, crossing out, writing, crossing out,
and beginning again. She was working on *Out in the World* and at the same
time rewriting the last act of *In the Summer House*. Oliver Smith had an option
on the play and planned to produce it on Broadway. The hope of an actual
production fortified Jane as she worked on the play and made it possible for
her to give it an ending. But the novel would only go so far and no further:
seemingly, it couldn't be finished.

There remain seven notebooks of that novel, a series of fragments
difficult to seam together with any continuity. Yet it is possible, even from
the fragments, to guess at Jane's intention. And we know, since she told
Paul, what she thought the work should be. She wanted, she said, to write a
nineteenth-century novel. She had in mind something of the quality of
Balzac, the creation of a world of sensory and realistic detail. But in addition
she wanted her characters to be representative, each of them to represent an
abstraction, almost in the sense of a morality play.

In fact what developed in the novel was a recounting of her own journey
out into the world. *Out in the World* is more directly autobiographical than
anything else Jane ever wrote. *Two Serious Ladies* had been autobiographical in
a different way. That novel had been an act of dissection, an arbitrary
splitting of her own being, while the narrative voice remained distinct and
separate, commenting, sometimes sardonically, upon the actions of the
characters. But Jane felt that *Two Serious Ladies* was a failure, and not even a
novel. To her it was still separated from life in the outer world by that gulf
the child Mary had felt in "A Stick of Green Candy."

Out in the World reproduced the shape of Jane's own experiences.
Though she made certain factual changes, she was writing of her own
present and past. It is a novel with a double focus, with two main characters

whose lives barely intersect. First there is Emmy Moore, fat and in her mid-forties, who has come to the Hotel Henry in a little town in New England to be alone and to write. The second character is Andrew McLain, a soldier in his early twenties, who falls in love with another soldier. Jane, though not fat and forty-five nor a private in the army, is both Emmy Moore and Andrew in a way she had never been either Mrs. Copperfield or Miss Goering. She is immersed in their consciousness and does not hold herself apart from them, nor they from her.

Alone and in a hotel room, Emmy Moore writes a letter to her husband Paul (whom Jane also calls Mr. Copperfield in the notebook):

> Dearest Paul:
>
> I cannot simply live out my experiment here at the Hotel Henry without trying to justify or at least explain in letters my reasons for being here, and with fair regularity. You encouraged me to write whenever I felt I needed to clarify my thoughts. But you did tell me that I must not feel the need to *justify* my actions. However, I *do* feel the need to justify my actions, and I am certain that until the prayed-for metamorphosis has occurred I shall go on feeling just this need. Oh, how well I know that you would interrupt me at this point and warn me against expecting too much. So I shall say in lieu of metamorphosis, the prayed-for *improvement*. But until then I must justify myself every day. Perhaps you will get a letter every day. On some days the need to write lodges itself in my throat like a cry that must be uttered.

Emmy Moore tries to explain to her husband her ideas about women. She has a concept of three distinct types: Western women—who are manly and independent, Turkish women—who are soft and feminine and dependent, and Oriental women—"who could easily be just as independent and masculine as the women of the Western world." She realizes that her concept is "puerile" but that doesn't stop her from feeling it to be true. She believes, too, that by some accident of fate, she, who was meant to be a Middle Eastern woman, was born in the Western world. She admits to despising herself for her dependency. She can use her feminine intuition with great skill, but that too she despises as a method of achieving power.

> I want you to know the whole truth about me. But don't imagine that I wouldn't be capable of concealing my ignorance from you if I wanted to. I am so wily and feminine that I could live by your side for a lifetime and deceive you afresh each day. But I will have no truck with feminine wiles. . . . I shall try to be honest with you so that I can live with you and yet won't be pitiful. Even if tossing my feminine tricks out the

window means being left no better than an illiterate backwoodsman, or the bottom fish scraping along the ocean bed, I prefer to have it this way.

As Emmy discards her wiles in life, so Jane discards her writing wiles in *Out in the World*. There is in this novel none of the witty detachment, the sardonic grace, the playfulness that was part of her craft in *Two Serious Ladies*. It is as if she were hoping to break through to something entirely different from what she had done before, something both classical and more representative, at the same time.

In an early notebook Jane had had a character named Mother Sender say, "But then it is likely that very few of us have the patience or the courage to arrive at the point where we are really sucking at the bone of our lives. . . ." And it was just this sucking at the bone that Jane demanded of herself now.

Just so, Andrew, before he can go out in the world (by falling in love with Tommy), must ferret out his own lies and examine the secrecy that has been his protection:

Looking back on those early days he realized that he must have seemed nothing like the others; he did not allow himself any close friends or companions. He was fearful that too much proximity would reveal the difference he was concealing from them with badly suppressed excitement. . . . His painstaking travesty had indeed lent to his face a look of flushed headiness that rendered him suspect to his companions though he had certainly not been aware of this: His eyes too had a dangerous sparkle. Very rapidly the lie changed until it was not his family that he was concealing any longer but a private monster whose shape was not even visible to himself. Like other odd children he was in the end simply concealing an oddness. He could not remember when the lie melted away so that he could no longer feel it. Poison ceased to drop into his heart . . . little by little the lie vanished. His breast was emptied of the bitter vial. There was a possibility, he realized, that it had not vanished but engulfed his spirit so totally that he could no longer find it anywhere. This latter possibility he sincerely believed to be the more likely one.

Andrew meets Tommy at camp, an army camp unlike any that has ever existed, where Tommy is cooking over a bonfire (as Jane had met Cherifa over a cooking pot outside her hanootz). After the meeting Andrew feels that his life has changed but he cannot tell whether something has been given him or "on the contrary taken away. It was almost as if he had been robbed and as a result felt exhilarated." But what touches Andrew more than anything else in his relation to Tommy is the sense that secrets are being revealed to him. He who has always been so secretive is now finding out the secret of another:

> . . . the heavy wave of peace and exaltation so overwhelming that Andrew felt his heart submerged resulted not from the stuff of the tale he was hearing but from the increasing certainty that he was hearing secrets. Everything Tommy told him he saw immersed in the magical light that enchants certain secrets, secrets unannounced as such. . . . As he listened to the dreary account he felt increasingly exultant. His own silence always so oppressive that it burned his throat like sand now seemed to evade him; freer now than himself it seemed to mix with the dark evening . . . this silence of his which until then had been a manifestation of misery became a reflection of his own intuition and of his own purity—so that what had always been an ugly cage was transformed at that moment into a wonderful church.

Further, Andrew must examine his own parents, strip them of the myths that have held him since childhood.

He must remember that his father was once well-to-do and then one day lost his business, was once able to challenge his wife with arguments of his own, but then in time lapsed into passivity. Andrew recalls a meal he and his parents shared at a hotel, where he examined his mother's face, which was partly hidden by a veil. He watched her every motion as she ate, seeing the "scattered and malevolent" look upon her face, seeing her with his father.

> Andrew averted his eyes from his father's countenance, but even without looking up he knew what he would find there, a face devastated by the absence of wrath, though Andrew did not understand that he was seeking wrath in his father's face. He knew that when his mother had won her point, as she always did now in any discussion, he could not so much as glance at his father without feeling sick.
> He could see his mother's eyes black and piercing, hunting her husband's face for the vanished prey. . . . He did not know that like himself she was seeking the wrath so necessary for her life.

All of this relentless sucking at the bone is in pursuit of a vision, a new way of seeing. As a child Andrew had had one intimation of that kind of seeing, and in his love for Tommy there is the possibility of a return to that vision. He remembers that

> he was walking along the road to his grandmother's house. It was in the summertime and he had not been to visit his grandmother for a year. The stone wall at his left was high enough to prevent his seeing over it.

It was warm near the wall and the air was still, though across the road a cool wind was making the grass wave. He would reach out frequently as he always had to touch the warm stone. He was barely conscious of his surroundings when he reached for the wall and felt the wind blowing through his fingers. Automatically he turned and looked at his hand. There was a breach in the wall. He could see fields and blossoming orchards that he had never known existed. In the distance there were cows standing in the pastures and blue oats curving in the breeze. Some of the cows were in the shadows and others flamed red in the sun. The fields of oats and the pasture land too flashed in brightness and then darkened as he watched. Only the blossoms close to him remained brightly in the light of the sun.

He stood still: The breach had not existed the year before.

. . . For many years he approached the breach with mixed feelings until his grandmother died when he was thirteen and they ceased going to the house. . . .

After Andrew meets Tommy, he once again has the sense of that breach and all that it can mean to him; only this time he feels the breach within himself. "In reality his heart was the wall and it was as if a part of it had crumbled in the night. There was a breach made through which the wind could blow."

No longer to be in the world as part of a travesty is what Andrew is seeking, just as Emmy Moore is trying to evade travesty in her writing, is trying to utter the cry that is lodged in her throat.

But Emmy, finishing her letter to her husband, feels a sense of despair. She feels she has said "nothing at all." She feels she has not justified herself enough.

Automatically she looked around the room. A bottle of whiskey stood on the floor beside one of the legs of the bureau. She stepped forward, picked it up by the neck, and settled with it into her favorite wicker chair.

And Emmy, sitting there, unable to write, sees a representation of power made impotent:

. . . the distinct image of a giant steamship lying on its side. She turned her head slightly to the left as she had done in actuality to avoid the sight when the Hewitt Moores had taken her to see the boat dragged up from its ocean bed several years ago. . . .

In effect, Jane is Emmy Moore (or Emmy is Jane), unable to break through her writing, her power made impotent. For she is anchored by her sense of sin—not just the sin of her failure to write, but the opposing and even greater sense of sin that will be hers if she breaks through the block.

What has happened in Morocco has opened up new possibilities for Jane. The change is evident in the astonishing, even classical grace of the prose, in the way she relinquishes her old wiles in the service of a new clarity. But with the new possibilities comes an even greater fear of sin. She is turned back upon herself.

So Jane wrote and crossed out and wrote and crossed out, "very nearly throwing everything into the fire (mentally)." Then, like Emmy Moore, she started to drink—but gin, not whiskey, and almost an entire bottle at that. Soon she was "very cheery indeed." And (with Nora and Cory) she went out—not to the local bar and grill as Emmy Moore did—but to the Monocle. There she met an Algerian belly dancer and talked Arabic to her. And then the next morning she went back to her desk and started again.

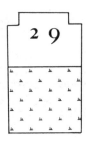

29

WENDELL WILCOX, A PROFESSOR AT THE UNIVERSITY OF North Carolina, was living in Paris that winter and spring of 1950 and met Jane at Alice Toklas's.

Alice Toklas had asked me to tea one afternoon and when I got there, there was Jane. Meeting Jane was not like meeting anybody else. There was no feeling either of restraint or expectation, but rather one of having known her for a long time, except one hadn't. She was the very easiest person to be with that I have ever known.

We went to lunch together the next day and then again nearly every day after. I can't even remember that we made arrangements. She would call me and come by or else I would go for her to the Hôtel de l'Université where she was staying with a friend, a very tall American woman in early middle life. Jane and I would wander around and eat and drink here and there, talking about nothing in particular, Jane speaking mostly of her personal friends as if I knew them too. I have forgotten now most of the names. Libby Holman quite a lot and some others. Jane looked very much like her pictures, except that in the flesh she was much more appealing, and did not give so much the effect of being a little girl who was dressed up and showing off. Though that element was often there. She liked very much to go into shops and try on clothes which she had no intention whatsoever of buying. I think there was a touch of fetishism there. She loved wearing somebody else's clothes. Particularly if they were utterly unsuitable. She came to dinner one night wearing a sweatshirt that belonged to the woman she was living with. When the sleeves were not turned up, they came well below her fingertips. She was in a very good mood and ready to cause the small commotions which she enjoyed. When the food came, she looked in everybody's plates and began saying that they had more meat than she did. She called the waitress and said that poor little Madame Bowles was always given the smallest piece of meat and asked if she might not be given a little more. . . .

Jane at this period complained that she was very short of money and led me into the cheapest restaurants she could find. She seemed very nervous about the state of the food in these places and on two occasions got up and went into the kitchen to talk to the cook and examine the state of the food. Someone she knew of had been poisoned by canned food of some sort.

The odd thing was that these commotions which she so loved to cause never seemed at all burdensome and the French put up with them without complaint. I was never in the slightest put out by them, and I am easily put out. This was due I think to something essentially Jane that made one let her go on unresistingly. This is hard to describe because I never had the sensation that I was watching a performance on the stage. Yet it was of course a performance. It makes Jane sound formidable whereas she was not in the least so. I believe, however, that much of the time she was consciously performing.

One day in one of these cheap eating places I made a mistake and was surprised with the results. She was talking about her family and I asked her what her maiden name had been. She glared, struck the table and said, "Auer. Now you know." It took me a moment to answer while she remained suspended. Finally I asked if they were related to the musician. She hesitated and then said, "Yes."* Her tension dropped, and we went on as we had before I had been so careless.

We never really talked of anything but her friends. Never said anything about books or music. She was going about at the time with a copy of *Le Deuxième Sexe* under her arm. We did say something about that and for some reason talked about Kierkegaard.

We talked, however, about Jane's writing. I was intensely admiring of *Two Serious Ladies*. I told her what I thought about it, but she felt embarrassed by the fact that her writing was not as smooth and orderly as Paul's. I tried to explain to her that though Paul was extremely accomplished and had spots in his work which were entirely his own, nevertheless he wrote a conventional novel basically and that it was in a way his exoticism that carried him. God knows Jane's stories were exotic but the really exotic element was Jane herself. Both the story and the telling are completely natural in Jane and come from nowhere outside herself. No one but Jane could have written a line of them. I talked in this way to her and tried to make her feel less desolate about her work.

She was at that time writing a book. The male characters annoyed her

---

*There is no other evidence than this statement that Jane was related to Leopold Auer.

to the extent that when she had to talk about one she would turn to the back of the book where she recorded their doings and where their presence could not contaminate her ladies.*

What most of her fears consisted of I don't know. I have seen her at night walking slowly along grazing the walls with her hands. She was afraid, she said, but of what?

To Wilcox Jane was one of the people he had most loved in his life. To Gore Vidal, who had met Jane the summer before in Tangier, she was "unbearable." (Jane, in turn, disliked Vidal, referring to him as "Mr. Gorvey" to Paul, who was very fond of him.)

In 1976, writing about Tennessee Williams and his "Monster Women," Vidal said, "I could never take any of them from Carson McCullers to Jane Bowles to Anna Magnani. Yes, yes, yes, they were superb talents all. Part of the artistic heritage of the twentieth century. I concede their talent, their glory, their charm—for Tennessee but not for me. Jane ('the finest writer of fiction we have in the United States') Bowles was more original. She thought and talked a good deal about food and made powerful scenes in restaurants."

Ned Rorem came to Paris while Jane was there. He had also seen her in Tangier the summer before and had watched her carefully, observing her "making a mountain out of a molehill. She and Paul had a kitten that wasn't well. Jane was wringing her hands. They called the hotel doctor in. Paul took her very seriously in all this, though he knew the effect she had on others."

In Paris, however, says Rorem, "Jane was very kind to me. She helped me to find a place to live. She took me to a restaurant. I remember a valet of Apollinaire was there. I found that I wanted to make a good impression on her. It became important to me that she admire me."

To Wilcox, Jane said that she was frightened for Rorem because of the dangerous life he was leading. She took him to Rorem's "small room, where he was supposed to be wretched and contemplating suicide. Fortunately he never did."

After Cory left, Jane found herself in financial difficulties. She even suggested to Wilcox that she move into his room with him, but she never carried through the suggestion. At the time Jane was receiving $100 a month from the Author's League, along with option money from Oliver Smith for *In the Summer House*, but she was spending more money than she had. And Cory, who had paid for many of their joint expenses, was no longer there to pay the bills. Jane sent for money to her bank in Tangier. When she received no answer, she called Georges Bernier. "I must see you," she said. "It's very urgent." Georges went to meet her in a café. Jane explained that she had sent letters to the bank in Morocco repeatedly without receiving any answer. She

---

*Jane may have said this to Wilcox, but in the notebooks there is no such separation.

Libby Holman, Morocco, 1948.

*Outside Tangier, 1949. Jane at center, to her left
the Hon. David Herbert, to her right Truman Capote, Paul.*

PHOTO BY CECIL BEATON

Paul and Jane, outside Tangier, 1949.
PHOTO BY CECIL BEATON

Opposite: *A costume party at the Hon. David Herbert's, Tangier, 1949.*
from left: *the Comtesse della Faille, Jay Haselwood, Jane.*

Above: In the Summer House, *December 1953.* In the center:
Judith Anderson and Mildred Dunnock.
PHOTO BY EILEEN DARBY

Above: *Cherifa*.

Opposite top: *Mohammed Temsamany, 1954*.
PHOTO BY KATHARINE HAMILL

Opposite bottom: *Ahmed Yacoubi*.
PHOTO BY KATHARINE HAMILL

Paul, mid-1950s.
PHOTO BY KARL BISSINGER

asked him for advice. "Is this a good business letter?" she said. She showed him what she'd written. "It seems she'd already sent it," Rosamonde Bernier remembers. "The letter went, 'Dear Mr.—: Unless the money arrives by Tuesday, I'll shoot myself.'"

It was as it had been before, in Mexico and in New York. Each person who met her saw a different Jane: the helpless Jane, the helpful Jane, the enraging Jane, the endearing Jane, the kind Jane, the anguished Jane making scenes. But whatever the effect on others, it was always intense and puzzling. "It was, of course, a performance," says Wilcox. Yet watching, no one was sure. She was performing, but then maybe she wasn't performing. She seemed to be playing, and yet was she playing? For a moment they thought they knew; then they weren't quite sure. Perhaps she didn't know herself. Only in her work: there she knew she wasn't performing. But there, the more she discarded her playful wiles, the more she was blocked.

IN JUNE, PAUL RETURNED TO LONDON FROM CEYLON AND INDIA. THEN HE came to Paris to be with Jane. Wilcox saw them together several times:

"Paul had the gift of immediate affability, as did Jane. But there was a great difference. I remember a gathering one afternoon in a very large apartment. Paul sat on the floor with his back against the wall. There was a semicircle of young people about him. He sat in their midst, tossing a coin into the air and catching it repeatedly. It gave him a somewhat sinister air, as if he were aloof, occupied with something else, and only giving a small part of himself to his admirers."

That June, Carson and Reeves McCullers were also staying at the Hôtel de l'Université. Jane and Paul frequently had breakfast with Carson in her room. Carson was having her own difficulties at the time, although she was a favorite of the literary establishment wherever she went. Jane was very jealous of her, as she was indeed of all women writers, and now she said about Carson's work, "Her freaks aren't real." She felt she wrote too easily about the freaks who were such a feature of her work, thinking to make them attractive by superficial means, whereas to Jane the more peculiar people were, the more difficult it was to write about them, the more one had to labor to make them "real."

In July, Paul left Paris to meet Libby Holman in Málaga. For a month they traveled around Andalucía, soaking up atmosphere for an opera based on García Lorca's *Yerma*, which Paul was composing, in which Libby would star. Jane, alone, went off to New York, having been led to believe that at last *In the Summer House* would be produced there. But it was another false alarm, she wrote to Alice Toklas. Toklas in turn wrote to Paul that the news that Jane's play was not "going on in New York was a frightful disappointment to

me. It was what she so greatly needed—and would have given so many
people pleasure."

But to Samuel Steward a few months later, Alice Toklas wrote:

> Jane Bowles' play never came off in New York—someone told me—it
> may even be true—that she messed things up by falling in love with the
> actress who was to be the leading lady—who wasn't interested. Dear
> Jane—she could have used a theatrical [success?]—she left here at the
> height of a successful love affair and she should have concentrated on
> her play—which Thornton [Wilder] liked a bit. She is to her misfortune
> true to type. . . .

The "successful love affair" in Paris that Alice Toklas refers to was
apparently with Nora. Ned Rorem also remembers her as Jane's "girl
friend." Wendell Wilcox, who met her with Jane several times, remembers
Nora as "a very handsome blond young woman who affected a pleasantly
louche appearance. At night she wore a black dress, the neckline of which
descended to the waist, a fashion which was then being worn in Paris. And at
times she wore a black cape which added to her clandestine air and
emphasized her blond beauty."

As for the actress in New York that Jane was supposed to have fallen in
love with, there is no other evidence that this happened. The story may have
been another part of the sexual mystique that surrounded Jane.

Even though the production of her play was not realized that season,
Jane stayed on in the city until winter. Much of the fall she seems to have
spent with Libby Holman, whose son Topper had just died in a mountain-
eering accident. Several people who knew them make a point of mentioning
what a great help Jane was to Libby during this tragic period.

While in New York she did manage to write a nonfiction piece for
Mademoiselle on her experiences in Tangier. Published in April 1951 as "East
Side: North Africa," it was an account of her visits with Cherifa and
Cherifa's sister, Betzoule, and Zodelia. In the mid-sixties, Paul revised the
article, changing the narrator from the first person to the third, and excising
the direct comments on the women and the society. The revision was
included in Jane's collection of short fiction as "Everything Is Nice."

In its original form the piece ended with one of Jane's most moving
disclosures of her own puzzlement at what the town—the medina of
Tangier—and its women actually meant to her:

> When I reached the place where I had met Zodelia I went over to the
> wall and leaned on it. Although the sun had sunk behind the houses in
> back of me, the sky was still luminous and the color of the blue wall had
> deepened. I rubbed my fingers along it; the wash was fresh and a little

of the powdery stuff came off; but no matter how often I walked through these streets reaching out to touch the chalky blue wash on the houses . . . on the walls, I could never satisfy my longing for the town.

I remember that once I reached out to touch the beautiful and powdery face of a clown because his face had awakened some longing; it happened at a little circus but not when I was a child.

In March 1951 Jane returned to Paris, to work once again on *Out in the World* and on the ending of *In the Summer House*. Truman Capote was in Paris and had a room next to Jane's in a

pleasantly shabby hotel on the rue du Bac. . . . Many a cold evening was spent in Jane's snug room (fat with books and papers and foodstuffs and a snappy white Pekingese puppy bought from a Spanish sailor); long evenings spent listening to a phonograph and drinking warm applejack while Jane built sloppy, marvelous stews atop an electric burner: she is a good cook, yessir, and a kind of a glutton . . . she is also a spookily accurate mimic and can re-create with nostalgic admiration the voices of certain singers—Helen Morgan, for example, and her close friend Libby Holman.

In a story written years afterward, "Among the Paths to Eden," Capote endowed his main character with some of Jane's characteristics, the stiff-legged limp, "her spectacles, her brilliant and poignant abilities as a mimic." The surfacing of these characteristics in his fiction was a measure of the intense effect Jane had upon him, Capote wrote.

But that winter Jane had an entirely different effect upon Alice Toklas. Jane had been a puzzle to her before, but now Toklas felt she had the "answer" to her, after seeing Jane with Libby Holman, who was also in Paris:

Jane is strange as an American but not as an Oriental—especially an Oriental D.P. It was to this conclusion that seeing her with Libby Holman brought me. If accepting this makes her more foreign it at least relieves the strain—that morbidity—she originally seemed at first to be consumed by. . . .

It was not morbidity but mystery that Carl van Vechten had seen in Jane in January before she left New York. In two photographs he took of her then, her image seems to be at some indefinable depth from the lens. It is as if she could be caught only through a series of screens, or behind her own doubled image. The portraits are harsh, unflattering in the conventional sense. She seems both young and old, male and female, weighted.

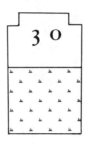

3 O

HAVING RETURNED TO TANGIER, PAUL WAS WORKING at his usual pace, writing his new novel *Let It Come Down*, doing articles for *Holiday* and *The American Mercury* about the Sahara, and also composing *Yerma*. A collection of short stories, *The Delicate Prey*, had been published to excellent reviews in the United States and in England.

Alice Toklas had written to him about *The Delicate Prey:* "The memory this morning is that your delicacy is perfect, precise and poignant, but the macabre fate, though inevitable, that overtakes most of your prey, is not to my taste."

About Toklas's comment, Paul writes to Peggy Glanville-Hicks, "It seems to me one could say that about life itself."

But though his work was going well, though he had by now established a literary career, Paul continued to have the sense that his life outside of his work had little meaning. In February he wrote to Peggy Glanville-Hicks of his daily existence, and added:

> Inside I am waiting to escape to somewhere else. I don't quite know where. Naturally one always wants to escape if one has no reason for being anywhere. And I have no reason for being anywhere, that is certain. If I work, I don't think of that, and feel the escape urge less, so that the work is largely therapeutic. But when one feels that the only reason for working is in order to be able to forget one's life, one is sometimes tempted to consider the work slightly absurd, like the pills one takes to make one's digestion easier. There should be something else in between, but what it is, is anyone's guess. Some will say one thing, others something else. I suppose the trouble is that one thinks one's life instead of living it. Occasionally one enters into contact for a split second, when the wind blows across one's face, or when the moon comes out from behind a cloud, or a wave breaks against the rocks in

some particular way which it would be impossible to recognize or define. Then one catches oneself being conscious of the contact, and it is lost. Thus, a great desire to lose consciousness. Yet in sleep nothing is different: there is always the same cage around.

Like Jane, Paul was also preparing his own journey out into the world. He mentioned to his friend Brion Gysin that he longed to have his own car. Brion told him to buy one, that he could afford it.

This shocked me. I had never thought of myself as a possible car owner. Nor had it occurred to me that money was something that could be spent. Automatically I always had hoarded it, spending as little as possible. Brion's suggestion was like the voice of Satan. I began to look at cars, and within two weeks I had bought a new Jaguar convertible.

Paul hired a driver, a young Moroccan, Mohammed Temsamany, whom he dressed in a military-looking uniform with shiny boots and puttees and with a visored cap. In the Jaguar they drove south to Marrakech and then to Fez, where Paul began to see a good deal of the young Moroccan painter Ahmed Yacoubi, whom he had first met in 1947. When Paul heard from Jane that she wanted to return to Morocco, he suggested that he drive to the French border to pick her up. Paul invited Ahmed to come along with him.

With Temsamany in his uniform and Ahmed in his white turban and jellaba, Paul drove through Spain.

We nearly had trouble at the cathedral in Córdoba. As we entered, both Temsamany and Ahmed washed their faces, rinsed their mouths, and gargled with the holy water in a fount by the door. Then they squared off and began to spit it at one another. I hurried them out of the building before the sacristan, who had witnessed the shenanigans from the other end of the cathedral, could get to us.

Jane was in very good spirits when they picked her up at the border. During the trip south, however, she objected every time Paul drove. She insisted that she always knew exactly what Paul was thinking. She said she felt as if she herself were driving when he drove and she could not relax.

When they returned to Tangier in late June, Paul and Jane went again to the Farhar. The house in the Casbah needed repairs—new pipes and walls and ceilings and a stairway. Jane was the one who kept track of the repairs, while Paul went off for a month to Xauen, an isolated town in the mountains, to work on *Let It Come Down*.

The change in Ahmed's position with respect to Paul became very clear to Jane on the trip and in Tangier. What Paul had been able to do for Jane many years before in *Two Serious Ladies*, he was now doing for Ahmed and his painting. Though Paul himself was not a painter, he had a very good critical eye and was able to make suggestions that Ahmed could incorporate into his work. It was always part of Paul's talent and personality that he took great pleasure in lending himself to the creative world of other people, seeing their world through their eyes, and yet helping them as a guide.

There was a great irony in Jane's jealousy, since it was Jane—at least as far as Ahmed Yacoubi remembers—who got Ahmed interested in painting when she met him, through Paul, in Fez in the spring of 1948. At that time Ahmed was still in his teens. "I was doing sculpture when I was very young, but my father said to try something else because it was against the religion to make idols. I was trying to do some drawings with goat dung mixed with water, but it was Jane who first got me to using paint."

Ahmed had progressed so well that Paul could now write with pride to Peggy Glanville-Hicks, "Ahmed has been making a good many magnificent paintings. . . . The new ones are far more striking than the previous ones, more complicated and sophisticated, but they have lost none of their madness and directness. . . ."

While Paul was in Xauen and afterward when he returned to Tangier, Jane went on with her life with the grain-market group, pursuing Cherifa and Tetum as she had before. She kept trying to work on the novel *Out in the World*, trying to find a place where she could work quietly, either in a room in a hotel or somewhere in the medina, but she was continuously being distracted.

She'd try to force herself to be more disciplined. She would say to Paul, "I'm seeing too many people and it's terrible for me." But she could not stop herself. Then too she was drinking a great deal at parties and at the Parade Bar. Paul would tell her she was drinking too much and she would become very angry. She would say to other people, "Paul thinks I'm a heavy drinker." But she would not change her habits, even though there would be constant arguments between them about the drinking.

"She became increasingly recalcitrant about showing me any of her work because of her block or whatever you want to call it," Paul remembers. "She wasn't able to carry anything through to completion and she hated everything she was doing. She wouldn't show her work to me and didn't even want me to mention it to her. Nor would I have dreamed of insisting. She wouldn't have done it. She'd have refused."

Though Jane did not say anything to Paul about her jealousy of Ahmed, these feelings did begin to invade the novel she was writing. Andrew and Emmy Moore had been the main characters of *Out in the World* as she had originally conceived it, but now she began to focus the narrative on Agnes Leather, a young woman in love with Andrew. In one fragment from a notebook she writes of Agnes:

She sees Tommy and Andrew as a union. Actually of course she is terribly jealous of them—and by referring to them constantly as a union—and particularly in lecturing Tommy about it she manages to assert herself and embarrass them terribly. . . .

But at the same time, Andrew and Tommy continue to reflect her own situation with Cherifa, which she now sees with a sharper eye.

Theme of Andrew's life:
Tommy is the wall which prevents his entering into his life and which he must scale, but he is the breach in the wall too through which other fields can be seen. The road from behind the wall is through Tommy, but he mistakes this and thinks that only by reducing Tommy to something that bears his stamp and then ridding himself of the boy (as a sacrifice to his life that is to be) will he find that life—. But he cannot find his life because he cannot capture Tommy in order to lose him—thus the mad dance begins. . . .
He has interfered with Tommy, nature's child, and discovered in himself another person—a full-fledged militant man—domineering and not shy at all. He is shocked a little since this seems to be the same size as he is—and yet had remained hidden to himself thus far. . . .
He [Tommy] refused to admit that anything had happened between them. His way of punishing Andrew is to look completely bland or at least disinterested. . . .

But the doubleness of this vision, Andrew and Tommy as herself and Cherifa, and also Andrew and Tommy as Paul and Ahmed, of whom she is jealous, cannot hold for Jane. The novel breaks into fragments. More and more characters appear. Situations and characters seem to dissolve into each other. Jane tries to grasp the idea of the novel intellectually. "This is a book about travesties and about two different generations," she writes. "Emmy Moore represents the one and Andrew McLain the other."
But the theme of Agnes Leather's jealousy appears again:

Agnes Leather can hardly wait in the morning to rush over and join the boys in their renovated cabin. To make them love each other more is her conscious objective but underneath it all she feels sure that Andrew loves her best because she's a girl. However in order not to bring this to a head—she has a suicide plan. She says it's because her life, as it is then, that spring, with picnics indoors and out is exactly what she wants and that it is the right moment to kill herself. One day they go to a picnic and Andrew says, "Oh! shit." She has brought the food—far too much bread as usual. . . .

And now it is Agnes Leather's consciousness that more and more —despite the fragmentation—takes on the mark of Jane's own life in Tangier, her doubt about the meaning of her own experience, her fear that she is not "in" life:

> She could not remember when this conviction that just beyond her reach was the sensitive and complicated and violent world of human beings—had not been rooted so deeply in her heart that it had seemed to her that it was part of its very shape and substance. At the same time she actually expected that some day she would change her present heart for another—or that some breach would be made so that the light would come through. She did not like to go with other educated people because she was afraid they might find this out and know about her heart even more thoroughly than she did herself . . . the situation of the world was of course very depressing to her and she hoped that the earth would not blow up before she could consider that she was actually living on it. The climactic atmosphere of the epoch made her feel frantic and in some way enfeebled. . . .

In early November Paul and Jane drove to Fez, where Ahmed was still living. While driving in Fez, Temsamany had two accidents. "One night," Paul wrote to Peggy Glanville-Hicks, "an evil invisible woman appeared to him as we were going over the Col du Zegotta. The car skidded and spun abruptly around, so that it was facing the opposite way. He cursed her and she left. Jane was so upset that she was ill for two days."

In the second incident Temsamany was "attacked by a djinn while driving in the Oued Zitoun. The djinn seized the steering-wheel and jerked it out of his hand while he was shifting gears. He had announced the day before that a djinn was hovering around and wanted him to have an accident, but no one paid any attention. The car went full-speed into a stone bridge. Naturally it [the car] has to be rebuilt."

Jane returned to Tangier with Temsamany to have the car fixed. As the house was still being worked on, she took a room at the Hotel Rembrandt. When Paul returned to Tangier late in November, Ahmed came with him to stay.

Through Paul, Ahmed met Isabelle Gerofi, who managed the Galli-mard Agency, a bookshop in Tangier, and who arranged for a show of his paintings. In a letter to Peggy Glanville-Hicks in December, Paul reports:

> The show has been on for almost three weeks, and crowds still gather along the boulevard to gape. But what is better is that he has sold twenty-eight paintings, which is unheard of, considering that they are all utterly unintelligible to the people of Tangier. I think that the real

reason is that the principal connoisseur of Tangier, who has a house full of Modiglianis and Soutines, bought thirteen all at once, and that impressed the follow-suiters. Anyway, Ahmed takes it quite as a matter of course, says it is Allah who really does the paintings in any case, so that they would have to sell. To him it merely means that Allah wants him to have some money, and he goes out evenings in the moonlight alone and intones long prayers of gratitude to his friend Allah for being so good to him.

At the same time that Ahmed's career flourished and Paul took pride in it, Jane was caught, unable to progress in her writing. To her friends in Tangier she seemed to be as she had always been—worrying about her work, of course; that was Jane—but also witty, delaying, captivating with that elfin charm that was her great power. Yet though to others she may have seemed perennially young, the sense of time in her own life was beginning to alter for her. Of Emmy Moore Jane writes:

At the party in Andrew's house [she] is addressed as Mrs. Moore. All at once she feels that to be her age is her responsibility—that hidden behind all her problems was her age—waiting for its natural dress —which she has denied it. She sickens and sees all this clearly in a flash—tries helplessly to set the table. . . . Did Emmy Moore lose her age when she was little?

Jane is almost thirty-five years old. She has delayed and delayed throughout her life, as if by holding time back, she could make a constant present out of existence, but now time itself begins to force its meaning on her. In the novel there comes to Agnes Leather a sense of another kind of time, brought on by a warm day in winter:

Usually such unseasonable days had a very depressing effect on her. This had been true ever since she was a little child. She had thought, then, that such days belonged to another year—a year behind the celebrated year with four seasons which everyone talked about, and this frightened her. She had told her father about the two years, but he had explained that there was only one year—and that all the days of the year, even the warm winter days and the cold summer days, belonged to one year and that the year belonged to nature. She pretended to believe—in fact she wanted to think the way he did, but it was already too late. . . .

That there is a year behind the "celebrated year"—that there is a time beyond clock time—old feelings long held off, return now, slipping in where narrative might have been, replacing the "and then" and the "and then" of the novel Jane tries to force into being.

TOWARD THE END OF THE YEAR JANE DECIDED THAT SHE WOULD GO TO New York. Though Morocco was the place she loved best, her sense of Tangier and her being there had become clouded by Paul's interest in Ahmed. Perhaps she took the accidents to the car as omens. She still hoped for a production of her play on Broadway. If it was a success, she would be able to recoup much of what seemed to be lost.

In January 1952, she left Tangier, departing as usual, in a flurry. Paul wrote to Peggy Glanville-Hicks: "Her Siamese cat had fallen from the ceiling of her room in the Rembrandt, and was incapacitated. Its teeth however were still sharp. We bought penicillin and Terramycin in Algeciras, rushed to Gib to meet the *Saturnia*."

After Jane left, Paul remained in Gibraltar to attempt to secure Indian and Ceylonese visas and passage for himself and for Ahmed. With her on the boat Jane had taken a large collection of Ahmed's paintings. She was to try to arrange a show for him in a gallery in New York.

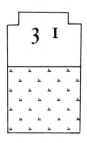

31

JANE ARRIVED IN NEW YORK IN MID-JANUARY. SHE would stay in the United States for more than two years, occupied with the production of *In the Summer House* and its final rewriting. The play in its original form was already in repertory production at the Hedgerow Theater of Moylan, Pennsylvania, directed by Jasper Deeter, the gifted founder of Hedgerow, and Catherine Reiser. Mike Kahn, Libby Holman's nephew, had shown Deeter the script of the play in 1950. Deeter admired the play; he thought it sensitive, comic, and Chekhovian, and entered into an agreement with Jane for repertory production. Jane received $100 in advance royalties. The play had its first production August 23, 1951, while she was in Morocco.

Because of Jane's previous contract with Oliver Smith for a professional New York production, her agreement with Deeter stipulated that no critics be invited to the performance without her permission. The Hedgerow production was an intelligent one, faithful to Jane's original intention, but Jane and Oliver Smith were after bigger game than small repertory theater, even if it was excellent repertory. She wanted a popular success on Broadway and Oliver kept assuring her that she would have what she wanted. But getting backers and money for a play about mothers and daughters—a dark, convoluted, though comic play—was not easy in 1952. While she waited, Jane kept reworking the last act. She spent most of her time with Libby in Connecticut and in Oliver Smith's house on Tenth Street.

There was also Paul's continuing success to contend with. *Let It Come Down* was published in February and reviewed on the front page of *The New York Times Book Review* by Robert Gorham Davis, who found it "more continuously exciting" than *The Sheltering Sky*.

> . . . [It] has more shape and style as a novel. It drives its central
> character relentlessly toward doom, toward the final orgiastic shudder,

with the nightmare clarity, the hallucinative exoticism, of the best of Bowles' short stories. And as in the short stories, artistic power and inhumanity go together.

Though Jane may have responded to the fact of Paul's success with *Let It Come Down*, she did not react to the novel itself as intensely as she had to *The Sheltering Sky*. She never felt that this novel predicted or even reflected her own life.

The hero of the novel, Nelson Dyar, whom Davis calls a "moral idiot," comes to Tangier in a sudden and desperate move to escape his own meaningless existence in the United States. In Tangier he is drawn into and finally willingly succumbs to the corruption of the European-Moroccan world. Dyar's destiny is not, however, the working out in prophecy of Paul's own individual sense of destiny. Rather it is a doom Paul foresaw with detachment, as in "Pages from Cold Point," that of the civilization from which he had come. In the novel Paul draws a parallel between the corruption in Tangier and the corruption in New York. At a party someone says to Dyar:

"Are you from New York? . . . Then you must see how alike the two places are. The life revolves wholly about the making of money. Practically everyone is dishonest. In New York you have Wall Street, here you have the Bourse. Not like the bourses in other places, but the soul of the city, its *raison d'être*. In New York you have the slick financiers, here the money changers. In New York you have your racketeers. Here you have your smugglers. And you have every nationality and no civic pride. And each man's waiting to suck the blood of the next. It's not really such a far-fetched comparison, is it?"

Jane did not think—or did not let herself think—about the doom of civilization, as Paul did. As always, she made a great point of avoiding political discussion.

Paul has recounted how she avoided these conversations:

I went to a dinner party where I found myself the only man at a table of many women. Among them I remember with certainty only three: Esther Strachey Arthur, Elsa Schiaparelli, and Janet Flanner. I was not supposed to be there at all, having been included only at Jane's insistence. It was a very good dinner, and it lasted for a long time, what with the wines and the conversation. Suddenly one of the ladies, adopting her most jovial manner, said, "Now, little Mrs. Bowles, suppose you give us *your* ideas on the world situation." Jane put down her napkin and murmured: "Excuse me a moment." Then she left the room. We waited for her to come back, but there was no sign of her. After a while I went to see what was wrong. I found her asleep; she had gone into another room and curled up on the divan. "What else could I do?" she demanded when I ridiculed her later.

But now though she refused to talk about politics—except to say that she was for Adlai Stevenson and hated McCarthyism—she did speak of certain nonpolitical changes taking place in the country. She was disturbed by the new importance of television. "A whole generation will grow up without knowing how to make its own games," she said. It seemed a world less capable of play, and a world in which change came faster and faster.

On Jane's return from Morocco Gordon Sager spent some months living with her at the house on Tenth Street. "I suppose she was losing some of that incredible youthful buoyancy she'd had. She'd been so full of vitality. I remember her getting up on a table in a club one night in 1946 and pretending to be La Pasionaria of New Rochelle. No, she wouldn't do that in 1952. But then that was to be expected. She was older. I was older. I probably wasn't even aware of any change then. She was still marvelous company."

He does remember one upsetting incident from that winter. "It was early one evening and Jane had gone into her room to take a nap. She often took catnaps. I went into her room after a while and she was lying on the bed in a flimsy nightgown, without a cover over her. The window was wide open and the snow was blowing in on top of her. And she was sound asleep. No, she wasn't drunk. She was sleeping. It frightened me. It seemed suddenly so irrational to be sleeping uncovered in the cold. I woke her up and that was all."

Natalia Danesi Murray remembers going with Janet Flanner to Treetops while Jane was staying there. "Jane was very amusing and a good talker. She was very intelligent and sophisticated and difficult too. She was different from anyone else I'd ever met. While we were there, Jane told a story. I can't remember the details of it now, but I remember the effect it had on me. It was a story of a fire, a fire she had seen or imagined, I don't know which. It was one of the most terrifying stories I had ever heard."

Still, along with the occasional darkening, there was the "old" Jane. In the summer of 1952 she went with Oliver Smith to Newport to visit Sylvia Marlowe. She brought her cat along, the same one that had fallen from the ceiling of the Rembrandt Hotel. Jane insisted that her cat would only eat crabmeat. Sylvia became furious at the idea of indulging a pet in this way and told Jane so. Jane said, "Sylvia, you've changed. You used to be such a nice, sweet girl. Now you're a monster."

IN THE EARLY SPRING OF 1953 MIRIAM LEVY HAPPENED TO BE IN NEW YORK AND she went to see Jane. It had been thirteen years since they had met. Their daily lives couldn't have been more different. Miriam had had three children. She was working on intercultural education in Saint Paul, she was on the board of the local NAACP, and she was involved in the fight against McCarthyism in Minnesota.

"Jane was staying at Oliver Smith's. When I arrived, there she was at the top of the steps waiting for me. She looked strange. I didn't know if she was drunk or on drugs. And the place was an appalling mess. The kitchen—well, there was no place to start. We were going to have lunch, but she was very vague about food. She opened a can of sardines. I had the feeling she wasn't well. At one point she said, 'I have to go into the other room and lie down.' I said, 'Can I do anything?' She said, 'No.' She went in the other room and passed out. Later she came back.

"It was all kooky, the mess and the people wandering in and out, and that sense that nobody cared about anything."

Jane seemed very preoccupied with her own world. There was a lot of talk with people who came and went about the production of her play. Miriam felt as if she and Jane had almost nothing to say to each other.

But then at one point Miriam began to talk about her involvement with the fight against McCarthyism. "Suddenly Jane came to life. All those people had been wandering in and out of the apartment and she was distracted, paying attention to them. But suddenly what I said mattered to her. Everything else that I'd talked about before—the intercultural education or whatever—it was like the Jewish refugee problem in the thirties. It was as if I were coming from outer space. But this she really connected up to, when I started talking about McCarthyism. (It was, I later decided, because of Paul and his position as a former Communist and his fear that in coming to the United States he might not be able to leave.) It was very odd to me because her interest was so sudden and so intense and so personal—whereas I was doing all this on the basis of some principle. I was so far from being a Communist myself it wasn't funny, but I felt I had to help test the situation and take a stand on principle."

Miriam carries in her mind an image of Jane that day, listening with her head to one side, now and then laughing hysterically, her eyes luminous in their nearsightedness. Once Miriam reminded Jane of their childhood episode of the car and the ruddy-faced man at whom they had spat. She mentioned something about his having been the lover of Jane's mother and it was at this point that Jane became indignant.

"We kept sitting there for hours. The people who came in were talking about casting Miriam Hopkins in the role of Gertrude. That went on and on. We went out for dinner and then we went over to Libby Holman's town house—Libby wasn't there. Paul came in with Ahmed Yacoubi. Yacoubi had some paintings with him. Jane and Paul wanted me to buy some, but I didn't."

PAUL HAD BEEN IN CEYLON AND INDIA WITH AHMED YACOUBI THROUGH JUNE 1952. Then, based in Tangier, they had traveled to Spain, Italy, and England. They arrived in New York in March 1953. Though Paul was very worried that his passport might be confiscated because of his having been a Communist, he had come to do the music for Jane's play, which was now assured of a Broadway production late in the year. Through Jane's efforts Ahmed had had a show at the Betty Parsons Gallery in New York and another was being arranged at the Weyhe Gallery. Both Paul and Ahmed were staying with Libby Holman at Treetops.

Though Paul and Jane had long ago chosen to have separate sexual lives, Jane was not prepared for either the intensity or duration of Paul's relationship with Ahmed. Ahmed Yacoubi wants it made clear that his relationship to Paul was not a sexual one. But what was important to Jane was the intensity of Paul's feeling for Ahmed and of his involvement in his creative work. Even now she did not speak of her jealousy to Paul directly. Only once Paul asked her what she thought of Ahmed and she said, "He has holes for eyes."

Then too, she had much in her own life to preoccupy her. She was involved in a difficult love affair, again one in which she saw herself as the aggressor and the other woman as the innocent. She was also caught up in the coming production of her play, and in the rewriting of the last act, which had never seemed "right" to her.

But then something happened between Paul and Ahmed and Libby Holman that Jane could not ignore.

In 1948, when Libby made her trip to the south of Morocco with Paul, she had suggested marriage to him. Libby told Paul she had discussed it with Jane and Jane said she was agreeable if that was what Paul wanted. Libby assured Paul that Jane would always be able to live at Treetops with them. When Paul didn't say anything, Libby added, "I don't think she really likes the idea, though, because I think she really wants to be Mrs. Bowles herself." And that was all that was ever said about that.

Now, at the beginning of May 1953, Paul decided to return to Tangier.

Libby, who was very honest and direct, came to Paul. "I've fallen in love with Ahmed," she told him. "I feel so guilty but I can't help myself."

Paul returned to Tangier and Ahmed chose to stay with Libby.

Shortly after Paul's departure, Jane went to Ann Arbor, Michigan, for a production of her play at the Mendelssohn Theater. Early in June, on her return to New York, she received a telephone call from Libby at Treetops. Some kind of incident had almost happened because of Ahmed and Libby was very angry. Ahmed later told Paul that Libby thought he'd tried to drown her six-year-old son in the swimming pool, but it was all a misunderstanding.

Libby said she was going to call the police. Jane told her not to but instead to put Ahmed on a boat back to Morocco. Libby agreed if Jane would keep Ahmed with her at the town house until passage could be booked on the next available boat to Morocco. Jane's first concern in all this was for Paul. But it is also likely that, angry though she was at Ahmed, she understood how complex the situation at Treetops must have been for him. He was sharp and street-wise, even crafty, in the world he had come from. But he had been thrown into a completely strange world of great wealth and sophistication, where the limits of his own position and his own power were not made clear to him.

Ahmed returned to Tangier by the middle of June and went to see Paul. In a letter to Virgil Thomson written in July, Paul reported:

> Ahmed returned from New York alone about three weeks ago and went directly to his home in Fez. He seemed extremely distraught, and certainly there is no better medicine for that than to be in the most familiar surroundings until one calms down and gets bored. So I encouraged him to return to his family without settling down here at all. Whether he went or not I don't know. At least he left Tangier for the south.

By late July Ahmed was once again with Paul.

Temsamany recalls that Jane spoke to him about the incident: "Libby Holman she loved life and she had everything gold. Yacoubi went riding in her Jaguar. He'd point something out and say, 'I like that,' and the secretary would write it down.

"Libby had a young son. Yacoubi pushed him in the pool or made some kind of trouble. Libby said to Jane, 'I'm going to ring up the police.' Jane said, 'No, it's your own fault.' Jane said, 'Put him on a boat and send him back to Morocco.' All this Jane told me.

"Paul came back and he was very sad. He said, 'Look what I thought, look what I believed.' I said, 'It's your own fault.' Then Paul said, 'He thought if he were with this rich woman he'd have everything.' Then he said,

'Right now we go to Fez to his mother.' Paul and myself, we went to Fez. I parked the car and knocked at the door. His mother came out, I said, 'I'm terribly sorry because Paul Bowles took your baby over there and he didn't come back.' I told about Libby Holman. His mother said, 'Well, if the woman was rich . . .'

"We came to Tangier. I saw a shadow behind a tree. That was Yacoubi waiting for me to leave, so he could talk to Paul alone. 'That's Yacoubi,' I said. And Paul forgave Yacoubi. But Jane, she never forgave Ahmed for what he did to Paul."

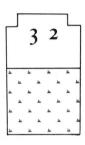

3 2

*I*N *THE SUMMER HOUSE* WAS PERFORMED FROM MAY 19 to 23 at the Lydia Mendelssohn Theater of the University of Michigan in Ann Arbor. John Stix was the director. Miriam Hopkins played Gertrude Eastman Cuevas, Mildred Dunnock was Mrs. Constable, and Anne Jackson played Vivian Constable.

Marjorie Eaton, who played a small role, one of the Mexican servants, kept a diary of the production. "At the beginning, when we had our rehearsals in New York, Miriam Hopkins was very friendly with the rest of the cast. But as the opening got nearer and nearer in Ann Arbor, she began to panic. No one could communicate with her. When we had our rehearsals she insisted on sitting in the audience and watching us. Stix had been with the Actors' Studio and we were working with improvisation, which we loved. But after Stix had rehearsed with us, he had to rehearse the play a second time alone with her.

"Finally we came to the dress rehearsal. And, of course, at that point, Miriam had to be there. But once she was on the stage, she got absolutely stuck. She was paralyzed; she couldn't move. Then Estelle Hemsley went up to her and slapped her on the face. Miriam started crying and then Estelle went out to get her a glass of water. Afterward Miriam thanked her."

Stix, who was very young at the time, was intimidated by Miriam Hopkins, who, though a Hollywood star, had not worked in the theater for many years. For the character of Gertrude she insisted on dressing in a very stylish manner—she had with her her own clothes from Bergdorf Goodman. In the play, however, Gertrude was supposed to be tacky in her dress. But Stix either said nothing to Hopkins or she would not listen.

In addition to Stix's problem with the star, there was also the problem of the last act, which was still being rewritten. Kenward Elmslie, the poet, went out to the opening with John LaTouche: "It was total lunacy there. Up to the last minute people kept pressing Jane to make changes in the script. She was also under other pressures, not to let the other people down, Oliver

Smith and Roger Stevens and others who had made the production possible. Yet it seemed to me that being under pressure was almost natural to her. She always had a terribly precarious balance, but somehow she knew how to maneuver."

Tennessee Williams also came out to the opening. He described the play as

a piece of dramatic literature that stands altogether alone, without antecedents and without descendants, unless they spring from the same one and only Jane Bowles. It is not only the most original play I have ever read, I think it also the oddest and funniest and one of the most touching. Its human perceptions are both profound and delicate; its dramatic poetry is both elusive and gripping. It is one of those very rare plays which are not tested by the theatre but by which the theatre is tested.

But the play opened not just to poor notices, but to violent attacks. The *Detroit Times* reviewer said:

All the efforts of a splendid cast and lively direction failed, in our estimation, to keep *In the Summer House* from degenerating into a verbose plea for understanding on the part of the playwright and into a pointlessly morbid study of the psychic difficulties of as useless a bunch of characters as we've ever seen assembled on a stage. . . .

The chief weakness in the play is that all the important characters were, in varying degrees, mentally deranged . . . the daughter is psychotic and the mother is inhumanly ambitious, brittle and superficial. The daughter is drawn cruelly by the author—a doltish, lumpy and dull girl who provokes a feeling of revulsion and fear. . . .

Nor was the *Detroit News* reviewer more enthusiastic:

In the Summer House starts with Miss Hopkins on a balcony, delivering one of the longest monologues ever written for the stage, while roly-poly young Rosina Fernhoff, in the character of her daughter, sits in a summer house, stage-right, and makes an occasional plaintive interjection.

That strange opening leads an experienced observer to suspect that the play will be heavy with significance, full of profound speeches a little on the vague side and, probably, symbolic. That suspicion proves to be a sound one, long before the halfway point is reached. But nobody attempting prophecy in the first act could imagine such a shebang as the third act proves to be. . . .

The story of *In the Summer House* chiefly involves a number of females from California, all of whom seem to suffer from serious nervous disorders. Miss Hopkins plays a bossy, shrill neurotic, with a marked speech compulsion. Miss Dunnock enacts a doting mother who becomes a dipsomaniac. Her daughter, the victim of an understandable murder, early in the proceedings, is played by Anne Jackson as a spoiled, conceited young silly. Miss Fernhoff, as the other daughter, portrays a certifiable lunatic, of the most stupid, stolid and clodlike sort.

All those female crackpots, plus two men, get into complications which rather delightfully involve a roistering Spanish family. . . . But not fifty funny Spaniards could save *In the Summer House* from going down its dreary course, from a fair beginning into pretentious, wordy nonsense.

The title seems to imply that poor Molly, the daughter, is trying to make a refuge for herself, amid all the vexations which are, you'll agree, likely to afflict half-wits who push their girl friends over cliffs.

Oliver Smith's flexible and atmospheric settings are the best things in the play, by about two city blocks. He and Roger Stevens are the producers.

"Pointlessly morbid" . . . "useless" . . . "deranged" . . . "provokes a feeling of revulsion and fear" . . . "neurotic" . . ." They were not only judgments upon the play but judgments upon Jane herself. For the play was inseparable from Jane. As Tennessee had said, "[It] stands altogether alone, without antecedents and without descendants, unless they spring from the same one and only Jane Bowles."

In the Summer House begins in a garden "somewhere on the coast of Southern California." Molly, who spends much of her time dreaming and reading comic strips in the vine-covered summer house, is eighteen with a somnolent, impassive face. Her mother, Gertrude, a widow, is "a beautiful middle-aged woman with sharply defined features, a good carriage and bright red hair. She is dressed in a tacky provincial fashion."

The play opens with a long soliloquy by Gertrude in which she rails at Molly for lolling in the summer house hour after hour. "You can't even see out because those vines hide the view." She speaks of her dissatisfaction with her own life, having to take in boarders to make ends meet. She says she is thinking of marrying Mr. Solares and going to Mexico with him. Mr. Solares is comical and inept, but he has money.

Knitting furiously, Gertrude recalls Molly's father, a man who wasn't rich enough, a man who refused to worry about earning money, no matter how Gertrude lectured him. She lost all interest in the marriage, she says, and would have given it up, but she found she was pregnant. "You were my reason for going on, my one and only hope . . . my love."

But recently Gertrude has come to have the "strangest feeling" about Molly. "It frightens me . . . I feel that you are plotting something. Especially when you get inside that summer house." Gertrude alternately harangues and threatens her daughter, who answers only in monosyllables.

Mr. Solares and his family appear with a huge picnic lunch. They joke and sing and eat voraciously. A new boarder arrives, Vivian Constable, a fifteen-year-old girl with wild reddish-gold hair, her eyes seeming to pop out of her head with excitement. She is wild and aggressive in seeking her own pleasure. She pursues Gertrude avidly and even invades Molly's summer house. Behind Vivian, always hiding in the shadows, is her mother, Mrs. Constable, who is worried about her "poor bird."

In the course of the play Vivian drowns—either by falling from a cliff or being pushed from it by Molly. Gertrude marries Mr. Solares and prepares to go off to Mexico. But before she leaves Molly declares her love for her mother so violently that Gertrude is frightened. However, she goes to Mexico and Molly marries Lionel, a young man who works at a nearby restaurant, the Lobster Bowl. (He is thinking about becoming a religious leader or of getting into politics. "I don't look forward to either one of them," he says.) He and Molly stay, in a chaste marriage, in a room above the Lobster Bowl. Mrs. Constable, with Vivian dead, has become an alcoholic and hangs around the restaurant to be close to Molly and Lionel.

In the last act Gertrude, unhappy with her life in Mexico, returns to reclaim Molly from Lionel. In one version of this act Gertrude drags Molly away, after convincing her that she is violent and dangerous to others, and Lionel is left alone. In another version, Molly runs out and kills herself. In the published play Molly rushes off after Lionel, and Gertrude is left alone.

In Vermont, in New York, in Paris, and again in New York, Jane had tried to find the right ending. She had begun the play in the mid-forties when she was living with Helvetia. Helvetia was putting pressure on Jane to leave Paul and to stay with her, just as Gertrude tries to force Molly to leave Lionel and come with her. Helvetia, like Gertrude, did go to Mexico, though not for her own marriage, but to see her daughter, who had married. When she returned from Mexico she complained bitterly about the noise and the confusion, just as Gertrude does. Helvetia's attitude toward her own dead father is reflected in Gertrude's attitude toward her dead father. (This play too is a work about missing fathers. Molly's father is dead—she dreams and hides in the summer house. Vivian's father is dead—her wildness is unreproved. Gertrude's father is dead—she still longs for his approval.)

As she harangues Molly, Gertrude is Helvetia, but she is also Claire, as

Jane remembered her from childhood. The overprotective, indulgent side of Claire appears in the character of Mrs. Constable. Lionel is the Paul figure in the play, though his character is not clearly defined. What is clear, however, is that he is the only one who understands Molly. He is her only hope for getting away from her mother—if she can get away.

In *Out in the World* Andrew had faced the same problem of getting away from his mother. He had a "conviction that his own going away was like no other going away in the world . . . he was not like other boys who wanted to go away. . . . He and his mother were isolated, sharing the same disgrace, and because of this sharing, separated from each other. . . ." In the notebooks is the implication that they are locked together by an unde-fined sin.

In *In the Summer House*, however, sin is given a palpable form for the first time. It is not the vague sin, hinted at but never explained, that appears in Jane's other works. The sin is named as murder and Gertrude claims to know that Molly has committed that sin. In giving the sin a name, Jane violated something of her own sense of mystery, but she was responding to what she took to be the demands of the medium. She spoke to Paul about the choices she had made. "I can't quote her," he says, "but the gist of what she had to say was that in the theater you had to be 'yenti.' You had to make everything so clear that nobody would miss it. You had to open up the material, dramatize it, and lay it on thick—all those things that she didn't like. She felt that you couldn't hint in the theater."

But if the theater was "yenti" to Jane, it was also the playing out of play; it gave physical body to the imaginative life now so blocked in her fiction. In this play performed before other people, there was hope for acceptance and, perhaps, hope of a redemption of sorts. But unfortunately there was no redemption and little acceptance from those who saw the play. With the sin named, with the material opened up and dramatized, there remained some fundamental irresolution in the play—as if it did not want to come to an ending. Like Jane's life, the play was based upon a precarious balance, the absence of finality, even the evasion of ending. All of the endings, even the final one, seem forced. And the dilemma portrayed on the stage seemed to reviewers to be nothing but the trivial and neurotic arguments of "female crackpots."

Like Emmy Moore, Jane had not "clarified or justified enough." At Ann Arbor she must have thought of her father, who had taken such pride in going to the university there, and how he had judged her for "dramatizing" her troubles. Jane's mother did not come to the opening. (Kenward Elmslie does remember, however, that the first person that Jane called after the opening was Claire.) Of course Jane continued to get great support from those who were close to her, from Oliver Smith, from LaTouche, from Tennessee, and from others. Oliver, who had helped her for so many years, was persuaded that on Broadway the play would still have the success it deserved.

Once Jane was back in New York she was put under great pressure to revise the script for the Broadway opening. There were also many changes made in the cast. The principal change was that Judith Anderson would play the role of Gertrude Eastman Cuevas. Her presence in the cast reassured the backers, but it created a new, formidable problem for the play. Judith Anderson, unlike Miriam Hopkins, was a star of the theater with a remarkably commanding stage presence. *In the Summer House* is a play of extremely delicate balance, in which the dualities are very subtle. It is also a play that has much in it that is mysterious, that cannot be "explained." Judith Anderson with the power of her presence threw off the balance of the play, and Stix, who was even more intimidated by her than by Miriam Hopkins, did not know how to restore that balance. The actress kept asking Stix to clarify her role, to clarify the motivation, but his clarifications were not helpful and without appropriate direction the star's personality rushed in to fill up the mysterious gaps in the play.

According to Marjorie Eaton's diary a first rehearsal for the Broadway production of the play was held in New York on November 2, 1953. She also noted a special rehearsal on November 15 in Oliver's house. The play opened on Thanksgiving, November 26, in Hartford.

"Everyone was terribly disturbed because Stix was blanked out by Judith's personality," Marjorie remembers. "The backers were very nervous. The show was to open in Boston on Sunday, November 29, at the Wilbur Theater. In Boston there was a change of directors. José Quintero came up from New York and worked with Stix. Then Stix left. It was a very embarrassing position for him and for everyone."

The pressures on Jane to make the ending more palatable to a Broadway audience increased. According to Paul, who had arrived from Tangier to help with the music, a psychiatrist was brought in to explain the motivation of the play: "He kept wanting to know more about Gertrude's father." Paul also remembers that Jane wanted him to decide things for her. He refused and, even though she said she couldn't make a decision, she was able to rewrite some scenes very quickly on the road, including one excellent scene for Mildred Dunnock, in which Mrs. Constable returns to the Lobster Bowl and finds Molly and Lionel alone there.

Both in Boston and in Washington, where the production went on December 14, Quintero worked late into the night with Jane and Judith Anderson. Then the next morning they would tell the cast about the changes that had been made.

Tennessee Williams remembers having heard that "Judith wanted things changed at the end and Jane kept agreeing. I kept telephoning Paul and Jane to keep the original script."

The play opened December 29 at the Playhouse Theater in New York, produced by Oliver Smith and the Playwrights' Company. Besides Judith Anderson and Mildred Dunnock, Elizabeth Ross was in the cast as Molly and Jean Stapleton as Inez. The reviews were far better than in Ann Arbor. Many reviewers praised the play, but the praise was mixed with reservations. Brooks Atkinson wrote:

> It is going to be difficult today to do full justice to Jane Bowles' *In the Summer House*. Perhaps it is going to be impossible. Scene by scene her play is original, exotic and adventuresome, but very little of it survives the final curtain. From the literary point of view it is distinguished: it introduces us to a perceptive writer who composes drama in a poetic style.
>
> With Judith Anderson and Mildred Dunnock giving the finest, most imaginative performances of their recent careers, *In the Summer House* also has theatrical distinction in a production beautifully directed by José Quintero. But when the play is finished it leaves one theatregoer in a muddle about the character and with a feeling of flatness about the whole play, as if the total achievement were unequal to the labor and talent involved.
>
> Of course, a theatregoer must consider the likelihood of his being the element that has failed. Perhaps he is expecting something that Mrs. Bowles does not intend to deliver or that is alien to the chiaroscuro style she applies to her theme. . . .

Atkinson went on to attribute the flatness of the play to its vagueness. "Did Mrs. Cuevas's daughter murder Mrs. Constable's daughter?" he asks. "Why does Mrs. Cuevas marry the Mexican for whom she has so much contempt . . . ? In the last scene, what is it that Mrs. Cuevas recalls from her youth that prevents her from persecuting her daughter?"

He also attacks the characters as "amusing exhibits of one form of neurosis or other, but they are not interesting in themselves." Like the Ann Arbor critics, Atkinson felt that the characters, because of their singularity, were of clinical interest only, that they had no relation to the rest of the world.

Whatever the critical judgment, the actors in the play admired it intensely. They attribute its critical and commercial failure to circumstances surrounding the production. Elizabeth Ross to this day regrets that she played Molly as she did—too passively, without vitality. But neither the directors nor Jane gave her a key to the part and she herself could not get hold of it, as she felt she should have.

Judith Anderson recalls that "the disaster started with Stix. I asked him about the play and there was silence. It needed a great imagination to accent the character of Gertrude. She was someone I hadn't played before. I was numbed. I begged for another director. I wasn't freed until Quintero came. But even then I wasn't freed completely. There wasn't enough time to find the character. In Boston and in Washington we only had eight rehearsals. And then we came to New York. There were good notices and bad notices.

"I thought Paul and Jane the maddest couple I'd ever seen. She had one skirt and two coats and a suitcase with a hole in it. He was elegantly dressed and had matching luggage. They were very devoted to each other.

"I can't say that I knew Jane. She was so different and so fey with a funny little smile—a lost quality. I remember one of her gestures—how she would cup her chin in her hand.

"I remember too that Jane was always across the street in a bar talking to the bartender. When she was with me, in front of other people, to embarrass me she'd say, 'Do you love me?' knowing how I felt about that kind of thing."

Mildred Dunnock, who was in the production from the Ann Arbor opening through the New York closing, recalls her own experience of the play:

"The first act sprang from Jane as a complete whole. She didn't know the mechanics of playwriting and yet she wrote two excellent women's roles. One problem with the play was that the young people were not very well drawn. The interest of an audience—in those days at least—did not go to middle-aged women. But I believe Jane was not so interested in the young people as in the older women. The young people weren't properly integrated into the story. The boy-girl thing was never resolved. But Jane had examined the women intimately and she knew their effect.

"The night before we opened [in Ann Arbor], while we were doing the scene on the beach, I threw a sausage toward Miriam. It seemed the right thing to do at the time. The sausage hit her on the back. She turned and said, 'Did you hit me with that sausage?' She was very upset. When Judith took over, I said to her, 'I just want you to know I'm going to throw that sausage.' And Judith understood that.

"It was a questionable play in terms of selling it to investors. So everyone counted on Judith Anderson's selling it. But, in terms of playing, her presence caused a problem. It wasn't just a matter of Judith's willfulness, but it was also her position as a star that didn't permit the ensemble playing necessary to the play.

"When José Quintero came, he was susceptible to Judith. She had for some years occupied the position of leading tragedienne and also sex symbol. The persona of Judith distorted the play and changed its value.

"So the play fell apart, probably because people who adored Jane had not the objectivity to deal with the inadequacies of the script. Yet Stark Young, the greatest drama critic I ever knew, brought me a reliquary the night of the opening. And he said to me, 'You'll be a long time finding a part like this.' There was music in it, an inner kind of thing rooted in intuition, that demanded the closest attention in playing it.

"In Washington there was a moment during the rehearsal when I suddenly did something, I turned as if I'd heard something offstage.

"Judith said, 'What are you doing?' She wanted that bit eliminated. But I had to find the way to that character. There was a rehearsal call for the next day at two. In the morning I left a note saying, 'If that's eliminated, I'm leaving the play. I won't stay if I'm not allowed to play the character as I want to.' Then I went out and walked the streets of Washington until two. I didn't want Jane to see me and persuade me differently. They left it in.

"Jane was so vulnerable and appealing and had such extraordinary talent. I think she enjoyed working in the theater. It was not like writing alone. There wasn't that kind of loneliness. I know her life was never an easy one. She was like a naïve and sophisticated child. But I felt there was nothing she didn't know.

"There were great needs in her. In a sense she was a little like an animal. You felt you must not satisfy any of her needs unless you satisfied them all. In the play too there were those vast needs that were not satisfied—a kind of animality—but there was also a great strength."

SO JANE WAS BACK WHERE SHE HAD BEEN: THE FOOD THAT WAS "SWEET AND natural" to her was still "foreign" food to others. Though, under pressure, she had made many changes in the last act to justify it psychologically, the play still left most of the audience puzzled, even angry. Katharine Hamill remembers that "the second time I saw it, I heard a woman say to a man on the way out, 'Don't look so downhearted, it's over now.'"

If there was intense admiration for the play among Jane's friends and admirers, the larger world still felt her work singular and strange. As Alice Toklas wrote to James Merrill:

> Jane Bowles' play would appear to have affected the audience strangely —no one agreed and that may have been the producer and actors' fault more than Jane. She is a strange creature. . . .

But two days later, in response to a letter from Mercedes de Acosta writing in detail about *In the Summer House*, Alice Toklas made a harsher judgment of Jane. It was as if she, who prided herself on being a sensitive observer, had to have an answer to Jane, even if it meant dismissing her.

> When I asked you to tell me about Jane Bowles' play it was not to ask you to take time to analyse it in detail as you did but what you had to say

fascinated and interested me beyond words—for it was an exact portrait of Jane herself and as I suspected the play is nothing but a projection of herself—ergo neither she nor the play are adult. As you so very clearly saw. What in her seemed based on fear—her strongest realist emotion —you have put your finger on—fear of taking an adult attitude to her weakness—more particularly even fear of facing adult responsibilities. If mistakenly I mistook the reason of her fears the moment you gave the right one we were agreed. And I was relieved for it had worried me a bit—of course it diminishes one's interest in her to have the answer. Years ago we took our nice intelligent Bretonne servant to keep house for us in Spain. As she was lonesome we found a French maid who was working in the household of the French consul and saw that they saw each other as often as suitable. Jeanne was pleased with the new acquaintance but not overjoyed. After spending a long [evening] together Jeanne returned and observed—I didn't know why I didn't like her more but now I know—*Elle est sotte.** If I wasn't shrewd enough to find it out for myself—I do thanks to you know now what worried me and why there could be no real pleasure in knowing Jane. . . .

IN THE SUMMER HOUSE CLOSED ON FEBRUARY 12, 1954, AFTER A RUN OF LESS than two months. Those who cared for the play—and by now there was almost a cult—hearing of the closing, rushed to the theater and fought for seats. During the performance there was much laughter; at the final curtain there was great cheering. Following the performance there was a wild party.

To an interviewer from *Vogue*, as she prepared to leave the United States and return to Morocco, Jane said, "There's no point in writing a play for your five hundred goony friends. You have to reach more people."

*She is stupid (foolish).

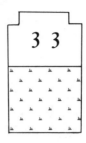

33

"(J)UST AFTER THE PLAY CLOSED WE WENT TO MOROCCO with Jane and her cat," Katharine Hamill and Natasha von Hoershelman remember.

In Tangier they saw a different Jane, speaking Arabic, always trying to get on with the Arab women, sitting in the grain market on a stack of wheat.

"We met Cherifa. She was handsome and had gold teeth. Like Janie she was unpredictable—except in one thing. She tried to get every nickel out of Janie that she could.

"We also met Tetum. She was in the coal market, a woman about forty-five. She was furious because Jane had taken Cherifa to the doctor's. There was a great jealousy between Cherifa and Tetum. They weren't in love with Jane; it was clear that they just wanted to get as much as they could from her—although they would never get rich from Jane, because Jane didn't have any money. Jane didn't have any illusions about their feelings. She didn't care whether they liked her or not. She wanted to be in that life. But yes, she did love Cherifa.

"When we visited, Jane was living in the Rembrandt Hotel and Paul was living in the Massilia Hotel with Ahmed. Jane was constantly looking for a place to live. We asked her, 'Why don't you live in the house in the Casbah?' She said, 'It's too narrow.' It was true, though she did live in the house on and off."

Both Natasha and Katharine had the feeling that in Tangier Jane was very dependent on Paul, more than she had ever been in the United States. "During the month that we were there, Jane would have lunch every day with Paul. She would speak to him on the phone for half an hour arranging it. Often the two of us would join them.

"One day Temsamany and Ahmed cooked a meal for us. We all sat crosslegged on the floor and smoked kif after the meal. Ahmed had cooked the soup. We told him it was a very good soup. He said, 'Betty Crocker, Betty Crocker.'"

Natasha and Katharine remember that Jane's main interest in Tangier was the daily life of the native women. "Except for a few visitors and Jay and Bill, who ran the Parade Bar, and David Herbert, she saw almost no one but the women.

"We did some traveling together while we were there. In one place Jane wanted to go into a house in the Jewish Quarter, where only Jews were allowed. They said, 'No Nazarenes.' She said, 'I'm Jewish.' No one believed her."

AFTER NATASHA AND KATHARINE WENT BACK TO NEW YORK, PAUL BECAME ill with typhoid. While he recuperated, Jane went every day to the hotel and cooked his meals for him in the kitchen. By this time Jane had left the Hotel Rembrandt and had moved into the narrow house in the Casbah. Ahmed lived with her until Paul recovered completely from his illness.

Tennessee Williams and Frank Merlo arrived for two weeks and Jane spent a lot of time with them, but after their departure she was again left to her own devices—and to the thought of her own writing. Every day news came from the rest of Morocco of attacks or massacres in connection with the growing independence movement. But in Tangier, in the International Zone, things went on as they had been.

Now Jane would sit each morning in the room of her house overlooking the sea and try to write in a leatherbound notebook Paul had given her on his return from India. There had been another flurry about the play in the *New York Herald Tribune*. Walter Kerr had written that Jane's remarks to the *Vogue* interviewer were the most cheering he'd heard in a long time. He praised her as the author of "a tantalizingly imperfect play" who did not carp about criticism, but was realistic in her assessment of the demands of the theater.

> The fear of becoming a hack has, I think, kept many a talented man or woman from becoming a useful playwright. The theater is—if there is no other word for it—cruder than some other arts need be, it is cruder in the sense that it is more direct, more concrete, more expansive, more explosive.
> . . . The hack may say what he means and say it flatly. The talented man may say what he means and say it richly. But the talented man who insists upon his right not to say it all, to hug his meaning like a secret close to his breast, to serve his goony friends rather than the gaping audience, is better off out of the theater.
> All hail to Jane Bowles for her happy pronouncement.

Jane agonized and made jokes about the publicity, but it was only a temporary distraction. The question before her at the moment was to begin again, to write another play. But she was in a block worse than any she had had before. She was trying to write as Emmy Moore had tried to write—being direct and honest, trying to toss her feminine tricks out the window. She was trying to rid herself of the passion for secrecy in her work, she for whom secrecy had always been the absolution from guilt. But now, as she wrote, the characters slipped and did not take hold. Further, she kept being overwhelmed by the material, the nature of which seemed impossible to put into language. This material was rooted in a sense of her own duplicity.

In a fragment of a play she began in New York, while she was still revising *In the Summer House*, these words appear:

> She believes that she has a second heart and because she believes this she can accept a lie and protect it. Her wild clinging to this false trust is a result of her not wishing to discover that she has only one heart after all. . . . She protects her lie—She guards her false trust in order not to fall into her single heart—
>
> The single heart is herself—it is suffering—it is God it is nothing— . . .

Now in Tangier, in the notebook Paul had given to her, she wrote the most clear statement she would ever make about her work and her block—and her life:

> The double heart. Not a drama, but both families. The final painful experience. There must be no more pain like this. Death is better than a long murder, the murder of a life—the murder of a life is—
>
> Might bring into sharper focus what is surrounding and seeming to be outside. When the inside is dying, there can be a new joy, a joy so false that one can be shaken with mirth, as one never is, can never be, when the joy is a true joy and the inside is not dying.
>
> A play. There comes a moment when there is no possibility of escape, as if the spirit were a box hitting at the walls of the head. Looking at the ocean is the only relief. I have trained my eyes to look away from the beach where they are going to build the new docks. I cannot look at that part of the beach unless I think of my own end, curtail my own sense of time, as Paul says that we must all do now. I can do it, but it's like: "You too can live with cancer." When I was little I had to imagine that there was some limit to physical pain in order to enjoy the day. I have never yet enjoyed a day, but I have never stopped trying to arrange for happiness. My present plan to get Tetum into my house is as good as any other. It is at a very pleasant stage of development—still like a daydream. Nothing has changed. My father predicted everything when

he said I would procrastinate until I died. I knew then it was true. In America it was terribly painful to know this as a child. Now that I am nearly forty and in North Africa it is still painful.

A play. Is it writing I'm putting off, or was it always something else—a religious sacrifice? The only time I wrote well, when I passed through the inner door, I felt guilt. I must find that again. If I can't, maybe I shall find a way to give it up. I cannot go on this way.

I love Tangier, but like a dying person. When Tetum and Cherifa die I might leave. But we are all three of us the same age, more or less. Tetum older, Cherifa a bit younger. I'd like to buy them meat and fish and oil so that they will stay alive longer. I don't know which one I like best, or how long I can go on this way, at the point of expectation, yet knowing at the same time that it is all hopeless. Does it matter? It is more the coming home to them that I want than it is they themselves. But I do want them to belong to me, which is of course impossible. . . .

If I have broken through my own prison—then at the same time I have necessarily lost whatever was my place of rest—Tangier cracks—

I love it—But it can no longer contain me. . . .

LATE IN JUNE OR EARLY IN JULY, JANE SENT FOR TEMSAMANY. SHE TOLD HIM TO go to Cherifa. "She said to me, 'I'll give you anything you want if you get me Cherifa,' " says Temsamany. "She asked me to go and arrange it so Cherifa would come to the house. Cherifa didn't want to go with Janie because she was a European. Cherifa was thinking what is going to happen to her life after having been with a European. She was a lesbian before, but with Moroccan women. Everyone knew her lover was Zohra, who was married to Glegga. But Cherifa came."

Jane had done in life what she could not do in the writing block: she had forced a change.

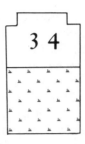

3 4

Late in July, Jane wrote to Katharine and
Natasha of what had been happening to her in the two months since they had
left. The letter is astonishing in its directness of feeling and in its wit, in its
sense of at first being an observer in the Moroccan daily life, but then at last
of being in that life.

Darling Natasha and Katharine,
I never stop thinking about you but too much happened. Please forgive
me if this is not an amusing letter. . . . I think I had better simply write
you a gross factual resumé of what has happened. Then if I have any
sense I shall keep notes. Because what is happening is interesting and
funny in itself. I am a fool to have lost two whole months of it. I have no
memory—only a subconscious memory which I am afraid translates
everything into something else, and so I shall have to take notes. I have a
very pretty leather book for that purpose.

   The day you left I was terribly terribly sad. I still miss you—in the
sense that I keep thinking through it all that you should be here and how
sorry I am that you left before I could truly take you into some of the life
that I love.

   . . . I went down that long street, way down in, and landed in a room
filled with eighteen women—and a dozen or two little babies wearing
knitted capes and hoods. One lady had on a peach satin evening dress
and over it the jacket of a man's business suit. (A Spanish business suit.)
I had been searching for Cherifa—and having been to about three
houses all belonging to her family I finally landed there. I thought I was
in a bordello—the room was very plush—filled with hideous blue and
white chenille cushions made in Manchester England. Cherifa wore a
pale blue sateen skirt down to the ground and a grayish Spanish
sweater—a kind of school sweater but not sporty. She seemed to be
constantly flirting with a woman in a pale blue kaftan (our hostess), and

finally she sat next to her and encircled her waist. C. looked like a child. The woman weighed about 160 pounds and was loaded with rouge and eye makeup. Now I know her. An alcoholic named Fat Zohra and one of two wives. She is married to a kind of criminal whom I believe knifed his own brother over a card game and spent five years in jail. The other wife lives in a different house and does all the child-bearing. Fat Zohra is barren. There was one pale-looking girl (very light green), whom I thought was surely the richest and the most distinguished of the lot. She wore a wonderful embroidered kaftan—a rich spinach green with a leaf design. Her face was rather sour—thin compressed lips and a long mean-looking nose. I was sad while they played the drums and did their lewd belly dances because I thought, my God if you had only stayed a day longer but of course if you had perhaps they wouldn't have asked you in (Cherifa I mean); they are so leery of strangers. In any case at the end of the afternoon, (and part of my sadness was an aching jealousy of the woman in the blue kaftan), Cherifa took me to the doorway and into the blue courtyard where two boring pigeons were squatting and asked me whether or not I was going to live in my house. The drums were still beating and I had sticky cakes in my hand—those I couldn't eat. (I stuffed down as many as I could; I loathe them) but I was really too jealous and also sad because you had left to get down very many. I said I would of course but not before I found a maid. She told me to wait and a minute later came out with the distinguished pale green one; Here's your maid, she said. "A very poor girl."

Anyway a month and a half later she became my maid. I call her sour pickle and she has stolen roughly about one thousand four hundred pesetas from me. I told C. about it who advised me not to keep any money in the house. She is a wonderful maid—an excellent cook and sleeps with me here. I will go on about this later but I cannot remotely begin to get everything into this letter. . . . You will want to know what happened about Paul, E., Xauen.

Paul went to Xauen for one night, having sworn that he would not spend more than one or two nights at the Massilia. He came back disgusted with Xauen and then started a hopeless series of plans—plans for three of us in one house . . . I even planned to live in the bottom half of a policeman's house in Tangier Balia—(the place with the corrugated tin roofs), while Paul and Ahmed lived in the little house in the casbah. I felt Cherifa was a hopeless proposition—and had no particular desire to be in my house unless there was some hope of luring her into it. (Maid or no maid.) In the hotel I did try to work a little. But it is always impossible the first month and the wind and the rain continued. The rooms were very damp and cold and one could scarcely sit down in them. I became very attached to the French family who ran the hotel.

We stayed on and on in an unsettled way. In the beginning E. would come by every day with her loud insensitive battering on the door, and her poor breezy efficient manner and I would try desperately not to smack her. I felt I could not simply drop her and so would make some half-hearted date with her always before lunch so that we could go to Georgette's. E. filled me with such a feeling of revulsion that I almost fell in love with Georgette. I never allowed E. within a foot of my bed from the moment you stepped on the boat. I have never in my life had such an experience. Nor will I quite understand what possessed me. Some devil but not my usual one. Someone else's devil. In any case she started taking trips—the first time she came back, when I heard the rapping I said, "Who?" and she said, "The family"! That was it. From then on I could barely stand to be in the same room with her—and I hated myself for it. All this revulsion and violence was on a far greater scale than the incident deserved but it must have touched something inside me—something in my childhood. I have never been quite such a horror—some of it showed outwardly but thank God only a bit of what I was really feeling.

. . . Paul had typhoid in the hotel and that was a frightening mess for two weeks. We were both about to move into our houses—he had found one on a street called Sidi Bouknadel, (overlooking the sea), and I was coming here. Then he had typhoid and then Tennessee came, for two whole weeks. I moved in here while Paul was still in the hotel. For a while Ahmed and I were living together while Paul lingered on at the hotel—in a weakish state. He is all right now. Ahmed stayed here during the whole month of Ramadan (the month when they eat at night), and I was with him during the last two weeks. Not very interesting except that every night I woke up choking with charcoal smoke, and then he would insist that I eat with him. Liver or steak or whatever the hell it was. At first I minded terribly. Then I began to expect it, and one night he didn't buy really enough for the two of us and I was grieved. Meanwhile in the daytime I was in the hotel preparing special food for Paul to bring his appetite back. There were always four or five of us cooking at once in the long narrow hotel kitchen—the only room that looked out on the sea. Meeting Tennessee for dinner and Frankie (they were at the Rembrandt) was complicated too. Synchronizing took up most of the time. We were all in different places. Ten—and Frank at the Rembrandt.

I have kept out of the David [Herbert] life very successfully except on occasion. I could not possibly manage from here nor do I want to very much, though I love him and would hate never to see him. . . . The ex-marchioness of Bath is here for the moment. . . . I went to a dinner party for her in slacks. A thing that I did not do on purpose. . . .

The night I got *Vogue* in the mail—which quoted the remark you might have since seen about writing for one's five hundred goony friends etc. I went out and got drunk. I was terribly upset about it—though I knew what I had meant I had certainly not made the remark expecting it to be quoted or I would have elaborated. I hate being interviewed and something wrong always does pop out, every time. I meant "intellectual" which Walter Kerr in the *Trib* seems to have understood, but at the time I was worried about my friends—the real supporters of the play and the contributors to whatever chance it had—financial and otherwise. Anyway I was sick at my stomach. I did go to the Parade and did get very drunk. This pitch-black boy seemed charming so I latched on to him as one does occasionally. He was a kind of God-sent antidote to the quotation which I was ashamed of. Paul tried to console me saying that nobody much read *Vogue* and that it would be forgotten. Of course later Walter Kerr devoted a column to it in New York and it appeared in Paris as well where there is no other paper for Americans, so if anyone missed it in New York they have seen it in Paris or Rome. I now think of it as a kind of joke. Every letter I receive has the article (Kerr's article) enclosed—with its title—"Writing Plays for Goons"—they come in from all over Europe and the United States. I keep teasing Paul about the scarcely-read copy of *Vogue* lying on the floor of the beauty parlor. So much for that. . . .

One day before Ramadan and before Paul had typhoid I went to the market and sat in a gloom about Indo-China and the Moroccan situation and every other thing in the world that was a situation outside my own. Soon I cheered up a little. I was in the part where Tetum sits in among the coal and the mules and the chickens. Two little boy musicians came by. I gave them some money and Tetum ordered songs. Soon we had a big crowd around us, one of those Marrakech circles. Everybody stopped working (working?) and we had one half-hour of music, myself and everybody else, in that part of the market—(you know). And people gathered from round about—just like Tiflis. Tetum was in good spirits. She told me that Cherifa had a girlfriend who was fat and white. I recognized fat Zohra—though I shall never know whether or not I put the fat white picture in her mind or not. I might have said "Is she fat and white?" I don't know. Then she asked me if I wouldn't drive her out to Sidi Menarie—one of the sacred groves around here where Sidi Menarie (a saint) is buried. They like to visit as many saints as possible of course because it gives them extra gold stars for heaven. I thought—"Natasha and Katharine will be angry." They told me to stick to Cherifa but then they didn't know about fat Zohra. After saying this in my head I felt free to offer Tetum a trip to the grove without making you angry.

Of course it turned out that she wanted to take not only one but two neighbors and their children. We were to leave at eight thirty A.M., *she insisted*. The next day when I got to Tetum's house on the Marshan with Temsamany (nearly an hour late) Tetum came to the door in a grey bathrobe. I was very surprised. Underneath she was dressed in a long zugdun and under that she wore other things. I can't describe a zugdun but it is quite enough to wear without adding on a bathrobe. But when they wear our night clothes they wear them over or under their own (which are simply the underpeelings or first three layers of their day clothes, like in Tiflis). She yanked me into her house, tickled my palm, shouted to her neighbor (asleep on the other side of a thin curtain) and in general pranced about the room. She dressed me up in a hideous half-Arab half-Spanish cotton dress which came to my ankles and had no shape at all. Just a little round neck. She belted it and said "—now go back to the hotel and show your husband how pretty you look." I said I would some other day; and what about our trip to the saint's tomb? She said yes yes—but she had to go and fetch the other two women who both lived in a different part of the town. I said would they be ready and she said something like, "Bacai—shouay." Which means just nothing. Finally I arranged to come back for her at three. Rather infuriated because I had gotten Temsamany up at the crack. But I was not surprised—nor was he. Tetum took me to her gate. "If you are not here at three," she said in sudden anger, "I shall walk to the grove myself on my own legs." (five hours, roughly) We went back at three and the laundry bags were ready and the children and Tetum.

"We are going to two saints," Tetum said. "First Sidi Menarie and then we'll stop at the other saint's on the way back. He's buried on the edge of town and we've got to take the children to him and cut their throats because they have whooping cough." She poked one of the laundry bundles who showed me a knife. I was getting rather nervous because Paul of course was expecting us back roughly around seven and I know how long those things can take. We drove along the awful road (the one that frightened you) toward the grove—only we went on and on much further out and the road began to bother me a little after a while. You would have hated it. The knife of course served for the symbolic cutting of the children's throat though at first I had thought they were going to draw some blood, if not a great deal. I didn't think they were actually going to kill the children or I wouldn't have taken them on the ride. We reached the sacred grove which is not far from the lighthouse one can see coming into the harbor. Unfortunately they have built some ugly restaurants around and about the lighthouse, and not far from the sacred grove so that sedans are now constantly passing on the highway. The grove itself is very beautiful and if one goes far enough inside it, far away from the road, one does not see the cars passing. We didn't penetrate very far into the grove because being a Christian, (oy!) I can't sit within the vicinity of the saint's tomb. Temsamany spread the tarpaulin on the ground and the endless tea equipment they had brought with them and they were off to the saint's leaving Temsamany and myself behind. He said, "I shall make a fire and then when they come back the water will be boiling." They came back. God knows when. The water was boiling—we had used up a lot of dead olive branches. They sat down and lowered their veils so that they hung under their chins like ugly bibs. They had bought an excellent sponge cake. As usual something sweet. I thought, "Romance here is impossible." Tetum's neighbors were ugly. One in particular—"Like a turtle," Temsamany said. She kept looking down into her lap. Tetum the captain of the group said to the turtle, "Look at the world. Look at the world." "I am looking at the world," the other woman said, but she kept looking down into her lap. They cut up all the sponge cake. I said, "Stop—leave it, we'll never eat it all." Temsamany said, "I'm going to roller skate." He went off and we could see him through the trees. After a while the conversation stopped. Even Tetum was at a loss. There was a little excitement when they spotted the woman who runs the toilets under the grain market—seated not far off—with a group, somewhat larger than ours—but nothing else happened.

I went to look for Temsamany on the highway. He had roller skated out of sight. I felt that all my pursuits here were hopeless. I looked back over my shoulder into the grove. Tetum was swinging upside down from an olive tree, her knees hooked over a branch, and she is, after all, forty-five and veiled and a miser.

There is more to this day but I see now that I have done exactly what I did not want to do. I have gone into great detail about one incident, which is probably of no interest.

But as a result of that day Cherifa and I have been much closer. In fact she spends two or three nights here a week in dungarees and Haymaker shirts. She asked for five thousand pesetas (about one hundred and fifteen dollars), so that she could fill her grain stall to the brim. I have given her so far fifteen hundred pesetas. She sleeps in dungarees and several things underneath. I shall have to write you a whole other letter about this—in fact I waited and waited before writing because foolishly I hoped that I could write you "I have or have not—Cherifa." The awful thing is that I don't even know. I don't know what they do. I don't know how much they feel. Sometimes I think that I am just up against that awful hard-to-get Virgin block. Sometimes I think they just don't know. I—it is difficult to explain. So hard to know what is clever manoeuvering on her part—what is a lack of passion—and what is fear—just plain fear of losing all her marketable value and that I won't

care once I've had her. She is terribly affectionate at times and kissing is
heaven. However I don't know quite how soon or if I should clamp
down. I simply don't know. All the rules for playing the game are given
me by Paul or else Temsamany. Both are men. T. says if you don't get
them the first two times you never will. A frightening thought. But then
he is a man. I told Paul one couldn't buy desire and he said desire can
come but only with habit. And never does it mean what it means to
us—rather less than holding hands supposedly. Everything is very
preliminary and pleasant like the beginning of a love affair between a
virgin and her boyfriend in some automobile. Then when we are finally
in bed she says, "Now sleep." Then comes either "Goodbye" or a little
Arabic blessing which I repeat after her. There we lie like two
logs—one log with open eyes. I take sleeping pill after sleeping pill. Yet
I'm afraid to strike the bargain. "If you do this I will give you all of the
money—if not—" It is very difficult for me. Particularly as her affection
and tenderness seem so terribly real. I'm not even sure that this isn't the
most romantic experience in a sense that I have ever had and it is all so
miraculous compared to what little went on before. I hesitate to rush
it—to be brutal in my own eyes—even if she would understand it
perfectly. I think love and *sex*—that is tenderness and sex beyond
kissing and les caresses—may be forever separate in their minds, so that
one might be going toward something less rather than more than what
one had in the beginning. According to the few people I have spoken
to . . . they have absolutely no aftermath. Lying back relaxing—all that
which is more pleasant than the thing itself if one is in love (and only
then) is nonexistent. Just quickly "O.K.? now we sleep." Or a rush for
six water bowls—to wash the sin away. I'm not even sure I haven't in a
way slept with C. Because I did get "Safi—naasu?" ("O.K. now we
sleep.") But it does not mean always the same thing. I am up too many
trees and cannot write you all obviously. Since I cannot seem to bring
myself to the point of striking a verbal bargain—(cowardice, delicacy,
love?) I don't know—but I simply can't—not yet. I shall have to wait
until I find the situation more impossible than pleasant—until my
nerves are shot and I am screaming with exasperation. It will
come—but I don't believe I can say anything before I feel that way. It
would only sound fake. My hunch is she would go away saying never.
Then eventually come back. At the moment, no matter what, I am so
much happier than I was. She seems to be getting a habit of the house.
Last night she said, "It's strange that I can't eat eggs in my own house
but here I eat them." Later she said that her bed at home was not as
good as mine. Mine by the way is *something*—lumpy with no springs
—just on straw—a thin wool mattress, on straw. At home she sleeps in
a room with her great-aunt. The great-aunt on the floor. Cherifa on the

bed, natch. She's that kind. I find her completely beautiful. A little smaller than myself—but with strong shoulders—strong legs with a good deal of hair on them—at the same time soft soft skin—and twenty-eight years old. Last night we went up on the topmost terrace and looked at all of Tangier. The boats and the stars and the long curved line of lights along the beach. There was a cold wind blowing and Cherifa was shivering. I kissed her just a little. Later downstairs she said the roof was very beautiful, and she wondered whether or not God had seen us. I wonder. I could go on about this, dear Katharine and Natasha, and I will some other time. I wish to Christ you were here. I can talk to Paul and he is interested but not that interested because we are all women. We see each other almost daily—his house is not far from here. And it is a lovely walk. Outside the walls of the Casbah —overlooking the beach and the ocean. Most of my time is taken up with him or Cherifa—or the house and now work. I am beginning again to work. Before she came I was such a nervous wreck I couldn't do anything. Also I was in despair about all the world news and as I told you Paul's illness—everything was a mess. Now I am in a panic about money and though I will write a play—I must write other things too for immediate cash. Not that I don't have any for a while but I must not use it all up before I have completed at least enough of a play for an advance. Thank God I am in a house and not in a hotel. Although the house has cost me a good deal until now it won't henceforth because I've bought most everything I needed except a new bed for upstairs. I shall fill the house with beds—traps for a virgin. I feel happier now that I've written you. All the time I have been saying—I should write about *this* to N. and K. but it seemed impossible—utterly impossible to make a resumé of all that happened before. And as you see, it was impossible. I have not even found it possible to write in this letter why Tetum swinging from an olive tree in her cloak and hood should have precipitated all this—but it did. I think Cherifa got worried about losing me to Tetum—she was so worried she asked me for a kaftan right off. Then started a conversation, a bargaining conversation which resulted in her coming here after Ramadan to spend the night. But I can't go into that now. I always let Fatima (sour pickle) decide what we are to eat. It is all so terribly simple—all in one dish. Either lamb with olives or with raisins, and onions, or chicken with the same or ground meat on skewers or beef or lamb on skewers (you remember how wonderful they taste). Or a fried potato omelet with onions, or boiled noodles with butter or eggs fried in oil and always lots of black bread and wine at five pesetas a quart (excellent). I've had guests once, Tennessee in fact, white beans in oil and with salt pork like the ones I cooked for you. Lots of salad—cucumber, tomato and onion, all chopped up, almost daily.

Fresh figs, bananas, cherries. Whatever fruit is in season. Wonderful bowls of Turkish coffee in the morning which is brought to our bed (when she is here as she happens to be now for a kind of a week-end) or to me alone. And piles of toast soaked in butter. At noon we eat very little. Usually if Cherifa isn't here (she supposedly comes twice a week but that can include two afternoons) I go over to Paul's for lunch —except that he never eats until three thirty—sometimes four. I get up at seven and by then I am so hungry I don't even care but I like seeing him. We eat soup and bread and butter and cheese and tuna fish. For me tuna fish is the main diet. I love this life and I'm terrified of the day when my money runs out. The sex thing aside—it is as if I had dreamed this life before I was born. Perhaps I will work hard to keep it. I cannot keep Cherifa without money, or even myself, after all. Paul told Cherifa that without working I would never have any money so she is constantly sending me up into my little work room. A good thing. Naturally I think of her in terms of a long long time. How one can do this and at the same time fully realize the fact that money is of paramount importance to one's friend and etc. etc., that if there is to be much sleeping it will most likely be against their will or something they will do to please one—I simply don't know. Possibly if it came to that I might lose interest in the sleeping part, possibly why I keep putting off the bargaining—but the money I know is paramount. Yet they are not like we are. Someone behaving in the same way—who was not an Arab I couldn't bear. All this will have to wait for some other letter. Perhaps it is all a bore, if so tell me. But I thought since you have seen her and Tangier that it would interest you. . . .

Please write. I shall worry now about this messy letter.

All my love, always,

J. Bowles.

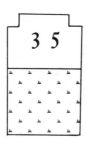

35

THE NAME CHERIFA MEANS A "DESCENDANT OF A saint." Cherifa was born in 1928 (approximately) in Mraier, Fahs, a village near Tangier. Her father was a cherif—he could trace his ancestors back to the prophet Mohammed. And through him Cherifa could bear the title. She was one of five children. Her father died when she was a small child —another of those absent fathers.

When Jane met her in 1948, she had been selling grain in the market for years. She was a woman of great vitality, with a wild humor and sudden terrible rages.

If in Cherifa there was a "wild" woman, there was also a fearful woman. During the years that Jane pursued her—up until the time she came to Jane's house in the medina—Cherifa was, according to Paul, terrified of Jane and her friends. Though she was willing to violate many of the precepts for women, she still had a sense of the necessity for keeping up appearances.

The combination in Cherifa of the wild and the cunning, the fearful and the tough, the powerful and the childlike, was very appealing to Jane. Though Cherifa was illiterate, she had a basic intelligence that was tuned to survival and profit. She was devoted to her family, particularly to her sister and her sister's children, and her scheming was directed toward getting things for them more than herself. She was a very amusing and talented mimic. Like many other Moroccan peasant women of her time, she practiced magic.

I met Cherifa several times in 1977. I had been told stories about her, by Paul, by other Europeans, and by Moroccans. Many of the stories involved her use of poison, her use of magic, her greed for money, and her wild rages. I was told one myth about her that as a child she was stolen from her family and kept prisoner in a cave. One version of this story had her being raped by the woman who abducted her.

It was Temsamany who took me to meet her at her house in the native quarter of Emsallah. I was prepared for a woman of enormous, almost mythical proportions. Instead I met a slight, rather wizened woman, wearing a ski cap, sweater, and jeans. She and Temsamany drank and laughed together. She joked with him about her affairs with women when she was young. She did not speak English—though she apparently understood a good deal more than she said she did—so Temsamany translated for me, when he wasn't caught up in the spirit of the conversation and the food and the drink. Sitting, watching the two of them laughing and joking, understanding nothing but the hints that physical gestures can give, I was made aware of the impenetrability of their world to me. We sat in a windowless room, perhaps seven feet by ten feet, opening into another room with a stairway to a higher floor. Temsamany and I sat on a narrow couch that lined one wall. Opposite us sat Cherifa, her legs drawn up under her in tailor fashion. On the floor was green linoleum. The walls were bare except for three small pictures of Cherifa's sister, who had recently died. Cherifa, who was then not even fifty, seemed much older because of the many lines on her face. Yet there was something ageless in her expression, something watchful and self-protective, and when she got up she moved quickly and with great energy.

When she was asked a direct question about herself—at least if Temsamany did in fact ask her what I asked him to—she responded vaguely and evasively for the most part. Yet now and then she answered directly. This is Temsamany's version of those few direct answers:

"Cherifa was born four kilometers from Tangier. When she was four or five she was always happy. She was exactly like a knife.

"Cherifa knew Paul first. When Jane came, Cherifa was wearing a hat. That was the beginning of love. Cherifa didn't speak English and Jane didn't speak Arabic, but it was heart-to-heart together." And Cherifa added that her years with Jane were her "happiest years."

My next visit with her was six months later, on my return to Morocco. I went with Naima, a young Moroccan woman who acted as a translator. We had great difficulty finding Cherifa's house, as it was dark and there are no numbers in the Emsallah, and I had only my memory to guide me. Finally we showed a woman a picture of Cherifa and the woman took us to Cherifa's door. Cherifa had not been expecting us. She had been drinking.

We sat in the same windowless room as on the previous visit. Three of Cherifa's nieces, gentle, pretty girls, sat quietly with us. In this gathering of women Cherifa took on another presence. She was demanding and insistent and angry, her face harsh, even malevolent. She said she wanted money for answering any of my questions. How much money? Naima asked her naïvely. Enough to spend the rest of her life in comfort and security, she said.

She repeated her statement over and over again. She wanted money and enough money. The anger and rage in her face gave her demands the pressure of a physical force. I am no bargainer, to begin with, and I also knew, from what I had been told by Paul and others, that the few dollars I could offer her would be nothing to her. But there was something about the force and the rage with which she demanded the money that set up an intense resistance in me. (Although I did not know it at the time, Naima later told me she was very frightened by Cherifa. She had never met a woman like her. When Cherifa threatened and cursed, her nieces said to her, "Don't talk that way, it isn't nice." And Cherifa answered, "I'll talk any goddamn way I want to.")

I got up to go. I said that I did not have the kind of money that Cherifa wanted and that I was sorry that she would not speak to me. I picked up my things. Then Cherifa changed her mind. After all, she told Naima, she would say some things to me. But first she told one of her nieces to go out and get an orange drink for everyone. She pulled from her pocket a large wad of bills. Naima later told me that she had never seen a peasant woman with such a large amount of money.

Much of what Cherifa said after this was again evasion. Whether it was deliberate evasion or whether it was only her way of speaking and narrating, or whether she was dealing with what she thought was expected of her, I don't know. Once, she returned again to her first meeting with Jane:

"Janie used to love me because I dressed like a man and sold grain in the market. I was 'strict' like a man. Janie used to say that she loved me because she never saw a girl like me in the whole world."

Cherifa spoke of the house Jane had given her. She said she had threatened Jane that she would leave her if Jane did not give it to her. She spoke of Jane's later illness and of her seizures. She imitated one of Jane's seizures. She spoke of how she took care of Jane and how she herself became ill afterward.

I came away from that visit shaken by the swift change from intense rage to sudden adaptability, by the statements that were alternately naïvely self-condemning and self-praising, by what was hidden behind the hawklike, sometimes smiling, face.

It seemed almost easier to accept the vision of a mythical magic-making Cherifa than to try to account for the inconsistencies and changes. But after all, I told myself, it is not so hard to understand that adaptability. It is what made her survive so well. If she could not get money, enough money, then at least she would rather be "in the book" than not "in the book"—whatever being "in the book" meant to her.

For a Moroccan woman to enter into an arrangement with a European or American woman, as Cherifa did with Jane, was unusual, even unprecedented in Tangier. (Or, if there were precedents, they were kept secret.) There was, of course, a long tradition of young Moroccan men entering into such exchanges with European men. In fact, the exchanges had been celebrated in literature in the works of Pierre Louys and Gide and many others. A young

Moroccan man was not condemned by the society for such a relationship as
long as he made it clear to other Moroccans that he was doing it for money
and for security. It was also understood that within the relationship there
would be a struggle for power, a game called *tla el fouq*, the game of top dog.

But that was between a man and a man. Between a Moroccan woman
and a Western woman there were no rules or even expectations. It is true that
Cherifa had had lesbian relationships with other Moroccan women. But
those relationships, though regarded with contempt by the men, were not
judged finally and severely. She was still a member of society and not
ostracized. But for a Moroccan woman to be with a European woman, that
was something else again. Cherifa was risking a great deal. At least, that is
what she conveyed to Jane.

Jane knew, as she says in the letters, that it was the desire for security
that drove Cherifa, yet Jane wanted there to be more between them. She
wanted there to be passion and love beyond the economic bargain being
struck—so, at least, she seems to be saying to Katharine and Natasha. But
Jane being Jane, no one really knew what she wanted. Most of her European
friends thought it was a great joke, though Jane protested that she loved
Cherifa. A few close friends believed her, but even they could not rid
themselves of the sense that Jane was playing a game.

The writer Christopher Wanklyn arrived in Tangier in 1954 and met
Jane and Cherifa. "I had started to learn Arabic as soon as I arrived. Jane
suggested that I come and listen to her and Cherifa. Cherifa wasn't there all
the time, I remember. She was in and out. When she was at Jane's she would
drink and Jane would say to her, 'Don't drink so much.' Cherifa got drunk
very easily.

"Jane treated Cherifa as a friend but also as her child. Cherifa was very
demanding. Most often Jane would give in to her. To me it was a game that
Jane enjoyed playing. Once I remember Jane and Cherifa and a Moroccan
friend and I were going somewhere. As we were getting into the car, Jane
said, 'Ask Cherifa if she's gone to the bathroom. I'm not talking to her.'"

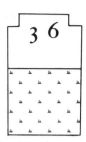

3 6

At the same time that Jane was out in the world, striking her bargain with Cherifa, she was also writing—or trying to write. She was at work on a play.

But the play kept fragmenting. Her work had become the burden on her back. She'd say to others, "I must write, but I can't." Paul urged her to work, but she would say to him, "What's the use of my working? You're so much more successful than I." Then to other people she would say, "Paul's the writer in the family, not I." Still he kept after her. "I know you believe in me," she would say, "but leave me alone." But then, he felt, when he left her alone, she would not work, and again he would be at her about working.

He did not believe that his success was the reason she was not writing. "It would make me feel very badly if I believed it, but I don't believe it. The things that stopped her from writing had nothing to do with me.

"Her own method of work was at fault. The weight of the work was too heavy for her to pull. She didn't know how to get into training to pull such a heavy load all at once. What she wanted to do was more than she could do, more than perhaps anyone could do.

"She never had the sense that she had a body of work behind her. It was as if each new work she began was from scratch. She refused to pay any attention to what had gone on during the writing of *Two Serious Ladies*. That was one thing, that was finished, she said. This had to be entirely different, with a different style, a different subject matter. And besides she felt that *Two Serious Ladies* was ridiculous, a joke, too light. I disagreed with her violently.

"She didn't want to have learned from past experience, because the past experience didn't come up to her expectation. There's a character in 'A Guatemalan Idyll,' a little girl, about whom Jane wrote that she could fall into the same pile of glass over and over again and scream just as hard the last time as the first.

"I used to talk to Jane by the hour about writing. I'd say to her, 'Just for the first page, say she comes in, sees this, does that.' And she'd say, 'No, no, no. That's your way, not my way. I've got to do it my way and my way is more difficult than yours.' 'But why do you want it to be so difficult?' I'd ask her. 'Why don't you make it simpler? Leave the difficulties for the later scenes?'

"No, it all had to be difficult from the first paragraph in order for her to have respect for it. 'Well, it would be easier the other way,' I'd say, and she'd say, 'I know,' but she wasn't interested in making it easier. When she finished a thing, she wanted to be able to say she'd done it all herself. She had to make everything herself. She couldn't use the hammer and the nails that were there. She had to manufacture her own hammer and all the nails. She was a combination of enormous egotism and deep modesty at the same time. You could see that she thought no one was as good as she, but then she'd say, 'I'm not good at all.' If you started to make comparisons with other people, then you could see very quickly where she put herself with respect to them."

DURING THE YEARS THAT JANE PURSUED CHERIFA UNSUCCESSFULLY, FROM 1948 on, Paul had regarded that pursuit as a game. Seeing Jane with the Arab women, he felt that she was "playing house." He saw her as someone who liked to have lots of people around her whom she could control, and he thought that control was an essential part of the game. If he objected to the game, it was because he felt Jane was using it as a distraction, as a substitute for her own writing.

But now that Cherifa and Jane had struck the bargain, Paul saw something much more dangerous in the situation. Cherifa was around a lot of the time, often drinking, often bringing her friends to the house in the Casbah to drink with her. Paul remembers them as tough women like Cherifa herself, one of them the madam of a brothel, the wife of a famous gangster; he did not like to see Jane with these women.

Jane, in turn, had her objections to Ahmed Yacoubi, who was living with Paul in the house on Sidi Bouknadel, outside of the Casbah. She still had not forgiven Yacoubi for the pain he had caused Paul because of the incident at Libby Holman's. To her friends, when she spoke of him, Jane would say, "Yacoubi, ech!" To Paul she only said that she was upset about the way he was spending his own time. She said it wasn't so much Yacoubi himself that she objected to as it was Paul's immersion in Yacoubi's career.

Then one day, late in the summer of 1954, Jane reported to Paul that she had found some packets of *tseuheur* under a pillow and under a mattress in her house. *Tseuheur* is used by Moroccan women for magical effects; it is made of antimony, pubic hair, and menstrual blood, among other things. Jane rather casually told Paul of her discovery. He was alarmed and he told Yacoubi, who became very frightened.

Ahmed had always disliked and distrusted Cherifa. He mocked her because she was a lesbian, but he was also afraid of her. He refused to eat any food that she cooked, and he always did ritual washing and praying after seeing her. He called her "haya," a cobra or a powerful poison. When Paul told Ahmed of the packets, Ahmed said of Cherifa, "She's a witch."

He refused to go to the house in the Casbah anymore, because Cherifa was there. He said that Cherifa was trying to "get" Jane, and that then she would try to "get" Paul. He insisted that Paul not visit Jane in her house, that if Jane wanted to see Paul she must come to visit him at the house in Sidi Bouknadel. And Paul agreed to his demand.

When Paul told Jane what Yacoubi had said, and added that he had agreed not to come to the house in the Casbah anymore, she became very angry. She insisted that Yacoubi was simply trying to come between them, that he wanted to keep Paul away from her. Paul said that Yacoubi was not pretending, that he actually was frightened of Cherifa. Jane told Paul that no one knew who had left the packets of *tseuheur* there, because there were always lots of women around, any one of whom might have done it. She had showed the packets to Cherifa, who had said that they were very bad and that a jealous neighbor must have left them. But Yacoubi was adamant in his demands. And besides, Paul told Jane, he himself was afraid of Cherifa.

Jane did go several times to see Paul in the house on Sidi Bouknadel. But when she came, Ahmed made her feel like a guest. She didn't feel at home there and she reproached Paul for what Ahmed was doing. She began to attempt to salvage what she could in terms of appearances. Finally she said to Paul that she was not jealous of Ahmed—"I don't mind what you do, but I do mind meeting you when you're walking in public beside him." She said she didn't like the idea of Ahmed's name being coupled with Paul's on any occasion—at a party, even at an exhibition. She said it was bad for Paul, and bad for the two of them. Paul listened, and he agreed to do what Jane wanted.

That summer Jane's friends began to notice a great difference in her. Clemence Bonnet, whose family ran the Atlas Hotel, where Jane would later stay, recalls the change: "I had first met her a few days after she came in 1948. She was bigger than life. At the same time she gave one a sense of her delicacy. She had wonderful manners, she never made a faux pas, and she was envied by others. She was unpredictable and she would laugh a lot. Though she was always indecisive herself, she gave good advice to others. But then one moment in her life—in 1954—something changed. Then she was always pushing people away. She'd say, 'I must write, but I can't.' That's all she would say. She was very secretive about her own affairs."

David Herbert remembers that she felt "kicked out" by Yacoubi. "Because of her unhappiness she was drinking more."

That fall Jane came to the house on Sidi Bouknadel less and less. In her depression she may have gone to stay with a friend on the Old Mountain, though no one's memory of this is clear. Beatrix Pendar, who had known Jane in New York in the forties, and was now living in Tangier with her husband, does remember that she would barely eat and would see no visitors, not even Paul. "Jane felt that there was no room for her in Paul's life," says Beatrix. "At the same time, she was in agony about her work."

In 1950, when Jane had been working on "East Side: North Africa" for *Mademoiselle*, she also wrote a fragment of a conversation between an American husband and wife in Morocco. She calls the husband Mr. Copperfield (as if her fiction is the text of her life). It is the most directly autobiographical rendering of a conversation between herself and Paul that she was ever to write. But it was not from memory. As she had written Katharine and Natasha, "I have no memory—only a subconscious memory. . . ." The conversation is a reconstruction out of that subconscious memory, a searching for what went on between herself and Paul in the spaces between the words.

In the fragment the husband and wife are seated at a little iron table in front of a hotel. A washout in the mountains has prevented their continuing on their journey. Mr. Copperfield, anxious because of the extra money the delay will cost them, becomes suddenly irate at the sight of the "jumble of Oriental and Western costume" the villagers are wearing.

"The whole civilization is going to pieces," he said irritably.

"I know it," she replied in a sorrowful tone. Her answers to his ceaseless whining over the piecemeal disintegration of Moslem culture . . . had become increasingly unpredictable today because she felt he was in a very irritable mood and in need of an argument—She automatically agreed with him.

"It's going to pieces so quickly too," she said. Her tone was sepulchral.

He looked at her without any light in his blue eyes. "There are places where the culture has remained untouched," he announced as if for the first time. "If we went into the desert we wouldn't have to face all this.

"Wouldn't you love that?"

He was getting back at her for mourning with him over his remark. He knew perfectly well that she did not want to go to the desert and that she did not believe they could keep running away from the industrial revolution. Without really knowing he was doing it, he provoked the argument he wanted. . . .

The sun was beating down on her chest making it flame: Inside her heart felt colder. It was hard to believe that deep inside her breast there was always a cold current that seemed to run near her heart. It was true. She did change. Sometimes she would run to him with bright eyes.

"Let's go," she would say. "Let's go into the desert." She never said this unless she was drunk. . . .

"Sometimes I feel like going," she said, just to keep challenging. "But it's always when I've had something to drink. When I've had nothing to drink, I'm afraid." She turned and faced him. He saw that she was beginning to look hunted. Like herself he did not want to express more than crankiness. But it was too late. Her eyes expressed pain.

"Do you think I ought to go?" she asked.

"What?"

"Do you think I ought to go?" she asked him.

"Go where?"

"To the desert—to live in an oasis."

She was pronouncing her words slowly. "Maybe that's what I should do, since I'm your wife."

"You must do what you really want to do," he said. He had been trying to teach her this for twelve years.

"What I really want to do—Well if you would be happy in an oasis maybe I would really want to do that?" She said these last words hesitantly and the questioning note in her voice was sincere.

"What?" He shook his head as if slightly caught in a spider web. "What is it?" He was pretending not to have heard, more for his own benefit than for hers. He was not a faker.

"I meant that maybe if you were happy in an oasis I would be too. Wives get pleasure out of making their husbands happy. They really do, quite aside from this being moral."

He did not smile because he was in too much of a bad humor.

"You would go to an oasis," he said, "because you wanted to escape *Western* civilization."

"My friends and I don't feel there is any way of escaping it—and I'm not interested in sitting around and talking about industrialization all of the time."

"What friends?" He liked to make her feel isolated.

"Our friends." She had not seen any of them for years. She turned on him with a certain violence. "I think you come to these countries so that you can complain. I'm tired of hearing the word 'civilization.' It has no meaning or I've forgotten what it meant anyway."

They both secretly rejoiced that they were not going to feel tenderhearted after all.

He did not answer her.

"I think it's uninteresting," she went on, "to sit and watch costumes disappearing one by one. It's uninteresting to mention it."

"They are not costumes," he corrected her. "They're simply the clothes they wear."

Her heart was bitter too. But they could not both reflect the same sorrow. She thought this would seem indelicate. It would happen some day surely that this little argument (which was their marriage melody)* would be silenced and they too would be lost in that world of grief so heavy that those who share it cannot look into each other's eyes. . . .

And now the marriage melody was changing, just as she had always feared it might. She was seized by a grief, but not a grief Paul shared. The grief arose out of her increasing sense of what Paul was to her and her increasing fear that she would lose him.

It was not just that in his complexity he mirrored her being, but in that complexity he sustained her. He was her tie to her writing (her "religious sacrifice"); he was also her tie to her daily life and he kept her from falling out of that daily life. But he was also like Mr. Copperfield, in *Two Serious Ladies*, who stands apart from the two women, yet is the balance point of the work. So Paul, apart from Jane through their separate sexual lives, enabled Jane to maintain her own balance. Even the life with Cherifa had its meaning for her only if Paul was there to know of it, perhaps to laugh at it, even to be angry about it.

In *The Sheltering Sky*, at a time of acute stress for himself, Paul had been able to make use of the marriage material, to use it therapeutically and to use it artistically as a point of departure for the work. But to him *The Sheltering Sky* was fiction, not life. What he had written he felt had no real connection with Jane and himself. Jane, however, had taken it as prophecy. She could make no distinction between the life and the work, in that the one predicted the other.

She had always feared that to use the marriage material directly was to endanger it. Perhaps she remembered how she had mocked Elsie Dinsmore and Elsie's father. Jane did not have to be reminded of the consequences of that. Yet now the course of her own creative development was leading her to write, to feel she had to write, of a man and a woman together—in a way she had not done in *In the Summer House*. But the one life of a man and a woman together that she knew of was that of Paul and herself, and she could not endanger that marriage. With the marriage threatened, in her life as in her work, she was blocked.

LATE THAT FALL PAUL PERSUADED JANE TO GO WITH HIM AND AHMED TO Taprobane, an island off the coast of Ceylon that Paul had purchased in 1952. At the last minute Jane prevailed upon Temsamany to come along with them as company for her. In December 1954 the four set out by boat for Ceylon.

---

*This phrase is crossed out in the notebook.

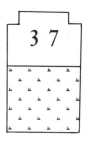

3 7

PAUL HAD FIRST SEEN PICTURES OF TAPROBANE IN 1949 while visiting David Herbert in England, and he was immediately entranced by it. When he saw the island on his first visit to Ceylon in 1950, he decided he wanted to own it. In 1952, when he discovered that it was for sale, he bought it.

Taprobane is a very small island of black basalt rising sixty feet above sea level. It is a short distance out to sea from the mainland and from the town of Weligama. When the tide is low, it can be reached by wading across the shallow water. At other times, a boat is needed to make the crossing.

In 1910 a Count de Mauny-Talvande constructed a large octagonal house on the island. The house has no doors. There is a large central octagonal hall, called the Hall of the Lotus because of the motifs carved upon its pillars and roof. The domed roof, thirty feet high, is supported by eight square pillars and sixteen light columns. Around the Hall of the Lotus is a series of small rooms, open alcoves, whose side walls can be let down on chains. Curtains can be drawn to shut off each alcove from the main hall. The Count de Mauny had surrounded the house with a carefully selected botanical garden.

Paul has described their arrival and Jane's reaction to the island:

When we got to Weligama and she saw the island of Taprobane there in front of her, a mere tuft of rain forest rising out of the sea, she groaned. We waded across and climbed onto the jetty. A newspaper photographer from the *Times of Ceylon* snapped our pictures as we did so. Then we came to the gate, and she looked up the long series of stairways through the unfamiliar vegetation, toward the invisible house. "It's a Poe story," she said, shrugging. "I can see why you'd like it." I had prepared her for the nightly invasion of bats (flying foxes, they call them), but she had not expected so many, she said, or that they would have a three-foot wingspread and such big teeth. Once it was dark you could no longer see them unless you pointed a flashlight out into the trees. This was a regular and compulsive action on the part of us all when we first moved into the house. Each one of us had his own flashlight, which he used going from room to room. There was no electric power on the island, and the house had only one bright oil lamp, which was generally in the center room where the problem was to protect it from the sea wind that always blew through the place. But since the central room's ceiling was thirty feet high, there were many shadows even there. The rest of the rooms were dimly illumined by the wavering flames of inefficient old oil lamps and candles.

Right away Paul began a daily routine that never varied, a discipline that would enable him to finish his new novel, *The Spider's House*. At six each morning he put on a sarong and walked across the island (a very short walk), watched the sun rise from the south point, and then set to work writing.

Jane was planning to work on a new play. She had in mind, she told Paul, a drawing-room comedy with drawing-room conversation, that would not be a drawing-room comedy at all. But she could not work here any more than she had been able to work in Tangier. And in addition she was physically very uncomfortable. It was too hot for her, hotter even than Panama, she said.

At first, Temsamany remembers, Jane had terrible difficulty falling asleep; there was no liquor available. He and she were sleeping in adjacent alcoves. "She'd say to me, 'Timmie, turn on the light' [the one bright oil lamp], and I'd get up and turn on the light. Then I'd lie down. Then she'd say, 'Timmie, turn off the light,' and I'd get up and turn off the light. Then she'd say again, 'Timmie, turn on the light.'

"Then Jane and I went to Colombo and there we found some liquor. Jane would pour some for herself and then for me. We were drinking and dancing like two kids. It was heaven after being in jail. But then we went back to Taprobane."

On Taprobane, Jane began drinking very heavily, a fifth of gin a day, Paul says, though she did not get drunk. On the island she had no escape from not being able to work. Further, she was confined in what was essentially one large room with Paul and Yacoubi and Temsamany. To Tennessee Williams Jane wrote, "The bats hang upside down from the trees at night and in the morning they all fly off at once with a great noise." She signed her letter, "The Spider's Wife."

Suddenly her hair began to fall out in great hanks and she became terrified that she would be bald within a year. She had periods of terrible depression and hysteria that were a nightmare to her. At times she was distracted by visits to neighbors on the mainland, particularly to the local Burghers, who were "staid members of the Dutch Reformed Church, spoke an archaic English, and were touching in the way that only a group about to disappear can be."

But then she returned to the island and the house that was one large room, where Paul was working, finishing *The Spider's House*, and Ahmed Yacoubi was painting, getting ready for an exhibit of his work in Colombo. So she and Temsamany drank.

Ahmed Yacoubi remembers that Jane was very upset on Taprobane and attributes it to the strangeness of the environment. "Jane hated it on Taprobane. It rained every day. There was no electricity and no water. At night there were noises of a devil dance on the mainland. Once we went to the dance and saw a person ill lying on a rattan cot. There were sheets upon him and his face was covered. Then they killed a black chicken at dawn."

Paul realized that Jane was upset, but there was a self-protectiveness in him, which guarded his work, which would not let him see what was happening to her. Further, Jane, or at least a part of her, wanted to protect him—even against herself—wanted him to be able to go on and finish his novel, as she was not able to finish her play.

To Paul in July 1948 she had written how frightened she was when the doctor had told her there was something "organically" wrong with her heart. "I would so much rather have been the neurotic faker than someone really ill. . . ." But now, on Taprobane, she did not know whether she was "organically" ill or not. The only thing that was certain to her was her sense of nightmare.

What she did not know, as every day she consumed large quantities of liquor, a fifth of gin—dangerous enough alone—was that the alcohol combined with the Serpasil, a drug she was taking for high blood pressure, was doubly dangerous. The combination of alcohol and Serpasil brings on severe depression. Also, despite the drug her blood pressure was probably out of control. Medically it would be expected that she was suffering from hypertensive encephalopathy, a brain condition associated with high blood pressure. This was in addition to the effect of the alcohol on her brain. Both are experienced subjectively as a terrible diminution in the capacity to think. But still Jane went on drinking. As she had written to Katharine and Natasha, "I am as indestructible as an armored truck."

Peggy Guggenheim came to visit and in *Confessions of an Art Addict* she offers a memorable account of Taprobane:

Paul Bowles had invited me to Ceylon, where he had bought a little island. It was the southern-most inhabited spot in the Indian Ocean, fantastically beautiful and luxuriant, with every conceivable flower and exotic plant from the east. The house resembled the Taj Mahal, as it was built in octagonal form. We all lived there together in separate rooms divided by curtains, we being Paul, his wife Janie, Ahmed, a young

Arab primitive painter of great talent, and an Arab chauffeur, who seemed rather sad without the Jaguar car, which had been left behind in Tangier, Paul's other home.

In order to get to the island one had to pick up one's skirts and wade through the Indian Ocean. There was no bridge or boat. The waves usually wet one's bottom, even though the distance one walked could be done in one minute and a half. It was terribly unpleasant to go about all day with a wet bottom, but there was no other way. The beauty of the surroundings made up for all the inconveniences, which were many. There was no water on the island and the servants had to carry it over on their heads. This made bathing, apart from sea-bathing, virtually impossible. But there was a raft just below the house and the swimming was superb. The beach opposite was skirted with coconut palms, and there were narrow fishing craft with beautiful Singalese fishermen riding them astride. It was another dream world. . . .

Peggy Guggenheim remembered that Jane was very depressed. "I think she was having a nervous breakdown," she said. "Paul was working and he was occupied with that and with Ahmed. He was very paternal with Ahmed."

Peggy asked Jane to go with her to India, but Jane refused. They did go to Colombo, however, where they spent a week together. They shared a hotel room and, at one point, Jane said to Peggy, "It's like being married again." Peggy, who was only interested in men, thought Jane's statement astonishing. "That's not what I call being married," she said.

The presence of Peggy Guggenheim on the island precipitated a fight between Yacoubi and Temsamany. "We were having lunch together," Temsamany says, "curry and all that. It was very good, but I don't like rice. Yacoubi said to me, 'This woman, she comes to you or me?' Temsamany, who thought Yacoubi was after Peggy for her money, made a snide remark. "Yacoubi said, 'I'm really mad at you.' We both got up and went away from the table. He came at me with his knife. He tried to cut me and he cut me. I took his knife and threw it into the sea, onto the rocks. I said, 'What will I do to you now, after what you have done to me?' He started to cry. Then I started to cry. We embraced each other. He went down to the water and got his knife from the rocks."

After Peggy Guggenheim left for India, Jane came to Paul and said, "I can't bear it here. It's not Ceylon or Taprobane. It's me." She said she couldn't work and she felt isolated and she wanted to go back to Tangier. She asked Temsamany to return with her. "She was both sad and mad," he says.

Jane had been at Taprobane for two months when she left for Colombo to arrange her departure by ship for Morocco. Paul and Ahmed and Temsamany went with her to Colombo, and then Paul and Ahmed returned to Taprobane. To Jane, who was still in Colombo, Paul wrote on February 24,

> Three letters arrived for you this morning. I send them now with this. Ahmed says not to lose his nickel belt and his Rolex wristwatch, and to excuse him for reminding you of them; he thinks you'll need both on the ship. . . . Actually everything will be perfectly all right without him [Temsamany], so I hope you have been able to persuade him to go with you. Ahmed at last has what he wants, which is really nothing more than complete charge of the house, servants and marketing; he went today and astonished everyone in the market with his purchases and haggling; I haven't seen your pills, so I imagine you took them with you. You might drop me a line before sailing, IF you do!

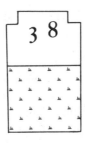

FROM TANGIER IN LATE APRIL OR EARLY MAY, JANE
wrote to Paul:

Dearest Bupple:

It has been very difficult for me to write you. I have covered sheet
after sheet, but now I am less troubled in my head for some reason.
Maybe because I hit bottom, I think. And now I feel that the weight is
lifting. I am not going back in that wild despairing way over my
departure from Ceylon, my missing the end of your novel, the temple of
Madura, that terrible trip back alone (a nightmare to the end because it
was the twin of the other trip I might have made with you). It was better
toward the end, but I hit bottom again in Tangier. The house reeked of
medicine and there was the smell of other people's stale soup in the
velvet *haeti* and even in the blue wall. I put my nose on the wall. It was
cold and I could smell soup. The first day I was in the house the whole
Casbah reeked of some sweet and horrible chemical smell which
doubled its intensity with each new gust of the east wind. The Arabs
were holding their noses, but I didn't know that. On the first day I
thought I alone could smell it, and it was like the madness I had been
living in. A nightmare smell coming up from the port, and a special
punishment for me, for my return. I really felt very bad. I can't even
remember whether or not Cherifa came to me here that first night in the
house. Truly, I can't. On the second day the barber came over to me in
his white and black hood and asked me to go to the Administration
about the smell. He was holding his nose. "There are microbes in the
air. We will all perish," he said. As he spends his entire time in the
mosque and is one of the few old-fashioned Arabs left in the quarter, I
was amused. The smell is gone now. The sewer pipes had broken, and
they were dumping some chemical into the sea while they were
mending them. And from that day on I felt better. And the house smells

better—at least, to me. Fatima said: "Naturally. Filthy Nazarene cooking. Everything made of pork. Pork soup, pork bread, pork coffee, an all-pork house." But now there is kaimon, and charcoal, in the air. I feel so much better. But I am terrified of beginning to work. I don't know what I'll do if that nightmare closes in on me again. I am sorry too that you have to live through it. I won't go near you if it happens again. Actually I cannot allow it to happen again. But I must work. I had some shattering news when I returned . . . *le coup de grâce* . . . my taxes. Clean out of my mind from the first second that I banked the money. Somewhere way back, someone, either you or Audrey [Wood—Jane's agent] warned me not to consider the money all mine, and I was a fool to forget. Having never paid taxes. . . . However, I suppose it is understandable. The slip of paper doesn't say much, not even what percent I am to be taxed. Perhaps all that has gone off to you. In view of the condition I was in this winter and on the boat, I should think this blow would have landed me in the hospital. In fact I went to bed and waited. But I got up again the next day alive and sane still, though my head was pounding with blood-pressure symptoms. I had to get out of that state, obviously, and I did.

. . . I shall wait in Tangier and I shall lead my life as if it would go on. I cannot face the possibility of its not going on. Yet I would be unwilling to stay here if it meant your giving up Temsamany and the car. I consider them essentials, just as there seem to be essentials to my life here without which I might as well be somewhere else. Maybe I'll have to be, but it is best to face that when it comes, in two months or with luck, later. I have pulled every string possible in the sense of looking for a job. I can only do it through friends. There is a terrible depression in Tangier. Hotels empty, the Massilia closing, and ten people waiting for every job. Most people think I am mad, and that I should write or live on you, or both. It is not easy to make friends take my plight seriously. Not easy at all, unless I were to say that I was starving to death, which would be shameful and untrue.

. . . But although Ceylon was wasted and I did not see the temples, or even Kandy, it has changed my life here to a degree that is scarcely believable. I very swiftly reduced expenses to a scale so much lower than anything C. has ever expected of me when I was here that she is at the moment back in the grain market. I think it is a healthy thing for C. to go to the market in any case, even if the funds were more adequate. Ramadan she will be going there a lot.

I am now exhausted. Ramadan would be an ideal time for me to escape to New York, I suppose, but I don't want to, until I know that I can come back here or that I can't, at least, not for a while—that is, if we are both too broke. I'll face that later too. If I go downhill again then I suppose I would go home. Finding it impossible to work again is the only thing I fear . . . the hell with Ramadan. I am rather grateful that C. does want to go to the market during that time. Because she can't come here in a straw hat, but must keep going back to the bottom of Emsallah to change into a veil and white gloves, it will be difficult for her to come regularly.

. . . As for C. and all that, I shouldn't even bother writing you about her since it is such a fluctuating uncertain quantity. At the same time I feel this terrible compulsion to write you about the geographical location of the grain market in relation to Emsallah and my house, and the awful amount of travelling she would have to do if she went often to the market during Ramadan, just to get in and out of her straw hat. I doubt that she will go often once the *aïd* is over, but we'll see. I certainly do not wish to interfere with her work, ever (!). I have no right to, since my own position here is so precarious, and in any case I shouldn't. She has now expressed a desire to travel and to play tennis. Now I do have an upper hand that I never had when I spent more money. What is it? I suppose one must close one's fist, and allow them just the right amount of money to make it worthwhile and not shameful in the eyes of the neighbors. I understand many more of the family problems than I did. It was difficult before to find one's way in the maze. But for "the moment," I know that is over. Will explain when I see you, maybe, if I don't forget to. I'm sure you can't wait. I remember the glazed look you always got when I mentioned her before. I think however if that nonsense began again I would give up. If I could only work now I would feel quite peaceful.

Tangier looks worse. The Socco in the afternoon is mostly filled with old clothes. A veritable flea-market that I'm trying to preserve. I've been booming away at Phyllis about it, because she knows the new Administrator. I also asked her about my hair. She has me down on a list. It says: Janie, Grand Socco, hair. Which is just about it, isn't it? The same obsessions, over and over. When I am sure about my hair I will write. But I think the news is good. You will never know what that nightmare was like. I know you thought it was in my mind. . . .

The baqals announced a three-day close-down in commemoration of the upset here two or three years ago, and they were closed one. *Plus ça change*. Now my left hand is tired. Please write, and especially about your book, and don't above all scold me or put me in a panic. We'll talk about it all when you come, if you ever do. I wonder if instead you'll go to England? Anyway, Bubble, I think the trip has done some good. Much love. I hope you are well and that it got really hot. Write everything.

"Now I do have an upper hand," Jane writes. But if she had the feeling she was in control of the situation with Cherifa, there were others who felt her position was more precarious.

Beatrix Pendar, whom Jane saw frequently that spring, remembers Jane and Cherifa together. "Jane first brought her to me in 1954. She was wonderful-looking, with big earrings and a large hat, a woman with a lot of wit and virility. I told Jane she looked like a man. At that time Cherifa was substantial, hefty, square. Beside her Jane looked very young and fragile, though she too was strong and had an enormous amount of vitality—almost virility—in her makeup.

"To me Cherifa was like a scorpion or snake. She had no sympathy. She was always trying to get money from Jane, pressing her like a lemon. She was insisting on gold teeth for herself and for money for her sister's children. She was the one in the family that provided food for everybody. Jane would bring Cherifa along when she came and would say, 'Cherifa wants to see you.' And I'd say, 'Cherifa doesn't give a damn whether she sees me or not.'"

Although it is difficult for Beatrix Pendar to separate in memory 1954 from 1955, the years she spent so much time with Jane, she feels that "even in fifty-four Jane was already beginning to feel Cherifa's possession. Jane would say to me about Cherifa, 'I'll give her everything I have. I'll leave it to her when I die.' I would say to her, 'You'd better be careful,' and she'd laugh. I never understood Jane's sensibility. She was intent on creating a world that was amusing and that would amuse others. She didn't know how dangerous it was. The unconscious, the primal spirit, is very strong in a woman like Cherifa. I felt Jane had no spiritual imagination. She didn't realize the knife had two sides. Yet she must have known that she was living with a woman who had power over her food. She liked danger, I think."

FROM JAPAN, WHERE HE WAS TRAVELING WITH AHMED YACOUBI IN APRIL, Paul sent a letter to Jane:

> What a shame we (you and I) went no further than Ceylon, because I know for certain you would love Hong Kong and Japan; they both have everything you are always searching for. However, you are satisfied with Tangier, so there's no point in trying to get you to wander elsewhere. . . . What a pity we didn't go in 1938! Not that it's ruined, but it's so far that you'll never want to go. . . . Anyway, I have been finding it all delightful, and only wish you were here, too, to see it with [me]. . . . I hope all is well, with you and the house and Tangier. Hasta luego and much love,
>
> > Bupple
> > Ahmed sends many salutations.

In the early summer Paul and Ahmed returned to Morocco. He had finished *The Spider's House* on Taprobane and now, in Tangier, he set to work trying to finish the Lorca opera. He rented a two-room cabin on the Old Mountain, where he installed a piano, and would go there to work every day.

On his return he had found Jane deeply involved in her life with Cherifa and in her social life. Paul asked her how her play was going—the drawing-room comedy that was not a drawing-room comedy. It was no good, she said, and she was no longer working on it. No good, why? She would not say any more about it. Was she working on something else then? Again he tried to talk to her about her work, to press her to a regular discipline, but she would not be moved. He was convinced that the life with Cherifa and the social life with others were the distractions that stopped her from working, were nothing but a fantasy she was playing out.

Several friends of Jane's, among them Gordon Sager and Beatrix Pendar, began to notice that Paul was becoming much more impatient with Jane's indecisiveness. Of course, Jane had always been indecisive—that had been part of her charm. Her indecision would involve everybody around her in its complexities. "In New York, in the forties," says Beatrix Pendar, "everyone considered Jane's indecisiveness charming. But now she was older and it wasn't so charming anymore."

Christopher Wanklyn remembers her obsessiveness and her indecision of that time: "A lot of her obsessions were about food. She'd go to a restaurant and she couldn't make up her mind what to have. She'd give dinner parties and she'd keep going over and over how many grams per person she would need."

But Jane's compulsiveness was offset for him by other things he gained from her—even from that compulsiveness. "Jane broke down the world into tiny little things that she was obsessive about—symbols, finally. Nothing, no matter how small, was trivial to her. She was marvelously generous and intelligent and she taught her friends the private language of her vision, though a good many people did not understand her.

"She spent a lot of time with people in Tangier who were regarded as strange or odd by the rest of the European community. I wouldn't have found them interesting or amusing, but with Jane—through her—I saw them differently. I had the feeling that Jane would have invented them if they didn't exist. Her life was invention as much as her work. There were no barriers between them. Perhaps that's why she couldn't finish anything. There was no relief for her in daily life.

"Anyplace she went became part of the theater she was continuously creating. She never spoke in abstractions. She always celebrated the actual thing and related it to people and what they were about. The objects she chose in her own home were not for decoration, but for association. She loved the cheaper Moroccan objects. She loved naked lightbulbs. She had one hanging in the house in the Casbah. She liked linoleum. She had a cat she called Berred; that's the word for a cheap kind of enamel teapot.

"She was also a great help to me as a writer. I would show her what I was working on and the things she said to me were invaluable."

But to Paul the combination of her intransigence about her work (that she would not be moved, that she would accept no suggestion) and the indecisiveness, which by its very nature seemed to ask for help, caused him more and more frustration. Caught up in life with her as he was—it finally didn't matter that they had separate daily lives—he felt responsibility for her and for her talent as if she were a child. But after all, she was no child.

Finally he said to her, "I don't want to see you unless you're working."

He said it with the intent of pushing her to work. But it did not have that effect. Jane took his words to mean simply what they said. In despair she went to stay with Beatrix Pendar and her husband. To Beatrix Jane said that Paul didn't care for her anymore, only for her work.

Of course, Paul did not stop seeing her. After a week she moved back into her house in the Casbah. Nothing had changed. They went on as they had before. He was working. She was not working, ostensibly. At least, she was only writing now and then. The antagonism between Ahmed Yacoubi and Cherifa had not abated, but now Paul did on rare occasions come to Jane's house in the Casbah. Mostly, though, Jane went to see him in his new apartment, on the eighth floor of a new building, located in what was then the outskirts of the city.

But around them their world was changing. As part of the independence movement, each day fifty thousand people demonstrated in the city for the return of Mohammed V to the throne. The police used tear gas to prevent riots. Dozens of people were wounded by shrapnel, though there were no deaths reported.

However the independence movement affected Paul personally in his daily life, he had been able to use it as material for his fiction and thereby objectify it. In *The Spider's House* he had written of the struggle between the revolutionary Istiqlal and the traditional Moslem religious world. He had been able to call upon all that he had observed in Morocco over the years and all that he had learned from Ahmed and other Moroccans, and had written an objective, even prophetic account of the opposing forces in the Arab world. At the same time he had used the struggle to examine what Morocco meant to him, why he had come there, and why he had stayed.

For Jane no such objectivity was possible. Christopher Wanklyn remembers that "once, during the early days of the independence movement, Jane came into the house while I was shaving. She was wearing an enormous hat and she said, 'They're on the march again.' Was she frightened? Yes, she was, but in all that Jane did, there was some theater."

There may have been "theater" in Jane's presentation of her fear, but that didn't mean that she wasn't fearful. In *Out in the World*, Jane had written of Agnes Leather that "the climactic atmosphere of the epoch made her feel frantic and in some way enfeebled." What was going on in the city "enfeebled" Jane. The sounds of the tear-gas bombs exploding and the marching added to her already existing sense of powerlessness about her work and her life.

IN NOVEMBER 1955 MOHAMMED V RETURNED TO THE THRONE OF MOROCCO. IT WAS just at this time that Cherifa decided to make a crucial move. She went to Jane and demanded money.

"At the time that Mohammed V returned," Cherifa says, "I said to Jane, either give me money or I'll leave. And Jane said, I'm sorry, that she didn't have any money but that she'd give me the house on Amrah."

Jane then went to Paul and told him that she wanted to give the house to Cherifa. Paul agreed to do what Jane asked. He would sign the house over to her and she in turn would sign it over to Cherifa. The actual transfer would take many weeks because of the legal technicalities, but the papers had already been drawn up by the time Jane left Tangier for a trip to New York in February 1956.

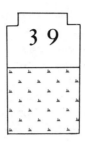

39

IMMEDIATELY AFTER HER ARRIVAL IN NEW YORK, Jane went to Chicago to see her mother and stepfather, who had just had a coronary thrombosis. From Tangier on March 25 Paul wrote to Jane that the transfer of the house had been completed.

In his letter he urged Jane to contact Themistocles Hoetis, an American editor who was interested in republishing *Two Serious Ladies*. Jane had been ignoring the whole matter:

> He says he has the rights, and all he needs is your signature. If I were you I'd give him permission, but put a time limit on his rights. . . . For God's sake, be businesslike about it, even though there is no immediate money involved. My saying that may sound silly, but one can usually advise others better than one can take care of one's own interests, no?

Paul added that he had decided to sell Taprobane.

> I am absolutely against any kind of rental. When I go out I want to sell it and get the cash. Maybe we could all go to Ceylon for the Kandy Perahera. Do you like elephant processions?

From Treetops, where she was staying with Libby Holman, Jane wrote to Paul (the letter has been lost), reproaching him for not saying anything about Julian's heart attack or about the suicide of Mary Jane Shour. Paul answered:

> I don't know why you think I fail to read letters; it certainly isn't true, nor can it be borne out with regard either to my lack of reaction to your news about Julian's coronary thrombosis and Mary Jane Shour's suicide. . . . I don't know what I could have said about Julian's attack. I looked at the letter again to be sure you were no longer going to be in

Chicago by the time my answer reached you; when I realized that you would be at Treetops, I thought it unnecessary to comment. For some reason I thought you already had told me about your cousin's suicide. I still think you did, months ago. Is it possible that you just learned about it for the first time? It seems to me we were discussing it last year, one day at your house in Amrah. If I had thought it was new news I should certainly have remarked about it, but I assumed you had forgotten that you had told me. . . . I have the check for 500 pesetas which I shall give to Cherifa. We saw her briefly last week one day at twilight. She was a combination of the Tailored Woman and the Haidous el Kebir. . . . *

After staying with Libby for several weeks, Jane went to California to visit Oliver Smith. Leonore Gershwin remembers meeting her then: "I met her at a party. She was so shy she stayed in the other room all the time. I went in to talk to her. She was very worried about Paul's business affairs at the time, and I offered to help her with some business matters. Jane asked me to lunch and the whole time she spoke only about Paul. She carried on about his agents not treating him properly."

Jane returned to New York, where Roger Stevens, on the basis of *In the Summer House*, which had been included in Louis Kronenberger's *Best Plays of 1953–54*, gave her an advance to write a new play.

Jane sailed for Tangier in early June on the liner *Queen Frederica*. With her on the voyage were Tennessee Williams, Frankie Merlo, John Goodwin, and Lilla van Saher. Jane confided to them her feelings about Ahmed. Yet though she was angry at Ahmed and still suspected him of trying to break up her marriage with Paul, before sailing she had asked a friend to locate a special kind of parchment that Ahmed liked to use in his work.

Of that crossing Tennessee Williams remembers that "Jane was the only one I associated with. I suspected Frankie Merlo of having an affair with someone else, and he probably was. Jane was soothing. Even if she had her own anxieties, they never obliterated her interest in others or her compassion for them."

On her return to Tangier Jane went to live in the apartment next to Paul's, on the eighth floor of a building called the San Francisco. Whereas earlier Cherifa had maintained her own residence and only visited Jane, now she moved in with her. She was to stay with Jane full-time and to work for her in the house. It is not clear whether Cherifa's agreement to be with Jane full-time was tied to the transfer of the house or whether that decision was

---

*Haidous el Kebir was a generic title Ahmed Yacoubi had given several large drawings. *Haidous* or *abidous* is the word given by the Berbers of the Middle Atlas to their musical and choreographic spectacle. Paul meant that Cherifa was wearing some outlandish combination of European and native clothing. She often did.

made independently. In either case, when she came to the house, Cherifa's pride probably demanded that she should come as a servant. Otherwise, in the eyes of Moroccans, she would be classed as a whore.

Upon her arrival in the household, Cherifa made it clear what her position would be. She would not do any drudgery. She would run the household. She would hire the other servants. As for the house in the Casbah, Cherifa rented it out to a Moroccan family at a substantial profit.

Almost immediately after Cherifa moved in, she and Jane began to argue about household matters. "Cherifa would get very angry," says Paul. "She would leave and come back the next day. She had taken some clothes with her, but not all of them. She had come back to bargain. It was a matter of *tla el fouq*, bettering her position. Cherifa had to command. She made it clear to everyone that she wasn't really a servant. She was in charge of the other servants. She had Aicha working for her half the time. Cherifa woke up in the morning, clapped her hands, and had food brought to her on a tray. She'd send Aicha to the kitchen five or six times. Aicha was running for her more than for Jane."

Jane seemed to take the fighting for granted. Her relationship to Cherifa by this time was oddly maternal. She felt a great responsibility for her. After all, she was the one who had induced Cherifa into the situation. Jane once told Paul that all the other women in her life were mother figures, but of Cherifa she said, "I think of her as my daughter, my child."

Paul had always felt that Jane was very maternal and had told her so. She'd said, "Yes, but I'm not going to have any children, if that's what you mean." She said she was terrified of the idea. Then she'd add, "Why bring more life into this world? The babies who aren't born are luckier."

There was an element of "playing house" in the arrangement between Jane and Cherifa. Even the arguments—the arguments between Jane and Cherifa and between Cherifa and the other servants—were part of this play, a reminder to Jane of the world of women of her mother's family that she had known so well. Cherifa contributed to this "playing" by her talent for mimicry. She was always getting dressed in costumes and doing imitations of Americans or Europeans or other Moroccans that she knew.

Jane may have recognized something else in her need to have Cherifa living with her. In one of the later notebooks for *Out in the World*, Agnes Leather decides to invite Sister McAvoy to come and live with her in a house she will rent in or near town.

This plan, preposterous as Agnes knew it would appear to an outsider, did not seem so to herself. She needed to mark her separation from another living being more desperately than most and so the urgency of her need blinded her to any incongruity in the means she used to justify it. In order that she might live out such a feeling of separation in a truly vivid way, she needed to move into a house with whomever she was going to be separated from. . . .

And, in fact, at just about this time—according to what Jane told David Herbert—the relationship between Cherifa and Jane ceased being a sexual one. "Jane said that she and Cherifa were intimate only during their first year or so together."

The presence of Cherifa in Jane's house was also, in part, an imitation of the presence of Yacoubi in Paul's life. In some way it made her feel that her marriage was less endangered.

There was always a good deal of going back and forth between Jane's household and Paul's. Isabelle Gerofi and her sister-in-law Yvonne Gerofi were invited to tea that fall at Jane's. "Though Jane had invited us," says Isabelle, "she was so busy with what was going on, she hardly spoke to us. She'd talk to Yacoubi. Then she'd sit for a minute. Then she'd ask for Cherifa. She kept walking in and out of the room. Paul too. There was a parrot, Seth, and a cat, Berred. Jane was always worried about food for Berred. Berred would sit on Paul's lap. When he stood up, he said, 'Excuse me, Berred.'"

The enmity between Cherifa and Ahmed had not disappeared, though it was mostly submerged. Cherifa, envious of the attention given to Ahmed, asked Jane for paints and crayons. Jane got them for her and Cherifa did a few drawings, which Jane tried to sell to her European friends.

Ahmed and Temsamany disliked and were suspicious of each other as before. Some years earlier, Ahmed tried to assert the superiority of his position. Temsamany became furious and went into Jane's apartment, saying he was going to quit. He would not be the chauffeur anymore. Jane started crying and then Temsamany started crying. Paul came in and saw them both with their hands over their eyes. To him it was "shameless to be weeping over such a thing." Yet later he knew, or felt he knew, why Jane was crying. "She had established a daily life and any change in it would open up the threatening void."

With all her involvement in her own household and Paul's household and with her dinner parties and her social life, Jane was still trying to write, working on the play for which Roger Stevens had given her an advance. She attempted to arrange her life so that she could work, but she couldn't manage it. When she tried to work at home, the servants kept calling her. So she tried to find a place to work outside of the house. She would go to one friend's house for a day and try it, then go to another's. But it didn't help. She was unable to write continuously and with the kind of discipline Paul had, whether he was working on his music or on the travel articles he was now writing for *The Nation*.

But then Jane did take great pleasure in the distractions of the household, in cooking, in drinking with her friends. While Tennessee Williams was visiting, he and Jane spent every afternoon at the beach. When he was ready to leave, he asked her what she would like as a present. "A leg of lamb," she said. Tennessee bought her the lamb as she'd asked. Then each day until she used it, she would go to the butcher's where her lamb was being stored and say, "I would like to see my leg of lamb, please."

As always, she loved to give advice to her friends and, on occasion, even tried to reform them. Tennessee once appeared in her apartment with a packet of opium that he had bought in the Grand Socco. Jane said, "Let me see it." He gave it to her and she took it into the bathroom and flushed it down the toilet. "Well, that's that," she said when she returned. Paul was horrified. Tennessee only laughed.

At this time Jane even attempted one public act of reform—her only political act. When the new administration in Tangier decided to tear out the great trees, planted by the French in the Grand Socco, Jane took a petition among her friends, trying to get signatures to ask that the trees be left standing. Her petition was, not surprisingly, unsuccessful.

IN AUGUST JANE RECEIVED A LETTER FROM OLIVER SMITH IN WHICH HE TOLD her that John LaTouche had died. Jane and Touche had always had a special feeling for each other, though they had quarreled often enough. His death was a great blow to her. She had the sense of the multiplication of terrible things around her: the death of Mary Jane Shour by suicide (just as her father Louis Shour had died), the illness of Julian Fuhs (and what would happen to Claire if she were left alone?), the death of Touche, and Jane's own fortieth birthday approaching—with no work behind her—or so she felt. Time was passing, to be replaced only by loss. And all the while, she knew she evaded, seeking protection in daily life by evading. Only in the writing was there no protection.

When Jane was younger, despite her anxieties, in her work there had been a unifying force, a sense of dualities, opposing each other, then combining, then opposing—a sense of two becoming one, of one becoming two. But in an untitled play she was now working on, even duality had lost its force. Writing of a marriage between Claude and Rita, and of a love affair between Rita's nephew, Gabriel, and Beryl Jane, Jane seems to be trying to find parallels and contrasts between the love affair and the marriage. But neither the love affair nor the marriage achieves substance. It is as if there are too many opposing forces to sort out.

The love affair is played out in a restaurant bar. It could be the Lobster Bowl of *In the Summer House* with a change of menu. Jane considers one possibility:

Beryl Jane fights against giving in to Gabriel—(a possible scene in act 2 when she goes to bed with him—seems to give in to his ideal, seems to be his—then becomes stronger than ever, having had him?) Then he must give her up even though she now has a physical hold on him.

Then a further possibility presents itself. Rita appears in the bar-restaurant, very depressed. Gabriel goes to comfort her. Now Beryl Jane tries to make him come to the cabin with her: "I'm asking you straight out before it's too late. Don't you desire me?"

Yet Jane, dissatisfied, tries again, another version of what happens between the two lovers:

BERYL JANE: Gabriel . . .
GABRIEL: What?
BERYL JANE: What time are we going to go back to the cabin?
(They stop dancing and stand still in the middle of the floor.)
It's because you've got so much on your mind all the time. You might forget . . . about the cabin. I don't think we should go there so late that we're both tired, you know.
(She stops and looks at him, a very peculiar expression on her face. She seems almost frozen, but she is compelled to go on. Then, in a strange childish voice:)
I get so tired at night. It's because I get up so early. I get so tired.
(He doesn't answer. His eyes are blank.)
Like a kid, isn't it? I'm like a little girl?
(There must be something terrifying about this scene. Her smile is crooked, as if she were being trampled inside.)
Don't you think so?
(An almost repulsive innocence.)
I still play marbles with my brother. And I climb apple trees.

She kept writing scenes over and over again, knowing she was blocked. In one of the pages of her notebook she begins a note to Paul:

Dear Bubble—
I have not been able to get to work yet! isn't it awful—mostly my own lackadaisical mood—and the fact that I have reached a difficult and perhaps impossible point in my play. I feel some *drama* is required—and to generate the heat that drama requires—well, I don't know if I will be able to. . . .

But if Jane could speak lightly of her lackadaisical mood to Paul, the notebooks themselves show her far from lackadaisical, as she is unable to work her way out of the block. In the writing she is being overwhelmed by alternatives that continue to multiply. The script keeps falling to pieces.

Most, if not all, writers at one time or another in their professional lives run into a block. In every writer this block takes a different form. It is so intimately connected with both life and work that it seems to resist all disentanglement. Yet by its very impenetrability it insists maddeningly to the writer that there must be an answer—in the work, in the life, in the life, in the work: Is the block a technical problem, a stylistic problem? Is it a matter of focus? Is the theme insufficiently clear, or too clear? Or is it not a technical problem at all, but something finally rooted in one's own being? Is it a failure of feeling? Are the characters "freaks" and not "real"? Do they have too many ways to go because they have no center? Or have I (the writer) lost my own center? Or is it only this place where I write, or this time that is wrong for me? Or is there something in these scenes, no matter how fragmented, that is hiding what must be said? Can I not see or must I not see what I must say? So the questions come one after the other until even the questions themselves become part of the block.

Finally Jane judged her block to be her own failure; she did not blame outside circumstances. It was what happened to *Out in the World* all over again, but now it was happening in a play, in a medium she always considered "simpler" than fiction.

She tried to appease the demands of her condemned and condemning imagination. "I must write, but I can't write," she said to her friends, holding on to life and its pleasures and its games. But just as she herself had written, "There comes a moment when there is no possibility of escape, as if the spirit were a box hitting at the walls of the head."

IN NOVEMBER PAUL LEFT FOR ENGLAND WITH AHMED, EN ROUTE TO CEYLON, where he planned to sell Taprobane. Jane chose to stay in Tangier. On February 1, 1957, she wrote to Paul:

> I have been trying to write you for days but unsuccessfully. The fact is that I have been having the same trouble with my work that I had in Ceylon and before I left for Ceylon. I don't know whether to keep writing through the block or to get out of here now or in a month or two before I come to the end of my money. I know I can get passage back from somebody but there is always the question of leaving a little behind for Cherifa. I hope that I will come out of this all right. The fight against depression again is serious since failure follows me into my dreams, and I have been awake for many nights, as I was in Ceylon. But there is no heat thank God. If I left I would borrow from Libby and pay her back out of my months' checks there. I would give the money to Cherifa that I would be saving by living at Libby's. I don't really want to do this

though it might be the nicest thing I can do. C. doesn't want me to either and she is very happy to have the house and says that I must not worry. She even said that with the rent she gets for the house she can live with her family and contribute her bag of flour a month and so you have done that much for my peace of mind, at least. Naturally she has gotten used to more than a bag of flour a month and I wonder if I shouldn't whip myself out of here no matter how much I dread doing it. The longer I wait the less I will have to give her unless I asked Libby for an outright gift of a couple of hundred dollars. Actually before I left Libby said to me, that I shouldn't worry about money and that if I needed any to let her know. Then there are the little cats whom I adore, and C. herself whom I can't bear to leave, and you too who will be returning and I would not like to miss you though I am sure that you would probably not want to see me if I don't have a play done, and it would be a sad encounter to say the least. Actually I cannot picture any of this happening. I cannot picture leaving, nor can I picture your return and my having nothing to show you after all this time. Maybe none of this will happen. I hate to think of it and I get into a kind of terrible panic when I do. Still, if for *some reason* I did have to leave I would naturally pay the rent here until June or whenever the contract is up and lock the door. But I would not leave the cats, naturally. They would have to come along. Ira read my fortune and said that someone's death was going to oblige me to travel across water, and that as a result of this death I would inherit a little money. I don't believe it of course but it did occur to me that I should tell you that in case of any emergency or even if I suddenly became a lunatic and felt a compulsion to go just because I didn't want to, that I would put all of your things into the apartment here and lock the door leaving the key with Christopher [Wanklyn] or Ira. The person who was going to die was a woman and I can't think of anyone but my mother who might leave me a few hundred dollars, but I do not really believe in cards.

I filled a notebook with my notes and suggestions for my play and even started writing the dialogue. And now today for the first time in a week, I had a flash of an idea and so I will see if [it] does not help. It is impossible to write a play in the dark without having some idea of where one is going. I did get an idea but it was so definite that I couldn't go against it either. For nearly a week I have had dreams of not being able to go on with it and then my head got into such a bad knot that I took a lot of Equanil and knocked off work. Today my head feels better—less knotted. I wrote you a long beginning of a letter but it was so confusing I thought I would tear it up, and I did tear it up, but at least I had been writing *something*. And then after I had written you the first really sad page of the letter I tore up, I made some lentils and I got an idea about cutting out one of the characters in my play. In fact two of them. One was a girl and the other a dead man. Like Gertrude's father in *"Summer House,"* who became such a bore to all of us. I think the girl was cut out because of a dream I had, about her and her girl friend. I dreamed they hated me and that they could never be in the play. I must write it. But am I fooling myself by insisting that I will? And by fooling myself robbing C. of the last money that I can call my own? I am convinced that I should not think in these terms. Well I will go on trying really hard for another month and see how I feel after that. I am sorry to bore you with this but I must at least mention my work or you will think that I am getting along beautifully and that makes me even more nervous. I will let you know if and when I get over this hump. I gather you are working as usual and I suppose Ahmed is too. . . .

On February 15, 1957, Jane's story "A Stick of Green Candy" was published in *Vogue*. It had been lying around in a closet for years, since 1949, when she had written it. When Frankie Merlo was in Tangier in the summer of 1956, Jane had let him read the story and he had taken it back to the United States and sent it to *Vogue*. Jane did not even mention the publication in her letters to Paul. After all, it was "old" work. What mattered to her at the moment was the play she could not write.

On February 24, two days after her fortieth birthday, she wrote again to Paul:

Dear Paul:

I have just had my fortieth birthday the day before yesterday, and that is always, however long one has prepared for it, a shock. The day was not as bad as the day after it, or the following day, which was even worse. Something coming is not at all like something which has come. It makes trying to work that much more difficult (or could it possibly be more difficult?), because the full horror of having no serious work behind me at this age (or successful work, in any sense) is now like an official fact rather than something in my imagination, something to be feared, but not yet realized. Well, I don't suppose you can understand this, since when you reached forty you had already quite enough stacked up behind you.

I realized about your birthday, but I don't think I mentioned it in my letters, or thought of it at the time I wrote you. Anyway, it is over. I did not tell anyone mine except Cherifa, and I celebrated with her on the night of the twenty-first because on the twenty-second an old man from Xauen, an uncle or grandfather, was expected at her house. . . . I am still determined to write my play, and have no intention of going back to New York until my money runs out. I have somehow, thus far, staved off the terrible depression that was coming over me when I wrote you last—staved it off perhaps simply because I cannot ever again be the way I was in Ceylon. I mean that I will do everything in my power to pretend that I am not, even if I am. It was too horrible. And so I knocked off work entirely for a week and then went back to trying to write the play. My mind is not a total blank, which is more than I can say of the way it was before. Whether it will get beyond that, I don't know. I am sure you will come out all right because you always have.

Seth said his first word yesterday. "Dubz." He said it clearly three times, and again this morning. I daresay it is because Seth sits in the bathroom a lot and I am always lunging in after Dubz [a cat] to stop him from using the tub, and of course calling out: "Dubz!" at the top of my lungs. I hope that he will keep saying it so you will hear him when you get back. . . .

Radiant sunshine, balmy weather and scarcely any rain. The beaches are crowded. . . . Apparently there is more drink then ever in their world, only not as openly. There seems to be not much fear about. Ramadan is in less than forty days, and I dread it as usual. Seth is so terribly noisy that I have to put him out on the terrace in order to do any work. I am furious that you are living in Colombo and have an oscillating standing fan. I would have loved that. If you like Weligama so much why don't you keep it . . . or aren't you prepared to live alone there? Actually I don't think you would like that for long. But maybe you won't be able to sell it. Your life in Colombo doesn't sound too expensive thank God so I imagine you'll stay there until you sell the house. Seth is driving me mad.

Dubz just fell into the toilet up to his waist and I had to help him to dry off . . . Cherifa bought Seth a length of strong wire which she has fastened around his cup and the bars of his cage so that he can no longer dump his seeds on the floor. It is to be a great saving in money and I am glad. He just said "Dubz" again. I try to say it over and over again to him so that he won't forget.

From Colombo Paul answered Jane:

I should have written you in time to wish you a happy birthday, but perhaps it's just as well I didn't, if you got into such a state about the fact that it was number forty. Do go on with the play so I can see it, forty or fifty notwithstanding.

In mid-March Jane received a letter from her agent, Audrey Wood:

I do think, Jane, it would be politic if you were to write Roger Stevens some report of your work on the play. After all, he was good enough to put up money for you, sight unseen. A great deal of time has already gone by. . . .

On April 6 Paul wrote to Jane from Nairobi:

. . . I haven't started a new book, but at least I sold the pieces I wrote on the trip out—the *Holiday* piece on Tangier and the short story, which *Harper's Bazaar* took. So I don't feel quite as useless as I did. . . . I think you should conquer your embarrassment if you really want Seth to say: "I am Seth." Or you could go in for something more recondite like: "My name is Seth." Which sounds like an autobiographical novel's title . . . something awful by Robert Graves on Biblical times. . . . I send much love and hope to see you in another six weeks.

PART THREE

1958 - 1973

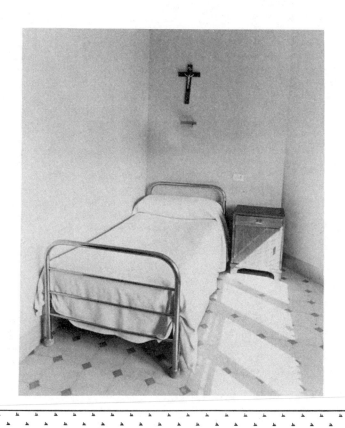

Overleaf: *Jane's room, Clinic de Los Angeles, Malaga.*
PHOTO BY JAMES KALETT

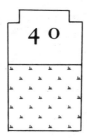

4 0

IT WAS APRIL 4, 1957, DURING THE MONTH OF Ramadan. Jane was "doing Ramadan," fasting as the Moslems do during the daylight hours. In the course of the afternoon there was apparently some kind of argument about food between Cherifa and Jane or between Cherifa and the other servants. At the end of the argument some food was thrown out in a rage.

Around five o'clock, angry and upset, Jane went to Gordon Sager's apartment house, rapidly climbed the three flights to his flat and asked him for a drink. He gave her a cognac. She drank it and then drank several more. She left Gordon's and hurried through the few blocks back to her own apartment building. She did not take the elevator. She ran up the eight flights, dragging her stiff leg. Soon after her return she began to vomit and kept vomiting all night long. She was barely able to speak and had difficulty seeing.

Christopher Wanklyn remembers: "Paul was coming back from Ceylon. I was living in his apartment at the San Francisco. The morning of the fifth I got a call from Cherifa to come over. There was Jane lying down, with a slice of lemon tied with a cloth onto her forehead. She had great difficulty speaking. She said, 'What is worse than baisar?' [Baisar is a very thick pea soup that Jane detested.] Jane was always talking in riddles anyhow. It occurred to me that she was talking about majoun and that she and Cherifa might have eaten it the night before. Jane was saying that her field of vision wasn't clear. 'What's happened to me?' she asked. I called a French doctor. Then I called Gordon. The French doctor came and said Jane had had a little stroke. Cherifa was able to say very little about what had happened. I thought she was probably ashamed of having given Jane the majoun. Cherifa hadn't been drinking because of Ramadan, so I thought that was why she had taken the majoun and Janie then must have shared it with her."

Gordon Sager, who admits that his memory of those days is not very clear, does remember that Christopher called him to tell him of the attack.

"Jane had partial paralysis of her limbs, partial blindness, and some difficulty with speaking. But she did say to me, 'I guess I got loonier than I intended.'

"She asked me to write to Libby. Whether she asked me to cable to Paul, I don't know, but I did anyhow."

Cherifa tells the story of that night, with Temsamany translating: "The night of the stroke Jane was drinking. Cherifa was waiting for her. Jane was drinking without eating. That night Jane couldn't see. When Jane came she was throwing up. Jane had a telephone. Paul was in India. Cherifa called Christopher Wanklyn and he came. They put ice on the top of her head. Cherifa was scared. Jane didn't know what she was doing. The doctor gave her sleeping pills and told her to relax. Cherifa was with her day and night. After that Cherifa was sick with her kidneys."

Cherifa tells the story again, with Naima translating: "The night of the stroke, it was Ramadan, Jane was drinking at Gordon's. She ran up the stairs. She had liquor and kif. She went into the bathroom and poured cold water on her face and on her eyes. She couldn't see. She said because of the liquor and the kif. Then she couldn't speak. Cherifa ran for Christopher Wanklyn. He called three doctors. They put ice on Jane's head."

In Jane's papers at the Humanities Research Center there is a slip of paper signed by a Dr. R. Spriet, a diagnosis made apparently several days after the "attack": "Cerebral spasm with confusion and mental torpor for several days, but no sign of cerebral hemorrhage or of cerebral thrombosis."

After Jane became ill the conviction grew among many Europeans and Moroccans in Tangier that Cherifa had poisoned her. The stroke, they believed, was brought on by slow poisoning, part of an attempt on Cherifa's part to gain control over Jane. The story persists in several variations, the most common being that Jane told Cherifa, "When I die, I'll leave you the house," and so Cherifa poisoned Jane.

Truman Capote, writing of Jane as "that genius imp, that laughing, hilarious, tortured elf," gives another variation on the poisoning theme: "The late Mrs. Bowles lived in an infinitesimal Casbah house . . . with her Moorish lover, the famous Cherifa, a rough old peasant woman . . . an abrasive personality only a genius as witty and dedicated to extreme oddity as Mrs. Bowles could have abided. ('But,' said Jane with a cherubic laugh, 'I do love Cherifa. Cherifa doesn't love me. How could she? A writer? A crippled Jewish girl? . . . All she thinks about is money. My money. What little there is. And the house. And how to get the house. She tries very seriously to poison me at least every six months. And don't imagine I'm being paranoid. It's quite true.')"

There are others who see the poisoning story as myth. Edouard Roditi, who had known Jane in New York in the thirties and forties and then in

Tangier in the sixties, says, "That Cherifa poisoned Jane is part of the myth of the Tangier expatriate group. The fact is that Moroccans go in for magic, but I don't think this magic works."

Gordon Sager says, "There's much talk in Morocco about poisons that attack the central nervous system. I think Cherifa may very well have engaged in magic, but I think that is probably as far as she went. Cherifa, while illiterate, was no fool. She knew Jane was not really well. I thought she was very good with Jane when she was ill."

Maurice Grosser, who painted one portrait of Jane in the thirties and another in the forties and who now lives in Tangier, says, "There were all sorts of stories about Cherifa poisoning Jane. Datura poisoning is not uncommon there. It's thought of as a way of making someone helpless so you can control them. But it's very hard to know what happened to Jane. Tangier gossip is enormous and elaborate and fantastic."

As for Temsamany, he said, "I think Cherifa was afraid that Jane would someday say, 'Our dream is gone' and would leave her. To have her all the time in her hands was what she wanted. I swear Cherifa was giving her stuff to make her in love with her. There is a potion to give more love. Cherifa bought it from other people. I don't think Jane knew Cherifa was doing that. At the beginning Jane's love was a normal love, but later she was even more in love."

THE FUNCTION OF MAGIC IN THE MOROCCAN CULTURE IS A COMPLEX ONE AND difficult for an outsider even to begin to understand. Although the present Moroccan government frowns upon all forms of magic, it is still possible to buy potions for spells on the streets of Tangier. Moroccan folklore is filled with references to magic and spells. The anthropologist Edward Wester- marck in his *Ritual and Belief in Morocco* devotes hundreds of pages to various magical practices and spells and ways to avoid them. He shows that women in particular are feared as practitioners of magic. That "woman is an unclean being" is a basic part of the folklore; uncleanliness is defined as a "magic force productive of evil." And old women are particularly dangerous.

Given the ambience of the world of Tangier, it is not surprising that many Moroccans and Europeans would conclude that Cherifa had poisoned Jane. To believe that she poisoned Jane to gain power over her was a way of making sense of a relationship no one had been able to comprehend and also a way of making sense of Jane having a stroke at forty. And then of course there was Cherifa's appearance and personality, which would make this assumption reasonable: that she was so powerful in her effect, that she was so wild and violent in her rages, that she was a peasant woman who came from a world that believed in spells and potions.

But whether Cherifa used magic or did not, whether she used poison or did not, certain facts about Jane have to be taken into account that have nothing to do with Cherifa. Jane had had inordinately high blood pressure for years. She had a hereditary predisposition to vascular illness. Her father had died of hypertension when he was forty-five. Her maternal grandmother had died of a cerebral hemorrhage in her early sixties. Jane had been taking Sparine to reduce her blood pressure, but she had also been drinking a great deal. Sparine and alcohol in combination are deadly. Sparine makes the effect of the alcohol more intense. The alcohol makes the effect of the Sparine more intense; it can cause the Sparine to reduce the blood pressure too quickly. Too rapid a drop in blood pressure can cause a transient episode of ischemia, a spasm in a blood vessel, which may lead to a stroke in someone predisposed to vascular illness.

The poisoning by Cherifa has come to be another part of the myth that surrounds Jane. But given Jane's physical and emotional condition at the time of the stroke—blocked in her work, anxious about the marriage, fearful because of Paul's absence, haunted by omens: the suicide of Mary Jane Shour, the death of John LaTouche, her father's death in his forties—she needed no other poisoner than herself. Her own spirit was "a box hitting at the walls of the head."

Paul did not receive Gordon's cable until he got off the boat in Las Palmas. By the time he got back to Tangier it was six weeks after Jane's stroke. Jane had spent the time at the home of Patricia Ellis, a friend who lived on the Old Mountain. Jane seemed better than Paul had feared, though her eyesight was still affected and she also showed an odd aphasia, getting certain words wrong, which everyone thought quite amusing. She would mix up genders, for example, saying *he* instead of *she*, and give the antonym of a word instead of the word she intended: e.g., *fat* instead of *thin*, *high* instead of *low*.

Remembering what Ahmed Yacoubi had said of Cherifa, to say nothing of his own suspicions of her, Paul tried to go over with Jane what had happened that night. He asked her whether she had said, "What is worse than baisar?" Knowing her as he did, he felt sure she was saying that she had taken some majoun that had been given to her by Cherifa. He had heard that majoun can cause the aorta to burst, and he considered that the majoun might have caused Jane's stroke. But Jane denied that she had said anything about baisar. She only said, "Well, I may have had a puff of kif."

Gordon Sager had notified Libby Holman after Jane's stroke. On May 2 Libby wrote to Jane:

> I cabled you yesterday as soon as I got Gordon's letter. I am so worried about you because I know how hard it is for you to have anything wrong with you, more so than any of us because you get so wildly imaginative about everything.

I want you to call on me for any help you need and don't hesitate to
have Gordon cable me collect for anything. . . .

On June 1 Libby sent another letter:

The typed letter I received from you yesterday was absolutely
miraculous. You will kill me for this, but it was better than some of your
letters before you were ill. . . .
    Oliver called Saturday night and had heard from Truman who had a
letter from Cecil who had heard from David Herbert about your
illness—so I told him the truth and he promised not to get hysterical nor
to notify your mother—He seemed terribly concerned about you but
was calm and said he would write you a letter at once. . . .
    Janey, the financial end will be taken care of to your satisfaction. $175
a month as you asked. I will ask Polikoff [Libby's lawyer] to send you a
check monthly if that is the way you want it. I suppose you already have
the $500 I sent last week. So I shall send the monthly amount beginning
July 1. If that is not enough, please don't hesitate to let me know. . . .

Katharine Hamill and Oliver Smith each volunteered to send Jane
twenty-five dollars monthly to help her with her medical expenses. The
attack had been diagnosed differently by a series of Tangier doctors as a
"spasme cérébral," a "small bleed," a "microlesion," and a "gros accident
cérébral." By the beginning of July it had become clear that Jane was
suffering from a permanent loss of vision; she had a homonymous hemian-
opsia (or hemianopia) of the right side. What this meant was that from either
eye she could not see the right side of the visual field.
    On July 11 Paul wrote to Peggy Glanville-Hicks that he and Jane were
getting ready to go to London to see a neurologist:

She has no desire to go, nor have I, not really, but it seems necessary,
since the cerebral spasm has left her unable to see clearly enough to read
or write, and that of course has to be corrected if possible. She is
obsessively terrified that her mother will hear of it and drop dead of the
shock, so please don't discuss it with anyone who doesn't already know
about it. Such things have a way of getting around in the most
mysterious fashion. She had told no one of it at all, and suddenly letters
began arriving from unlikely people asking me for details, because they
had heard from Themistocles Hoetis who had heard from Gore Vidal
who had heard from Truman Capote who had heard from Cecil Beaton
who had heard from David Herbert that Jane had had a stroke and that I
refused to allow her to have a doctor because I wanted her to die
immediately. Too many gossip vultures hovering overhead. Anyway,

she is much improved and far from dead, and we are planning to go to London later in the month, just for a few days. Ahmed is in Fez visiting his family. . . .

Jane seemed better, but on July 21 she suffered two epileptiform fits, which further impeded her vision, and which threw her into a state of terror. Soon afterward she and Paul went to England to consult a neurologist. A woman in Tangier had persuaded Jane to first see some Scientologists in London. "We went to this ghastly apartment," Paul remembers. "A man and woman, an unbelievable couple, were the practitioners. The man took Jane into a corner. He was saying something to her like, 'Pick it up, put it down. Pick it up, put it down.' Jane looked terribly confused. He finally said, 'We're waiting for her to break.'"

Paul took Jane to the Radcliffe Infirmary at Oxford. According to the records of their neurological department, as reviewed by Consultant Neurosurgeon C. B. T. Adams, FRCS, Jane was admitted August 6 with very high blood pressure. To the attending physician she detailed the events of the day of the stroke: the fasting, the drinking of alcohol, the taking of hashish, and then the vomiting and becoming unconscious. When she came around, she said she saw things "crooked" and she could not talk. Though the ability to talk gradually came back, she continued to have difficulty in finding the right words to say what she meant. Her convulsive attacks had begun two weeks before she was admitted.

From what she told him, the attending physician recorded that she was "highly strung," that she had been of a nervous disposition since childhood; that she was afraid of close places, hated the sea, landscapes, and forces of nature; and that she had long had unusual compulsions that made her go into dangerous situations. He added that she had difficulty making up her mind, even about a menu. For the last seven years she had had terrible pressures within and on her head—as if there were steel bands about it. (This symptom is regarded medically as one associated with depression, unconnected to high blood pressure.)

She reported that she had had a series of severe depressions, before and after she had gone to Ceylon, where she had "wept most of the time." Just before the stroke she had had another serious depression. She was, at the time she was admitted, terrified of being alone. She could not rid her mind of obsessive thoughts.

The attending physician suggested the possibility of surgery to remedy the homonymous hemianopia, but that suggestion made her even more anxious.

Jane was in the infirmary only twenty-four hours when she begged Paul to take her out. After an additional day at the clinic, Paul managed to have her moved to Saint Mary's Hospital in London, where she was put under the supervision of Dr. Harold Edwards, FRCP. There she had a complete set of neurological tests to determine the size and location of her brain lesion. She was also seen by the noted eye specialist P. D. Trevor-Roper.

The Saint Mary's Hospital records from 1957 have been destroyed, but Paul remembers that the doctors said that her lesion was not operable, and that the damage to her vision was irreversible. It was suggested to her that she could compensate for her visual difficulty by using her remaining field of vision. He remembers too that one doctor said to her, "You're not coping, my dear Mrs. Bowles. Go back to your pots and pans and try to cope." In private conversation another doctor said to Paul that Jane was so "high-strung," it was unlikely she could learn to adapt to her visual impairment.

Dr. Edwards, now dean of Saint Mary's Hospital Medical School (University of London), does not remember Jane as a patient. However, he is able to make some general statements about what her condition must have been. Commenting on her speech difficulty—her dysphasia (or aphasia) —and the impairment of the functioning of her right hand, he says, "She had a dysphasia associated with a sudden happening in the left cerebral hemisphere, and apparently also a right hemiplegia. I would have expected that her speech would have recovered less readily than her limbs.

"Her visual condition would have made reading very difficult. When we read, we're always scanning several words in front of our gaze, involuntarily. With the hemianopia, her reading would have been reduced to a childlike way of grasping words."

Since it was her brain that was affected, what was involved was not simply seeing, but the whole question of imagining and understanding. "If you were to devise how best to undermine the mind of a writer," says Dr. Edwards, "you couldn't think of a more effective means than this."

Upon her release from the hospital Paul and Jane prepared to return to Tangier by ship. But then she developed a new symptom—intense palpitations of the heart, which came on as she was walking in the street. Paul suggested that she readmit herself to the hospital, but she refused and they boarded the ship for Tangier.

From Tangier, Paul wrote to Virgil Thomson on August 31:

On the ship the palpitations became alarming, and led to a further epileptiform seizure, with resulting mental confusion, amnesia and complete hysteria. I tried to get her into the hospital in Gibraltar, which she resisted violently after accepting and refusing it several times, and we came here.

Virgil had sent a check from the American Institute of Arts and Letters to help pay for Jane's medical treatment. Paul accepted the money gratefully, saying that Jane was preparing to return to London:

The simple fact of the matter now is that Jane has lost her nerve and is at the brink of a mental breakdown. When things get to that point there is no end visible; a sort of spastic stubbornness puts her into direct opposition to any therapy a doctor can offer. She is convinced no one can diagnose her illness and that suicide is the only solution. Her main obsession at the moment is to return to London immediately, and see either the neurologist who just released her or some other.

. . . it looks as though she would be going back and quite soon. This time they must take into account the psychic side of the question; if they had done that two weeks ago when she was still in the hospital all this wouldn't have been necessary, it seems to me. During the ten days she was in St. Mary's she had all the essential tests: X-ray of brain and heart, various blood tests, electroencephalogram and arteriogram, and the possibility of brain tumor was removed, as well as the necessity (that is, the feasibility) of surgery. But the facet of her emotional reactions to the illness was left untouched, and that is at least fifty percent of her present trouble; that much should be apparent even to a neurologist. At the moment she has a general practitioner and a psychiatrist working on her every day, and that plus massive sedation is keeping her going—I mean conscious and able to talk coherently.

To Peggy Glanville-Hicks on September 3 Paul wrote:

It is much worse than it was last month when we set out. Now it is purely a question of her mind. Evidently the trauma caused by the loss of vision and the actual inability to identify objects and ideas (an inability of which she has always been all too conscious even while she has been suffering from it) has been too much for her and she has retreated into a world of fantasy for the time being. . . . However she is far from docile and it is very difficult to do anything with her particularly inasmuch as her conversation is as lucid as she chooses to make it at any given moment, depending upon the effect she is intent upon making. . . . I have never seen anyone in a state like Jane's, able to talk clearly and yet capable of absolutely no contact with anyone. All the words as if spoken to herself. She won't take a step unless one propels her by the arm, and then the motion is somnambulistic and uncertain . . . she mutters to herself from time to time: "Complete isolation, complete isolation." And that seems to be what it is. . . .

One of Jane's doctors in Tangier arranged for her to see a psychiatrist who had written some monographs on black magic. The psychiatrist came to see her each day and she seemed to be calmer with him, but within two or three hours after he had left, she was again in a state of terror. On September 10 Paul wrote to Virgil Thomson:

> To communicate at all with her one was obliged to discuss her return to London; she could not hear anything else, literally. Her burning desire was to go back to Dr. Edwards of London. So I wired him that, and he wired back that he advised immediate rehospitalization. When I relayed the news to her, however, she made an abrupt shift and decided she preferred Radcliffe Infirmary at Oxford. I wired there and they accepted her. When she heard this news, once again she rejected the prospect, claiming that they would torture her there. At the same time she was increasing her intake of drugs at an alarming rate, and in spite of a daily absorption of a quantity and a variety of calmants that would have put a horse out, failed to sleep or relax at all. There was also an undercurrent of violence in her behavior which worried me terribly, directed principally inward, but taking the form of unreasoned hostility to others at times, so that she was impelled to take hold of heavy objects with the idea of hurling them across the room. It seemed time to take action, and fortunately a friend, the ex-wife of the son of old Otto Harbach, offered to accompany Jane to London. I think she had things to do there, and was glad of a free round-trip air passage. I was completely worn out by that time, having had to be available constantly since I returned from Ceylon in May. (It was a nightmare I hope never to have to repeat.) . . . The last forty-eight hours were pretty awful for everyone; as the time drew near Jane became much worse. She was convinced she was being sent to be tortured, that she would never come back again, and her ability to describe and discuss her own state lucidly, at the same time being imprisoned in it, was perhaps the worst part. . . .

On September 5 Jane returned to London accompanied by Anne Harbach. She went first to Oxford and was readmitted to the Radcliffe Infirmary. The hemianopia had improved and now only affected the lower right quadrant of her vision, but she continued to have severe difficulty in reading and writing. She was also still disturbed that she might have a brain tumor. Tests eliminated this possibility.

The records show that she was in a state of extreme anxiety and depression. A Dr. Tennant was called in, and it was decided that Jane should be moved to Saint Andrew's, a psychiatric hospital in Northampton. When Jane left the Radcliffe Infirmary, an attending physician, Dr. Pennybacker, recorded that the prognosis "must be guarded. The most pressing problem is helping her to accommodate to her condition."

In late September Paul went to England to consult with Jane's doctors at Northampton. Ahmed accompanied him, as he was about to have a show of his paintings at the Hanover Gallery in London.

On October 2 Paul wrote to Virgil Thomson:

I am on my way to London from Northampton, where I've been seeing Janie. She seems a little better than she did last week; in fact, for long periods she appeared to be her own usual self. It was only at moments of emotional stress that one could sense that anything at all was the matter with her. Principally, she seems profoundly unhappy and depressed. They want to try electric shock . . . but since she herself must sign the release permitting them to administer the treatment, and since she is apprehensive about its efficacy, she is receiving no treatment at all for the moment. Which isn't much use, of course. But I think the security afforded by the place itself, as well as the routine it imposes, has done her some good. Eventually I hope she will come around to asking for the treatment, so I can see with my own eyes just what its result will be, before I return to Tangier. Naturally she wants very much to go back with me, but that is quite out of the question. She is under heavy and regular sedation, which rules out being on her own for the time being. I feel that if she would only make up her mind to take a minimum of four treatments, we would know better where we stand, and since all the doctors concerned, both neurologists and psychiatrists, insist that in her case, which is akin to the wartime cases of blitz-shock, electroplexy is more than likely to produce a beneficial result in the shortest possible time. She sees its effect on the other patients around here, and rejects it, without understanding that the others are manic-depressives, schizophrenics and alcoholics on whom it is often tried without much hope of being successful. Sometimes it doesn't seem wise to have her in such an atmosphere—certainly not for longer than is necessary. The doctors, however, ridicule the idea that the surroundings could have a bad effect on her. The first day I went out, I found her playing ping-pong; she also does weaving as occupational therapy. But naturally all of that bores her to distraction, as do the other patients, and her only expressed wish is to leave. The most painful moment comes each time when I say good-bye to return to London; she is convinced that I'll never come back to see her.

In London, Paul became seriously ill with Asian flu. He spent nine days in bed with a high fever. While he was ill he made use of the fever to write a story, "Tapaima," about the effects of an imaginary South American drink. On the tenth day, with his fever down, he got up and went out. The next day he was delirious and ended up in a hospital, where he had to stay for a month. When he recovered, he went to stay with Sonia Orwell. While he was in the hospital, Jane had a series of electric shock treatments. According to Dr. I. E. J. McLauchlan, consultant psychiatrist at Saint Andrew's, "It seems that her depressive illness responded well to EST (course of seven treatments) and she was certainly a good deal better when she left our care. She also had supportive psychotherapy, occupational therapy and medication. According to the records, Mrs. Bowles was undoubtedly very much improved by the time she left hospital, but I think the prognosis was regarded as somewhat uncertain." On November 11 Jane left the hospital and went to join Paul. From all appearances, the electric shock therapy had produced some relief in her depression and anxiety. While she was in London, she also saw the eye specialist Dr. Trevor-Roper again. He noted a great improvement in her visual condition.*

In mid-November Paul and Jane and Ahmed returned to Tangier. There Jane was put under the care of Dr. Yvonne Marillier-Roux, a compassionate and skilled woman, originally trained in Paris as a homeopath. On prescription from her, Jane was taking Epanutin, to keep the epileptiform fits under control, Amytal, a barbiturate, and two other medications, Medinal and Lipiodol. With her visual problem improved, she could even joke with Paul about "coping with her pots and pans," after trying for hours to write a single sentence in a letter.

But then an incident occurred that put an end to Jane's efforts at coping. Ahmed was arrested by the Moroccan police. (Under the new administration Tangier was no longer part of an international zone).

According to Yacoubi, "I was accused of attacking a boy, but it was all politics. They put me in jail."

Yacoubi had always been free with his political opinions, proclaiming them loudly as he sat having coffee at the Café de Paris. Apparently he was politically suspect by the new government. Early in the fall of 1958 the father of an adolescent boy accused Yacoubi of having had sexual relations with his son. The police had called Ahmed in for questioning in early September, but then released him. When he returned from his exhibit in London, he was told to come to the jail in the Casbah. He was immediately imprisoned. At first Paul thought it was a matter that would be resolved quickly, but as time wore on and Yacoubi was not released, he became very apprehensive. Paul and Jane would go to the jail to take him food, but Yacoubi lamented that his three lawyers, who were taking all his money, could do nothing for him. The situation in Tangier suddenly became fearful

---

*Dr. Trevor-Roper's records indicate that the hemianopia had virtually disappeared when he examined her after she left Northampton. This is very puzzling in view of a subsequent examination (seven months later in New York) which shows the hemianopia still existing.

to Paul and Jane: "partially because the police were making wholesale arrests of certain European residents, deporting some and packing the rest off to jail, we decided to get out of Morocco and not return until the new regime had attained its balance."

They left all their possessions in their apartments, shutting the doors behind them. Paul gave the Jaguar to Temsamany. (Six months later, Temsamany sold the Jaguar and went to Germany to work.) Cherifa fled to relatives in the hills.

After stopping in Lisbon, Paul and Jane went to Funchal, Madeira. From there on February 17 Paul wrote to Peggy Glanville-Hicks:

> Jane was just recuperating from her illness when the trouble struck, and she has got consistently worse as a result. I felt I couldn't go off and leave her there [Tangier], especially since the lawyer thought it likely that she too would be interrogated. That simply wouldn't have done at all. So she is here and isn't well. She can do nothing but sit silently all day and stare into space. . . .

On March 8 he wrote again to Peggy:

> I'm trying to write a new book, and would like to find the right place in which to do it. Jane may possibly go back to Tangier this month or next. She won't say whether or not she really intends to, but at any rate she is much better in her health than she was when we came, except that of course she is under such heavy sedation that her spirit seems to weigh many tons, and not being able to read or in any way divert herself, she requires a good deal of time and attention. But the great thing I have been able to do during the past month is to get her working for the first time since her stroke, and that I consider a victory of the first magnitude. Of course, she insists that unless I am present with her she won't be able to continue, but I have proven that it wasn't really physically necessary that I be there all the time—only morally necessary. I suppose such a necessity is just as real, or perhaps more so, at least as long as one thinks it is. . . .

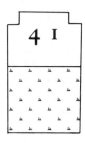

IN FUNCHAL, PAUL RECALLS, JANE WAS WORKING ON A novel she had begun earlier.* *Going to Massachusetts*, the title given to it by him, is a work about destiny—how one avoids it and seeks it at the same time—and about the isolation that comes from the knowledge of that destiny.

Bozoe Flanner, who has lived for ten years with Janet Murphy, in a state of dependency upon her, decides she must go to Massachusetts to be alone. She takes the bus, but gets off before it gets to Massachusetts. From her room above Larry's Bar and Grill in a town nearby, Bozoe writes to Janet:

I have only a few things to say after all these many years of suffering—By suffering I mean living. There isn't any use in my trying to pretend that I do not believe we were put on this earth to suffer. I do believe it—But not clearly enough. Not clearly enough to give a lecture on the subject certainly nor even to argue with a friend—who believed we were put on this earth to seek happiness—Now of course it is a time when collective suffering engulfs us all yet I would like to know—before it is too late—what I was seeking what I was seeking when I was still this overgrown individual—Bozoe Flanner—whose spirit never found its proper shape—like a bad f[l]ower—one whose—I could only suspect. . . .

---

*As with Jane's other unpublished work, the notebooks and the typescript of this novel are undated. It is probable, however, that she began working on it after she began the play about Beryl Jane and Gabriel.

Jane starts, then stops, crosses out, then begins again. She had done this
n her manuscripts before, but in these notebooks there is evidence of an
urgency that takes the reader back to "Camp Cataract" and beyond that to
Two Serious Ladies. Bozoe Flanner's life and words seem an inevitable
development of the imaginative course begun in those works. It is as if Jane
had heard the warning of Mrs. Perry in "Plain Pleasures": ". . . if she doesn't
watch out her life is going to be left aching and starving on the side of the
road and she's going to get to her grave without it."

Bozoe Flanner desperately seeks absolution from some nameless sin:

To think of the world—filled her with dread and desolation. She feared
that her place on earth—would be contested before she had found
it—The fact that she was free to find it—and had not done—so—made
her ashamed—guilty—: She was very conscious of the advantages she
enjoyed as a citizen of a democracy—and because she lived in
misery—and without courage—she thought that God would abandon
her sooner or later—to a totalitarian world. Other people—she
considered victims of the times they were born in. . . .

At times she was frightened at the failure of her spirit—and so
ashamed of it—that she felt the entire world—might turn totalitarian
because of her. It was about such things that she would talk to Janet
Murphy . . . "I know that God isn't going to make America go
totalitarian just because I'm such a failure," she would say to Janet
Murphy, "but I feel like somebody who really believed that He
might. . . ."

Her opposition to the totalitarian state was not the clear-headed
opposition of an individual who has enjoyed his rights—in a comparatively free world—For she had not enjoyed her rights: She had enjoyed
nothing because she had not felt ever that she was fulfilling her
destiny—Because of the failure of her spirit—she felt that she actually
deserved a totalitarian state and in her less balanced moments—she even
feared that she might bring one on: at such moments she imagined that
if she could save her own soul through sacrifice she might symbolically
save humanity as well—: But since she did not love humanity nor care
therefore whether or not it was saved except for her own sake—there
was no question of the real sacrifice. . . .

She was so desperately seeking absolution for some nameless sin that
she could not yet love humanity. . . .

Because she felt severed from her destiny she clung hard to her daily
life with Janet Murphy with a grip that she could not break—though it
was her own—and it was not her own will that in the end had finally
broken it: Bozoe Flanner loved Janet Murphy and her life in the
apartment over the garage with the desperate longing a dying person

feels—for grass and the smell of salt water and flowers—But a dying person remembers the smell of the sea and the smell of the flowers when he was not dying—and Bozoe Flanner could not. . . .

Jane makes a note to herself of the myths that are necessary for existence: "In collective egos—Between the pain of being oneself and separated from one's maker there is one's maker—One is never quite totally in the world: It is intolerable to be in this world without a myth."

In her working notes for the novel she wrote: "This is a book about isolation—how one seeks it when one is isolated like a double cell. . . ."

Before going to Massachusetts Bozoe speaks to Janet of her journey: "I was born to make this voyage—I have never spent a moment of the day or night free from this knowledge," she says, pounding the table.

Janet Murphy's answer to her is, " 'Your life is your own, Bozoe.' At which statement Bozoe would fly into a rage: 'My life is *not* my own,' she would scream at her. 'Have you missed the whole point of my life?' "

But it is precisely Janet Murphy's "missing the point" that holds Bozoe to her and makes her get off the bus before she gets to Massachusetts. Janet's denial of Bozoe's dilemma "gave Bozoe a certain freedom to repeat herself endlessly although it locked her securely into a cage. . . ."

And Jane, writing the novel of that endless repetition, prints a note to herself:

I am going to write this BOOK.

Though her vision was improved, some profound alteration had taken place in her internal vision. She felt she had lost the capacity to see and render her inner world.

Each afternoon in Funchal, Paul would come into Jane's room and would read over with her what she had done. "I was trying to persuade her she could still write. I would read it and say, 'It's marvelous,' and she would say, 'You're just saying it. It isn't true. I can't think the way I could. I can't visualize.' "

By March 29, when Paul once again wrote to Peggy Hicks, Jane had stopped writing:

I'm trying to get Jane to go to New York, because she can't continue with the life she is leading here: staying in bed all day unconscious, and doping herself at night. She will end up by being totally paralyzed, which she says she wants, in any case. Her morale is worse than ever, but there is nothing really the matter otherwise. She simply isn't interested in anything, short of going back to Tangier, which is out of the question since she is wanted by the police there. . . . I've never had a problem like this and it occupies every moment of the day after twelve, and of the night until one or two. We're getting nowhere, I can't work at anything, and she becomes more embedded in her obsession every day. . . . The doctor here found her blood pressure "fantastically high," and changed her medication, and . . . he also told her she risked a further stroke if she underwent any great nervous strain. She welcomed the idea, thinking another stroke would mean death, but he disillusioned her, saying it might mean only complete paralysis, and that one couldn't choose which areas of the brain to affect. That sobered her a little, I must say, but two days later she was off again. If I can, I'll get her to go to New York. I feel certain that any outside change would be for the better, would stop the wheel of compulsive thoughts from turning. If I could only get her out into the street for a quarter-hour walk it would help, but she refuses everything. Of course she has had far too much horror coming directly on her release from the sanatorium; the lawyer's last letters are too much . . . the police are searching for Cherifa because Jane signed over the house to her, but evidently Cherifa has fled to her relatives' hut in the hills, since they can't find her. . . .

Paul's way of saving himself—his work—was made impossible by what was happening to Jane. In the letter she had written to him after her return from Ceylon, she had spoken of her nightmare and said, "I am sorry too that you have to live through it. I won't go near you if it happens again. Actually I cannot allow it to happen again."

But the nightmare had happened again, and far more intensely than in Ceylon. Now they were on an island of their own making, alone, together. Sometimes Jane would say to Paul that she felt the stroke was Jehovah's wrath. And he would say to her, "You don't really believe that," and she would say, "I don't believe it, but I feel it."

Between Paul and Jane it had always been as it was between Mr. and Mrs. Copperfield. Paul had given Jane's fears their "just due." But now Paul felt that would be inhuman. That he did not do so convinced her even more that her fears were justified.

Under the unrelenting pressure of Jane's obsession and what was happening to them, Paul, at one moment, threatened suicide. He kept trying to get her to go to New York, but she refused. The choice was taken away from her, however, when her passport expired and the American embassy in Lisbon refused to renew it. The FBI opposed renewal because Jane had once been a member of the Communist party.

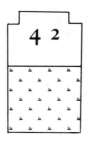

4 2

IN MID-APRIL JANE ARRIVED IN NEW YORK FROM
Lisbon by plane. Paul had telegraphed Tennessee, who was in Florida; he
volunteered to come to New York to meet Jane at the plane and also offered
her the use of his New York apartment.

Katharine and Natasha also invited Jane to stay with them. Katharine
remembers her arrival:

"The plane was supposed to arrive very early in the morning. We called
to see if it was coming in on time. They said no, it would be two hours late
and would land in Boston. But a short while later there was Tennessee with
Jane at the door. He had flown up from Florida to give Jane the keys to his
apartment and then he went right back."

Katharine and Natasha were not prepared to see Jane so ill and so
disturbed. They had to go to work that morning, but they called Florence
Codman, who came to stay with Jane. Then Katharine took the afternoon off
to be with her.

"Most of the time she couldn't sit still. She had to keep getting up and
looking for her medicine or checking on her passport or looking for her
mirror or for her wig. She had to do it herself. She wouldn't let anyone help
her.

"Then she'd have long spells of silence. She was very depressed. She
understood what everyone said to her, but she would hardly speak. She was
trying to work out what was wrong with her, why she couldn't write. She
went to sleep on the couch and slept all curled up in a little bundle. We were
frightened to leave her alone."

Soon after her arrival Jane had an epileptiform fit. Katharine and
Natasha took her to a doctor, who gave her more medication and found that
her blood pressure was dangerously high.

Further, her difficulty with language worsened. "Once," says Natasha,
"she came to the country with us, to our house in Pennsylvania. We went by
train and as the train was going through the tunnel I put my hand on hers,

remembering how she had always been so frightened of tunnels. But Jane said something like, 'That's over with. It's of no importance.' As if now she was in the real terror. And when we got to the house, Katharine said, 'The bathroom is upstairs. The yellow toothbrush is yours.' Jane said, 'What is yellow?' Katharine said, 'You know what blue is?' Jane said, 'Yes.' 'And what green is?' Jane said, 'Yes. But I don't know what yellow is.' "

Disturbed by her condition, Katharine and Natasha arranged for a nurse to stay with Jane during the daytime at Tennessee's apartment. For a while John LaTouche's mother came to be with her at night.

In reply to a worried letter from Katharine about Jane's physical and mental state, Paul answered:

> What you say about Jane is extremely upsetting. Does the doctor think her present state is a temporary exhaustion due to the trip, or a return of the same trouble she had last summer? You use the word "confusion," which makes it sound more like the latter. Confusion implies the adjective "mental," which is something I had hoped was all finished by the shock treatment. (Please read this to yourself and not to Jane.) During the entire time since she left the hospital in Northampton she has been completely normal from that point of view. Emotionally no, because she has never been emotionally *normal*, and since her illness she has been even more inclined than usual to worry. But still, I should say she has been herself, but more so. I just had to argue her out of her worrying afresh each day and get her to admit that there were other things to discuss besides the one or two topics that obsessed her. Since leaving the hospital she has not once been incapable of admitting the absurdity of her worry. (It was her inability to step out of line and see herself that made the shock treatment necessary, according to the doctors in England.) But I don't know. Your letter makes it sound as though she had taken a very definite turn for the worse, both physically and otherwise. In the first place, since she started taking Epanutin she has had no convulsions. The last convulsion took place in early February en route to Madeira. For a month after that she took Epanutin regularly, two a day, until she came to Lisbon, where the doctor here suggested that she stop and pay attention to getting the blood pressure down. For that he gave her Hepadesicol and Serpasil. She responded extremely well, and the last time she visited him, a week before leaving, the blood pressure had fallen in what he said was a spectacular fashion. I think I wrote you what it had been and what it was the last time he took it, and I can't remember the exact figures now, but it was in the neighborhood of 150 over 80, I think, having gone down from something like 220 over 150. Of course, like all the other doctors, he gave us nothing written, so there are no records. One of the great

troubles is that Jane never takes the medicine regularly unless one keeps at her constantly, which I did. However, I can't see how, even if she neglected to take *any* Serpasil for a day or two, the pressure could have risen so dramatically in so short a time unless something else is very wrong.

I'm trying to convince myself that it wasn't the fact that I let her go alone on the plane which has made her worse. She insisted that she didn't dread the trip, and I'm convinced that she didn't, at least consciously, because I should certainly have known it if she had been dreading it. What she said she dreaded was seeing her mother, which I understand, since she has kept up the pretence of being well ever since her stroke, and it has involved such a tremendous structure of lies that she automatically overestimates the adverse reaction her mother would have when the whole edifice collapsed. I can see that, and even at the beginning I was not a partisan of keeping everything from her mother; however, I had to play along in spite of myself, since Jane's mother is not my mother.

The immediate situation worries me terribly. Obviously you can't be a nurse to Jane, and if as you say she really needs a nurse, then I don't know what to do. I can go back to New York, but what will I do with her when I get there? I suppose that's my problem; it's one I can't see any solution for, at least from here. John Goodwin wrote me saying he thought I should be there, and I can see that he's right. But there seems to be an element of immediacy in it all that throws me. What matters seems to be this very week,—not next month. All my possessions are in Tangier and I want very much to get them out before leaving this part of the world. . . . Does Jane feel she can't leave New York at all for the present? I wish she'd write me and give me an idea of what she is thinking about. Did she get my letter telling her Cherifa was not and had not been in jail at all? . . .

On May 2 Paul wrote to Jane from Lisbon:

No news from you, which is rather worrying to me. I wish you'd write, if even a few lines, to let me know how you are. I've had two letters about you—of course—one from Katharine and one from John Goodwin, both of whom told me that you weren't very well. But I should like to have one from you, yourself, if you can type a short one, just to let me know in your own words how you feel.

I am wondering, too, whether you want me to try to write your mother, or whether you will be sending signed notes like the one you sent last week for me to post here . . . I'm perfectly willing to try and compose some Jane-like notes, only I don't think I could counterfeit your signature very well. But let me know what you want me to do, and as soon as you can, so that not too much time will go by without your mother's having a letter.

Did you manage to hang on to your money, travelers' checks, and the Libby check? That is another thing I must hear about . . . whether you have money and whether you need any; and if you do need some, be sure and say so, because I still have some, as you know, and will send it. But don't say you don't need it if you do, please, because it will just make everything more complicated later. I've been hoping to hear from you for the past ten days. Both Katharine and John told me you had had a convulsion shortly after arriving. That must mean you neglected to take your Epanutin, because you surely wouldn't have had it had you taken it. Have you got the various papers I gave you the night before you left? I mean the ones listing your medicines, the treatment you had in England and where each treatment was given? . . . I know you said you'd probably lose them, but you couldn't very well have lost them, since they were in the small grip along with the medicines themselves. . . .

. . . I hope you got my letter telling you that Cherifa had not been in jail and was not in jail, and hoped for some money. . . . I've heard nothing since that letter of Temsamany's which came over two weeks ago, but everything was obviously all right at that time, and there's no reason to think it would have changed since.

In the second week of May Jane tried to answer Paul. Her aphasia was far more disabling than it had been, even after her stroke the year before. She was unable to read what she wrote, but she forced herself to type. "I hope you can read enough of this to understand and don't let it frighten you," she says to him. Even with her difficulties with the language, the sentences are undeniably Jane:

Dearest Paul

I am sorry to have waited so long and I was very happy to read your letter and to know that you for the moment at least were happy set and able to eat and therefore I presume to work—or you must be by now on your way to it. I dreamed of happiness and felt it in my dream as solid as gold. It was this afternoon I dreamed of it and I had the doubtful satisfaction of knowing that at last there was something in my life that was not facke or open to doubt in any way. I have never known such misery and so I shall perhaps servive. I hope to survive because I am natural, like that wretched woman in my story. There is nothing you can do except write me that there is some hope that we may go to mexico. I could fly because that I could then go to when the time came.

I have not asked the doctor yet about altitudes—what affecrt they would have on me even if only temporarly. There I could find a maid or two at least and you would be there if I could get back to work. I think of these things when I feel hopefull but when I don't see any way out of here I am desperate. Berred and Cherifa I can't bear to think about and must tretend there dead. . . . The most important is my eyes or that field of visian—whatever it was called—not the field of visian itself because that is gone but the ability to read—there was a special word for that but I can't remember what it was we used it all the time. That is surely the tragedy if there is one unless it is simply the fact that don't like to write anyway. Libby is drumming up money from sourse and another—some from Oliver—and some John Goodwin and some from Katherine and twenty five dollars from Natasha when she has her tooth work finished. She herself has contributed the sum you're already familiar with and will continue too for life. I think this is very sweet of her and the work she is doing with my pasport and calling up these people to ask for a small sum of money from each for as long as I need it is invaluable. I will have no place to live soon and the rent will have have to be payed but according to Libby there will be enought from the various soursces. Diane has has reappedred as if by a mirictle because I didn't know where to reach her and simply ran into her at least Natasha. She wants to take an apport with me and since there is no other place except an old lady's home or home for dissabled people scince for for various reasons nobody have me. Dionne is reatly improoved after two years of Inalisis and very warm. Mrs. Latouche is spending the nights with me and a nurse the dayse. It is simply because I cannot be alone I am too frigtened after the fit which took a long time coming on and I would no way to comunicate if it happened when I was alone here. Libby does not think I should be in fact she says it is out of the question and thinks there will be enough money for medisons and rent and a maid between the groupe. She is writing you all about it very soon, but she is terribly busy and I do not see her very much. It will be a good send to have Dionne because lauliness is my toupbist problemme ple the fear of being alonge because of these ghastly fits. I am staying leave on the hope that some day I will be able to write again—at least to be indepemdent. I started three days ago to have fit but I took a dillantine and it stoped it in the midle. Dyane saw it happening the palpatations and insanne pullse beating I called the doctor but the fact that it did not come to its conclusian but that I was able to stop it is hopefull. There is so much hopelessness in this situation that I did not write you. But I am not crazy and was never crazy and only fear will drive me crazy. The fit was very unpleasant and terrifying because I—I have lost my place and so cannot find it again. Surely you can make some sinse out of this letter and last enough read most of it. It is very difficult for me to write Bubby but I will certainly write again tomorrow or even later tonight. Please do write my mother and sign it with an initial which I often have done to her when I did not happen to have a pen. I feel better and I take my pills three times aday it is a struggel now for survival. I don't think you should mention suiside as glibly as you have on occasion—but I don't think you would use that way out really. This may sound like a nonsequator but I am in a hurry and I reffer to a coversation we had in Portugal. You threataned suiside if you had no money or if you were trapped with me and I didn't cheer up or if you were trapped in America. Naturaly I have been in a bad state but I have to face it and not die of it. It will be wonderful if the pills really work but it will take a few monts two now won't it. It is awful writing this way not not rereading. I hope you are working and this letter reaches you wherever you are. I suppose Spaine is you nesxt stop if Portugal proves impossible for any longer. You ask me about money and I know you have any money very much but perhaps you could pay the doctor in London. The episode in Tangier has nearly broken my heart but not know I am getting cold and forget when I can. I am not actually but I preffer to pretend it is something that the didn't happen. Please for God's sake don't send me any masages saying that Cherifa is waiting for my return or expecting. I will only go back if you go back because the government has changed. Libby is still expecting to have a production in the near future so do not go too farway. I cannot write you too much because it brings the whole tangier horror back and I am utterly lost here in America and without you. Portugal was a ball compared to this, but people have been wonderful to me and Dian is coming to live with me a sublet apartment. I cannot live with Libby and she will explain that to [you] herself. She has been sweet and making great efforts collectin the Jane Bowles fund, which I started telling you about eartlier in in the letter. Please Paul wrok or you might as well be here in an offict which I never want you to be. Katherine has just arrived and she will mail this letter toninght so I must finish it before we sit down to dinner. She promises to explain what is happening because I am incabable of explaing it except that I will live in an aportment with Dyan for the nexet few month untill I say what will do next. Perhaps Mexico will be the answer but I must have somewhere to live now since Tenessee will be returning soon. I think that I I will make it somehow and above all for you do your work and don't go too Japan because you will be hearing from Liby soon. I hope you can read enough of this to understand and don't let it frighten you. There is no time for corections. It is like being naked and I hate it. I feel better then I did when I hit the "lows" as Libby calls them. My blood pressure was down today and I lost or rather gained five pouns. The readin is the saame. I hate to send you a letter like the is but it is better then a—nothing isn't it. But I was very sad and couldn't. Please wright me above all—and the less about Tangier the better unless the morrocon Government wants to make you president. I will write again and so will Katharine. Please pay money I owe in England. The rest is being taken care by friends—Katharine will explane.

Much Love—as ever—J.

By chance Natasha had met Jane's old friend Dione Lewis in the street. Hearing of Jane's illness and that Tennessee Williams would soon be returning and needing his apartment, Dione offered to find a place where she and Jane could stay together, sharing the rent. Dione had had a series of emotional problems and had been in psychiatric treatment for several years; she felt very sympathetic to Jane's difficulties and wanted to help her. She found a summer sublet, an apartment near Park Avenue on East Seventy-ninth Street, which rented for $150 a month. Libby paid Jane's share of the rent.

When Dione had to be out, she arranged for friends of hers, unemployed actresses, to be with Jane. Dione was angry that many of Jane's old friends and acquaintances—except for Katharine, Natasha, Florence Codman, and John Goodwin—would have little to do with her now that she was so ill. "Their attitude to Jane had always been that she was a pixie. If she did something cuckoo, well that was Jane, and it was very funny. But now when she needed them they couldn't take her."

Many of the people who had known Jane were frightened by her state. They thought she was "crazy." This became part of the myth about her. In Patricia Bosworth's biography of Montgomery Clift, she describes Jane as the "quick-tongued fragile writer who was going slowly mad."

In her letter to Paul, Jane had said, "But I am not crazy and was never crazy and only fear will drive me crazy." She could not understand what was happening to her and no one could make sense of it for her.

In terms of current medical knowledge, her difficulty with understanding language as well as expressing herself suggests a global problem on the left side of the brain. Her not comprehending "yellow," for example, is a symptom of a "receptive" aphasia, associated with a lesion in the left cerebral hemisphere. That she could not "visualize," as she had said in Funchal, would suggest a lesion in the occipital region of the cortex.

As for the hemianopia, "even to a normal person," says Dr. Trevor-Roper, "it presents a grave psychological difficulty. Though her right field is gone, the patient persists in imagining a continuation of what she sees in the left visual field."

In this affliction the eye, in a sense, continues to "see." That is, the image falls upon the retina and the optic nerve transmits the signal to the brain. But it is within the cortex or even deeper areas of the brain that the breakdown occurs. In the most extreme case, in total cortical blindness, a patient is not only stopped from seeing but prevented from understanding what she would see if she could see; that is, from understanding what sight could do for her.

To Jane, who was never a "normal person," the hemianopia presented more than a "grave psychological difficulty." She took her stroke to be the punishment, so long evaded, for the sin or sins she had accepted as her own.

If there was at this time something frightening in Jane to others, it was in part the nakedness of her preoccupation with her illness, her obsession with what was happening to her and why it had happened. She had never been a stranger to anxiety. But now it drew upon the full force of her being, and few people could tolerate her presence.

"Of course she was difficult to cope with," says Dione. "But she always had been. If she wanted to do something, she did it and no one could stop her." Now the overwhelming anxiety did nothing to make her more compliant, but still she felt she needed someone to take care of her. "She was very frightened and didn't want to be alone. She was terrified too of not being with Paul. He was her rock.

"She'd say, 'I think God is punishing me for not writing. Of all the diseases I could have picked for myself this is the worst, not to see, not to be able to write.' She wanted her illness to be a stroke, something physical, not mental. I thought her intelligence was as clear as a bell, but I felt she should see a psychiatrist or a neurologist who was psychiatrically oriented. But I never said to her, 'You should see a psychiatrist.' Most people's reaction is, 'What do you think, that I'm crazy?'"

Jane's mother was also in New York at this time, about to have an operation for cancer. She still did not know that Jane was ill, nor that she was in the United States. Paul had continued to send letters to Claire, signing them "Jane." In a letter of May 14 Paul wrote to Jane that he had written another letter to Claire, "although I shuddered to sign your name, which to me looked like a very clumsy forgery. I hope to God she doesn't suspect anything."

About Tangier he added, "There is no particular news . . . so that even if I wanted to write you about it I couldn't. Temsamany writes that the police have taken his passport away from him and he despairs of ever getting it back. A. has had no trial and none has been set." However, within two weeks Paul received a letter from Ahmed saying he was free, having finally been brought to trial and acquitted in five minutes' time.

On the advice of Libby's doctor and of one of Dione's friends, Jane went to see Dr. Aaron Bell, a neurologist. He recommended that she go for speech therapy to Lenox Hill Hospital. Shortly afterward she wrote to Paul:

Dear Paul,

I personaly—Jane Bowles I mean—cannot write you today. It is imposible. There is no point untill you do come over if and when you do and you are once more joined together with your clothes. It is a time for me when silence is the best for both. I am thinking of going to a place where they correct speach (therefore reading) a type of therapy that is new and has had good resolts supposedly. I consulted a nuroligist to see if there was anything I could do with this terrifying life of mine and he said speache therapy. (i.e. reading) They go together and it is better to work at something anyway even if it turns out to be of no avail . . . what I have is called efasia. I cannot spell but that is what they say. I do not put much home in it but I must try anyway if I have the courage and if I think it will do me any good and if I can get the money. Naturally there is no limited time as usual but I suppose I could tell whether it was having any results or not. I will know more when I have been to the speeche center at Lenox Hill Hospital in a week and have consulted with the therapict there. I will know what it costs and if I can get any money for it which I am very worried about. I am not sure in fact I am pretty damned sure theat Libby doesn't want to spend any more on me—at least that she can't afford two for the moment while she is gurding he loins for Yerma. It will take a pretty sumn and know of it tax deductuble. . . . I cannot go on this way—just sitting. I simply cannot. Please please don't think that I mean that you should pay for this I don't. I know you couldn't afford it. It won't be any fun I know but anything to hasten this waiting if it is at all possible. I am desperate because I am know fascing heavy time in a way that I didn't even when we were together in Portugal. It is not possible that it got worse. But it dead. My health is alright. I did not want to write you because I didn't want you to think me miserable but I am sure you are used to that. This seems to me the darkest time but perhaps something will break and I will be cleare—cleare like I was in the air going to America. I love being in the sky and I did love being as close to the ground as possible [to you?]. I loved Tangier very much. More than I knew even with all that talking but it is my sight my friedem that I want again.

It is terrible to have to be taken care of. I cannot get around her at all. But I did go out in Tangier. I went out to market and came back and spent nightss sleeping alone and not being afraid. Dione of course has to go out a lot and I have seen a few friends. John has diligently taken me out on the average of once a week. I have the same horror of stirring that I did have in Portugal, but I have to stir now and then to go to the doctors. One night [a friend] too me to a dyke night club, It was like going there after I died. A girl started talking to me and wanted only to talk about north africa. She was an econimest and believe in evolution as the for the trouble between arab and french, inevitable evolution, if I had met her in Morocco I would have decided that she was a communist but here it is differant. She hated your book more than any book she ever read, (Sheltering sky) so I felt very flatered and famous. Please don't feel gulilty which I know is your way about any present mess I was in before or am in now was entirey of my own making and not yours. I am heart broken about my life with c. but it is not that nearly so musch as the preasant which frightens me. I shall write you more about that but it is not important. I simply want to send her some word that I am not coming back so that she can plan accordingly. I cannot send her money either. but to keep going to the bank untill it is all used up. The only other suggestion I have is that you send her the equivalent of one thousand pesetas a month and that she keep goint to the bank to untill the end of her life. I don't ask you to do this because we have so little money and if you are going possible to live in Mexico and I too in the end it will mean a great deal of defferand to us. Yes one can still live in Mexico and there is a small town even not far from Mexico city, but lower down. A friend of ours told me that we could live for nearly nothing. I suddenly remember that I did not tell the doctor that I could nor read—he tested me on writing. Naybe they were right in england. I will see what they say in the speach centar. Please Paul forgive this letter I am doing the best I can and it is very deppressing not to know the words much better know than I did when I was in Tangier. I must stop now and I am hoping to see you above all. Please make up something for my mother, based on this. She is fine. Julian wants to go on eith the farse at least untill she is stronger then I'll probably have to see he. I don't know. Like yourself Julian says that one must not try to think more than a day ahead. I can't go on. I am suddenly so deppressed by the fact that I forget to mention to the doctor that I could write to a certain extant but not read that I am appaled. . . .

"I can't go on," she writes. But she goes on, hating being taken care of, needing to be taken care of, fearing to be alone, hating being cooped up in the apartment, fearful of going out. Once she said to Dione, "Why don't we go to a neighborhood and sit on a stoop where there are people?"

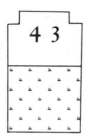

4 3

THE THERAPIST JANE CONSULTED AT LENOX HILL Hospital was James H. Dewson, a language therapist in the Department of Speech Pathology and Audiology. Dewson remembers Jane coming to see him in the summer of 1958.

"She walked with a shuffling gait, as if she were weighed down by many burdens. She was round-shouldered and her chest was caved in. She looked mousy in a way and yet at the same time there was something sexy about her, something girlish and flirtatious. One couldn't have an ordinary conversation with her. She'd be angry or she'd be witty, or then there would be a kind of childish joy, or maybe a terrible despondency." Then only twenty-four years old, Dewson tried to be adamant with her. He was determined to get her to read and write again. He insisted she write about anything and everything, no matter how trivial.

He was an energetic, bluff young man, just out of the army. Even then he knew he did not understand this complex woman. "She was way ahead of me with her wry smiles and her laughter. I felt I had to take a strict line with her because she was so wily. I tried to push her to the limits of what she could do.

"Like a schoolgirl she would stamp her foot and say, 'Don't make me do that.' She was very coy with me and yet she was desperate at the same time."

She came to see him twice a week. Sometimes she would return with something that was astonishingly complete and beautifully written. Other times there would be only a fragment of a sentence. He remembers that she said to him, "Every word is like chiseling in granite."

Dewson was sure that her problem was to some extent an emotional one. "She was a recluse. She didn't seem interested in life."

At the same time he recognized that she was suffering from a physical disability, from the stroke and its aftermath. "She couldn't see well because of the hemianopia. She would walk to the hospital for the appointment and she would hold on to the walls of buildings as she came. It gave her a sense of safety to do that, as she had no side vision. It was as if she were imprisoned in something.

"As with many stroke victims she was aware of her power within her head, particularly in terms of language, but she was not able to exert that power. She was a hand-wringer, I remember. She seemed to know what she wanted to say, but she couldn't get it out."

He pressed her hard and at times she became angry at him. She disliked him, as she disliked most doctors or therapists who treated her. "They don't see inside your head," she told Paul. Still, despite the fact that she did not like being pushed by Dewson, Jane did work very hard for him. She never came without bringing something that she had worked on. He was pressing her to write, just as she, for so many years, had pressed herself. She answered, "I can't, I'm not able to." Yet she kept trying. In that situation she was able to say things to him that she could not say to others. Whereas she had told Dione how she longed for Cherifa, adding, "For fifteen dollars a month you can have someone who will stay with you for life," to Dewson she said that she was afraid of her. He remembers that Jane talked about her a lot. "She was a presence in her life."

For several months that summer Jane worked with Dewson. She even brought Paul to the office, when he came to New York. And then suddenly Jane was gone. Soon afterward Dewson left Lenox Hill Hospital. He kept the compositions Jane had written for him. There was something about them, he felt, that was important. At the same time he felt burdened with the responsibility for them. A year after he left Lenox Hill, he destroyed them all.

But several of those compositions survive, Jane's own copies, in her papers at HRC. Reading them, one does feel the words are "chiseled in granite."

I don't know whether or not I understood you corectly—But it seems if I am corect—you asked me to write compositions for you. I can not. Please try to find some other way. I cannot write a composition. If I could I would. I don't think I have been able to for years anyway—and a this time it is completely impossible. If it is a failure of the will—then my will is sick—it is not lazyness. I am trying to read and I must say that I am doing well in that. If I could write a composition I would find my way out. But there is such a thing as a failure of the will which is agony for the person who suffers from it. I did not suffer a stroke for nothing at my age at age—and I have gone far away down the path   of no return. I must have started down that path when I was very young. I know that you want me to write something different—but I can't. I know that there are years of suffering ahead and that nobody can look into my brain. I know that they keep basket cases

alive and that you don't choose to express your oppinion on   this —because as you said it a unresolved—a religious or philosophic unresolved—problem—Are we to take our lives or anyone elses—to save ourselves or anyone else from unindurable pain. Is torment pain—the final the purest offering we have to make to a supreme being because if it is not then why is it concidered   a   sin
  to relieve
  One is alone finally and there is no doctor for the soul. I   one can find the strength to bow to the soul and accept it as existing beyond the ego—and beyond pain—perhaps the torment would ceise

I think I see know what is the matter but I cannot express it. It is my thinking itself that that does not work in some way—where any deduction is necessary—a joke which is at all complicated is impossibbly for me to conceive. Just as it is impossible for me to understand why—eleven subtracted from twenty five—. I think—I know this is gone—and the way to learn it again is I think—I know impossible. I read—and it takes me an hour or or more to complete a quarter of a page—some of the sense comes through but a lot doesn't and so I can in no way tell whether I have really read the sentence or not. If I could really describe this to you I would be alright—because then I could write. —and read and in other words function in the world—whether I was in bad emotional state or not. I would seek help for that—for a nameless deppression or a fear beyond the actuall danger involved. I have known those such [composition ends]

Once she had spent days trying to describe the bridge in "Camp Cataract," a bridge she was building in her imagination. And she had to struggle for detail after detail. Now she struggles to put together in language the details of daily existence.

I see the vanity table with its three way mirror. . . . The vanity table is divided in three parts—it can be pushed back—so that the mirror is are flush with—(God knows what) There is a glass top on the table itself covered with a doily of lace and the whole is an indetermaney color—grey—. There is a big bottle of equinal on the top of this table at which I am siting. The pills in the bottle are are white but they look blue because the bottle is of blue glass. There is a red box—oblong in shape—one cannot see the contents because the cover of bottle is covered and closed. I know it contains drops of some patent medicin. If I opened it I would see glass bottle. There is some eadecologne—a medium sized bottle with a black stopper. There is a stick deodorant

which has to be unscrued before using. The top is white when opened
but I cannot describe it. One bed closed and the other unmaid. I can see
the white wolen blankets pushed back on one of them—and in a messy
heap—on the cover shets-sheets [composition ends]

IN MID-JUNE PAUL RETURNED TO NEW YORK TO WORK WITH LIBBY HOLMAN ON
the production of *Yerma*. He stayed at the Chelsea and came to see Jane
several times on Seventy-ninth Street, but he was involved in rehearsing the
orchestra and chorus and soloists, in preparation for the opening in Denver.

With Paul in the United States it had become impossible to keep up the
pretense about Jane with her mother. And since Claire seemed to be
recovering well from her operation, Jane let her mother know that she was in
New York. According to Katharine and Natasha, Claire "had hysterics"
about Jane's stroke. Dione remembers that the reaction of Julian and Claire
was very disturbing to Jane. "If Jane had to be with her mother and
stepfather for a day, she couldn't stand it. Instead of their showing gentleness
and tenderness, she felt they were reproaching her. And I had the same
response. I thought they felt that Jane was playing a game, that she was
deliberately posing to make herself look ill. He, more than she. Claire might
have been different without him, but she was having her own problems."

Claire and Julian were both having serious difficulties: he had been in a
concentration camp during the war and his eyes and heart had been affected;
she was just recovering from the cancer operation. Burdened by the cost of
their own illnesses, they were barely managing to support themselves. Claire
knew that Paul didn't have the money for expensive medical care for Jane. If
Libby didn't continue to help her, what would happen to her?

Jane felt both Julian and Claire were reproaching her for "acting" ill.
Jane insisted that she was not dramatizing her illness, yet at the same time
she felt she had brought it upon herself. As she had written to Dewson, "I
did not suffer a stroke for nothing at my age." She does not know, nor can the
doctors tell her, what part of her difficulty is organic and what part is
psychological (and therefore "neurotic faking?"). She only knows that she is
in constant terror and that it is getting worse and yet she cannot explain to
anyone what is happening to her.

For Dewson she writes:

There are three people in here. Mother—my mother myself and a
monster. The monster is not to be reconned with. I cannot deal with the
monster. It is not my fault. It is not my fault. Even if I could explain
what it is that is missing it would help because I would still be where I
am—no better off. There are no accounts to settle. Just the accounts of
decinsy—decency . . .

IN AUGUST, LIBBY AND PAUL AND THE CAST OF *YERMA* WENT TO DENVER for the first tryout. From Denver, Paul wrote to Jane that they were going to take the production to Ithaca and he hoped she would come to the opening there. He added, "My mother and father are driving up sometime next week, I think, in case you would like to go with them."

Jane did not go to Ithaca, but Claire went there and spoke to Paul about Jane. Though Jane was resolutely against hospitalization, both Paul and Claire agreed that it was necessary. Claire returned to New York and finally prevailed on Jane to enter the psychiatric clinic of New York Hospital —Cornell Medical Center in White Plains. "Jane's mother and stepfather wanted me to drive her up there," Dione remembers, "but I said no. I said to Jane, 'Please don't go.' But our sublet was up in the apartment and we had to get out and there was nowhere else for her to go. So her mother took her there. What else was she going to do? If she had tried to keep Jane with her, she would have ruined her own marriage."

When Jane entered the hospital on October 1, her blood pressure was very high, 260/160. The second night she had a grand mal seizure, followed by a petit mal seizure on the next night. She was given barbiturates, Dilantin and Serpasil to treat her seizures and her blood pressure. Within a few days her blood pressure was lowered to 220/120 and there were no recurrences of her epileptic attacks.

Her neurological examination in New York had confirmed that she had a right homonymous hemianopia, right-sided hyperflexia, and Hoffmann and Babinski signs, all indications of brain impairment. A Bender gestalt test also showed evidence of organic damage. Her electroencephalogram showed a moderate abnormality over the left occipital, parietal, and temporal areas, consistent with the cerebrovascular accident she had had. There was one puzzling aspect of her condition from a medical viewpoint: a striking absence of optic fundi findings; that is, there were no changes in the vascular system in the eye. This is paradoxical and unexpected in view of her long-standing high blood pressure and the stroke.

But if the doctors were puzzled by this incongruity, they were even more puzzled by her personality. They found her seedy-looking and bizarre. They thought her relationship to her husband bizarre, her sex life bizarre, even her published writing bizarre. They found it puzzling that she kept referring to her difficulty in abstract terms, trying to describe a disconnection with things around her, yet saying there was something in it that was not subjective. Nor in her conversation did she seem to want to unburden her feelings. They did recognize her intelligence and her sense of humor, but as soon as they tried to test her capabilities she became anguished. In the hospital she seemed to sit alone a lot, and those relationships she formed they saw as clinging.

Katharine and Natasha visited her in the hospital. "She claimed they weren't doing her any good, but obviously they were doing her some good. She said no one came near her, but obviously that wasn't true," Katharine says.

"Then she said, 'How can anyone afford to keep me here?' We told her, 'It's because of your stepfather, who knows somebody. You're getting a special rate.' Jane said, 'Do you mean I'm on scholarship?' "

Florence Codman went to see her in the hospital and was shocked at her condition. "Jane needed more attention than most of us. With her imagination she needed someone who was close to her to be there."

Dione also went to visit. "She had a crush on a patient named Matilda. That was what saved her."

When Claire was not able to visit, she wrote to Jane four or five times a week. Once when she came, she brought Helvetia Perkins with her. Jane had not seen Helvetia for years, but in January 1958, having heard of the stroke, Helvetia had written to her:

Dearest Jane,

I've been terribly sad—and sorry—to hear about the trouble you've had. I would have written before—only I felt you were perhaps in no mood to hear from anyone, and I was afraid to sort of break in on you. Now I can't hold out any longer. You must be going through a wretched time, and I am so very, very sorry though this, I'm afraid, can't be any comfort to you. I have come down here to sit through the winter months, and as usual—if I come down—have ended up at the Chelsea, which I don't seem to be able to get away from. As usual too, I have very few engagements and am living exactly as I do in East Montpelier! This, I guess, would be true—wherever I went—so things haven't changed much for me though underneath them, inside and out, little dislocations and movements happen, now and then, and make tiny differences. And I love my room—it is long and skinny. You'd hate it—but it's comparatively quiet and the sun, when there is any, comes pouring in.

. . . You will never be forgotten, Jane, certainly not by me, nor, I'm sure, by anyone who has ever known you. . . .

With my love to you, always,
Helvetia

P.S. If I can do anything here, for you or Paul, I'd be glad to—so please ask him to let me know. . . . I wish I could draw a medieval student, but I never could make one!* Love again, H.

---

*The borders of Jane's notebooks are filled with caricatures of curious faces. When asked what they were, she would answer, "Medieval students."

On board the Orsova, *en route to Ceylon,
December 1954.* From left: *Paul, Ahmed Yacoubi,
Jane, Richard Rumbolz.*

Taprobane.

Returning to Tangier, 1956, John Goodwin and Jane.

Jane, Tangier, early 1960s.

*Tangier, early 1960s. Paul second from left, Cherifa
sitting on floor, Jane peeking from the back,
Sonia Kamalakar extreme right.*

Julian Fuhs and Claire (Jane's mother).

Jane with Leonore Gershwin.
COURTESY LAWRENCE STEWART

Jane's unmarked grave, San Miguel Cemetery, Malaga.
PHOTO BY JAMES KALETT

Though Jane may have felt that the doctors in the hospital could not get inside her head, though she may have hated her psychiatrist there—as she told Paul and Dione—yet her condition did improve. By November she was talking of going back to Tangier.

In mid-December Paul came to White Plains to get Jane and they returned to Morocco by boat. In a letter to Virgil Thomson, Paul described their trip and Jane's condition upon her arrival in Tangier:

Dear Virgil:

I'm sorry I didn't manage to get in touch with you during the last week of New York. I wasn't my own master from the moment I got Janie from the hospital. The great worry was about whether she would be able to make it to the ship before deciding against going at all. I could see the signs of that calamity approaching, and I didn't want to give her a moment to sit and begin to brood about it. The ship sailed with us on it, and the trip across was difficult. Jane was beset with every sort of symptom at all hours of the day and night. Her heart beat too fast. She felt her blood pressure in her temples. Her head ached. She was nauseated. She was jittery. She had no appetite, save at four in the morning, when she ordered in sixteen sliced-chicken sandwiches without mustard. (This was routine throughout the voyage.) I was trying to write an article for *Holiday* in record time—the length of the trip—seven days, and needed complete solitude, or at least quiet for a few hours during each twenty-four. All passed. We got to Algeciras, where Jane decided the police would very likely arrest us. They didn't. She refused to come to Tangier until I had sent a telegram to the police asking them if we might return. This I did. Suddenly it became the worst thing we could have done. Now it would be impossible for us to return. It was too late to recall the telegram, and I refused to send a second asking them to pay no attention to the first (as she suggested!). We decided to stay in Algeciras until we heard something. The next day a cable from the American Consul arrived. It said we might return whenever we wished. The following day we came here, where Jane immediately became another person entirely. She began to laugh and take pleasure in food, and become her old normal self, more so than she has been at any time since the stroke. So I'm gratified, of course, and delighted that I managed to get her out of New York in time. I think all will go well now for a while, perhaps for good, or until some external situation changes everything. . . .

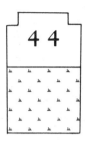

44

Jane returned to Tangier to take up her daily life, as if the continuation of what had been could ward off her terrors of the future. Things were not, however, just as they had been.

Though Jane's physical and mental condition had improved, she still had great difficulty with reading and with the physical act of writing. Her aphasia had almost disappeared, but she was unable to deal with numbers. To add or subtract the simplest sum was impossible for her. She was physically more frail than she had been. She fatigued easily. She had to be careful with alcohol, and was allowed only small amounts of red wine.

There was also still the possibility that she might suffer from an epileptic fit at any time, and she was terrified of being alone. As Dr. Roux agreed that she should have someone with her all the time, she hired a Spanish woman, Angèle, to be her companion. Between Angèle and Cherifa and Aicha, the cook, Jane was never alone.

In the eyes of those who knew her, the Jane after the stroke was a different woman. To one man, "before the stroke she was the kind of woman you would make a pass at, but not afterward." To David Herbert she was oddly "more sane." To Paul, although in some ways she was "Jane, only more so," it was as if she were not running on full power, as if there had been a disconnection within her, and the lightning-quick changes in her feeling and thinking had been slowed.

But to those who met Jane now for the first time, she was beguiling and puzzling, entrancing and aggravating, funnier and more vital than anyone they had ever met. In the summer of 1959 Roberta Bobba was traveling through Morocco. "I was on my way to Algeria with my friend Betty, but I couldn't get a visa. I ended up staying almost a year in Tangier.

"The first time I saw Jane was at the Café Flores, a small bar across from the French consulate. She had weird hennaed hair, almost orange, a color that I later came to see many Arab women used. She looked like a little waif, with a dragging gait. She was wearing a cloth coat and looked dowdy, even mousy, except for her hair. But that was the last time I noticed what Jane wore. From then on it was only her conversation that mattered."

After it became clear that she was not going to get a visa to Algeria, Roberta moved into the Inmueble Itesa, an apartment building across from the American consulate, where Paul and Jane now had flats. Roberta saw Jane daily.

"As far as I knew then, Jane wasn't doing any writing, only writing letters to Libby. It seemed strange to me that so many of her hours were taken up in running the house. There were always great conflicts going on. Cherifa was there and also an Arab cook. They'd spend hours deciding who would go to the market and what they'd get. Jane would start laughing. Jane and Cherifa would argue a lot and sometimes Jane would get mad. Once Jane said, 'She only wins half the time.'

"As for Cherifa, I thought she was a stupid woman. But let me say, to be honest, that Cherifa despised me on sight. Jane's interest and mine was in talking. That shut Cherifa out, since I only spoke English. My friend Betty was funny and animated. She would make faces. Cherifa adored that, but she was hostile to me. Sometimes when we went to dinner at Jane's, a fight would start. Jane would say of Cherifa, 'She's just jealous.' Then Betty would get up and dance and sing and Jane would laugh. When Jane, Betty, and I had dinner together, we would eat at one table. Cherifa and the other women ate at another.

"The first time I saw Cherifa she was wearing a veil. I assumed she was a servant. The next time I saw her she had on man's pants and a man's shirt and an ascot and her hair was pulled back. The effect was sort of male. I think Jane made a doll out of her.

"Jane told me that Cherifa threatened to kill her several times. She said it was part of Cherifa's conversational charm.

"Since I couldn't talk to Cherifa, I didn't pay attention to her. I found her to be a pinched-face little woman, not attractive, with a childlike nature. She knew I was gay. As far as I knew that was a gay relationship between Jane and Cherifa. That relationship embarrassed me—and I'm not one to be easily embarrassed—so we didn't discuss it, though Jane did tell me once that she had to teach Cherifa to make love. But I believe that Jane was not homosexual by instinct or nature. I never felt that in her.

"Jane was interested in me because I was doing interesting things, having adventures, just going off and traveling when I wanted to.

"She had a great ability to laugh and play. Part of what she enjoyed in the Arab women was that they were so playful. All those endless discussions, whether to have turnips or beets—and she, Jane, playing too, but a kind of queen."

Six weeks after Paul and Jane returned to Tangier, Paul went back to New York to do the music for Tennessee Williams's *Sweet Bird of Youth*. By

July he was back in Tangier and with the aid of a Rockefeller grant was recording Moroccan music throughout the country.

Roberta Bobba remembers that Jane was exceedingly protective of Paul. "She would talk about how serious his work was. Her job was to see that he wasn't disturbed. On one of his trips Paul's driver had an accident with the VW and it was out of commission. Jane asked me if I would drive Paul since I had a camper. I said I would but by this time Paul had asked Christopher Wanklyn. Betty and I did go with them on one long trip, about a thousand miles, into the Sahara. Jane had prepared a box of food for the journey. In it were all sorts of fabulous delicacies, including caviar and fillets of anchovies.

"Paul would chat with the head man of the village before recording. Once I asked him, 'What do they think of having women here?' He answered, 'They don't know you're women.' We were wearing pants and sweatshirts with hoods. 'But,' he said, 'even if they did know, they wouldn't think about it. You're Western and you aren't anything to them.'

"My conversations with Paul were instructive. I was willing to be instructed. Betty and I amused him. It was a fair trade. I found him polite, but cold. I think he loved Jane as much as he could have loved anyone, but that's not saying a lot."

Roberta remembers feeling that it was very important to Jane that she was Paul's wife. "I knew some gay women who were married, who did it for family pressure or for the sake of appearances. But Jane really took on the role of the wife. She didn't do it for form's sake. She put on a great production in terms of the home, though I had the feeling that Paul couldn't have cared less.

"If it hadn't been for Jane," Roberta concludes, "I would never have stayed in Tangier. She was argumentative, but she was a hell of a kick."

Lawrence Stewart, who was later to write an excellent book on Paul's North African work, met Paul and Jane in 1960. He was Ira Gershwin's literary secretary and was traveling with Ira's wife Leonore at the time. Leonore had met Paul and Jane earlier, in the United States.

At first Lawrence was put off by Jane, as he recorded in his diary: "Jane's strategy was to move, speak, and react with exaggerated slowness. When we arrived at the restaurant, she announced that she didn't know why she had come, she hated Arab food. Paul smiled and talked amiably through all of this, and ordered a number of dishes (a beef stock with lemon slices in it, shishkebab, chicken with almonds and grapes, and a French pastry chicken pie . . .). The soup arrived and Jane, peering at a basket of sliced wheat bread, complained, 'The bread's too thin.' Only the most insistent solicitude on our parts, capped by Leonore's pressing two slices of bread together to fabricate a thick one, got past that difficulty."

In his diary Lawrence also recorded Jane's anxiety—which he thought was excessive—about what was happening in Tangier at the time. A series of changes was being instituted by the new government, including revocation of Tangier's status as a free port. "Jane kept harping on the subject with a sense of urgency. 'The revolution is only five years away and what will I do when it comes? Where will I go? Paul won't be here.' She asked these not as rhetorical questions but as though she expected that we could give her definite advice. Leonore suggested the American consul. 'Oh, he'll have gone by that time,' answered Jane."

But if he began by being irritated by what he thought were Jane's attempts to provoke reactions, Lawrence soon became devoted to her. "To this day I have never understood how anyone could have met Jane and not cared for her intensely.

"Most people who knew Paul and Jane did not care for both of them. Usually whoever liked the one didn't care for the other, or even actively disliked the other. There was something about them that made them, each in their own way, lightning rods for other people's fantasies. But I cared for Jane and I do care for Paul.

"To me they often seemed to be exchanging places. Paul would be reassuring when Jane was anxious, but then when Paul was agitated about something, it was Jane who insisted that Paul always saw the dark side of every situation."

Jane often spoke to Lawrence about leaving Tangier, though that, he thought, was a fantasy. When he left, she said to him, "We live on people passing through."

Ned Rorem was "passing through" Tangier in 1961. "I spent a month in Morocco and I saw the Bowleses often. I dined with them every night for a week. They would eat at eleven. Cherifa was in jeans. She cooked the meal and waited on the table. She was all smiles.

"Jane took me to the bookstore and to Madame Porte's for tea. I was sitting there with her when Ahmed Yacoubi came in. He came over and sat down for a minute. Later she told me she didn't like Yacoubi." (Yacoubi by this time was engaged to an American girl. Soon after he moved to the United States.)

"Jane was very outspoken about herself," remembers Rorem. "She had a magic quality. She could also be such a pain in the neck. Once we were going on a picnic. It took about four hours just to get out of the apartment. She couldn't make up her mind whether to take chicken or not take chicken. . . ."

But if Jane said to Lawrence Stewart, "We live on people passing through," as if through their eyes she saw her daily life differently, yet in her daily life in Tangier she "lived on" people who were there.

The painter Ira Yeager lived in Tangier in 1960 and 1961, when he was in his early twenties. He saw Jane often and met many of her friends.

"I met Paul first. He invited my friend Stuart and myself to the house, and there we met Jane. She was wearing an old green polished-cotton skirt, an ivy-league shirt, and flat shoes, like penny loafers. She was slim. When she met me she gave me this up-and-down look, her eyes slightly squinted, as if she were taking everything in at once.

"Jane and Pamela Stevenson, a young American woman, and Stuart and I would often go to lunch and spend the afternoons together. Pamela had been married three times. Her last husband had been a member of the camel corps of the French foreign legion. She loved exotica. She was very beautiful and terribly spoiled. Her father was a psychiatrist and her mother a psychiatric social worker. She said she was a Communist and sent money to Fidel Castro. She would eat nothing but escargots, spaghetti, and chocolate ice cream, and she drank only Coca-Cola.

"Pamela talked like a little girl. She loved animals and anything she did had something to do with animals. She smoked Black Cat cigarettes and went to the Owl Cleaners.

"She used to dress in that silver mail that belly dancers wore in Algeria. She would give parties wearing that and gold lipstick and gold fingernail polish. She had an old neutered male cat who was very bad-tempered and would often attack her. She would move back and forth between Tangier and America, always taking with her an old refrigerator and stove. Everyone thought she was a character out of one of Jane's books.

"She took the walls out of her house to make it into one big room. The roof fell in and she thought it was wonderful. Frogs and birds were living there. She would say to Jane, 'Oh, Janie, you're so wonderful.' I do think Jane found her a little bit of a pest.

"Stuart and I had a little shop in Tangier, selling jewelry and other crafts. Pamela was our only customer. If Pamela bought something, we'd be able to go out to eat that day. Often we went to a restaurant called The Three Pelicans, run by a middle-aged Englishwoman with a mustache, who was married to a fat younger man. Janie was fascinated with Mrs. Pelican, as she called her. She would laugh about her and swoon over her at the same time.

"When the four of us were together, we'd laugh a lot. It was silly and carefree—fun and games. That's the way we were with each other. Sometimes when we went to Jane's apartment we would see Cherifa. Cherifa would mimic Pamela—she was a remarkable mimic—and Pamela would laugh, giggling like a little girl. I thought Jane was wonderfully funny. I knew she was frightened and nervous and afraid to go out and to be alone, but somehow at that time those weren't the things I thought about. I knew she had been sick, but I never treated her like a sick person."

Ira Yeager remembers that Jane had another very good friend at the time, Sonya Kamalakar. "She was a Georgian princess and she was married to an Indian, Narayan. She was a funny little lady, short and fat, and her teeth were missing in the front. He was small and very delicate. They would have esoteric salons at their small house, which they called the Villa Darna.

The first time I met Narayan I thought he was a servant. He wore a white jacket and pushed a tea cart, from which he served nasturtium sandwiches. In fact he was a holy man. After Sonya died, he became a Franciscan monk, wandering through Spain."

The Kamalakars were often in great financial difficulty. They had come from France to Morocco in 1955, to participate in a scientific expedition. They had invested all their funds in the expedition, and when its leader disappeared with all the funds, the Kamalakars were stranded.

"Sonya would often ask Jane for help. Jane would usually do what Sonya asked, but sometimes she would become impatient with her."

David Herbert remembers that Jane "adored Sonya. She was like one of the ladies in her writing. One night I was at Jane's. Sonya sat in the middle of the divan all night. I said to her, 'Darling, haven't you been there long enough?' 'No,' she told me, 'Janie told me not to move because there's a large hole under me.'"

PAUL REGARDED JANE'S FRIENDS WITH A CERTAIN DETACHED AMUSEMENT. "SHE always cultivated the most eccentric characters. I'd ask her if she would ever write about them and she'd say no. What she liked about them was that they did what was unexpected. That was far better for her than people who were reliable or predictable. Her friends were usually naïve people. Sonya was naïve, innocent, and wide-eyed. Jane would have her to tea and serve caviar and smoked salmon. Sonya would sit there licking her fingers, saying, 'This is so good.' I've never seen anyone more self-indulgent in my life, but as she was eating she'd turn to me and say, 'Do you think Jesus will forgive me?' Jane liked the childlike in everybody.

"Jane was a great confidante of many people, men and women. They'd come to see her, shut themselves in with her and talk, and then they'd feel better.

"Pamela Stevenson moved into this building because she had a fixation on Jane, not a sexual fixation, but it couldn't have been stronger if it had been. She had to see Jane all the time and confess to her. Pam had had three husbands and was very neurotic. She had fallen in love with a Spaniard and she wanted to know how to get him, as if Jane could tell her how. What Jane tried to do was persuade her that she really wasn't interested in the Spaniard at all. What she was interested in was that the Spaniard wasn't interested in her. She lay in her bed for nine days, living on canned spaghetti, wearing black lingerie that she had bought especially for the occasion, waiting for the Spaniard to come and ring her bell. 'You're not interested in him,' Jane said to her. 'All you're interested in is your black underwear. You wouldn't mind who came in as long as he saw you in your black underwear.' The Spaniard never came, but Pam got over it finally."

In Jane's papers there is a letter from Pamela that shows the intensity of the effect Jane had on her:

Dearest Janie—

I am writing to you because your image has taken up housekeeping in my head, like a disgusted god who unwillingly symbolized an unbounded state of being. I am sure you are groaning, which bears out my feeling that you are there unwillingly; however, you are not so unwilling as not to be there. I enjoy your company intensely, although at times it is damned uncomfortable to have another person living inside one's skull, especially when the person doesn't want to be there a great deal of the time. I wish you would stop walking around in those Arab slippers in the middle of the night, but on the other hand if you weren't around I wouldn't have the benefit of certain exquisite insights of yours that I could never hatch by myself. . . .

Of course not everyone thought Jane's insights were "exquisite," as Pamela did. Paula Wolfert, who was living in Tangier in the early sixties, thought that "Jane was an oddball, friendly with old women like Sonya.* She was very amusing but sometimes sharp-tongued and sarcastic in what she said about others. I felt she did a lot of game-playing."

"I don't really know what Jane was like. She was always listening to me talk about all the things I was doing. She also liked 'girl' talk. She was interested in my emotional life with my husband.

"I called her once when I was pregnant and thought I was having a miscarriage. Jane came right over with the Spanish woman Angèle. She stayed outside while Angèle examined me. I didn't expect that Jane would be so modest."

Some people thought Jane was a poseur and a snob. "She was often abstracted, thinking of other things than what was going on around her," says Gordon Sager. "She seemed vague and people took that as a snub, but she would never have deliberately snubbed anyone."

To Libby Holman in 1960, several months after the terrible earthquake in Agadir, Jane wrote of some of the things that preoccupied her:†

Dearest Libby:

I am very sad not to have written you. It is too much of a task evaluating the whole situation and then writing what is important and

---

*Paula Wolfert was in her twenties at the time. Sonya Kamalakar was probably in her late forties.
†This letter is taken from published material, not from the original, and therefore does not show Jane's spelling errors or idiosyncratic punctuation.

what isn't. I can write down all my worries, and there are roughly about eleven major ones, including a very faint worry—not a worry actually, but an *awareness* that this is after all earthquake country, although we are not on the Agadir fault. That was such a nightmare. The reports on Agadir came here daily, and to top it off we had a tremor here. The people were so hysterical that they slept in the bullring all night. The Jews especially. I didn't know about it until the next morning. It is not fair to mention only the other worries since that one obsessed me for a good two months. Anyway, most of them will hold until I see you. But when will I see you? . . .

Things have changed considerably, but I don't think there will be a revolution this year (according to my spies) and maybe not for many more years, depending on what happens in the rest of the world, naturally. I shall ask your permission not to mention politics. I don't like them anymore.

The doctor does not want me to stay alone because of the danger that I might have a fit in the street or fall down and hit my head. I have a Spanish woman because she can keep accounts. My most solemn worry is about my work, and above all, do I really have any? Can I ever have any again? I will try to settle it this summer and next fall. (Within the next six or eight months.) For myself, anyway, because it has nothing to do with anyone else. Also there is nothing new except that I don't always know which is the stroke and which is the writer's block. I know some things have definitely to do with the stroke, and others I'm not sure of. The sheep festival is about to begin, in a month, and they are all buying their sheep now for the slaughter. I think that I will not be able to buy a sheep this year. They are too expensive for me, and Cherifa is having four teeth pulled, and later, a bridge made.

I have trouble with names, numbers, and above all the ability to add and subtract. I know perfectly well the general outlines. Two hundred dollars is less than three hundred dollars, and ten plus ten equals twenty, but the complicated divisions and subtractions and additions—! Adding more than two figures is impossible for me. That can be relearned, but I really need someone with me in this country, or they would all cheat me because I could not correct their own sums which are *always wrong*. So Angèle does that. I suppose that is the least of my worries, but I'm sure that none of this is psychosomatic, because I have no mental block about numbers, and they are worse than the rest. I don't think it would take more than six months to relearn the whole multiplication table. It is very funny but not bad, because I know what I need to know, and then can have someone else do the work. Some women are bad at computing even without strokes, and they are not as charming as I am. Don't ask Dr. Resnick anything. He might have discouraging news, and above all I must for once in my life keep my hopes up. Paul says that he spoke to the doctors and they said that nobody knew how much one could improve or how long it would take. The doctor in New York who sent me to that ghastly young man at Lenox Hill—I forget his name—said the hemianopia was permanent, but not the aphasia, which has proved to be correct. I now know the meaning of all words. They register again on my brain, but I am slow because there is a tiny paralyzed spot in each eye which I apparently have to circumvent when I'm reading. One side is very bad, worse than the other, but on the whole I'm getting much more used to it. Don't say anything to Resnick because he can't possibly predict anything, and anyway he is apt to be frank, and maybe he would say something depressing. Undoubtedly. I have an awful feeling that I've written this whole thing before. I will send the blood-pressure readings and ask if there are any new drugs besides Serpasil. My own doctor is pleased with me.

Libby, there is so much talk about myself in this letter that I think I must stop. I have left half the things out that I wanted to tell you about. At least there are no politics in this one. I was fairly poetic in the old days.

Much love,

J.

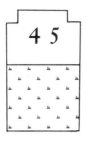

4 5

THERE IS SOMETHING ABOUT DAILY LIFE—DOMESTIC daily life—that resists narration in biography or fiction. It is a telling of another sort: Today I got up, I had breakfast, I read the paper, I went out . . . When tomorrow is today, again: I got up, I had breakfast . . .

Narration has the implication of a forward movement toward change. But daily life is the structure through which things can go on and on as they have been. It creates continuity without change, even as it allows the present to renew itself. It forms a background so habitual that it can be taken for granted. And the lives of others around us in our homes—and even the domestic animals—enforce that repetition and that continuity.

Before her stroke Jane had always lived in terror of the future. At the same time she had forced herself to go out and do that which frightened her. But there was also that in Jane that needed the security of daily life as a buttress against her terror. It is as if she always had a double narration in her life, the narration of the world of terror and the unchanging story which she herself had to create out of daily existence. She lived with the sense of being on an edge between them.

Now, after the stroke, her daily life assumed a desperate urgency. What others could take for granted—the habitual background of existence—she had to patch together minute by minute each day. Any action or gesture could reveal the world she had to evade—the world of her illness and the terror beyond the illness that the illness had come to replace. To the extent that these events and gestures were held safely within daily life, they guaranteed her own continuing existence. So that daily life, now, became her primary work.

Roberta Bobba found it strange that Jane could spend so many hours running the household. The painter Marguerite McBey remembers that "Jane did things with such difficulty. It took her twice as long to do something as anyone else." Watching her in the house, Isabelle and Yvonne

Gerofi had the feeling that "everything would fall on the floor. In everything she did she was clumsy and funny."

It is true that Jane's physical coordination had been affected by the stroke. Her right hand, in particular, did not function well, and since she was right-handed, that presented a serious problem. But beyond that there was a sense of willed delay in things that she did, an exaggerated slowness that Lawrence Stewart took to be her strategy. And certainly it was a strategy, an attempt at control, to hold on and to hold off at the same time.

The Gerofis remember how long it would take Jane to decide anything. "She would call up and say, 'I'll meet you in five minutes.' In five minutes she'd call and say, 'I'll meet you in an hour and a half.' Then the next time it would be three hours later. Often it would take most of a day to make arrangements. Once it went on for a whole day and we never did meet.

"She was interested in little things. She'd spend a lot of time thinking about what to wear. She'd call to ask which dress to wear to a party. Then she would hang up. Then she would call again. She had decided to wear the blue dress. Five minutes later she would call again. No, she would wear the green dress. It would happen three, four, five times. To choose a dress was not a matter of comfort or appearance. It was a matter of right or wrong. Each decision was a moral question. Once we told Janie about another woman who was also hesitant. Janie said it was important to make the right choice.

"Sometimes she would talk about salvation, but in such a way that we never understood what she meant."

It was not possible for Jane to let these decisions slip by, to make them half consciously. Even the smallest decision called for rigorous attention. To make the right choice between all the possible alternatives was the relentless burden imposed on her. That burden was the price she paid for daily life.

Her life was a continual effort at containment, but daily life can contain only so much. Outside are all the other things that can't be controlled. Things accumulate. Holding actions hold only for so long. Unexpected events break into daily life and form their own chronology.

Of the year 1961 Paul has written:

> Jane and I spent most of the year in Tangier, watching the city become progressively de-Europeanized. In spite of having come under Rabat's direct political control at the time of the sultan's return, Tangier had been allowed to retain its character until April, 1960. This delay gave local Europeans time to bring their businesses to an end and leave the country without undue losses. When the charter expired, Tangier's finances would be subject to the same controls as in any other Moroccan town. There was a great deal of uninformed speculation and needless anxiety among the European residents as to their future. Most of us

agreed that eventually we would be forced to leave; the arguments occurred over the amount of time we had left. . . .

Sometimes Jane would say to Paul, "We must leave," but they did not leave. And then it was only a statement of the moment. She did not want to lose the only daily life she had.

IN LATE DECEMBER 1961 JANE RECEIVED A LETTER FROM THE INGRAM MERRILL Foundation saying that she had been awarded a grant of $3,000 to write a play. The award was both promise and threat. Other people believed that she could still write, as she herself so desperately wanted to believe. It was a chance to begin again what had seemed so hopelessly blocked. But at the same time the possibility of regaining her powers was a threat. It brought into the immediate present all that writing had been and had not been for her.

To get back to work and still protect herself was what was necessary, to have her daily life and yet once again do what she needed to do, to give form to her imaginative life in language. But then, so much of her energy was consumed in allaying her fears of what was still to come. (What was still to come was never out of her mind for long, no matter how daily life held.) And she was still impeded by the hemianopia and the difficulty with her right hand.

She chose to begin a play set in Camp Cataract, the location of the story she had felt had been her most successful work. And soon after she began this play—as if again sexuality and writing were necessary correlates—she embarked on a love affair.

In February 1962 Jane met a woman we shall call Lady Frances. Frances was English, a writer, the daughter of a countess. She was very tall and thin, her face angular, the bones sharply defined, her manner self-assertive. She had published several works of fiction, which had been well received in England.

Jane would visit the Gerofis and talk about her passion, "but never in a regular sentence. Often there would be great sighs and she would say, 'Love is the most important thing in life.'" The Gerofis thought, though they were not quite sure, that it was another of Jane's jokes. Paul too thought of it as a joke. He found Frances unendurable (as he found all of Jane's lovers).

"She thought herself terribly intellectual. I remember having dinner with Jane and her downstairs many times, when I couldn't escape. Jane would be sitting there, slightly giggling to me, in an apologetic way, yet also sitting there thinking what a marvelous character she was. Frances would say, 'I shall now give you my impression of James Joyce,' and then she would hold forth for a half-hour. It was excruciating. Jane loved to have me at the

ble being horrified by her. And she would look across the table at me as if
o say, 'I can't stop her.'

"She would drink quite a bit. Once she got drunk and began to totter
and had to be put to bed. Jane put her to bed in the room with Cherifa. In the
middle of the night there was the most awful racket. It was Frances having a
nightmare. She screamed she was being murdered. And Cherifa made a
terrible stink about the whole thing. She went on for weeks. She called her
'the rooster.' She said that when she went to sleep, she began to crow like a
rooster. And that was a great joke, that Janie had brought 'the rooster' back
to the house.

"Those were the worst nightmare sounds I'd ever heard. Frances's
mother had just committed suicide in Gibraltar. Frances never had gotten
along with her mother. I think the whole situation gave her a certain glamour
in Jane's eyes."

The Gerofis have the impression that, as far as Jane was concerned, the
passion in the affair soon ebbed. She did, however, remain devoted to
Frances. In Jane's letters to her, there is a delicacy, almost a tentativeness,
and an attitude of protectiveness. If a number of other people in Tangier, like
Paul, found Frances too harsh in her self-assertion, Jane saw in her a painful
vulnerability.

In March, Frances left for New York, and several friends of Jane's, about
to make a trip to Marrakech and Fez, invited her to come along. Paul
encouraged her to go, as he wrote to his mother:

> I think it will be good for her, but the mere prospect of moving even for
> that short time has put her off her work. She is worried about being
> without a paid companion even for those few days. So far she hasn't
> been alone even for an hour, day or night, since she returned from
> America. Of course she won't be alone in Fez either, but she has grown
> used to having someone to obey her at every moment, and she feels lost
> if there is no one. Also she likes to be in immediate touch with her
> doctor, which is really not necessary. I think slowly she will have to
> break away from this routine, and become more self-sufficient or it will
> be very bad for her. And so I am all in favor of her getting out of the
> pattern this way. She's worried that I won't be able to take care of
> myself and the cat and the parrot. But the Spanish maid will be coming
> every day in any case to get my lunch, and I'll go out for dinners, so
> everything will be very simple, and I think I've finally convinced her of
> that. . . .

But in his next letter to his mother, Paul wrote:

Jane never did get away, even for a day. At the last minute she decided against it. Which is usually what happens. . . . Yes, she still has that Spanish woman to accompany her everywhere, but that is the doctor's fault; the doctor insists she can't take the chance of being alone for an instant for fear she will have a convulsion, although she hasn't had a sign of one in nearly a year now. . . .

Though Jane's health seemed much better in the early sixties, she was continuously suffering reverses. In September 1960 she'd had a hernia operation. In January 1962 she'd had shingles. In July 1962 she'd had to have a second hernia operation, as the first one had been unsuccessful. This time a large sheet of plastic screening was inserted into her abdomen.

These "reverses" did not have the immediate seriousness of the violent experience Jane had had in 1957 and 1958. They were a new kind of ordeal, the attrition of small illnesses. They too had to be incorporated into daily life, as just that, small illnesses and nothing more. To Paul, busy during these years with his project to record Moroccan music and with writing articles, these illnesses were a new pressure.

Our combined worlds orbited around the subject of her poor health. Each week she seemed to have a new symptom to add to the old ones; the horizon of her illness was slowly widening. It took me a long time to realize that my life had undergone a tremendous change. The act of living had been enjoyable; at some point when I was not paying attention, it had turned into a different sort of experience, to whose grimness I had grown so accustomed that I now took it for granted.

Now and then he would come upon her walking up and down in her room wringing her hands. She would refer again to the epigraph in *The Sheltering Sky*, the quotation from Kafka: "From a certain point onward there is no longer any turning back. That is the point that must be reached." And again he would say to her, "That's not so, it's not about you." And she would say to him, "Why did you use it, if you didn't believe it?"

Yet, if with Paul she spoke of her fears about the progress of her illness, with others, especially if they were in need, she hid the nakedness of those fears. When Tennessee Williams came to Tangier during the summer of 1962, in despair because of his breakup with Frankie Merlo, it was Jane who was able to console him.

At cocktail parties and suppers I sat in silence that was seldom broken. . . .

Moments of holy communion. . . .

One afternoon I was alone with Jane Bowles, and I said to Janie, "Janie, I can't talk anymore."

She gave me one of her quick little smiles and said, "Tennessee, you were never much of a conversationalist."

For some reason perhaps because it made me laugh, and laughter is always a comfort, as Janie was always a comfort, this answer to my anguished confession was a relief for a while.

In early September Jane and Paul went to New York, Paul to write the music for Tennessee Williams's *The Milk Train Doesn't Stop Here Any More*, and Jane to see her mother. Claire, who was now living with Julian in Florida, came to New York to see Jane. It was not an easy visit. After her mother left New York, Jane stayed on and saw a lot of Frances. Paul was concerned because with Frances Jane began to drink heavily. He prevailed on Jane to return to Tangier, where, he told her, she should be able to work on her play without distraction. She returned to Tangier on November 13 aboard the U.S.S. *Constitution*.

On December 5, from New Haven, where he was touring with Tennessee's play, Paul wrote to Jane, again trying to persuade her to work:

Characteristically, you say nothing about your work except to detail possible reasons for interference. But really, no work depends on the ability to find the perfect adjectives while one is writing it. And any process or formula which will make it possible to get the skeleton constructed (I know you always object to my terminology, because you imagine I mean a preconceived outline, as in school composition, which I don't), any method or trick or manner, is valid, as long as the thing gets on paper. Then you can look for your precise words. Anyway, I'm glad that at least you feel like working. . . .

And on December 11 he wrote to her again, telling her not to be distracted by the "mess" of daily life:

First, however, I should tell you that I got a letter from your mother who seems to be in a state of awful nerves because she hasn't received any communication from you save the cable, since your arrival. She said she had been trying to get me on the phone, but they told her I was out of town. For God's sake, if you haven't written her, do. But I suppose you must have by the time you will receive this communication. Actually you can't reply to it, I imagine, so that I can get it before I leave. But anyway. I was sorry to hear that as you put it, everything has got to be a mess in Tangier and therefore you haven't worked. That was the very thing we were making great resolves about while you were still here—that you wouldn't *allow* the mess-tendency to take over, because that has always been the pattern, and that has been exactly what has always got in your way. Of course everything's a mess, but *please* forget the mess now and then each day, because otherwise you won't ever work. The mess is just the decor in which we live, but we can't let decor take over, really. I know you agree in principle, but does that help you to leave the mess outside regularly for a while and get inside to work? Also I know it's easy to talk about and hard to do, but pretend you really live here in New York instead of there, and it might help. I mean, that you're only over there for a short while, and not permanently. . . .

Much love. I can't wait to get back and see you.

Bupple

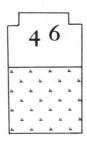

46

THE POET RUTH FAINLIGHT AND HER HUSBAND, NOV-
elist Alan Sillitoe, had met Jane and Paul during their first stay in Tangier
the winter of 1960–61. In May 1962 Ruth and Alan returned to Tangier with
their eight-week-old baby. For the first month or so they stayed at the Atlas
Hotel and ate dinner most evenings with Paul and Jane. Soon the Sillitoes
moved to a house on the Old Mountain, and by that time Ruth and Jane had
established a close friendship, different from any that Jane had formed in
Tangier.

Ruth was thirty years old, Jane forty-five. Ruth was, as yet, an
unpublished writer. Jane's career was, she said, in the past, forgotten if it
was ever known. The friendship between the two women was, however,
despite their differences, curiously equivalent. Both were Jewish. They
shared a common background and a common ethical sense. They did not
speak of literature, though Jane mentioned that she was trying to write and
couldn't. They shared the domestic daily life that women share. Ruth would
take her baby with her and visit Jane. "Cherifa and the other women were
sitting there. I remember a certain familial bickering, but it seemed a serene
place to be.

"Cherifa had a wicked smile and great charm. She wore a jellaba when
she went out, but in the house she wore blue boxer shorts or blue jeans, and a
T-shirt. She was always smoking a cigarette."

They were intimate friends without a personal knowledge of each
other's history. Jane said nothing to Ruth of her "amours." "Sometimes a
woman's name would come up in conversation and Jane would giggle, but
nothing more was said."

Looking back, Ruth has the sense that it was important to Jane that
Ruth think well of her. "In one sense Jane protected me from certain kinds of
knowledge about herself. As the mother of a child, I was someone for her to
wonder at. And I suppose I even connived at my own protection.

"I knew that Jane was ill. She knew I knew. Her life was tragic—we both knew it—but nothing was said about it."

Ruth remembers a phrase that Jane used when she was in high spirits, "giggling and snorting at the absurdity of her dependence on Angèle and Cherifa and the other women, and my domination by a nursing baby—the irrelevance of these outside attachments to each of us in our own essential isolation, the ridiculousness of the whole physical, female world (or so I interpret it). The phrase, spoken as though by a Girl Scout leader, was 'Get into position!' It always reduced us to helpless laughter.

"I remember the same phrase being used in quite other circumstances. When she was going to serve dinner (those nights we ate at her flat), we were all shooed into our places like a flock of chickens. At those times Jane was more than half serious. We did indeed have to get into position before matters could proceed. There was something rueful then in Jane's self-amusement, at her awareness of her need to have everything and everyone in place before she felt secure."

What Ruth recalls most clearly is Jane's laugh. "Her laugh was extraordinary. It was primal and anarchic, and yet there was something Nietzschean in its glee. That laugh seemed to dissolve everything. All considerations, whether the most stupid or the most tragic, were dispelled by it."

In February 1963 Ruth and Alan returned to England. Shortly afterward, Jane wrote to her:

Dearest Ruth,

This is just to let you know that I think of you all the time and wonder whether or not you will come back. I gave the letter to Fatima's husband,* in fact I read it to him in Arabic and he was very pleased indeed. . . . I am glad to write about Fatima and her husband because I don't want to get onto myself. Things are going badly for me. My work has come to a standstill, although I tried again this morning to start off on a new tack (spelling?). I did not scrap everything I had written but typed up the first eighteen pages of which I showed Paul ten. Paul was pleased and said that it sounded like myself and not someone else but he would have liked to see more. I would like to see more myself but I seem to have come to a dead end. I liked this letter best when I was writing about Fatima and her husband. Anyway I seem to get more and more discouraged and therefore it is difficult for me to write. I am afraid to

---

*Fatima was a Moroccan woman who had returned to London with the Sillitoes, to work for them.

have many mispellings which I think I warned you about in the past. In case you have forgotten, most of them are due to the odd affects the stroke had on my spelling but not *all* of them. There is no doubt that I spell better than I did before. (five years ago) It really is high time I got back to Fatima and her husband. This letter is going very badly.

About Fatima and her husband, I wish to tell you that Paul has forgotten how much money she gets a month, but I haven't! She gets fifteen thousand francs a month and that is what I shall tell Paul to give Fatima's husband. As I remember he was to get fifteen thousand more at sheep time but I am not as sure of this sum as I am of the other. Perhaps it was ten thousand? It is about time for the sheep money more or less so please write me what to give him.

Paul, whom I have just seen, told me that he was given money that was to be used each month for Fatima's husband's support but that no sheep had been mentioned. . . . Had you intended to send another check for that or is the sheep to come out of the check that Alan gave Paul for Fatima's husband. This is truly the kind of letter I love. The more I write it the better I love it. I hope you enjoy it as much as I do. Please study the wording of your reply so that I am sure to know exactly what to do about the sheep. The festival is still a month away but the longer Fatima's husband waits, the more expensive the sheep will get. He really should have bought it two years ago when it was a baby.

. . . Ruth I miss you so very much I do not dare to think that you might possibly not return. . . . I have only David [Herbert] occasionaly, (spelling) and Ira Cohn and Isabelle and every now and then as a great sexy treat—Mrs. McBey. I went to a fashion show at the Hotel Rif with Mrs. McBey and Veronica. One of the boys belonging to the cuban couple—Irving—loathes me. I have a feeling that I am going to be more and more hated as the years go by. I am thinking of leaving, but not yet. . . . Please write about the sheep. Tell me how you feel about London now, after your sad return because of your friend [Sylvia Plath]. . . .

In April, Jane wrote to Ruth again, telling her that Paul had rented a house in Arcila, a town on the coast, an hour's drive from Tangier. It was

very expensive but worth it because he can no longer work at all in his studio. The woman above him hammers brass trays all night until her croupier husband comes home from the casino at six, and the Yeshivabooka's who had moved into this building before you left, start cooking at seven in the morning. The kitchen wall is against his bed so he never gets any peace at all. . . .

Jane describes her own difficulties:

I haven't the energy to read since it's always a bit difficult for me because of that hemanopia trouble resulting form the stroke which you know about and which, although it is a thousand times improved, slows down my reading so much that I fall asleep with the light on. I managed to stay awake for one week reading a book called *Plain Girl*, a book for children with large print . . . after that I picked up a book called *Cybernétique et Société*! I bogged down after spending days on the preface which was purely tecnical and which required a working knowledge of physics. What is a working knowledge?

And then she adds:

On top of all this my bed seems to slant down instead of up which I would preffer and this too prevents me from reading anything because I am so exasperated all night. I wake up during the night and I realize that my bed is slanting down the very second I become conscious. I hope that some day this will all stop and that I will work a little because there is nothing else for me to do.

But then in a very Jane-like shift, with no transition, she is back to the details of her daily life:

I went to Sonia's yesterday and saw the Santscrit student who gave me news of the whole Lysergic acid set, headed of course by Sonia! I had not seen Sonia or anyone else—(nor the Gerofes) for ten days because Libby Holman was here with her abstract painter fisherman husband and she did not want to meet anyone nor go anywhere—so we stayed closeted for ten days. I did not write either letters or plays of course as you know. Her departure left me feeling sadder even than I had felt when she came and I am still trying to recover.

Early that summer Ruth wrote to Jane that she and Alan would not be returning to Tangier. Jane replied:

I am sad of course that you are not comming back but I can't say that I am in the least surprised. I expected it. By the time you had written me I knew anyway and—dispite my dissappointment—I think it is best for you. My life has turned into a veritable farce, schlepping between Arcila and Tangier as I do, and if I did not find it humorous I would weep.

Jane was giving Fatima's husband extra money from the Sillitoes' fund when he asked for it. Now she suggests that the Gerofis handle the money "because I am soft and . . . the Gerofis would be more business like."

Now with Arcila it is better that you do arrange something more satisfactory for the man because in anycase I am not going to be here all of the time. In the spring I will go to America if not sooner. . . .

I have just had lunch with Yvonne and the two girls at their house except that nobody ate any lunch. Noelle and I drank two litres of wine between us and even Yvonne had a little whisky. It seemed to me like some earlier time in my life, which was pleasant for a change. I turned up at Charles later with a lurching walk and slurred speech and he got rid of me as fast as he could. . . .

My mind is full of food that has to be taken to Arcila because there is nothing there to eat at all except some tomatoes and some giant sized string beans and sometimes fish is caught that Paul considers edible. Otherwise everything must be taken there in great baskets and burlap bags. You can imagine the lists that have to be made which is particularly difficult because Paul can never remember what there is left in the house when he comes here so that I am almost obliged to go there myself to see. It is easy enough to take the bus out there except that the seats have to be bought a day ahead . . . so as to be sure to get on the bus (there are two good ones a day—early morning and five o'clock) —but coming back of course is far worse because the bus starts at Larache and often comes through Arcila on its way to Tangier with no seats available at all. In such a case I just go back and spend another night in Arcila. It doesn't matter. . . .

In Arcila, Larbi Layachi was working for Paul. Paul and Jane had met Larbi while he was a guard at a café at Merkala Beach in Tangier. He had struggled since childhood to survive on his own and had spent a good deal of time in jail for minor infractions. Though he was illiterate, he had a remarkable gift as a storyteller, which Paul had immediately recognized. Larbi had spent months with Paul recording his life experiences on tape and these, translated, were soon to be published as *A Life Full of Holes*. Though Larbi had made some money from the sale of the book, he was quite content to work as houseboy for Paul in Arcila.

Larbi remembers taking Jane to the beach and to the market when she came to visit Paul. "In Arcila on Thursdays and Sundays she liked to go to the market and talk to the women. The women would laugh, they were so surprised she talked Mohgrebi so well. In the market she would buy a lot of things, things she didn't even need. Then she'd come back and say, 'Here, Cherifa, this is for you.' Cherifa would say, 'Are you crazy?' Jane would say,

'*Scoot*, be quiet you,' in a nice way. She wanted to help the poor people out in the market."

In Arcila, Jane also spent a lot of time with a young American writer, Alfred Chester. Chester had met Paul in New York and then had come to Morocco and taken a house in Arcila near Paul's. At that time he was writing a monthly article for *Book Week*, and in Arcila he did an article about Larbi and his book. Jane had read Chester's story "Berceuse" and admired it immensely. She also saw that he was very disturbed and moody, and spent a lot of time trying to help him.

One morning, however, Chester went to Paul's house in Arcila in a very excited state. He began to accuse Paul of working against him. There was a long and futile argument, and after Chester left, Paul wrote a letter to a friend in Tangier, Ira Cohen, saying, "Alfred being impossible. Am arranging to have him rubbed out next week."

Chester, who was also a friend of Ira Cohen's, saw the note and went immediately to the American consul for protection. Paul was called to Tangier for an investigation. The case was dropped, but Jane tried to make amends to Chester for what had happened, explaining to him that it was a joke on Paul's part. Chester in turn sent her a note: "I've returned the letter to Ira who assures me that you are right: it was a joke.

"Things wouldn't have come to what they are now had there been fewer professions of love and admiration, and more honest understanding and genuine interest."

Chester, who became very devoted to Jane, was later confined in a Moroccan mental institution and still later went to Israel, where he committed suicide.

IT WAS NOT AT ALL UNUSUAL FOR PAUL AND JANE TO FIND EACH OTHER'S friends difficult, even unbearable. When, for example, Allen Ginsberg came to Tangier to spend time with William Burroughs, Paul and Ginsberg became very good friends. Jane, however, found Ginsberg impossible. In 1958 he had called on the telephone and asked for Paul. Jane answered that Paul was somewhere in East Africa. Ginsberg then said, "This is Allen Ginsberg, the bop poet." "The *what* poet?" It took some time for Jane to understand the word, says Paul, but when she finally got it, she said, "I see."

"Then," Jane told Paul, "this complete madman asked me if I believed in God. 'Do you believe in God, Jane?' I told him: 'I'm certainly not going to discuss it on the telephone.' "

Further, Ginsberg later mentioned to Jane the effect William Carlos Williams's stroke had had on him—that he was no longer able to work—and Jane, in view of her own illness, found his remark insensitive and never forgave him.

THAT SUMMER JANE MET RENÉE HENRY AND FELL IN LOVE WITH HER.
Jane would speak of her grand passion to the Gerofis, but the relationship to
Renée was, she lamented, never a physical one. "She is afraid to be alone in
the same room with me," she said, and the Gerofis took it as another one of
Jane's jokes.

Rex Henry, Renée's husband, knew of Jane's infatuation. Now in his
eighties, living with his ailing wife in India, he writes:

> Our friendship with Jane started in the early summer of 1963. . . .
> David Herbert once said to me, "Of course Jane is in love with Renée,
> but it is you who are in love with Jane." The statement is somewhat
> terse, but not devoid of truth.
>
> My wife was in her youth considered exceptionally beautiful and
> many painters wanted to paint her portrait. When we were in Tangier
> she was over sixty, but still was considered very attractive. Jane fell
> deeply in love with her at first sight. Many other women and men had
> done the same. As it happens, however, my wife has only a religious
> form of sensuality and shrinks from the very idea of any form of
> physical contact. She is a Buddhist with strong mystic tendencies and
> feels more at home in India and in Ceylon than in Europe. But in her
> makeup there is a spontaneous outflowing of love—and this love of such
> a different kind or origin responded to the love Jane had for her. Let me
> say here that Jane in her behavior was incapable at any time of anything
> savoring of immodesty or vulgarity.
>
> I was fascinated by Jane and became devotedly fond of her. So for
> some time we were an almost inseparable trio, seeing each other
> practically every day. After lunch Jane would curl up on a sofa in the
> library and go to sleep. She was of an anxious disposition and easily
> frightened, often looking rather pathetic, but with her close friends
> completely at rest. Apt at times to be fussy and rather difficult as a
> traveling companion, she was happy and quiet with us, even on the long
> and tiring drive to our home in Marrakech.
>
> Jane was fundamentally—and beyond anything—interested in
> human beings and their behavior. . . . She seemed at times to view life
> through a microscope and therefore see a very small part, highly
> magnified, to the exclusion of everything else. . . . The continual
> exercise of her powers of observation had made Jane an exceptionally
> good judge of character. She would see through people immediately,
> especially if there was any "pretense."
>
> . . . Jane was sensitive, sensual, and erotic to a most unusual degree
> and the Tangier of that period (now totally different) gave to her life an
> excellent background, full of incentives. There is a point at which the
> only difference between eroticism and pornography lies in the attitude

of mind, . . . but that difference does exist. Jane was highly erotic, but never guilty of pornography. Her affective life was complicated to the point of being almost incredible in certain respects. She discussed it with me many times and in the most minute detail. Those long and extraordinary conversations I will never forget.

People in Tangier, generally speaking, heard that Jane was lesbian and that she occasionally drank more than was really good for her. They knew she had some trouble with one leg, that she had Moroccan friends and consorted with "peculiar" writers. (Chester, in particular.) The place, in any case, was a hotbed of gossip and this led to cursory judgments about Jane, as uninformed as they were unkind. It happened sometimes that these disparaging remarks were repeated by those whom Jane liked, even if they were not close friends, and it is in such cases that she was so tolerant and understanding, no matter how badly hurt she might and often did feel. She showed this same tolerance and understanding toward the behavior of others, no matter how odd it might be. (It often struck her sense of humor.) Her whole attitude of mind was to understand and not to judge.

. . . She could not, however, bear cruelty toward animals. She often protested at some risk to herself to Moroccans regarding their treatment of donkeys and dogs. . . .

In 1963 and '64 she was still brilliant and—before drinking—her mind was literally as sharp as a needle and quick as lightning. The one disability apparent during this "good" period was the difficulty of coordination when she wanted to write by hand. She therefore used a typewriter.

IN SEPTEMBER JANE'S MOTHER AND STEPFATHER ARRIVED IN TANGIER TO SPEND several weeks. When Claire's sister Birdie had died in 1961, Claire had inherited $35,000, so she and Julian were now able to take a tour through Europe and travel to Tangier. Jane had inherited the same sum. With this money and what she had received from Libby Holman she was financially independent for the first time in her life.

That month Andreas Brown, who was working for the University of Texas, came to Tangier to arrange for the purchase of Paul's papers by the Humanities Research Center. Paul wrote to his mother, "He wanted to buy $500 worth of old notebooks from Jane, too, but she is unable to decide whether or not she wants to sell them. Her excuse is that she is going to so many dinner parties she can't make up her mind."

In November Jane felt well enough to go with Paul and Christopher Wanklyn on a trip through the east and south of Morocco. The day they arrived in Marrakech, they heard the news that Kennedy had been assassinated. Jane was horrified, Christopher remembers, yet he had the feeling that what happened in America was very distant from her.

They set out from Marrakech, went over the Grand Atlas Mountains to the Anti-Atlas Mountains, and then on to the desert. Jane seemed in very good spirits, but after two weeks she said she wanted to return to Tangier.

One day after their return, Paul, Jane, and Christopher were in Jane's apartment talking and Paul turned on the tape recorder. On the tape, which is fragmentary and of poor quality, with voices often speaking at the same time, Jane's voice is surprisingly elegant in its articulation. Her shifts of tone and her phrasing are sudden and unexpected and funny. These cannot be conveyed in print, but still a transcription of the tape suggests something of the quality of Jane's conversation at the time.

JANE: I can't tell you—it was just awful. There were these two people originally from Texas—lately from Southampton—they're living in Southampton in the summer and they spend the whole winter traveling by plane. I don't know—they go to India—they go round and round the world [*she laughs*] and they stay at all the best hotels. And they're very simple people. He's a rather amusing man, much older than she is—seems much older—and—

PAUL: Who's older?

JANE: The man is—with this Texas accent and "Well, we just think it's awful expensive at the Minzah [*Jane mimics a Texan's accent*], so we went down to see the Velásquez, but they're such tiny little rooms, there wasn't room enough for our luggage." They have nine suitcases—Paul! Out. [*Paul has just gone out of the room.*] It was very depressing. [*"Depressing" is said with many different implications simultaneously. Christopher laughs. Long pause. The tape is unclear here. Christopher begins a conversation that has something to do with food.*]

JANE: . . : more complicated than that. It's higher-class than mayonnaise.

CHRISTOPHER: All I can think of is hollandaise.

    [*Paul returns*]

JANE: What happened? . . .

PAUL: I'm trying to get Harry. He didn't answer. He tried to get me.

JANE: Why is Harry coming all the time?

PAUL: All the time? I don't know what you mean by all the time.

JANE: Does he want to talk about his writing?

PAUL: I really don't know.

JANE: [*not clear*]

PAUL: What do you mean all the time? So far as I know he's only come once.

JANE: Well, he used to come with his novel.

PAUL: Well, last year he did.

JANE: Well, I wondered why he is coming this year.

PAUL: I don't know.

CHRISTOPHER: He finished it?

JANE: Yeah. ["*Yeah*" *with many implications. Pause.*] He's very nice.

PAUL: He's Mopsy, isn't he?

JANE: I don't know.

CHRISTOPHER: Yes, Mopsy has the hair and Flopsy has the mustache. That's the way I can tell them apart. Flopsy has the mustache that goes down and Mopsy has the hair that goes up.

JANE: Mopsy's cuter.

PAUL: Mopsy was to come yesterday.

JANE: He called up and said he couldn't.

PAUL: That's right and in his place Flopsy came without notifying me so I wasn't here. So then he called up today and said, "What happened? I came by."

JANE: I suppose he didn't realize that Mopsy had called up.

[*Paul, going out of the room, says, "What?" and shuts the door behind him.*] There's a disconnection. Even if he's on the same floor, he's in another room. [*She laughs.*]

PAUL: [*returning*] Well, after all, they live in the same house. One might know what the other is doing.

JANE: Not necessarily. They have three floors. It's like you and me. You go out before I can finish the story. I'm not finished with the story.

PAUL: [*laughing*] I didn't know you were telling a story.

JANE: [*laughing*] I'm telling the story of Flopsy and Mopsy.

PAUL: And Cottontail. I'm Cottontail.

It was the ellipsis in Jane's conversations that was so amusing to Paul. Yet at the same time the ellipsis made it very difficult for others to understand her. "We went out one day to go to lunch. We got as far as the corner across the street when suddenly Jane stopped and said, 'Oh, I'm so stupid, I forgot.' And she pulled a twenty-five-peseta note out of her bag and said, 'Would you take this upstairs and give it to Berred for her lunch?' There was a whole thing left out, of course. All she meant was, take it and give it to the maid and see that she buys the cat's food. When I looked at her and laughed, she said, 'Well, you know what I mean,' and she laughed too."

In these years there was much that Jane said and did that puzzled even her good friends. Isabelle Gerofi remembers that "once we went to a luncheon party, to which some very chic people from Italy had been invited. I asked Jane to come to my table. 'It's not possible,' she said. 'I have to sit with the Italian lady. You know about Italian people in the U.S. They're poor and they eat spaghetti.' But the Italian lady was very wealthy. We thought somehow Jane was persuaded that she was a poor lady and lost in society."

351

(Paul recalls this incident differently: "A society woman of Italian descent from Philadelphia was present at a party of David Herbert's. She was very big and had a strange build and was wearing a very odd dress. Jane thought she was a female impersonator—there had just been one visiting in Tangier. And she thought David had invited this 'poor man' and he was probably ill at ease. She decided to go and sit next to him and talk to him about various ways of preparing spaghetti. Later Jane realized that this woman was really a woman and she was terribly embarrassed; you couldn't speak to her about the incident.")

Of course, she knew she was puzzling, and she enjoyed it. Once, Paul recalls, she was sitting on the floor in his apartment, her back to the fire, gnawing on a bone with meat on it. She was munching loudly and with such gusto that a man who was visiting kneeled down next to her and watched her intently. She stopped gnawing and looked at him and said, "Do you want to know more about what I'm like?"

Even then, ill though she was, preoccupied with her fear of what might happen to her, it would be hard to say what she was "like." She was the Jane who was assertive, who would allow no one to criticize Paul, and the Jane who was shy and fearful. She was the Jane who was generous in helping others—who found a job for Larbi, who helped Sonya Kamalakar with the money for cancer treatments—and the Jane who was herself so needy. She was the Jane who said to Marguerite McBey, "Of course I always say right away that I'm Jewish and a lesbian," and the Jane who still hid much.

Even her hands were contradictory, Marguerite remembers: "She had marvelously strange hands. They weren't terribly feminine. They looked like hands that did something, but they were so soft, as though there weren't bones in them, as if when you touched them, they didn't resist you."

47

In late 1963 Jane met the Princess Martha Ruspoli de Chambrun at Sonya Kamalakar's. A descendant of Lafayette and the wife of an Italian prince—though long separated from him—wealthy in her own right, Martha Ruspoli was older than Jane by ten years or more. She was a handsome woman with a complex personality; she had a strong effect upon anyone who met her. Her style was a curious mixture of the theatrical and the intellectual. It was one of exaggeration, sometimes of sentimentality and then of sudden toughness.

In the small expatriate world of Tangier, where gossip was unlimited, people differed violently about Martha. Some thought of her as a woman of great intellect and perception. Others thought she was pretentious about her intellect, that she exaggerated and believed her own distortions. Some thought of her as compassionate, others felt she was completely self-involved. Some thought of her as a gifted raconteur, others found her dramatizations endless. Some people adored her, others feared and ridiculed her.

Brought up in England, she spoke six or seven languages. She had lived with her husband in Italy during the thirties, and then lived in Paris during and immediately after the war. There she studied music and yoga, and for a while worked as a translator and editor. In 1949 she came to Tangier. In her villa on the Old Mountain, she had a continuously busy social life. She was a collector, of objects of art and of stray animals.

She had had three children, a son and two daughters. After the death of her youngest daughter, she became interested in mysticism and archaeology. She had unearthed some ancient ruins in Morocco, but was forced by the government to stop digging. When Jane met her, she was in the process of writing a book, *L'Épervier Divin* (The Divine Hawk), a recounting of the Osiris legend through the accretion of detail from ancient Egyptian texts.

Jane was immediately intrigued by Martha, and asked the Gerofis to have a dinner for her. Later she invited her to the Itesa. But in fact it was Martha, according to what Jane told the Gerofis, who was the one who made the first physical advance in the affair.

To Jane sex had always been "in the mind," an act of the imagination. In that imaginative act she had seized upon lovers whom others might find unimaginable, but for whom she herself could feel desire. (To Paul Jane had often used the word *humiliating* in speaking of her love affairs. She had said, "It's all so abject." He always felt that her choice of lovers was determined by guilt, that she chose women others would be astonished by, to turn the guilt into a joke. "The knowledge of what she was doing kept her from enjoying it, and yet what can one do if one is compulsive, as Jane was?")

Jane's love affair with Martha was also an act of the imagination, but it was different from her other affairs. Martha, not Jane, had been the aggressor in the situation. And Martha was not the kind of woman to fit into another's imaginative world. In the situation Jane soon began to feel a terrible sense of powerlessness.

To the Gerofis, Jane said that Martha would make a first step and then pull back. "Janie would wait for hours and then Martha would come and say she had so much to do she could only stay a few minutes. But that's the way Martha is. It wasn't just with Jane that she acted that way."

To David Herbert, Jane said, "I'm not very happy with her. Occasionally she'll make a great play for me and then no more."

Jane did not have the feeling that she had had before—with Helvetia, Cory, and even Cherifa—that she was the pursuer and the other the innocent. Rather she had the sense that she herself was somehow the victim. But that Martha's mother had been born in Cincinnati, as had Sidney Auer, made the alliance seem ordained as well as protective. This shared past gave to the affair a sense of urgent necessity. It could help hold Jane in her daily life.

Rex Henry and his wife tried to warn Jane against the relationship. "My wife and I tried to persuade her not to give in to what would inevitably be a detrimental influence. Jane realized this and admitted it, but could not resist the need for a close companionship with a person of undoubted intellectual merit. In the early days of this association she used to come and talk to us about it and would see and admit the pitfalls, but the die was cast."

For her part Martha remembers an idyllic early relationship. "We used to eat together often, Paul and Jane and I, in 1964. Then Paul would go to his flat and Jane and I would come to my house and spend the night. We were very happy together."

AND ALWAYS IN THE BACKGROUND WAS THE FIGURE OF CHERIFA, WHOM JANE had incorporated into her daily life, whom she saw as her responsibility, her child. Martha felt that Jane had been taken in, that her conviction that Cherifa had sacrificed something to come with her was nonsense. She was being naïve, Martha told her—that in fact relationships like the one between herself and Cherifa were not infrequent between European and Moroccan women, only they were kept secret.

Martha never thought that Cherifa would want to poison Jane. "She would have wanted her to live for years, to get money out of her." She kept trying to get Cherifa to go, just as Paul had been doing, though to him Jane would respond sharply, "It's my business. I know what I'm doing."

Martha said to Jane, "You must get rid of her." Jane herself would admit, according to Martha, that Cherifa was "capable of anything," but then when Martha would press her to fire Cherifa, she would say, "She's not as bad as all that."

Cherifa was, as before, the head of Jane's household, in charge of the maids, getting, Paul was sure, kickbacks on their salaries. What concerned her most, apparently, as it always had, was security, for herself and for her family. Her own sexual relationship with Jane was ended by this time, but did she see in the other women a threat to her security? The Gerofis thought that Cherifa was jealous of Jane's "amours." But David Herbert was not sure. He remembers that at the beginning, "when Jane used to go out with Martha, Cherifa would help get Jane dressed and then give her a slap on the behind as she was leaving, but what she actually felt then, no one knew."

IN LATE FEBRUARY 1964 JANE RECEIVED A CLIPPING FROM LIBBY HOLMAN announcing the opening of *In the Summer House* in an off-Broadway production on the seventeenth of March. Jane was very angry and upset. She had signed the contract for the production reluctantly, after Paul had urged her to. The contract had stipulated that she had the right of veto in casting, but now it was too late for her to be in New York for the casting and the rehearsals. She felt that the producers didn't want her around, and had deliberately avoided letting her know the opening date. The play opened at the Little Fox Theater with Estelle Parsons as Gertrude and Leora Dana as Mrs. Constable. It closed after a run of a few weeks. Audrey Wood, Jane's agent, was stunned at the early closing and kept delaying telling Jane, but finally wrote to her about it. To Jane it was another defeat out of a life she might try to speak of as past, but one she could not finally relinquish. And then there was the new play she was still trying to write. How would its chances be harmed by this new failure?—if and when she ever finished it.

In May Lawrence Stewart returned to Tangier with Leonore Gershwin. He found Jane changed. She had grown heavier. "Her face was unwrinkled and her eyes were clear. She looked fine. She was still insufferably slow in making any decision, but she seemed more sure of herself and of running her life than she had been in 1960."

Lawrence had brought a message to Jane from Alice Toklas, telling Jane to write. Jane was upset. " 'Everyone is always bringing me messages from Alice,' she said. Later she was more conciliatory and spoke of Alice Toklas with affection."

To Lawrence it was clear that Jane's position was that she had once been a writer, but that was all over with now. She even said to him about *Two Serious Ladies* that it was really Paul's book, he had helped her with it so much. "We can't have two writers in the family," she added. At the time Paul was negotiating with director Robert Aldrich for the sale of the film rights to *The Sheltering Sky* and Jane was concerned that Paul get good advice on the negotiations. She kept asking Lawrence and Leonore for help.

Leonore recalls that she had brought Jane "some things I thought a woman in Morocco would need, petticoats and imitation-Pucci dresses. Jane generally wore the same thing, an A-line skirt, blue, usually, and a blouse and a scarf around her head. She had a trim little figure. She was very funny, with a witty sharpness."

Soon after Leonore arrived, she called Jane. "Jane came over with her friend Martha. She said to me, 'I'm a lesbian and this is my lover.' I felt like saying, 'This is nonsense.' I gave a dinner and Jane insisted that Martha had to come and sit next to her."

To Leonore Paul "still had the quality of golden youth. I was in love with him, as everyone was. Jane's love for Paul was more important than anything else. She would use any excuse to touch him. We'd sit there, he and I, on low cushions and Jane would be sitting on the floor. She'd lean over and touch him and say, 'You and your long legs.' We wanted to buy some rugs and other things in Morocco and Jane was reluctant to help us, but Paul said to help us so Jane did."

Jane and Lawrence and Leonore drove to Tetuán, an hour and a half from Tangier. "As usual with Jane it was difficult to go directly there," says Lawrence. "Paul had given explicit and clear directions, but Jane preferred to wander on her own. She didn't like asking questions when we got lost, because she said she feared complications. When we got to the shop Paul had told us about, I saw some rugs and other things I liked, and I began to try to bargain with the owner, with Jane translating. But when I asked Jane to ask the price of the runners, she said she wasn't going to bargain. I said I didn't want her to, that I just wanted to know the price. At this point Jane went out into the street. She said she found it all too painful. It was obvious to me that the shopkeeper, who was quite well-to-do, enjoyed bargaining, but that had no effect on Jane. She said she just couldn't bargain. She always felt so guilty, she said. Yet at the Marhaba Palace on that same night she lectured the owner shamelessly on the decline in the quality of his cuisine."

On the drive back from Tetuán, Lawrence recalls, Jane was sitting in the front with the driver and suddenly she began to speak of how Paul loved to eat the ice cream at Elizabeth's Tea Room in New York, during the years they were first married. It was for Lawrence one of those miracles of charm. "She talked with great ease and was wonderfully funny."

He remembers too that Jane lived in the apartment above Paul's, and to Lawrence's surprise she did not have a key to either Paul's apartment or her own. Serving Leonore and himself one day at Paul's she said to him, "You can either have Scotch or cheese."

But once when he was sitting alone in Paul's apartment, Jane came in, having just awakened from a nap. Paul had gone out looking for Larbi Layachi to have him autograph his book for Lawrence. Jane, not finding Paul there, became distraught. "I can still hear her wail, 'I'll never see him again, and what will I do?' And I thought—there was such terror in her voice—'My God, what can I do?'"

THAT SUMMER PAUL RENTED A HOUSE ON THE OLD MOUNTAIN. IT WAS ON THE edge of a cliff overlooking the sea, four hundred feet above the waves, and included twenty-five acres of forest land. Paul would walk along the edge of the cliffs, notebook in hand. He was working on a new novel, *Up Above the World*. Often Jane would come at noon and prepare his lunch for him.

Larbi worked for Paul again that summer. He remembers one day when Jane and Cherifa were supposed to bring lunch from the Inmueble Itesa.

"I was waiting for them and they didn't show up. I went out to look for them. When I got to the end of the property, there they were, walking, carrying the food. The taxi couldn't make it up the hill. Cherifa was mad at me. She said, 'How come you're sitting on your butt when we're bringing the food?' I said, 'How am I supposed to know what happened?' Jane laughed and said, 'How would he know? Be quiet, you crazy.' She said it to Cherifa in a nice way."

In July, Tennessee Williams came to Tangier with his friend Marian Vaccaro. He was so distraught about the death of Frankie Merlo that he did not stay. But he remembers going to the beach and talking to Jane, and again feeling comfort from being with her.

In September Jane's mother and stepfather came to Tangier a second time. Claire had been pressuring Jane to send her the money for the visit, and Jane finally agreed. During this visit Jane and Claire and Julian had dinner with Boo Faulkner, who was now living in Tangier. In the course of the evening something Claire said threw Jane into a rage. She screamed at her mother. Claire, defending herself, said, "Didn't I always do everything for you?" and Jane, still furious, said, "You gave me a governess I hated." Boo was astonished. It was the first time he had ever seen Jane angry with her mother; it was the first time he had ever heard her say anything about her childhood.

Jane's anger with Claire was certainly nothing new. Paul remembers that often when he brought Claire's letters from the post office, Jane would look at them and then throw them on the floor and stamp on them. Later she would read them and answer them dutifully. What was new was that the anger had broken through her control in her mother's presence. Still, it seemed only a momentary flare-up. That same week Jane could joke in a letter to Isabelle Gerofi, who was in a hospital in Belgium:

> I speak to Yvonne every day and she has been too busy to want anyone with her so far. At any rate my mother is leaving Monday. This is a kind of useless letter but I hope that Yvonne wrote you that she could have me at night(!) if she wanted me that late. By some miracle Sherifa gave her kind permission. . . . I am ready for a real lunatic asylum myself and tell Yvonne about it on the telephone every day.

To Ruth Fainlight that same month Jane wrote: "I have never really had it so good here in Tangier except much earlier when I was still in my thirties and I lived on the mountain and later in my own little house in the Casbah."

But then Jane went on to talk about a new worry. That summer she had signed a contract with Peter Owen, the English publisher, for publication of *Two Serious Ladies*. Thinking about the critical reception of the book and having to decide whether she should go to London for the publication caused Jane great anxiety.

> I don't expect to earn money on my book, but anything to forestall a bad reception, I mean one so bad that I will regret deciding to have it reprinted. I doubt that anything will help that except blurbs that will keep critics in check a little anyway. Thank God for Alan's.
>
> I could go on forever about all this, the pros and cons of going or staying here but I fear that the letter will turn into a fifteen page *ganze magilla* of "if's and but's" which I shall never send and then more months will go by and I will never write; but the letter could be used as

a document for some doctor who specializes in states of anxiety. . . .

I shall certainly write you again now that I've started but you may come to dread these tortured letters about tiny decisions. I am famous for them or I was when I was famous, with a few friends (most of whom are dead). . . .

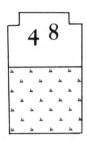

48

Though JANE WANTED *TWO SERIOUS LADIES* TO BE A success—dreaded that it would not be—at the same time she had a sense that it was the work of a girl from long ago, a girl who was now dead. To Lawrence Stewart she had said that that part of her life was finished. Yet to Ruth Fainlight she had written, "I hope that some day this will all stop and that I will work a little because there is nothing else for me to do." And again and again in 1963 and even in 1964, she had gone back to the notebook of the play she had begun in 1962, one more notebook of the many notebooks —fifteen years of unfinished work.

Though she had set the play in Camp Cataract, the characters in this play are not the characters of the story. According to the notebook, she began with three women and one man, Hortense, Miggie, Beryl, and Tommy. There is a convoluted love situation: Hortense is in love with Miggie, Miggie is in love with Beryl, Beryl is in love with Tommy, and Tommy is in love with Hortense.

But this is only the first interweaving. The characters never set. Their passions change, their personalities change, even their names change: a Bonzoe appears, a Teddie appears, a Loretta appears. To herself Jane writes: "Try the scene with a Miggie and a Teddie—or don't worry whether Teddie and Miggie are two separate people yet." Then she tries, "Loretta is in love with Bonzoe—but Loretta leaves—to go with Tommy—possibly—Try various combinations untill you get the right one."

Her working notes for the play are marked by a sense of mistrust of her own gift of invention, of her own imagination. She keeps trying to tie the characters to people she has known, as if she has given up trust in the process of fictional transformation that was always second nature to her. She writes:

Bonzoe is now like Teddy Grifiths [Griffis], a beautiful girl. . . .
. . . bring Miggie in as Frances—with a boney ugly face. . . .

Tommy wants Bonzoe too and Bonzoe finally sleaps with him because Miggie drives her to it. Miggie a kind of Helvetia driving Bonzoe to leave her—or . . .

She keeps tying the characters to characters in *In the Summer House*, as if that were a text of a safer reality:

Bonzoe in despair goes and sleeps with Tommy—certain that she will never get Miggie—she loves Tommy—he is the Lionel in this play. . . .

Bonzoe struggles to rid herself of Miggie even at the end when Miggie comes to her and declares her love—which Bonzoe then has to accept or reject (a) on mystical grounds—because she feels Tommy is right for her—(b) or because like Molly when she sees that Miggie loves her she does not want her. . . .

She tries to make the characters hold by seeing them played by a particular actress. "Could . . . Millie Dunnock be the other counselor?" "Try to make Nora come to life—a young Betty Davis—but ridden with guilt." She even asks herself, "Is it possible to change Miggie into more of a Judith Anderson person—or would that be too much like the *Summer House?*"

Most terrible of all for a writer, she has come to mistrust her own sense of language. Throughout the notebook she uses psychological jargon that she would never have used earlier. It is as if in accepting a language and framework not her own, she is invoking protection:

Hortense—is the only one who is truly schizophrenic—one day she splits at the camp. . . .

Hortense starts to be afraid of Bonzoe. . . . Her spurning of Bonzoe fed her nureausis and made it possible for her to live with herself. . . .

Bonzoe is young—very young—the boy is her father and she is in love with—Miggie—as the split between her unconscious hatred of Miggie [and] her conscious love and admiration deepens she gets closer and closer to the edge. . . .

Have Miggie be the capricious neurotic on[e] (like Jane) torturing Hortense. . . .

Hortense—canny—subdued dinamic quality—a masochist like Paul who is out to torture Miggie unconsciously. . . .

But the extraordinary thing in this notebook of fragments is the way in which the themes that had always preoccupied Jane are still the themes that surface here, that the cast of thought is still recognizably Jane, that the feeling is still recognizably Jane. The question of sin and the relation to God through love between women and women and women and men keeps recurring:

Tommy falls in love and associates or confuses love with a spiritual experience. He has love completely confused with God, if it is a confusion. . . .

Miggie has a very strong sense of sin—and to expiate this she tortures Bonzoe—with Hortense. . . .

Loretta is the sense of guilt in the play—equates Steve with God and her father. . . .

Then Lionel (Paul) and Hortense break Miggie's belief in God. The only person who can make her believe in God ever is a man. . . .

The word *God* appears again and again:

Each carachter carachter has his own conception of when he is pleasing God. . . .

Either people are afraid to mention God or else they are Roman Catholics. . . .

"I wonder too much about the nature of God to be in the state department. . . ."

She describes in one sentence the theme of her play: "This is about people who build up an artificial destiny or life through which nothing can pierce."

To Jane the writing in the notebook was nothing but failure. Yet, in its slipping and dissolving and fragmenting, there was a rendering of the process of her own life as she was living it and feeling it, nakedly, without wiles.

Her alternatives are clear: a world of slipping situations (and slipping feelings, where love goes to hate to sin to idealism to desperation), part of the artificial destiny to which she clings, and the world of the single destiny that is not artificial, the one terrible destiny she has always been avoiding.

"The play has no ending no solution," she writes. For there is no ending except the one ending that must be put off.

Still she tries to write. She goes back again, trying another combination. The empty pages face her, and she tries again to "suck at the bone of her own life."

IN THE WINTER OF 1964 PAUL COMPLETED *UP ABOVE THE WORLD*. HE thought of the writing as a

purely pleasurable pastime. I tried to recapture the state of mind which had produced the thrillers I had read to the seventh grade in primary school, to discover what result that point of departure might give now.

The ploy worked: I got caught up in the elaboration of the tale fairly quickly and knew I was going to finish the book.

What Paul got caught up in was a story of the torment and death of a husband and wife. The elderly Dr. Slade and his wife, Day, young enough to be his granddaughter, are on a second honeymoon in South America. They are affectionate with each other but their sex life is minimal, in part because of his health, in part because she avoids sex, for unstated reasons.

At a dingy hotel in a small town they meet a fat, disagreeable older woman, Mrs. Rainmantle. She is afraid to sleep in her room because there is no lock on the door. Mrs. Slade persuades her husband to take Mrs. Rainmantle's room, and she spends the night with the older woman. The Slades leave early the next morning, while Mrs. Rainmantle is still sleeping. As Day shuts the door she sees Mrs. Rainmantle in an oddly lifeless position, but she pretends to herself that it is not so. After the Slades leave, the hotel goes up in flames. The authorities believe that Mrs. Rainmantle died in the fire.

In fact Mrs. Rainmantle has been murdered by her son Vero, who has then set fire to the hotel. Suspecting that the Slades may be suspicious of her death, he contrives to meet them in the city. There he uses drugs to alter their minds, and ends by killing them. The Slades are condemned to death, never knowing why they are killed.

Vero is shown as obsessed by the evil in his own mother. He dreams of her:

Underneath the jovial flesh was the supremely calculating consciousness, the dark destroying presence. No matter what part she was playing (for her role depended upon her audience), to him her basic expression was always the same, cunning and omniscient, with an undertone of implicit menace, as though it had been universally conceded that woman's state, entailing persecution and suffering, included her right to seek vengeance.

In the world of this novel even love is obscene. Vero, dictating into his tape recorder, says:

In India, you know, there are people who claim that love is obscene unless both parties are so conscious of what they are doing—I mean so absolutely aware of themselves and each other during sex—that they can concentrate on God all the way through to the end, both of them. . . .

But there is not one character in the novel who is capable at any time of concentration on God or even on another human being. Under the influence of the drug administered to him by Vero, Dr. Slade comes to know "that soon there would be only the obscene reality of himself, trapped in the solitary chamber of existence."

Even here, in the unfinished notebook and the finished novel, the themes that preoccupy Paul and Jane are finally the same: the presence or absence of God, the presence or absence of love, the isolation of every human being.

But she carries into her fiction aspects of her daily life along with her moral dilemmas. There may be evil in Jane's work, but it is always hedged around by daily life, and finally limited by it. When Paul goes into his fiction, he discards daily life and hope. There gratuitous evil triumphs vengefully. It is an immoral world that God has abandoned.

In imagination he allies himself with irrevocable and destructive destiny. In imagination she knows of that destiny but allies herself with those who will delay it. None of her characters gives up the hope of happiness. She grants them what she had written of herself in 1954: "I have never yet enjoyed a day, but I have never stopped trying to arrange for happiness."

It is not by chance that the new novel Paul completed was *Up Above the World* and that the novel Jane never ended was *Out in the World*.

At the end of January 1965 *Two Serious Ladies* was published in England. Almost all of the reviews were very favorable. But Jane's attention was on Paul's work. He was just finishing *Up Above the World*, and they planned to take a trip to New York in April.

To Lawrence Stewart she wrote:

> We are both eager to have your opinion on Paul's new book. . . . I have a feeling it can be a great success, and I'd love to have your opinion and suggestions on how to handle it. Paul does not like to discuss it. . . .

Jane added that she had not written to anyone since before Christmas, since "a friend of mine here in Tangier died . . . and I was so depressed. . . ." The friend was Sonya Kamalakar. That she had died at a time when Jane and she were not on good terms caused Jane great anguish.

In April Paul and Jane sailed to New York. Paul went on to Florida to see his parents. His father had suffered a cerebral hemorrhage. To Jane Paul wrote:

> My father seems a bit better than when I arrived, but of course he cannot walk at all, or even move from his bed or chair without assistance, nor will he be able to at any time again. Each night after he is put to sleep, my mother and I discuss possible procedures to follow with regard to him. She is completely against putting him into a home, but she isn't strong enough to cope with him by herself. . . . The great

difficulty is that he has no idea where he is or what is going on. . . . The only sensible thing would be for him to be in a home where he would have constant medical care, but she won't consider that, so some sort of stop-gap has to be found.

In New York, Jane was staying with Libby Holman and her husband, Louis Schanker. John Goodwin invited Jane to visit him in Santa Fe with Paul, but she decided to stay in New York when she heard from Frances. Jane wrote to her:

Thank you for calling me. I wanted to call you but I had told you that I wouldn't unless you asked me to. It is an invasion of you're privacy I know and I thought it was best never to wake you up if the telephone was turned on and not to call and interrupt you in case you had friends. I wanted to call you very much and finally when you didn't write me I decided that you were either against seeing me at all or ill. I worried terribly about your being ill but still I never would have called. I am not going to New Mexico now that I have heard from you but I felt when you told me that I should go to Libby's that you might not want to see me again and I told you I was going to New Mesico. It came into my head because in the last weeks—or few days I had thought I would never see you again somehow and that New Mexico was best. Of course I could not do that anyway because there is not that much time left. . . . Paul left for Santa Fe and I think he was wise. He has always thought, as I have, that it might be a place to settle when Tangier proved impossible. I will surely stay here and may have to take a room somewhere because it is much too difficult either fitting my schedule to Libby's or inconveniancing all my friends. . . .

Robert Fizdale and Arthur Gold saw Jane during that visit. "We were all going up to see Jerry Robbins. Jane had great respect for him and she wanted him to direct one of Paul's novels if it were made into a film.

"We said to her, 'We have to be at Jerry's at seven-thirty, so for God's sakes, be ready.' She was staying at the Windsor at Madison and Fifty-fourth. When we went to pick her up, Bobby waited in the car, knowing that if we both went up we'd be delayed."

Arthur went into the lobby and called her room. She said, "You can't come up now. There's this terribly important call I'm expecting from a woman who is terribly prominent."

Finally Jane called down and told Arthur it was all right for him to come up. " 'You come down,' I said, but she said, 'You have to come up. The bedspread is caught in the door and I can't go in or out.' So I went up. There was an enormous chenille bedspread and it was caught in the door. I managed to squeeze in the room and both of us started pulling at it trying to get it out from under the door.

" ' While we're working on this,' she said, 'let's order rum and Cokes.' She loved them because they were 'yenti' drinks. And of course she loved the fact that the chenille bedspread was caught in the door.

"Then Bobby came up. He'd gotten tired of waiting in the car. He squeezed in the door. Then the bellboy arrived with the drinks. It was a little room and it was so crowded now that there wasn't any room for him. But Jane told him to come in anyhow. She tried to get him to move the bed. 'Oh by the way,' Jane said to us, 'do you have any money?' And to the bellboy she said, 'Bring us another drink.' "

IN MID-MAY JANE WENT TO FLORIDA TO VISIT HER MOTHER AND STEPFATHER. Neither Claire nor Julian was well. Claire had recently developed a heart condition and Julian was almost blind. From Miami Jane wrote to Frances:

> I seem to have bogged down in my depression and decided, at least, that you were right, "that it was useless to send you a letter about a decision which was already made and certainly now to late to change." It is a hair-raising document this letter, and the prose and cons of the decision to be made so minutely gone into that it really should be solde to a library for "Psychiatric research in extreme cases of anxiety."
>
> I shall certainly hang on to the letter but it does seem dead now and I only wish that I hadn't told you that you shouldn't call. Actually some of you're discretion *had* come off on me for a moment but of course at the wrong moment when it was entirely unnecessary. That is inevitable when one tries to please without quite understanding what one has done. . . .
>
> Now that I know more or less that you should never be subjected to any panics that have to do with me, I am likely to exaggerate the other way, which I'm sure you would rather I do than the contrary. It's true that it would be difficult for me to telephone you again before Thursday or Friday because he [Julian] would think me a "spend thrift," no matter who it was. Obviously if I called you every day as I long to he would think so even more and he would know how I felt about you. I don't care but my mother would mind his guessing anything and she knows me too well for me to hide much. She is quite remarkable in that way and wants me to be happy—however she would always hide that side my life. . . .

To Libby Holman Jane wrote of Frances:

Her fanatical secrecy about nothing at all is so irrational that I am frightened for her because of course I sniff a psychosis rather than a neurosis . . . (sniff, indeed) . . .

Perhaps I should not use the word psychosis in regard to F. but extreme neurosis—but I am no doctor. However I don't think White Plains would refuse either one of us. . . . Whatever I say I love F. very much—She is a tragic-fanatical-Electra kind of figure in a "tea pot."

On her return to New York Jane wrote Cherifa a letter in Spanish (it would have to be read to her), saying that she was trying to get in touch with Cherifa's nephew Hamed, who had come to the United States with a circus and was stranded. On June 2 Paul and Jane left by boat for Casablanca. Hamed returned to Morocco with them; Jane paid his fare.

From Tangier, Paul wrote to Virgil Thomson of their arrival in Morocco:

The day before landing, one of Jane's purser friends came up to her on deck and whispered that he had heard bad news a few moments earlier on the radio: Morocco was under martial law. This provided the expected effect: Jane went into one of her worrying states and refused to talk of anything else, so that as soon as we were on the dock the next morning she arranged to take a taxi directly to Tangier, rather than risk spending the night in Casa and going on by train the following day. So it cost $85 to get here, plus meals and drinks for Cherifa's nephew and the driver. But all was quiet, and indeed has remained so since. . . .

Jane has allowed herself to be caught up in the round of lunches and dinners; she complains about them afterwards, but, one supposes, enjoys them during. She's also writing, which generally puts her into a bad humor. . . .

I'm trying to prepare a volume of Jane's short stories for publication in England. The novel is still being a success there. I think the stories might be equally well received. . . .

It was Paul who was preparing Jane's collection of stories, since when her publisher Peter Owen had suggested it to her, she had shrugged the whole idea off. First of all, she said, she had no copies of her work. Paul told her that he had copies hidden away. Then she said that there weren't enough stories for a book. Paul converted "East Side: North Africa" to fiction, gathered the stories together under the title *Plain Pleasures*, and sent them to Peter Owen for publication.

Paul himself continued to work on a translation of a book-length story told to him in Mohgrebi Arabic by the young Moroccan Mohammed Mrabet. The book was published as *Love with a Few Hairs*. The collaboration between Mrabet and Paul was the beginning of a long and intimate working relationship.

ON HER RETURN FROM NEW YORK JANE WAS, AS PAUL HAD WRITTEN TO Virgil, caught up in the round of lunches and dinners, and she was also writing. But by that fall a great change had taken place in her. She was suffering severely from anxiety, depression, and insomnia.

It is true that Jane had always been anxious, always subject to depression, and that for years she had had difficulty sleeping. But somehow she had "coped." When Sonya Kamalakar died the year before and Jane had not made her peace with her, she had been very depressed, but had still been able to function. When, on her visit to Florida, she had seen Claire and Julian aging and ill, she was depressed, but she managed. But now her capacity to live her daily life began to erode away.

Under Dr. Roux's care, she continued to take multiple medication—for high blood pressure, for anxiety, to prevent convulsions, for insomnia. She was apparently still using Serpasil at this time. (Dr. Roux, either now or later, was trying other drugs, as the Serpasil caused Jane to be depressed, though it seemed the only effective way to control her blood pressure.) Jane had always been lax about taking her medication. But as her depression and anxiety worsened, she began to take the medications indiscriminately. The more indiscriminately she took the drugs, the more she became confused about what she had taken. And now, for the first time since her stroke, she began to drink consistently.

Worried about her condition, and particularly about her dizziness, she went to a doctor in Casablanca, who told her that there was "nothing new wrong" with her brain. To Libby Holman, after seeing the doctor, she wrote:

> I am really in a black state and trying to keep it from Paul as much as possible—which means that I don't discuss myself and my life and my work too much (just a little).

That fall, whether because of the anxiety and the depression or because of a specific physical illness—one of those "small reverses" that kept eroding her away—Jane spent much of her time confined to her room. In addition to her own physical and mental condition there were other pressures upon her. The affair with Princess Martha Ruspoli was causing her a great deal of anguish. Martha was working steadily on her book and she came to Jane's apartment frequently to discuss what she had done and to go over the manuscript with Jane. But Jane still had the feeling that, beyond these visits, Martha didn't have time for her. She was jealous of Martha and suspected that she was having an affair with a man. To the Gerofis, Jane said that it disturbed her that Martha was the "masculine one" in the affair. And she reproached Martha directly for "being like a man," achieving satisfaction too easily. As for Jane herself, according to Martha, she was unable to achieve sexual satisfaction in the affair. (It is Martha's opinion that Jane had never achieved sexual satisfaction in any situation. Martha thought it another form of Jane's need for self-punishment.)

Jane was also being subjected to pressure from Cherifa, who by now had become violently antagonistic toward Martha. Cherifa knew how Martha talked about her, how she urged Jane to get rid of her. Cherifa spoke mockingly of Martha as "Princessa." "I'm better than she is. I'm a saint," she would say to Jane, "and I have my papers to prove I'm a virgin." ("It was as if the two ideas were connected in her mind," says Paul, "a state of being holy because of never having slept with a man.")

Jane was pressed between Martha and Cherifa as if between mother and child. She was in a "summer house" of a different kind, where she was both mother and daughter, outrunning the dramas she had herself created.

Bewildered by what was happening to her, Jane kept trying to fashion a daily life, but it had a strange shape. Confined to her room, drinking, not eating regularly, she would fall asleep early and then get up at three o'clock in the morning and prowl around and eat. Paul had installed a small telephone between their two bedrooms—Jane's was directly above his—and she often called him. But she had the prospect before her that Paul was soon going to leave. He was going to Bangkok for an extended stay, starting the next summer. When he was in New York, Little, Brown had offered him the chance to write a portrait of Cairo for a series about cities. Paul had turned down Cairo, but had suggested Bangkok. Little, Brown took him up on his offer. It would be the first time since 1957 that Paul would be away from Jane for an extended and indefinite period of time.

Dr. Roux tried to control Jane's medication, by teaching Cherifa to give it to Jane, but Jane paid no attention to Cherifa's directions. Seeing Jane drinking, Paul tried to get her to stop. Dr. Roux had told him that Jane was to have absolutely no alcohol. "Do you want to kill yourself?" he'd say to Jane. "You're taking Epanutin and you're not supposed to have alcohol." "Leave me alone," Jane would say. "I know what's going to happen to me. I know I'm not going to get better. I have the right. . . ."

Cherifa, who liked to drink every night, would say to Jane, "You can't have any more," but Jane would simply take the bottle from her and pour herself another drink.

Still Jane kept trying to hold on to her life. She held to the affair with Martha as if that, above all, could save her. But as it happened, Martha's personality—the very things that made her survive in the world—began to work against Jane. Martha's combination of assertiveness and theatricality made her immune to Jane's imaginative power—or if she was vulnerable, she had a great capacity for self-protection. Jane's way of viewing the world, her microscopic examination of the smallest relations between people, her mistrust of abstractions, her attitude toward mystery and secrecy, her sense of sin, were all antagonistic to Martha's way of being.

Martha's mysticism was connected with a search for large abstractions. In her writing of the legend of Osiris, in the interpretations she made, in rendering the symbolic into the historical, in her very rhetoric, there was a sense of self-assurance. And then too, Martha's absolute immersion in her own daily life, her sense of her "place" in the world, and her capacity to get things done in that world, were all reproaches to Jane, or so she took them to be as she felt more and more powerless in the affair and in her own daily life.

Once during that fall Jane went to Martha and said, "I want to do something to make you hate me." Martha laughed and told her to "stop acting like a child." She considered it only more of Jane's need to punish herself.

Dr. Roux, Paul, Cherifa, and Martha were all equally helpless before the forces that had been set in motion in Jane. She had fought for so long, day by day, to be in daily life, putting off that point of no return of Kafka's: so many years of delaying, with continuous vigilance, watching for the return of old symptoms or the appearance of new ones. She had avoided for so long, carrying the burden of what must be or what would be, till the avoiding, the vigilance itself, became the burden. Of her unfinished play she had written that it "has no ending, no solution." But now something in her was driving toward ending.

And yet—and with Jane there is always an "and yet"—this picture of Jane, though accurate in the main, is incomplete. It makes her living presence darker than it was. For even at this time, Paul recalls, and later in the darkest days, there would still be, in and out of the darkness, her wit, her playing, her jokes, that part of her too, irrepressible.

ON CHRISTMAS DAY 1965, JAY HASELWOOD, PROPRIETOR OF THE PARADE Bar and one of Jane's closest friends in Tangier, died suddenly of a heart attack. To Libby Holman Jane wrote:

> The depression after Jay's death was bad and I did not start coming out of it for a month. For me it was the death of an eppoc—the spelling of that is driving me crazy but since Paul and I keep different hours and live on different floors I just can't correct anything. I know you wrote me it did not matter. If I have not written I had reasons.

The confusion in my life has been fantastic and I think impossible to write about. I am not sick but I am not well or I am having change of life and the dissiness gets better and then worse. . . .

Helvetia Perkins also died in December. (It is not clear when Jane heard of her death.) Jane had not seen her since 1958, and then only briefly when Helvetia had come to visit her in the hospital in Westchester. In the years since Jane had lived with her, Helvetia had changed. Her nephew Montgomery Orr remembers her from the early sixties:

She was short, determined, weathered, and had a haircut exactly like Gertrude Stein. She lived alone in a lovely house in Vermont then, but would make long solo auto trips, sometimes on business to Chicago, sometimes just to see the country or visit my mother who then lived in Montana. Always in the same tough tweed suit, and a brown crocheted cap, a little like a Peruvian ski cap, with ear flaps.

. . . She was also a determined liberal, shocking many of her old friends, and my wife Louise and me, when we visited her in Vermont in the early sixties with our daughter and a young man to whom she wasn't even engaged. At bedtime she asked, 'Would Bonnie and her friend like one room or two?' and either Louise or I blurted out, 'Two would be better,' squares as we were and are.

Helvetia died in Mexico on a visit to her daughter and son-in-law and grandchildren, to whom she was very devoted. At her death her daughter found among her possessions a portrait of Jane that Maurice Grosser had painted in 1947, a notebook of Jane's, and some books of Jane's from her years in Leysin. There was no trace of the novel Helvetia had worked on for many years, which she had shown to Paul when he was in New York in 1959. Reading it, Paul had been astonished. "I have never read anything that was so much like Jane's work."

Early in the spring of 1966 Jane received a letter from Farrar, Straus and Giroux, who wanted to publish *Two Serious Ladies*, *In the Summer House*, and her short stories in one volume, to be called *The Collected Works of Jane Bowles*.

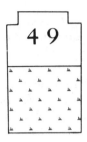

49

By LATE SPRING PAUL REALIZED THAT "THERE WAS NO question of leaving Jane in Morocco by herself in her present highly nervous state." They therefore worked out an arrangement that Jane and he would go to New York together. She would then take the train to Florida to stay with her mother, while he went on to Thailand.

In June, before sailing to New York, Paul received a telegram that his mother had died, and the following week another saying that his father had died. Although he had until now felt reluctant to leave Tangier, the death of his parents numbed his regret about going. "Very likely the shock made itself felt by leaving me in a state of indifference. I can only deduce that I felt profoundly guilty for having excised them from my life."

On the first day of July he and Jane sailed for New York on the *Independence*. After Paul left for Bangkok, Jane stayed in New York a few days, partly to see her editor Hal Vursell at Farrar, Straus and Giroux, partly to see her friends, including Frances. But in the city her anxiety became even more intense.

Estelle Lewis, Dione Lewis's mother, remembers that Jane called her up and asked her to come and stay with her. "I spent several days with her. She was staying at a hotel in the fifties. When I came into her room there was three or four hundred dollars cash on the couch. Jane had started drinking. She was waiting for her friends to call, but while I was there nobody else came to see her. She was very disappointed and she kept waiting. She wanted me to be with her all the time. I said, 'Now look, Jane, I can't be with you every minute. I have things I have to do.' She said something about my going to Tangier with her. I said, 'Listen, I have no strength for you, darling.'

"Mostly Jane would lie down and go to sleep. Then sometimes, when she got up, we'd go out and walk. We'd go into a department store and Jane would buy something and put it on her mother's charge account."

Dione came to see Jane. "She acted lost, as if she'd been shot out of a cannon." Jane was going to visit Frances, who lived on the thirty-third floor of a building near her hotel. "Jane had to get drunk before she could get in the elevator."

With the help of Richard Holland from Farrar, Straus and Giroux, Jane got on the train to Florida. In Miami she stayed with her mother. There she became more and more anxious and more and more depressed. To Hal Vursell she wrote of her intention to return to Tangier, and of her indecision as to whether to go through Algeciras or Casablanca:

> I don't see why you should take the time to read all of this but it is perhaps to justify and clarify to myself as well as to you my own impotence to make a decision in this tiny little nightmare among other nightmares. . . .

Frantic at not having heard from Martha since her arrival in the United States, she wired her and also wrote to Dr. Roux asking for news of her. Dr. Roux replied that Martha was very busy with visitors:

> I hope you've had direct news by now, and that you won't let your imagination lead you down dark paths, or toward suppositions one more grotesque than the next.

In fact Martha had written to Jane before receiving her wire, telling her how busy she was and adding:

> I miss you ever so much. Do let me hear from you and tell me you are well. Don't drink too much. Don't take too many drugs. Please give my regards to your mother and stepfather. With fond kisses. . . .

After receiving Jane's cable, Martha cabled her that she had written and on August 3 she wrote to her again:

> No news from you except that one letter just before you left New York on a journey which seemed such a nightmare that, believe me, had I had cash, I would have flown over to be near you—Well, you will be back soon now, I feel confident. We are already in August. . . . We had an abominable cook who, realizing that she was going to be fired, tried to poison us all! She *was* fired, and besides my socco activities, which take hours daily, I wield the pans and spoons.
>
> My poor book! I try to slip in an hour or so daily, but it is the mechanical work that takes so long. . . .
>
> Darling, are you all right? I think of you ever so often and miss you. How is your mother? She must have been so happy to see you after such a long time. . . . I am longing to have news of your arrival and your stay

with them. . . . For God's sake don't take too many medicines and don't drink too much! I hope you are well. . . .

I am very fond of you Jane, little one. Please don't be silly and don't "paint the devil on the wall" when he isn't there. . . .

On August 9 Jane wrote to Paul:

I have been so worried that the machine would not be back in time enough to write to you.* I certainly needed to send you more than a few lines. . . . I am sending you Peter Owen's account as I said I would. Julian says that if he gets thirty percent which is the final sum we settled on, as I remember, then his calculation would be about correct. I would earn about one thousand dollars according to Julian and I'm sure that you will agree with him. On publication of course I will get more.

I called up Dr. Dean [a local doctor], actually to have someone to hang on to while I was here because Naturally I was in a panic that I would somehow not be able to get out of here—which panic still exists but I do have Dr. Dean to hang on to. He gave me any number of pills in a brown paper bag. I thought he had brought some groceries with him (He came to see me—I did not have to go to there.), until he opened up the bag and showed me that it contained about fifty little celophane packets of pills each packet containing three tiny pills and these wrapped separatly although they are in units of three in a packet each one isolated from the other. I fear this will turn into a "building the bridge" at "Camp Cataract." I know that you will be carefull not to hurt Peter Owen's feelings about anything. The money has not yet arrived at my bank but that may be do to the strike which continues as you know by you're ships radio. . . . As for my health I am bewildered by the sensations I have—the same symptons as I have always had only much worse. I am going to the M.D. today and I will "Play it by ear." He is so busy that I could not get an appointment untill today which is the ninth. I arrived here on the twenty-seventh. I think Dr. Dean is writing you a letter saying Mrs. Bowles is much better than she thinks she is. I can't get a cabin to myself on the boat and there are slim chances that any will turn up at the last minute. I am returning to New York City on the 15 of August, where Hal has arranged three interviews for me. Each one in a dark bar. I am terrified and wish that I had never accepted because they will want to talk about Morocco, and books. I won't talk about the country I live in and can remember having red only a little of Susan S.[Sontag], Simone Weil, and you. The interviews are over by Thursday eveing at which point Hal will put me on a train to Stamford,

---

*Jane's typewriter had been broken.

arranging with Rose by telephone which train she's to meet.* Then I spend the evening with Rose and she will drive me out to Libby's the next morning. Then back to New York on Sunday with Rose, who will leave me there in order to go back to her house in the country or town. Who knows.

I am happy that Libby wanted to see me badly enough to make all these arrangements. . . .

I am delighted that you have liked your boat so far. It sounds wonderful. I'll write to Bangkok next. Martha has written me two of her usual sweet letters and even wired once because I told her how uncertain the mails were. I pray to God I'm on that boat by the twenty-second.

All my love,

J.

On August 13 Jane wrote to Gordon Sager about her return to Tangier:

I have been worrying about you and also I have been in a frenzy about the boats. I have decided . . . that I will leave here in August and arrive at Tangier on the date I will give you as soon as I have seen mother who is in the next appartment. If I should decide otherwise I shall certainly send you a cable. I shan't send you any more explanations or I would get into one of those long painfull recitals that you know so well. I am trying to remain precise, casual as well, as if the whole business didn't terrifie me. I am leaving the day after tomorrow for the Chelsea hotel. I am so deppressed that I can barely lift up my feet and drag into the next room. I shall now ask mother to correct this letter for me. If the boat, whichever one it turns out to be, arrives at some ungodly hour I don't know what I'll do. Hard to choose which port would be the worst for me . . . but I have decided to try getting off at Tangier unless they suddenly change plans. I mean the boat. If that happens I shall sit in Algecirras and send millions of wires before they take me off to the nut house. . . .

I had news from Martha three time but now I don't hear. She is probably very very occupied, in fact she wrote me that she was. . . .

Returning from Florida to New York, Jane had her "three interviews in a dark bar." Ned Rorem remembers seeing Jane that week. "I was to meet Jane at Virgil's to go to a party at John Koch's. At the party Jane sat in one place. She seemed scared to look to the right or left. I spent most of the time talking to her in the corner."

---

*Rose Minor, Libby Holman's secretary.

Jane spent the weekend with Libby and her family in East Hampton. The entire time she kept worrying about whether she would get to the boat. She had written to Paul, "I pray to God I'm on that boat," as if it were her only hope to get back to Tangier. Yet often in Tangier she would say to Paul, wringing her hands, that Tangier was bad for them. She would say that people kept telling her to go to the States to get proper care, and she'd add, "We've had enough of this life here." But now she had to get back to Tangier, back to her daily life, as if it were salvation.

ON SEPTEMBER 3 CLAIRE WROTE TO JANE:

Jane my angel:
   Your letter came today and I couldn't be happier . . . and don't laugh at me when I tell you your letter was perfect—not a single mistake. As I told you when you were here don't correct the letters you write me. I can always make them out and correcting takes so much of your time. I'm glad Martha, Gordon, and the Indian [Narayan Kamalakar] met you. Did you have any troubles at the customs? Am anxious to hear about the boat trip—Did you or didn't you share your room with someone?
   . . . Please Angel, have the wax blown out of your ears and your teeth cleaned. . . . Thanks again darling for your cable and letter and most of all for your visit.

I love you
Mother

On September 10 Claire wrote again:

Darling Jane:
   I thought maybe I'd get your second letter today but I didn't so I guess it will come next week. I went to the doctor Thursday for my yearly check up. He was very pleased with me. I read him the part of your letter about the physicist. He agreed with him 100% and he too said the brain gradually takes over to compensate for the damaged part. So that is such good news that we both should be very happy. He said that the balance of the body is mostly concentrated in the ears, so please dear, have the wax blown out. He also thinks you should at your convenience see a neurologist because perhaps now you do not need the strong medication you are taking. . . . Has your dizziness subsided any? Be sure to tell me. Have you heard from Paul. . . . I think it was wonderful of Martha to meet you at the boat. Didn't I tell you all would be right there. I hope it still is. I guess with Paul away your life is a little

easier and quieter. Angel, you should take this opportunity to write. You will soon be in the public eye here in America, so don't let them forget you. Devote part of your time to writing—you will be so happy you did—

Wednesday, September 14th is the Jewish New Year's eve. I pray to God to give you a healthy happy year and many many more to come—and that I will be able to be with you again. I can't tell you how I think of the time you were here, and how happy you made me. God bless you Angel.

all my love
Mother

P.S. I've forgotten—do I put garlic powder in the salad dressing—be sure to tell me.

On September 17 Claire wrote to Jane again:

Jane my angel:

Received your letter today, just two weeks after I received your first one—believe me I was commencing to worry. . . .

Darling you sound so lonesome. I'm sure you must miss Paul very much—but soon your friend's company will be gone and you'll have more fun—You say you are well—but you don't tell me if your dizziness is as bad as it was. While you are leading such a quiet life I would advise you to cut down on your relaxing medicines as much as possible. Take them only when you need them. Did you attend to your ears? . . . Again healthy happy New Year—Friday night, September 23rd starts Yom Kippur, the day of atonement. I'll pray for you. I love you so much.

Mother

On September 25 Claire wrote:

Jane darling:—

The "Day of Atonement" is over—it was yesterday. We don't go to temple, but nevertheless, I prayed that we all be written in the book of Life, with health and contentment.

. . . Do you still have [Dr. Dean's] pink pills or do you now take the liquid—Do you take your Serpasil—Have you been to Dr. Roux and what is your blood pressure? I'm anxiously awaiting your letter telling me about your dizziness. Is it as bad as it was—Have your friend's company left. I hate to think you are lonely—Be sure to tell me if Paul is staying in Bangkok. . . . Do you wind your clock every day—You know I put your jewelry in that gold bag—Did Martha like the bag you brought her? . . .

I miss you and love you, Angel. It was wonderful to have you with me.

Mother

P.S. Ever since your remark I am very conscious about "ing."

On September 28 Claire writes again:

Jane my Angel:—
   Received a letter from you today—and I'm wondering who addressed it and why—you still have not answered my many questions—about your boat-trip—did you share a cabin and was it agreeable—Have you had the wax blown out of your ears—I will do as you say and not mention your dizziness any more—except to say now you certainly do not have a tumor—your symptoms would be entirely different—violent headaches etc.—so get that out of your mind. In your next letter tell me how things are with Martha. If you still *like* her say "You enjoy being with her"—If you are still crazy about her say "You enjoy being with her *very* much" Did she like the bag—Your typewriter seems to be working right—Is it? I will not write you Sunday, because we are going to the eye-doctor Monday. Maybe I'll have some good news. We haven't been to the Chinese or steak place since you left. In fact, we haven't been anywhere. Hope Angel, you are getting some fun out of life—

I love you
Mother

Not to Claire, but to Paul, Jane wrote of what was happening to her in Tangier:

Dearest Bup:
   I did not think I could possibly send you the letter that I wrote you yesterday, because it was too full of neurological meanderings —opinions on my own state of being—doubts about not having been to a neurologist at all, finally, and mispelled words, etc. that I destroyed it. I did get to Florida and back and finally here to Tangier. I came much too early as far as Martha is concerned, because she is such a busy women still. It is hard for me to tell whether or not I shall ever see her as I did. She assured me that I would when she grew less busy but I see no end to it. I think she believes there is an end but I don't. . . . I may go to England if things do go on this way but it is too early for me to tell. The voyage back to Tangier was a night mare since they never knew really whether or not we could land in Tangier, untill the bitter end. It is always like that because of counter currents. Naturally I was worried all

the way by the thought of having to land in Algecirras by myself and to keep my eye on seven pieces of luggage. You can image what I went though. Thank God I had Dr. Dean to call up in Miami because my terror there of landing forever in a "rest home" was grave. I got dizzier and dizzier so I fuinally did call him. He said he knew a woman neurologist but by the time I got arround to making the decision to see one, it was too late for me to see her and catch the train. I myself was of two minds about ever seeing one and I do believe that if I did, it should be a first rate one in England, if any. I think my symptoms may be neurotic but I think more likely that I am possibly suffering from the equivalent of the fits that I used to have and have no longer, at least have not had for nearly three years. I have missed Rabit [Mohammed Mrabet] but have left a message with Yvonne for next friday which is the day on which he comes. If by some miracle they take me with them to Marrakesch, then I won't be here. However I will leave messages for him in anycase. He wants news of you which he has not yet recieved, so Mme. Jerofie said. . . . It does not look to me as if Martha would ever call me but perhaps she will again. The last two nights have been hell but your cat is fine and very happy at Martha's. . . . He is happy and plays with imaginary mice in the garden. I know that he is better off there and is part of their family—much more than me. I'm sorry to tell you that Berred died.

   . . . I miss you terribly and I know that it was foolish of me to come this soon. I could have stayed with Katharine. It doesn't matter. . . . Thank God for Dr. Dean in Florida. Otherwise I might never have gotten out of there. I was so frightened of loosing my mind and not being able to cope.

Much love naturally,

J.

Gordon Sager, who saw Jane often during this period, reports that she was seized with a new terror. "She would call me up eight or ten times in the morning. She wouldn't remember that she had just called me. She told me she was terribly worried about money. She would ask me to take her to her bank. Then she would want me to write a letter for her, asking for money from her New York bank. I'd tell her, 'Janie, you have plenty of money right here in Tangier.' "

Carla Grissman, who worked as a teacher in the American School, volunteered to help Jane. "I had met Jane in the fall of sixty-five through Isabelle and Yvonne Gerofi. Her style of expression was so extraordinary, not just her words, but her timing. Sometimes it was just one word and people would rock with laughter. Of course, you couldn't have a real conversation with Jane, not an analytic one, I mean. There would be sentences on one subject, and then there would be sentences on another subject.

"In 1966 when she returned from New York and began having so much difficulty, I thought it might be a help to her if she could begin writing again. I said to her, 'Janie, I'm coming and I'll sit here at the typewriter and you talk.' But it didn't work. She was combing her wig and looking miserable. Cherifa would be sitting in the other room on the floor. I remember she wore a knitted cap. Jane would get up and argue with her. Aicha would be sitting on the balcony with the baby. I kept coming even though it didn't seem to be working. Jane never said, 'Don't come.'

"She seemed so harassed. She couldn't make a decision of any sort. She would try, but then Cherifa would argue with her and then Aicha would say something. Then Jane would say she didn't have enough money to live on.

"I tried for weeks and weeks. Jane probably dreaded it. She seemed so preoccupied. She'd sit on her bed picking at her wig. She kept her money in a suitcase with a combination lock. She'd keep trying to get the combination right, but it was not easy for her. Finally I saw the writing wasn't going to work. But there was all this unanswered correspondence so I offered to type her letters for her."

On September 28 Jane began a letter to Paul, with Carla typing:

> Your letter was fascinating of course, but I have no news from here to give you. I'm worried about all kinds of things naturally but they don't bear writing about—and you are too far. I miss you very much but thank God you have landed somewhere, . . . and I am now not Carla Grissmann but myself continuing this letter. How I wish that I were with you now. . . . I hope you will write me even though I can't seem to answer you're letters and stick even the slightest bit of fun into mine. I wanted to say morcel of fun into mine. Not a very good word and I can't spell it anyway. I suppose I was trying to write 'titbit' If that is the correct spelling.

Jane gave up trying to write the letter, but the next day with Carla there and typing, she began again:

> I just got your second letter today, from Bangkok, of the 22nd and I wish more than ever that I'd gone with you. I seem to be very depressed, but don't worry. There's nothing you can do about it, and I hope that you do get out of that sticky climate. No, I don't think Martha would ever come out anywhere around there with me, her life seems very much booked up at the moment—her painter arriving soon and then Italy in the spring—I supposed you didn't ever really believe that I could come or that Martha would. . . .

In her next letter to Paul, Jane wrote, with Carla typing:

I'm very frightened being here by myself and never realized how complicated it would be for me. Gordon is trying to help me, although he gets very fed up since I don't understand very much, indeed anything, about how to handle the money. I always have needed more than I got and now I'm terrified of leaving things up to the last minute. I should have gone with you no matter how hot or uncomfortable it might be. I could have stayed in your room. It particularly worries me that you don't have any idea of when you're coming back, although I can well understand it. It terrifies me to live from month to month and so I have sent for extra money, via the bank, but even so until it comes I will be on tenterhooks, and *will* it come? I've had to drag Gordon to the bank manager because I can't express myself clearly. I still have money in the bank, though Gordon will find out how much. . . . I naturally want to be well covered, particularly with you not here. What can I do if I suddenly have no money—you were always here to handle these things. The only friend I have here now at hand who can help me is Gordon if he will and doesn't get too irritated—he said he would on Monday. . . .

I worry about your being in so much *heat*. . . .

On October 11 Jane again wrote to Paul, Carla typing:

Martha has been very sweet to me and I've seen a lot of her but that will cease I imagine as soon as her house guests come, the young painter, Tony, and his wife. They're coming to stay with Martha who is at this moment alone and doesn't like that very much, any more than I do. . . .

I have nothing but *complaints*, so I don't feel like writing as you must know by now, but *please* don't let me down, and keep writing to *me*. . . .

I am very quiet and don't find many amusing things to say or to write, that's why my mail is scarce, but I always remember that you said it's better to write a dull letter than no letter at all, so here is my dull letter, about as dull as a bank, but not as useful. . . .

Coming to see her day after day, Carla found that Jane was becoming more depressed and more fearful about money. "Once she owed the butcher eight cents for the cat's meat. She had no cash, so she insisted on paying by check. She couldn't say, 'I'll pay you tomorrow.'

"Sometimes during this period she would look like a little animal. She would stand buttoning and unbuttoning her sweater. She couldn't get the buttons right. She'd say, 'Where am I? I don't want to be here.' At other times she'd look delightful. At her birthday party at David Herbert's at that time she was radiant. But for the most part she looked old and lost. Once she almost burned herself in bed with a cigarette. But still, even when she was ill, there was her charm—it is impossible to describe. She had an extraordinary effect on me and on the way I look at people. Now whenever I go anyplace and I see someone strange or unusual I think, Go slow, don't judge, maybe this will be one of Jane Bowles's people."

Toward the end of October Jane received a letter from Carson McCullers:

Dear Jane,

It is marvellous to find all your books together in one volume—your curious, slanted and witty style has always given me boundless delight.

I am so pleased to know that a new and bigger audience can now share my pleasure.

Anyway, darling, bless you and thank you for your writing. . . .

Jane had Carla begin a letter:

Dearest Carson:

I was so happy to hear from you after all these years. I did not want to bother you, otherwise I would have given your name to my publisher and you might have written a short blurb. I can't write my letter, but am having it typed by a friend. Forgive me. [Jane could not go on. She became silent.]

She received a letter from her mother in response to one typed by Carla:

Jane my angel:

I was so happy this morning to receive your letter. . . . Am glad you are seeing more of David. . . . Too bad you didn't like the woman you shared the cabin with. Now you must tell me if you had the wax blown out of your ears. Are you making use of the clothes you bought. Does David like them? Please Angel, don't feel guilty about your short visit. What with the interviews and Libby leaving and the boat sailing, you couldn't help it. It was just one of those things. . . .

Darling don't worry about anything—everything will turn out all right—Are you in the mood to write a story? I love, love you

Mother

In this letter, in response to a request from Jane, Claire told Jane the balance in her savings accounts in New York: in one account there was over

$20,000, in the other almost $10,000. The numbers meant nothing to Jane.

To Libby Holman, whose nephew David had just visited Tangier, she began a letter:

> Dearest Libby,
>
> My eyes are bad again—won't focus at all. I got much too nervous taking those trips and trying to fend for myself on the boat I imagine.
>
> Anyway I am here but everything swimms before my eyes. It is a kind of "nervous breakdown" and I should never have gone. Or I should have stayed longer. It was folly to come back that quickly and I deeply regret it. I had no time to see anyone because of my obsessive terror that I would in the end not get back at all. . . .
>
> David Holman was very sweet. I wanted him to hide from you the state I was in—and it is not a state that is so noticable except that I am very quiet. I am writing these declarative sentences so that I can get through them before they turn into Gonza Magillas. At which point I would have to abandon them.
>
> I told David Herbert who wanted very much to meet David—I told him that I was very much frightened that if you heard anything about a nervous breakdown You would cut me off—I was half joking but it was a fear. David Herbert said I was crazy, but there is no limit to what I fear even so we went on with the conversation. Than David Herbert told . . . David Holman, which made everything terrible. Worse than that I told David Holman not to repeat it to you because it does sound crazy and he said he wouldn't dream of it so I'm repeating it to you and I'm sure Holman will tell you that I'm not crazy. Just depressed and with reason. I'm trying to Pull out of it But I realize that this little deception I was trying to get away with was not going to cease bothering me. Untill I came straight to you with it. . . .
>
> Anyway please don't cut me out because you think I'm crazy or for any other reason.

At the end of October Aicha went to the Gerofis at the bookshop and told them that there was no money or food in the house. Jane, she said, had stopped eating. Isabelle and Yvonne went to Jane's apartment and tried to go over the household accounts with her, to show her that there was enough money, that she did not have to worry. But she would not listen to them. "Paul had written to us, asking if we could try to get her to write to him, but she couldn't. She wouldn't even go out. Janie wanted Carla to go to the post office to send him a telegram, but then she changed her mind. She kept changing her mind. Carla tried to help. But even Carla finally gave up. Janie wouldn't listen to anyone. She just sat at home by herself."

Paul wrote to Jane telling her that he had received an early review of *The*

Collected Works that called her "a neglected genius." As for himself, he said, what he was doing was a bore. "I literally only sleep, work, and eat. . . ."

Jane sat at home with Cherifa and Aicha, taking her medication, one pill after another, sometimes many pills at a time. She was taking the pills that Dr. Dean had given her in Florida and also those that Dr. Roux had prescribed in Tangier, and was mixing them indiscriminately: Valium, Seconal, Serpasil, Mellaril, Epanutin, and phenobarbital among others. Dr. Roux was violently opposed to Jane's taking all the medications. She wanted her to take only the few essentials and those in carefully controlled dosages. Again she went over the medication with Cherifa.

According to Paul, Dr. Roux impressed on Cherifa the fact that Jane could die if she took too much medication. "Cherifa was afraid she'd be accused of wrongdoing if anything happened to Jane. To Jane she'd say, 'Give me that bottle. Do you think I want the police to come and find you dead when I'm in charge of you?' Cherifa would try to keep the medication away from Jane, but Jane would have hidden some away, so it didn't matter what Cherifa did." Cherifa soon stopped trying.

Those of Jane's friends who still came to see her also tried to get her to stop taking so many medications. But though she was fearful, though she kept saying she needed help, she would accept advice from no one. As Gordon Sager says, "She was very willful. She did what she wanted and she didn't do what she didn't want to do."

Dr. Roux wrote to Paul—as the Gerofis had also written—saying that Jane's physical condition was degenerating. Because of her immobility she was suffering from intestinal adhesions and might need to undergo another operation.

Paul was reluctant to return because it meant that he would have to give up his work in Thailand. But by December 9, as he wrote to Libby Holman, he had decided to go back to Tangier:

> I wouldn't be leaving so soon, but I've had a letter from Jane's doctor in Tangier saying she isn't at all well, either physically or psychically, and asking me when I intended to return. I wrote I'd try and be there at the end of January, but it doesn't look very feasible unless I pile all my luggage into a plane and go that way. And you know how I love planes. . . .
>
> I haven't heard from Jane in many weeks, and can't make her answer my letters. Or perhaps they merely get lost en route. . . .

In the midst of her immobility Jane received a letter from Frances, saying she was coming to Tangier. Jane drafted an answer to her:

Darling Frances—

I am in such a depression that I can't answere any of you're thoughtfully arranged questions. May I ask you one myself. Can you possibly go first to Paris—(France) as you say or whatever other place you are going and then come on to me. The room upstairs is a mess but I could fix it up. I suppose you can not do it that way around or you would have suggested it to me. My life is one of great pain and torment now and I don't see my way out of this trap. If I go to America there would be only the state Hospital and in England the same because I don't have the money to pay for a getter place. My deppression has gotten worse and worse and I don't know what to answer you about coming right now. I would rather not say anything today but I'm writing you know not to leave England or France without leaving me an address. I don't know yet Whether I I would rather go or stay. . . . You can tell by the way I write that I am in a bad way.

Love
Jane

on the other hand come I should say if you don't have any other place you'd rather go first. I'm a little bit hard up

Just before Christmas Jane received a letter from her editor Hal Vursell, enclosing a review of her book from *Life*.

Dear Janie,

I don't think one could ask for better than this. . . . So, if you were worried about what kind of critical notice you were going to get, I am sure that you can stop it now. . . .

I hope you are feeling better, darling. . . .

Jane never answered Vursell, but she managed to start a letter to Paul, though she never finished it:

I am afraid that by now it is too late to reach you for xmas and you're birthday. I feel quite sick about it and about not having written you. I have received all of you're letters and I don't think it was a good idea for me to stay here without you. The explanation of that will come later. [The Gerofis] have been very kind about helping me but you always did that month by month more or less and now I don't seem to be able to accept any reasurance about whatever financial arrangements I make. It is hell. You're own letter sounded so sad that I had to write you although I had far less to say than you and about my own my own confusion all of which Yvonne is trying to do her best to allay. I have no idea how to spell that word. Aisha to whom you sent the card is here and sends you love, or greatings as they do, and I did not tell Cherifa that the card was not for both of them, obviously. Mme. Roux may have written you by now . . . about the possible opperation that I might have but I think I shan't have it and that I shall just stay as I am. Enormously fat in spots because my digestion is at a standstill. I long for you to come home but I can't really tell from you're letters how terribly long this is going to take . . . Naturally I was horrified by you're letter about my book but it is exactly what I expected. As you remember I did not really want it republished at all. But you say that books are written to be punlished. . . . There have been no new terrors but they're will be I suppose. I am very worried about all kinds of things that I don't want to go into and can't. I did not write you for so long because I was in such a depression. Now it is something else. You're work seems very arduous and I'm sorry, almost in despair that you should be so lonely. Perhaps something will change.

On January 1, 1967, Claire called Jane from Florida and immediately followed it up with a letter:

Jane darling,

Just spoke to you and am more upset than ever. You seem to have no legitimate excuse for not writing me a line or two. I know you don't mean to worry me but I am actually sick from worry. I just spent $35 on a call to you and we both spent money on cables. If you are so worried about your money, a few lines from you would have saved us both that money. Jane, why do you need *so* much money. You must have some unusual expense that you're not telling me about. But if you need money so badly and quickly I'm sure one of your friends . . . would cash your American check immediately—but you can also write the Chemical Bank . . . and ask them to send you air-mail $1,000 from your savings account.

I had a letter from Paul who too is worried to death because he hasn't heard from you. I feel you are keeping something from me—and that worries me more than the truth possibly could. If we could afford it, even though it would be dangerous for us to buck the winter temperatures, we'd fly over in a minute—but it can't be so urgent if you are not willing to spend the money. You have 21,861 dollars in your savings account and close to $10,000 in the other bank. Darling, write to me—tell me what's upsetting and worrying you. Please, darling, I can't take any more.

> I love you
> Mother

On January 9 Dr. Roux wrote to Paul, reassuring him about Jane's physical condition.

From the psychic viewpoint there are more troubling problems. She continues to be in a state of depression with obsessive ideas (in particular the fear of not having enough money). In December she had a violent epileptic seizure (doubtless as a result of having taken too many whiskies on a jaunt with her friend Frances, who spent several weeks here). It has been three years since the last fit. Impossible to make her follow a regular medical treatment. Dr. Montsarrat and I have therefore given up trying, and Mrs. B. stays quietly at home with Cherifa and Aicha. She goes out very seldom, does not read, writes to no one, and spends all day ruminating. She never telephones me anymore. I am obliged to call her and to force her, from time to time, to come and see me. Perhaps your return will give her the necessary impetus to come out of her depressive state, but I am not certain. And in that case we shall speak with you, Dr. Montsarrat and I—on the matter of a psychiatric clinic. In any case we shall do our best until you arrive. Unless there is an unexpected change, she can continue her present mode of life until you come. I am extremely sorry not to give you better news.

To Libby Holman on January 20 Paul wrote that he was leaving Bangkok:

Dr. Roux writes me that Jane isn't well, and had a series of convulsions last month. Of course, Lady Frances was there, and I suspect that unwittingly she was the cause. She drives Jane literally mad every time she appears; I wish to hell she'd keep away. . . .

Now almost eighty, retired and living in Spain, Dr. Roux remembers how little there was that she could do for Jane from a medical viewpoint: "She was a patient of great charm, on the human level, but very difficult to deal with in medical terms.

"She had a wonderful sensibility. She felt more than other people. She had much spirit, much humor, she always found the comic in everything, even in her illness. She was very good, generous, charitable, human—with great intuition. She seemed to understand everything.

"She could not bear solitude. She wanted something alive around her. She liked someone to serve her, though she did not care about material things.

"Her arteries were not very strong. It was a hereditary problem. And then the drinking began very early. She did drink later, after the stroke, not a lot, but it was too much for her. She was frail, and often ill.

"She had a spirit which commanded her body. She was very changeable and unstable. It wasn't a matter of laziness in her that she didn't work. There was a basic instability. That was why she didn't read, why she didn't learn Braille. And the time became very hard for her to fill.

"For her it was fatal, the early life of pleasure, the drinking, the excitement, given her sensibility.

"And then little by little the arteries went. Reason went. She knew it was irreversible. And she spoke of killing herself, perhaps, but she did not kill herself because the vital force in her was so strong."

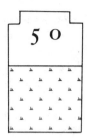

5 0

ON JANE'S FIFTIETH BIRTHDAY, FEBRUARY 22, 1967, Paul was en route to Tangier from Thailand. David Herbert organized a birthday dinner for Jane, to which he invited Yvonne and Isabelle Gerofi, Gordon Sager, and Carla Grissmann. Isabelle, knowing how Jane loved Pekingese dogs, brought with her a puppy she had just acquired. Jane kept the puppy on her lap during the party, but otherwise, Isabelle remembers, she barely responded to what was going on around her.

Jane's mother wrote to her on her birthday:

Feb. 22, 1967
Your Day

Darling:

Everyone is celebrating Washington's birthday, but we're celebrating yours—At the stroke of midnight we drank a toast to your good health and happiness. I'm wondering how you're spending your birthday—I hope you are celebrating in the way you most enjoy—

Angel, I think if you realized what a few lines from you would do for me, you'd force yourself to write—but if you can't, why don't you dictate a few lines to Gordon Sager, who would be glad to type them—

About 6 or 7 days after you receive this Paul will be home—Be sure you look nice for him he loves you so much—but no one can love you as much as I do—

Mother

The Gerofis wrote to Libby Holman about Jane's condition and in late February Libby and her husband Louis Schanker arrived in Tangier. Jane went with Isabelle to the airport to meet Libby. Jane was silent, except to remind Isabelle of a practical matter, that they must not take a "petit taxi," because it did not go to the airport.

When Libby got off the plane and saw Jane, she screamed with pleasure. She ran to her and threw her arms around her. In response Jane smiled vaguely.

On March 2 Paul returned from Thailand. Libby came to Paul in tears. "I can't take another hour of Jane," she said. "We're leaving on the first plane."

"It was the repetitions and the constant pulling down that was so hard to deal with," Paul says. "There was no hope in the world for her. There was nothing. It just went on and on and never stopped, over and over with the same things. And there was no way to reassure her. She said, 'I know that I'm disintegrating slowly. I'm aware of it and no one can tell me differently. I notice the difference from month to month. Don't tell me I'm going to get better. It's cruel to say that to me. I don't want to be a basket case.' That was her horror."

On March 10 Claire wrote to Jane:

Jane darling—
    I am shocked and grieved to hear you smoke so much and take nembutal—that's a sleeping pill and should never be taken except under doctor's orders—Julie and I each take one at night and you remember how dopey it made me. Please Angel, for Paul's and my sake don't take so many pills—You'll be more like yourself if you cut them out—I hope darling, you keep yourself clean—go to the hair-dresser every week so to be sure not to develop a scalp disease—Do you know darling what a few lines from you would mean to me? Are you going to deny me that—you know how much I love you—you mean life to me—and it's so empty when I don't hear from you because then I know you are not well. Just a few lines will do—

                                                          Love and kisses
                                                          Mother

Jane forced herself to answer Claire. In response Claire wrote:

Jane my Angel:—
    Imagine how happy I am to have your letter today. Darling, there is nothing wrong with you—your own father would have told you "to stop dramatizing your troubles." Darling, I was much younger than you when I buried your father and I had your knee to worry about—I did *not* give in—but carried on—you, too, darling are a strong minded person—and never again let anything get the best of you—I hope you and Paul are seeing your friends—especially David—did you go to the birthday party he gave you?
    . . . Be an Angel, darling, be your own sweet self and make me and Paul happy—I love you so much,

                                                          Mother

During this time there were moments when Jane seemed better, but then suddenly her recognition of the destiny that awaited her would return with even greater force. It was not simply that she let herself sink into depression. It was rather as if the strength and power of her personality now allied itself with the despair that was her only daily life.

Claire wrote to her again on March 30:

Jane darling:

You have always taken my advice—won't you please do it now—if you don't you will have to go to a hospital again—Believe me, Angel, there is nothing wrong with you that you cannot cure yourself. Force yourself to bathe and dress after you've had your breakfast—that isn't hard to do you've just talked yourself into thinking it's not worth while—How can you say that when the whole world is singing your praises—You must, darling, throw away every pill you are taking except the one for epilepsy and the one for blood pressure—don't you realize all the pills you are unnecessarily taking are responsible for the deep depression you are in—Angel, this can't go on—if you don't do it by yourself, you'll have to have the help of doctors and nurses—For my sake and Paul's, show us you can do it—I wish I could be with you darling—if you want me send for me—I love you so much,

Mother

In mid-April, on the advice of Dr. Roux, Paul took Jane to Málaga, where she was admitted to a psychiatric sanatorium for women.

To Virgil Thomson Paul wrote:

She could be lucid only if one managed, for a minute or two, to get her mind away from her "illness." Behind it all she seemed to be quite clear about her state, and could discuss it rationally now and then in moments of stress. Fundamentally the trouble was that she did not seem to care one way or the other. It was all happening in someone else about whom she didn't give a damn, and so she shrugged her shoulders. . . .

David Herbert went to visit Jane in the sanatorium. He brought her a group of excellent reviews of *The Collected Works.* "As reading was such an effort, Janie made me read them to her. She looked very sad and, for a little while, said nothing, then, hopelessly, she said:

" 'I know you mean this kindly, darling, but you couldn't have done anything more cruel!'

"I was aghast.

" 'You see,' Janie went on, 'it all makes me realize what I was and what I have become.'

"I was terribly upset. Janie, seeing this, looked up with a ghost of a smile. 'Give me the book,' she said. I handed her *The Collected Works*. With a trembling hand she picked up a pencil and added, 'of Dead Jane Bowles.' "

SINCE JANE'S CONDITION DID NOT IMPROVE, THE DOCTORS RECOMMENDED SHOCK treatment. It was Paul who had to make the final decision. He made it reluctantly. He wrote to Virgil Thomson:

> Unfortunately I have to take the final decision, after listening to the opinions of Drs. Roux, Monsarrat and Cotrina. The general health risk isn't so great, they seem to think, in spite of the arteriosclerosis, but my feeling is that it blots out whole departments of memory permanently, which isn't so good. Of course, she is dead set against it. But if she can't get well without it . . . ?

Paul remembers visiting Jane after the shock treatment. In the procedure, she told him, certain elements were placed on her scalp, which were referred to as blocs. She said she was planning to write a novel, *Dr. Cotrina and the Western Bloc*.

Sister María Candelas, who was a nurse in the Málaga sanatorium in 1967, remembers Jane as a patient with an "inferiority complex, perhaps because of her not too pleasing physical appearance at the time." Sister María recalls also that Jane was fearful that "her husband would forget her." But it was part of her illness, she adds. "For her husband did visit her with some frequency."

By late May Jane's condition had improved somewhat, but, Paul wrote, "not enough . . . to warrant taking her home, in spite of her heartrending pleas to be allowed to go back with me. One must have a nervous system of steel not to be shaken by paying her such visits. However, there's no point in talking about it. . . ."

In June, Isabelle Gerofi visited Jane at the clinic. "I'd been waiting a while in a small dark waiting room, when a nurse led Janie in. I remember the shock I felt when I saw how changed she was. She looked like a sad little old woman pensioner. She was dressed in a clean white blouse and a pleated skirt. As soon as she sat next to me, the nurse left, and we began to talk completely naturally, as if no time had passed since we'd seen each other.

"I suggested we go out for lunch and she accepted with a smile. The taxi let us off near the restaurant where I was planning to go. But then I saw a terrace bar nearby in the sun. I thought Janie would like to sit there first. It was there that through ignorance I made a great mistake. I allowed her to drink a Bloody Mary, although I did take the precaution when ordering of discreetly telling the barman, 'Very little vodka and a lot of tomato juice.'

Janie was on medication and should not have had even a drop of alcohol, but no one had told me that.

"As she drank, Janie became more at ease. She talked a little, but mostly she listened very attentively. I remember talking to her about a book I'd read. When lunchtime came we got up to go to the restaurant next door. But the little alcohol that Janie had drunk had affected her greatly. I had difficulty helping her maintain her balance. She held my arm and we walked together to the restaurant. People kept turning around and looking at us. We must have looked like two drunks leaning on each other. Suddenly we both burst into laughter at the idea of the scene we were creating.

"When we got to the restaurant and were seated, I suggested to Janie that she order shrimp cocktail, since she'd always liked that. She did, but she insisted first on having some white wine. During the meal, she picked at her plate rather than eating, and she kept asking for more white wine. Our conversation was friendly and easy and Janie several times showed that mischievous humor she'd always had, that was such a large part of her charm.

"After lunch I took her to my hotel. We staggered there as if we were walking on a path paved with irregular stones. Gradually, as we sat in my room, Janie passed into a deep sadness. And in the taxi that we took back to the sanatorium, she begged me to make sure that she would not be left there any longer. When I left her, I was very distressed."

AT THE BEGINNING OF JULY PAUL WENT TO MÁLAGA AND BROUGHT JANE back to Tangier with him. She was very thin, weighing about ninety pounds, but she seemed better. She was not depressed, although she showed a strange excitability that had never appeared before her treatment in Spain. She could not sit still for a minute. She kept getting up and sitting down, then getting up again, moving all the time.

Hal Vursell had arranged for *Life* magazine to do a story on Jane. In early August the writer Jane Howard and the photographer Terence Spencer came to Tangier for the assignment. Jane Howard's story was never published, though in 1978 an article appeared in the *Washington Post* based on her conversations with Jane. Jane Howard, who had never met Jane before, was probably not aware of the peculiar excitability that drove Jane to make facile statements about herself. Although the words are Jane's, they sound very little like Jane before she went to Málaga, the Jane who had always hated and feared interviews.

"I was unpopular myself in school," said Jane, an only child, "or at least I thought I was. I always went to sleep pretending I was one of eight children, all girls. It never occurred to me to want a brother. I probably liked girls in boarding school just to irritate my mother. I probably didn't transfer my affections to boys because I damn well wasn't going to, with her lurking around.

"My father used to call me Jim. He'd take me fishing when we went away summers, and I was a real little fisherman. But I was extremely feminine, and I still am. I used to love to hug my father because he had this very fluffy sweater. I slept with about eleven fluffy toys." (Even at fifty-two she slept with a stuffed koala bear, and "Fluffy" was her favorite nickname for her angular, Edwardian, meticulous husband.)

On September 3 Jane's mother wrote to her:

Jane darling:—

Haven't heard from you since my last letter, but have decided to go back to my old routine and write you every Sunday. . . . Now that Cherifa isn't with you (thank goodness) do you have to do the cooking? . . .

I hope sweetheart you are well and happy—don't tamper with your health. Please go to the dentist. I love you so much, it sometimes hurts.

Paul had fired Cherifa while Jane was in Málaga. For months Martha had kept insisting to Paul that Cherifa was bad for Jane and that he must get rid of her, but Paul, knowing Jane's feeling about Cherifa, had not been able to bring himself to make her go. However, shortly after he took Jane to Málaga he discovered a "magic" object in Jane's apartment.

Mohammed Mrabet remembers that "when Paul took Janie to the hospital I told him, 'Take this plant'—a philodendron—'out of Janie's house.' Cherifa said, 'The plant stays here or it will die.' She blocked my way. Then Paul came and took the philodendron. We bought a new pot for it. I took the plant in my hand. I found the magic packet. It was done up in a rag."

In 1974 Paul spoke of the incident to Michael Rodgers of *Rolling Stone:*

The maid was a horror. We used to find packets of magic around the house. In fact, in my big plant, in the roots, she hid a magic packet. She wanted to control the household through the plant. The plant was her proxy, or stooge, and she could give it orders before she left and see that they were carried out during the night. She really believed these things. *Rodgers: What was this packet of magic?*

Well, it was a mess. It was a cloth bound up very tight and inside there were all kinds of things . . . pubic hairs, dried blood, fingernails, antimony, and I don't know what all. I didn't analyze it, no Moroccan

would touch it, and I had to pick it up. Everyone around kept saying
don't touch it. I threw it down the toilet.
Rodgers: Why did you keep this maid around?
Mrs. Bowles wouldn't let me fire her. She said, "I hired her and when
I see fit, I'll fire her, but you can't." And unfortunately the maid knew
that. She was very hostile. She always carried a switchblade and when
she saw me alone she'd bring it out—swish—a real quick draw. [Bowles
gestures as with knife toward throat.] "That's what you'll get," she'd say
to me. She tried to put my eyes out one night. A monster, a real
monster. . . .

For years Paul had warned Jane that Cherifa was stealing money. "She
used to systematically get money from Jane. When Jane was so ill, Cherifa
kept at her about the money. She would whisper to Jane to give her money
while Jane was asleep. When Jane woke up, she'd say, 'I must give Cherifa
money.' I'd say, 'But you just gave her some.' Cherifa would be sitting
quietly in the corner. And Jane would say, 'Don't try to get in on this. I pay
her. I'll give her money.' "
When Paul found the magic packet, all of his suspicions and fears of
Cherifa erupted: his memory of what Yacoubi had said about her, his
suspicion of her behavior with Jane the night of Jane's stroke. He
remembered that his parrot had died of poisoning in 1966. And once again,
he thought, as many others did, that it was Cherifa who had poisoned the
parrot. And if she was capable of that, what might she have done to Jane or
still be doing? Though earlier, when Martha and Mrabet had pressed him to
get rid of Cherifa, he had done nothing, now he finally fired her.
Upon her return from Málaga, Jane at first seemed to accept Paul's
decision that Cherifa must stay away, though she was paid a salary. Jane
Howard reports that Jane used to sneak off to join Cherifa at the movies, and
quotes Jane as having said:

I feel guilt and affection for her. . . . If it weren't for us she'd never have
been introduced to European ways at all. She's a freak and I'm afraid
she'll get worse and worse as she realizes she isn't popular.

But to those who had known Jane for a long time, her vision of Cherifa
was not quite so flip. In the fall of 1967, in defiance of Paul, Jane took Cherifa
back into her household. To the Gerofis, "Cherifa was like a stone around
Jane's neck. 'I must call Cherifa,' she'd say, when she visited us, getting up
and calling her and sitting down and getting up and calling her again."
Even later, as she became increasingly ill, Jane would say to Dr. Roux
that she was afraid of Cherifa. Dr. Roux says, "I think she did much evil to

Jane, maybe by magic. She was like a faithful dog in a way. But at the end Jane came to be afraid of Cherifa."

LATE IN AUGUST, JANE HAD HAD ANOTHER OPERATION, FOR HEMORRHOIDS. To Libby on September 9 Paul wrote:

> Jane may have to go soon for another operation, but it's not certain. The stitches ripped out of the first, and she nearly died of pain for ten days, all without having the surgeon look at her because, as she claimed, he was "indifferent" to her suffering. When she finally went with Dr. Roux, they were horrified to see what had happened.

To Virginia Sorensen Waugh, Jane was able to joke, "I never thought the day would come when life would be one big pain in the ass."

Paul noticed a change in Jane, he wrote to Libby:

> As Jane recovers she gets onto a higher and higher horse, I find. And the reason for that is that she has suddenly cut out *all* medication, for the first time in ten years; as a result of "being on her own," as it were, she is extremely energetic, and the energy releases heretofore unsuspected reserves of aggression. So she has her own way or else.

On October 10 Jane's mother wrote to her:

> Jane darling:—
> I did not write you yesterday, Sunday, because I thought I'd get a letter from you today, surely—but I didn't—you must realize what anxiety does to me at my age. My blood pressure goes up until sometimes I think I'm getting a stroke. Why can't you school yourself to write me once a week—Is that too much for a 76 yr. old mother to ask? I always worry when I don't hear from you that something is wrong —and if God forbid, there is I'm sure if you asked Paul he would write to me—Are you all right—Are you still smoking so much—How are your hemorrhoids? What are you doing that you can't find time to write—I'm praying there's a letter on the way—
> Friday night, October 14th, is the eve of the Day of Atonement—the holiest day of the year for Jews—May God forgive us all our sins—I know you don't pray, so I'll pray for you—Besides David, who do you see—Is Tangier gay or quiet? Please I beg you write me a newsy letter—Have you gone to the dentist—Please answer all the questions I am asking you—because I am so unhappy when you shut me out of your life—You know I love you best in all the world—
> Mother

At the end of October Jane had to undergo another hemorrhoid operation. As always when she was ill, she tried to hide it from her mother. Paul wrote to Claire saying that Jane had a very busy social schedule. But to his friend Oliver Evans he wrote:

Jane had another operation two weeks ago today, and her pain seems to be increasing each day. She lies screaming all night, and there doesn't seem to be anything the doctors can do for her. No injection calms the pain. This preoccupation has kept me from doing much of anything, as I'm always on the alert for poundings on the ceiling by one of the maids, summoning me; it happens any hour of the day or night. The trouble is that she sometimes tries to get out of bed by herself, and falls, and that always makes things worse. Both the surgeon and her regular doctor are coming this afternoon. Not that they will be able to make a prognosis between them. I doubt that any doctor could. . . .

Once again she was on heavy medication.

When she began to recover Paul told her that she had received a letter from *World Authors*, requesting a short biography from her for inclusion in their next edition. He urged her to answer. Lying in bed, she dictated a brief summary of her life, while he typed the words she said. She began:

I started to "write" when I was about fifteen and was obliged to do composition in school. I always thought it the most loathsome of all activities, and still do. At the same time I felt even then that I had to do it.

And she ended:

It was only after the end of World War II that I came to Morocco. Paul had come ahead of me and bought a house in Tangier. From the first day, Morocco seemed more dreamlike than real. I felt cut off from what I knew. In the twenty years that I have lived here I have written only two short stories, and nothing else. It's good for Paul, but not for me.

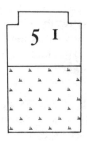

5 1

Suddenly, in late december, without notice to Paul or anyone else, Jane moved out of her apartment, taking Cherifa with her, and went to stay at the Atlas, a small hotel in the center of Tangier, close to the Parade Bar.

At first she would go to the bar at the Atlas and sit there drinking. There were many young American hippies in Tangier at the time, drawn by the easy accessibility of drugs. Soon Jane was surrounded by a group of them. She began to give away money to everyone around her, first cash and then checks. She gave away her clothing and all of her jewelry. Whereas the year before her depression had been centered on her terror of not having any money, now she squandered whatever she had.

No one could stop her. She was in a state of feverish activity and willed pleasure, similar to that of Mrs. Copperfield at the end of *Two Serious Ladies*. (When Miss Goering says to Mrs. Copperfield, "But you have gone to pieces, or do I misjudge you dreadfully?" Mrs. Copperfield answers: "True enough . . . I *have* gone to pieces, which is a thing I've wanted to do for years. I know I am as guilty as I can be, but I have my happiness, which I guard like a wolf, and I have authority now and a certain amount of daring, which, if you remember correctly, I never had before.")

Frequently Jane went from the Atlas to the Parade Bar, now run by Lily Wickman, a French woman with a gruff voice and a tough, sardonic manner. Jane at this moment conceived a passion for Lily, who as a young woman had toured Europe with her first husband in a motorcycle act called "The Wall of Death."

"You can't fall in love with a woman you've known for five years," Lily said to Jane. "And besides, my dear, I'm not a dyke."

"She'd come to the bar and drink," Lily remembers. "Then she'd want something to eat. She'd order a hamburger and it would come and then she'd turn and look at what the other customers were having. 'What is he having? I want that,' she'd say. 'But you didn't finish your hamburger,' I'd say.

"She drove me and the customers crazy, walking up and down, wringing her hands. The customers were complaining. She made them nervous. 'If you move again,' I said to her, 'I'll kick you out.'

"She went away and came back with a paper bag. She sat at the bar and started taking things out of the bag: a bottle of milk, a powder puff, other things. She took them out and put them on the counter. 'Now I'm not moving. Right?' she said.

"One day Paul called and said, 'Don't give her a drink.' When she came I said, 'No drinks, darling.' I gave her a Seven-Up. She drank it and spat it out right away. Somehow, I don't know how, some petrol had gotten into the Seven-Up bottle.

"When she was here, she kept repeating and repeating what she was saying. Then she'd take her wig off and put it on. She was, in fact, very gay when she was here. She was doing silly tricks with her wig. She knew a lot of people here. She would go into the kitchen and talk to the cooks and laugh. One day she came without clothes.

"Finally the customers began to be very upset. I called Paul. 'It will be all right,' Paul said. I said, 'She's driving me crazy.' 'Have a little bit of patience,' he said.

"She would invite me to go home with her. To placate her once I took a taxi with her. I got out at her house, then jumped back in again and drove off. Ten minutes later she called me. 'Why didn't you stay?' she asked me. 'I forgot my keys,' I said."

Boo Faulkner ran into Jane in the Fez market, opposite the Atlas Hotel. "She was in terrible disarray, terribly badly dressed. Her clothes were sort of hanging on her. Some woman took her back to the Atlas. It was sad and scary. To tell the truth, it frightened me and if I saw her again, I avoided her."

When Jane was young a great part of her beguiling charm was the sense she gave other people that through some force in her they were liberated. Now that she was out of control, that force had become terrifying. She had become a thing of embarrassment, a thing of shame, a thing to be avoided. Most of all, people were afraid that she might lose control completely. "It was frightening," says Paul.

She gave away all the money in her and Paul's joint account. But still she continued to make out checks.

"Jane had always loved money," says Paul. "But she hated the idea of loving money. It was wrong to her. Once when we had a visitor in the sixties, a wealthy woman who kept complaining about prices, Jane in her droll way said something silly about money, and this woman in a hushed tone said, 'We don't joke about money.' Jane had laughed about that for years."

Now people clustered around her as she continued to make out checks—American hippies, Cherifa, a man who ran a grocery store and kept selling Jane refrigerators. And still no one stopped her. "Even though she was so ill, her will was so strong," says Yvonne Gerofi.

One evening the Gerofis went to meet Jane at the Atlas and from there they all went to the Parade Bar. Isabelle remembers that "Jane had an excited, disordered conversation with a woman she barely knew. Lily called Paul. Paul came to the Parade to get Jane. She wouldn't go with him. She said she wanted to be with Lily and she went behind the bar. Paul asked her very gently to come and again she refused and then there was something like a small fight behind the bar between the two of them. And she went home with him."

Paul kept trying to get Jane to go back voluntarily to the sanatorium in Málaga. But she refused to go. He did not want to force her. He wanted her agreement. He kept talking to her and talking to her, but she kept refusing.

On January 9, 1968, the Gerofis went to Jane's apartment for dinner. She was more disordered than ever. At midnight she insisted that they take her to the Parade Bar.

On January 11, from the Hotel Atlas bar, Jane sent a note to Paul. It was written for Jane by Alfred Chester, who was visiting Tangier:

> Darling Paul—
>   It will be all explained—I mean, your financial dilemma—in one half hour. I mean, by me. It's true you should have a separate account. I have not spent as much money as you think. Please don't think it's your financial problem, *but mine*. We will talk it over and understand everything.
>
> > All my Love
> > Jane

They did "talk it over"; she stopped making out checks, but it was Paul's responsibility to cover those that she had written, amounting to almost $3,000. Now that she was once again home, Paul ordered the servants not to give her any liquor. She kept asking for a drink and they would not give it to her—she who had once said to Paul, "People want me to be amusing, so I have to drink."

She walked across the way to the American consulate. She lay on the floor and refused to get up. She said she wanted a drink. The consul general said, "I'm sorry, I don't have anything." She said, "I won't get up until you get me one." The consul general said, "I will take you in the car to Guitta's Bar." And Jane said, "You're a gentleman. I appreciate it very much. My husband won't give me any."

At home with Paul she would wring her hands, walking back and forth in a frenzy of anxiety, speaking only of the terror that was ahead, the terror that was coming. One day John Hopkins and Joe McPhillips were visiting

Paul when Jane was present, and she suddenly began to dance in front of the fireplace. It was a strange wild dance, says Paul, as if it were a striptease and yet she was fully clothed. He had never known her to dance like that and he stared at her in astonishment.

Jane received a letter from her mother, dated January 9:

Jane darling:—

At last! The first letter from you in seven weeks—I just don't understand—that Ramadan holiday comes up every year and this has never happened before—I'm a real wreck wondering what was happening with you and Paul—surely either one could have written a few lines—if you can't use your typewriter write a few lines by hand and don't keep me in a continual state of worry—I thank God you are well—

. . . The enclosed picture (in *Time*) gave me such a thrill—Did they ever publish that interview they had with Paul and you in Tangier? Are you ever going to write again—it's a shame to waste such a wonderful talent. Talent or not I love you to distraction.

> Mother,
> Please write

Every day now Jane went to Guitta's Bar. Madame Guitta did not want to serve her, but Jane insisted. And each day Paul would come to the bar and get Jane and take her home.

On January 15 Yvonne and Isabelle saw Jane in the Parade Bar. "She was in a very agitated state, a kind of frenzy," Isabelle remembers. She spoke to Jane quietly. "I asked her to agree to go to the clinic in Málaga. She became so furious. I had the feeling she wanted to kill me. 'No, no,' she cried out. But then she went into the garden and she walked by herself. When she came back in, she was quiet and she asked me to take her to the Viking Bar, which I did."

On January 17 Jane went to the bookstore that the Gerofis managed. She seemed to recognize no one. She went up to a clerk and asked to borrow two dirhams (a few cents). Then she picked up two books and started to go out with them. Aicha, who was with her, protested that she shouldn't take the books without paying. And Jane grabbed at her throat.

Now Jane agreed to return to Málaga.

"I had to get a man from the hospital, a Moroccan intern, to accompany me, in order to take her back to Spain," says Paul. "The intern had a syringe ready to give her medication if it was necessary. But there was no need for it. We took the ferry from Tangier to Algeciras, a two-and-a-half-hour ride, then drove from Algeciras to Málaga. In Algeciras, as we were getting off the ferry, Jane said, 'The whole world is full of refugees. We're so lucky that we got across with the war going on.' And we went along with it, the intern and I. Then she said, 'I don't think we can go back. But we don't need to think about that now. At least we're out of it and safe.'

"We arrived at the hospital at eight-thirty in the evening. It was silent and quiet as a tomb. It was completely dark, not a single light. Then a nun appeared with a candle at a barred window, way up high. She called out, 'Está cerrado. No puede entrar nadie!' [We're closed. Nobody can enter.] So we had to stay overnight in a hotel.

"By this time Jane was determined to get away. She had decided the intern was there to stop her from doing what she wanted to do. He wouldn't let her have a drink. He stayed in the room with her all night. According to him, she tried to throw herself out of the window, or rather she was determined to get out the window and escape from the hotel. He had to sit up with her all night. She didn't sleep. No one slept. She didn't seem to need any sleep. She went on and on. I don't understand how. Her physical mechanism seemed to be able to withstand everything."

IN A SHAKY, ALMOST ILLEGIBLE, SCRIPT SOME WEEKS LATER JANE WROTE A series of letters to Paul from Málaga.

Dear Paul—

Please try to forgive me for the way I've behaved. I am longing to come back and start fresh again. I was not drinking when I went away and I lived at the Atlas. I don't really know what I thought I was doing. I know that I have to fix my teeth—I had only a temporary arrangement on them which will have to be finished now. I've forgotten the name of the man [in?] Tangier (You use him too.) . . . I would like to live in my—house cook etc.

. . . Please Paul don't try to figure this out but believe me I want to go back to Roux and get going with my dentist. I'll try to explain to you someday about the Atlas but I don't even understand most of it myself. It is very hard for me to write with no machine and I wish you would explain this to Libby and my mother.

Dearest Paul—

Thank you a million times for ceeping in touch.

As you know its terribly hard for me to write—without a machine and I don't even know whether I still can use one it's been so long. I want very much to see you and get this way of life over with. I'm longing to come home and lead my life. I don't feel like writing because there is too much to discuss.

Actually there is nothing to discuss except the fact that I am not home and would like to be there as soon as possible I shan't write about anything but my dentist and ask how you are. The dentist should be in around a month if not know but it certainly must be soon. I sorry about having simply walked out and gone to the Atlas. I promise you I was not drinking. I want to go to dr I've suddenly

Jane's mother wrote to her April 10 and April 20. They are the last two letters from her that have survived:

April 10, 1968

Jane my darling

You have no idea how happy your letter which arrived a few minutes ago made me—

You say you are physically well—You must believe you are mentally well too—You tell me to keep my faith—I always have faith in God and you—and you, too, Angel must have faith in yourself—With the help of the doctor you will be well soon, believe me—Take cheer darling you are so much better. I hear from Paul regularly—and soon he will bring you to me, he promised. If you want me, when the time comes, I will come and get you—you know darling I am with you in thought always—Julian thanks you for worrying about him—he loves you and as always I adore you.

Mother

April 20, 1968

Jane my darling:—

Just had a letter from Paul in which he says he hasn't been to see you because he is having trouble with his teeth—but maybe by now he has visited you—

Angel, you must tell yourself you are a well person and believe in yourself. The letter you wrote me was wonderful—just like you used to write, so get well soon, and then Paul will bring you to me and both of us will be happy—

. . . Julian and I send you love and kisses—You are my life

Mother

In June Isabelle Gerofi went to Málaga to visit Jane. She recalls that "Jane had put on a lot of weight. It was a beautiful day and most of the patients were in the garden, walking or sitting peacefully. My impression was that Jane was very well liked by the others.

"We took a taxi to the Gibralfaro Restaurant. As we sat there looking at the wonderful view, Jane spoke gently and softly of her present life. At one point she laughed suddenly, one of her famous laughs. She had heard, she told me, an idiotic American conversation at the next table.

"After lunch we walked through the shopping street, talking. She asked me the time. She said she had to be careful to return to the sanatorium on time not to miss the departure of one of the patients, of whom she was very fond.

"At the sanatorium she took me to her room and suddenly she began to talk very seriously of her own condition. With great forcefulness and conviction she said to me, 'I must die, I want to die.' She said that the greatest proof of friendship I could give her would be to help her kill herself. When I protested, she answered that she knew that her illness was irreversible, that everything from now on would be decay, mental and physical. It was terrible to see her so lucid and so resolute about this and yet to find her, in part, just as she had always been."

Dr. Antonio de Linares Pezzi, the current medical director of the clinic, reports on Jane's history as a patient, as it is recorded in the clinic's files:

Señora Jane Bowles was fifty years old when she entered this clinic on April 14, 1967. She left July 26 of the same year, returned January 20, 1968, and was discharged again June 28, 1968. She was treated by Dr. Cotrina. The diagnosis was manic-depressive psychosis. The drugs that were used in her treatment were Tofranil, Largacticil, Epanutin, and Pueron. . . .

Besides psychological treatment and medication, she received electric shock, after having first been anesthetized with Narcovenol.

She seems to have taken alcohol and sedatives to excess. . . .

On June 28 Paul came to Málaga to take Jane out of the clinic. On the advice of Dr. Roux he did not bring her home to Tangier—which she desperately wanted—but took her to Granada, where he had arranged for her to stay for a while in a *pensión* run by the wife of an American expatriate. (Since she prefers not to be identified, she will be called Mrs. Hall.)

As Mrs. Hall recalls it:

"We had a letter from Paul one day asking if Jane could convalesce with us, as she had been ill in a hospital in Málaga. We agreed, as we had an enormous house with a quiet garden. We were not informed at all as to the type of hospital, or house, that Jane had been in, nor about the illness she was convalescing from—or, indeed, that we were to be a halfway house which would decide whether she was well enough to return to Tangier or whether she had to go back to Málaga.

"She arrived with Paul by taxi, and even though she was under heavy sedation it was obvious what was wrong with her.

"We were concerned because on the ground floor of our house my sister and I had opened a bar, the operation of which was a full-time job, from 7:00

P.M. to 3:00 A.M.; and Jane needed attention rather constantly.

"She was very gentle and quiet on arrival, and went almost straight to bed. She was *very* particular about personal cleanliness, and had a 'thing' about it. . . .

"She was terrified of locked or even shut doors, explaining that this was what the nurses did in Málaga, and that if only they would leave the doors open she could get well. The problem in our case was confining her to the family part of the house. She made frequent and sudden appearances in the bar, made up to the nines and wearing only a nightie—and insisting on alcohol which was not allowed her because of the drugs. She would become truculent when persuaded to go. She liked company and was very garrulous, and when she was not drifting she laughed and smiled a lot. She was always very polite and full of thanks for the least thing, which may have been just handing her her lipstick, as she always wanted to look nice.

"In long talks with Jane (and someone always had to stay with her as she was quite as likely to wander out into the street in her see-through nightie as she was in the garden), I found that she was convinced that her Moroccan maid, who had been with her for years, had cast a spell upon her, thereby putting her completely under her power. She was also convinced that the maid in question was robbing her of jewelry, money, and other personal possessions, and that she was conspiring with Paul to keep her in 'that horrible prison of a hospital' (her words) in Málaga. She became quite vehement about her convictions, and feared going back to Málaga.

"With her horror of being locked in a room, she could not be left alone, as then she would prowl around the house looking for something to drink, and given the bar this became an impossible situation.

"Jane required full-time attention day and night. At the end of a week or ten days Paul had to fetch her back."

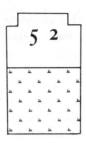

52

THE HOSPITAL WHERE PAUL LEFT JANE AFTER GRANADA
was a "casa de reposo," the Clínica de los Angeles in the hills just outside
Málaga. It was run by Dr. Rámos Ortiz with the assistance of a mother
superior and a group of nuns. The clinic, according to Dr. Roux, was known
for its humane treatment of its patients.

In September Paul, who had returned to Tangier, left to go to
California, where he had been invited to teach for six months at San
Fernando State College. There he taught advanced narrative writing and the
modern European novel. He found it difficult to accommodate to the United
States of the sixties, though he says, "The sojourn was not too different from
what I had imagined it would be, save that the people were better and the
circumstances of their lives far worse. . . ."

To Isabelle on October 22 Paul wrote:

> As you know, Jane's mother has been with her since I left. I wasn't
> really in agreement with the idea, but I couldn't do anything to prevent
> her. Now she is beginning to insist on taking Jane with her when she
> goes back to Florida. If only Jane would express her feelings on this
> subject, but she hasn't written me once and I have no idea if she wants
> to go with her mother or not. I must say that I can't help having my
> suspicions about my mother-in-law: Is she trying to influence Janie, to
> poison her mind against me? Mrs. Fuhs's letters are full of reproaches: I
> should be there, what am I doing here at this moment, etc. She knows
> perfectly well why I came. Also it seemed to me the most auspicious
> moment, precisely because Jane doesn't need me at the hospital. But if
> she takes her with her, there is nothing I can do about it. . . .

To Libby Holman on November 19 Paul wrote:

> The correspondence with Jane's mother has grown heavy and finally let
> up a bit. The diminution is due to the fact that she has been preparing to

leave Málaga and return to Miami Beach, which according to her pronouncements, she did today. At first she was extremely indignant and reiterated her intention of taking Jane with her. Then as time passed and she had the opportunity of observing her daily, she stopped saying that particular thing, and begged me to give up the work here and go immediately to Málaga. But she must have known I wouldn't do that, as eventually she began to deplore leaving Jane alone in the clinic. I too think it's bad, as Jane will inevitably miss her terribly. It's lucky (perhaps) that she was there with Jane so long, at least it is if Jane was happy with her. . . .

To Isabelle on November 28 he wrote:

Jane's mother is back in Florida. She keeps sending me tragic communications. According to her, Janie is completely ready to leave and to take up her ordinary life. If only she were right. She thinks it's terrible that Jane has to stay in the hospital two and a half more months, and I have to admit that bothers me, if in truth she is completely herself. Obviously she may risk becoming melancholic again. . . . But what's to be done? She's there and I'm here. If by chance you know anyone who's going to Málaga, I would greatly appreciate it if they'd speak to her for a moment and report their impressions to you. I know that won't help me any because even if she is in a perfect state, she couldn't go to Tangier and live in the apartment completely alone. What a problem. . . .

Shortly afterward Paul received a letter from Dr. Ortiz, saying that Jane's condition was much improved and that she was waiting for his return to go back to Tangier with him. Paul wrote to Dr. Roux about bringing Jane back and Dr. Roux advised strongly against it. She told him that he would not be able to give Jane the treatment that she needed, and that her condition would deteriorate.

In February 1969, after the school term was over, Paul returned to Tangier. He went to see Dr. Roux, who again tried to persuade him not to take Jane out of the clinic. "But she wants so badly to come home," he told her. When he went to Málaga to see Jane, as before, she begged him to take her with him. "But you weren't happy in Tangier, Jane," he said. "Happy, what's happy?" she answered. And so he took her back to Tangier.

When he got back to the Inmeuble Itesa, he left Jane in the car and went upstairs to see Cherifa, who with Aicha and Aicha's child had continued to live in Jane's apartment while she was in Málaga. He told her the doctor said she couldn't be in the house when Jane came back. " 'And Jane's arrived,' I said. I remember Cherifa said in a loud horrible voice, 'The bride has arrived,' and her eyes were narrow and fierce. I said, 'You have to leave so

Jane can come in.' 'You'll find out about this later,' she said and she left. When she was gone I took Aicha and went down and got Jane and we brought her up in the elevator. I told her I was getting rid of Cherifa and she was relieved."

But Dr. Roux's predictions were correct. Jane soon fell into a state of melancholy. She spent most of the time lying on the floor of the living room in Paul's apartment, looking at him, saying nothing. If she did speak, she would ask anyone who came if they would help her kill herself. She would ask for poison. She would say, "I want to die, but no one will help me. I know what's going to happen to me and I want to die before that."

Her physical condition was deteriorating rapidly. She had great difficulty moving by herself. The women who were working for her helped her out of bed and helped her to walk. At one point she apparently tried to throw herself out of the window of the apartment, but the sill was too high for her to climb onto it.

"And yet," says Paul, "I felt she didn't have a will to die. I always wondered if she were given something, whether she would do it. Would she have taken it? But I couldn't play around that way, of course. And I became an enemy more than ever because, although I sympathized with her desire to die and she knew I did, yet I couldn't admit it and I had to say, 'But naturally, no one's going to give you anything, Jane.' And yet if we'd been alone on a desert island, I probably would have given it to her."

During the four months that Jane spent in Tangier she did leave the house on occasion. Andreas Brown remembers going to a performance of *The Bacchae* at the American School, for which Paul had written the music. "Jane came to the performance, dressed in a beautiful caftan. She was very nervous, though everyone was excited about seeing her. David Herbert gave a dinner party that night to which she came. She said, 'Maybe I shouldn't stay, maybe people don't want me here.' But David was insistent and she stayed."

Once while he was visiting, Andreas went to the market with Jane. "The people in the market exploited her. She was disoriented and they tried to give her spoiled fruit."

According to Marguerite McBey, "The last time Jane was in Tangier, I felt she didn't want to stay. I couldn't bring myself to talk about what mattered. It was like putting a finger on a wound."

Joe McPhillips went to see Jane, remembering how lively she had been six years before. Now he saw her lying on the floor in Paul's living room, curled up into a small bundle, her feet inverted, her toes pointing toward each other.

Daniel Halpern, the editor of *Antaeus*, who was consulting with Paul about the magazine, was in Tangier that spring. "When anyone went out of the room and Jane and I were alone, she would say to me, 'Do you like me?'"

In a letter to Lawrence Stewart in May, Paul wrote that he had signed a contract with Putnam to write his autobiography.

> Taking care of Jane leaves me unable to work; I don't understand why. I suppose it's that having cast myself in the role of nurse I continuously play the part without meaning to. Unfortunately Jane is not improving; one would say she is determined not to. Three months have brought nothing good. If anything, she is even more distraught than when she came. . . .

Now Jane refused to eat. Paul kept trying to get her to take some food, telling her she must keep up her strength, but she refused him, and she began to refuse any medication. She would throw the medication on the floor and say, "I want to die. Please give me something so I can die."

Sometimes, Paul recalls, she would take medication or eat a small amount if Mrabet asked her to. "I think she thought it would have hurt him too much to refuse because he didn't understand. But she felt that I understood and that I was not helping her in the way she wanted to be helped."

David Herbert described Jane's last days in Tangier:

> Janie lay on the floor most of the day, staring at Paul. She would not eat and hardly spoke. There were still flashes of the old wit, but it was obvious she would have to return to the home. On her last evening I persuaded her, with great difficulty, to come out with me to dinner. She would only go to Guitta's Restaurant, where Mr. Guitta and his daughter Mercedes had served her for many years, and where we could eat quietly in the garden.
>
> Janie had taken great pains with her appearance as she knew how I loved her to look her best. Her hair was combed, her face made up and she was wearing her best black chiffon dress. By this time she could only walk with the help of two people, but she made a brave effort and we sat down to dinner. She was quite indifferent to what she ate.
>
> "Would you like a shrimp cocktail, Janie?"
>
> "What? Oh yes, if you like."
>
> "Would you then like lamb cutlets?"
>
> "All right."
>
> "What sort of wine would you like, red or white?"
>
> "Don't care."
>
> It was hard work but I talked away during the meal and at moments she responded.
>
> I was so happy to be with her again that I almost enjoyed myself.
>
> "What a lovely evening we've had, Janie. Just like the old days."

"Yes, wasn't it," said Janie, "except that I haven't opened my mouth once."

"Anyway, you are much better and I'm going to give a party for you."

"If you do, you'd better give it in the cemetery because I'm dead."

I realized that there was no point in prolonging the agony, as Janie was leaving with Paul in the morning. We thought she did not know this as he had decided not to tell her in case she worried all night. I dropped Janie home and said: "Good night, darling. I'll ring you in the morning."

"Do if you like," she replied, "but I shan't be here." And she quietly closed the door.

Although neither Paul nor anyone else had told her, she knew she was going back to Málaga, for the last time.

AFTER JANE'S RETURN TO THE CLÍNICA DE LOS ANGELES, PAUL WOULD VISIT her every six weeks or so, taking the ferry to Algeciras, then going by car to Málaga. He would go to the hospital and sit with Jane in her room. As he sat by her bed, she rarely spoke to him, only now and then saying, "Take me out of here."

In the spring of 1970 Jane had another stroke. One of the nuns told Paul that at a small party, a dance given for the patients, Jane began to dance "too wildly." The nuns stopped her and she became terribly excited and angry. Immediately afterward she had what the nun termed "a little accident."

"She made it happen," the nun said to Paul.

On June 11 Paul wrote to Libby after visiting Jane:

I got back from there a few days ago. Jane is in a terrible state. I don't think there is any hope that she will ever talk again, or move at all. The doctor seems to have abandoned hope, and says we can only wait. She did recognize me, I'm sure, but it was something far away and fleeting, the recognition. Everyone tells me she does not suffer, either physically or mentally, but *how* can one tell?

In early July, Narayan Kamalakar, the widower of Jane's late friend Sonya, was in Málaga and went to visit Jane. Narayan, a "holy man," was making a pilgrimage through Spain on foot. After seeing Jane, he wrote to Paul:

I won't be giving you a sudden shock when I say that Jane's condition is very bad. You saw her yourself not so long ago and are aware of this. I went to see the doctor the morning of the 3rd, but he did not show up and the nurse asked me to come again in the evening which I did and I saw him and had a long talk with him. He said it was better he was brutally frank and said he could hold out no hope and that inevitably Jane must now sink further to the point that she dies. You are aware of this and I am not suddenly shocking you in writing it. But what I did not realize till the doctor told me is that there is very little time now left. According to his knowledge and experience it is now only a matter of weeks or maybe a few months before Jane dies. I do not know, Paul, if you are aware of how little time is left.

The doctor then sent me on to the nuns that very evening. He telephoned them and I took a taxi from his office to the nuns. Hermana Asunción and a French/English-speaking lady called Lenore Werner* took me to Jane's room. Jane was not exactly in a coma but she was comatose. I stood for a while at the foot of Jane's bed and repeatedly said it was me Narayan come to see her, and, though she flickered her eyes and made vague sounds, that was all the response she made, and I am not sure that she was even aware she had a visitor. Hermana Asunción's and Mme Werner's efforts also were of no avail for me to establish contact with Jane and we had to give it up.

The two ladies then talked to me in another room. Although it seems cold-blooded on paper, I better put down the salient point of our talk as follows. It will be simpler and help you better if I put it down point by point:—

a) Jane is mostly in the comatose condition that I saw her in, but Mme Werner, who is the one who is now most with her and who actually looks after her, said that Jane is occasionally more lucid and aware, and that, at such moments, Mme Werner and she talk, and Mme Werner even reads to her. Both Mme Werner and Hermana Asunción said that Jane does not suffer mentally and that physically she is comfortable and not in pain.

b) Jane used to smoke a lot but she does not care for cigarettes now. Her appetite however is better and she eats all right.

c) Asunción first talked about the possibility of moving Jane back to Tangier and having her looked after in Tangier by a whole-time nurse, but when we discussed your situation, namely that though not poor you are not a millionaire and have to work hard at your writing to provide the means for looking after Jane, and secondly, you must find sufficient time undistracted for writing, and thirdly it would perhaps be risky and

---

*A patient who had been at the clinic for many years, who had recovered, but who stayed on.

certainly expensive and difficult to move Jane in her condition from here to Tangier, Asunción changed her mind and said perhaps it was better that they looked after Jane till she died.

d) Of course, this will occur to you automatically but I am just mentioning it as it occurs to me also that, in the above circumstances, it may be more practicable for *you* to move over to Málaga for the time that is left for Jane to live. Like that you will be here and not away. But this is something that only you can decide, namely if it is financially practicable for you to come stay here and work to meet any deadlines that you may have with publishers, etc. etc.

e) If I was a rich man I would defer my pilgrimage Paul and come right over to Tangier to you instead of writing all this cold-bloodedly. But my situation does not permit it, and apart from finance even passport-wise it is difficult, as I do not have a return visa to Morocco and it would take time to get a tourist visa etc. etc. However, and on the other hand, it is easy for me to get back to Málaga at short notice if *you* do come over to Málaga and need me at all as I shall be in the vicinity during the next 15 days and could get back quickly and cheaply by bus from Ronda to Málaga. I am leaving today for San Pedro de Alcantara and will spend 2 nights there. Then I will walk the mountain road, San Pedro de Alcantara to Ronda, 55 kilometers, which I estimate will take 4 days. So, a week from now I shall be in Ronda. . . .

f) Now, this is the most difficult thing to write cold-bloodedly and it is here I most wish I was with you physically and could say it instead of writing. But it is a situation that has to be faced, and since it is only *you* that can give the decision, I am obliged to write as follows:

As time is running out the decision has now to be made where Jane is to be buried when the time comes. Asunción raised the question and begged me to ask you to come to a decision. If the nuns do not have instructions from you at the time Jane dies they will be in a serious quandary and not know what to do, as people must be buried in Málaga the day they die, and thus there will be no time then for your instructions. The nuns want to do the right thing and avoid future sorrow and regret for you by burying Jane in the wrong cemetery. The situation at present is as follows:

1) Jane herself, when she was more lucid, had expressed a wish to be buried in the Protestant cemetery as you are Protestant.

2) When the Catholic priest who normally visits at the nuns was sick, he had asked his Jewish colleague to visit instead. The rabbi had tried to speak with Jane but she was not lucid at that time. The rabbi had then told the nuns that he was keen on Jane's being buried in the Jewish cemetery.

Thus, the problem is which cemetery? And the decisions can only be what *you* decide; and the decision should be sent to the nuns now.

So there! Paul that is all I can say. Except that my heart is with you, since I have the experience of Sonya's going 6 years ago and now 6 years later Jane is going, and they, Sonya and Jane, were close to each other, and in a week's time from now I will expect a letter from you waiting for me at Ronda when I arrive there telling me whether you want me to return to Málaga to you there, deferring my pilgrimage, or, whether I should continue on as you are unable to come now to Málaga.

Narayan

Despite what Narayan had said, Jane did not die in a few weeks. During the early fall she made the decision to convert to Catholicism. On the front of an envelope in a shaking hand she made a note to herself at this time:

When I begin Begin to feel too exalted I read one of Paul's poems. Even only a few lines brings me down to earth—earth.
List for here—the Commisseria
   dissen fectant
If possible go to that town that's near here
For Mother Superior 1 hun $200—100 for conversion

On the back of the envelope she wrote:

Ask the Mother to get my doctor for me—Speak to him abut the Jewish Faith and he [word unclear] it all beggan. . . .

It was the last thing she was ever to write.

When Paul came in October, Jane had converted. By this time she was blind. The nun showed this to Paul by passing her hand in front of Jane's eyes. There was no response. When Paul sat down next to her bed, she said to him, "You smell good." He understood that she was telling him she was blind. It was the only thing that was said between them about her blindness.

On his return to Tangier Paul wrote to Libby:

Jane lies out flat in bed. She cannot see, and she finds it hard to speak, but this time we were able to communicate because she was feeling better in general. (On my last visit she had grippe and was a little feverish.) Her mind seemed clear. (I don't know whether it's good or bad, but I suppose good.) She said her life was a tragedy, and she would not discuss her baptism to Catholicism. When I tried to see the religious medal she was wearing on a chain around her neck, she gently pushed my hand away, so I did not insist. At mealtimes she was fed spoonful by spoonful by a nurse, and she ate without any objections. (Here it was the most difficult part of all, persuading her to eat.) Of course she begged to come back here, or to go anywhere as long as it was out of the clinic. I promised her that as soon as she could walk I'd take her out. . . . The doctor says there is no therapy that can help because brain damage is irreversible. They do get Jane up and out of bed each morning, but she is very obstinate and does not cooperate, they complain. This is not surprising, as she has always been convinced that nothing can make her better. Nor do I blame her for not cooperating. I shouldn't myself under such circumstances. . . .

I know she would be very happy if you would write her. There is a woman who reads to her (mostly religious material) but she also reads letters if any arrive, and can translate from English. So *do* write her, please. Everyone imagines she is cut off from life, but she is hanging on very firmly, and is very aware. As I say, who knows whether it's better or worse thus? . . .

Paul had given his consent to the conversion—the nuns would not have accepted Jane otherwise—but he never believed it was a true conversion. He could not help suspecting that the nuns had exerted pressure on her. He felt disturbed by what he thought was their delight in her conversion and in the serenity they said it gave to her. When he visited, he noticed how when she let the cross drop from her hands, they would pick it up and put it in her hand again. It was another sign to him that she herself was not making the choice freely. Watching her he felt "that it was as though she were flying over an abyss. And then every once in a while when they'd come in and talk about Jesus, she'd look at me and smile and it was as if she were saying 'ossir.'"

When Jane's mother heard of the conversion, she would not believe it. She kept saying that Jane did not know what she was doing, that the conversion was not her own choice, that it was not the action of the real Jane. But in her early story "Plain Pleasures," Jane had written, "We each have only one single life which is our real life, starting at the cradle and ending at the grave."

From the time she was a child Jane had had the sense of sin—a sin that she could never define except to say that it was hers and original, that which separated her from others. Her life had been spent in the doubleness of the knowledge of that sin and the evasion of the knowledge. She had been obsessed by Elsie Dinsmore and yet had mocked Elsie's obedience to her father and her even greater obedience to Jesus. She had read Simone Weil's work over and over, feeling an identity with her, but then she had laughed and said, "But I have a sensual side too." For years she had spoken about sin and salvation—no one understood it. Most people thought it was Jane being funny, as when she'd said, "Most of all I want to be a religious leader," and then laughed and said, "But of course I'm not."

That sin which she took to be her destiny was inseparable from her imagination. Her writing became both the evidence of the sin and also—by some turn within her—the religious sacrifice that was its expiation. In her work, from the beginning, the themes of sin and salvation were unrelenting: in the words of Miss Goering as a child, baptizing Mary, "Dear God . . . make this girl Mary pure as Jesus Your Son"; in the words of Miss Goering at the end of her journey, ". . . is it possible that a part of me hidden from my sight is piling sin upon sin as fast as Mrs. Copperfield?"; in the words that tell of Sadie's life, "She conceived of her life as separate from herself; the road was laid out always a little ahead of her by sacred hands. . . ."

If in the earliest works there was a double edge—the sense of belief and the other side of belief, both present and united by her wiles—as the years went on, as her work became only unfinished work, the voices of sin and salvation became more urgent. "My life is *not* my own," Bozoe Flanner screams at Janet Murphy. "Have you missed the whole point of my life?" And of a woman in an unfinished play, Jane wrote: "She believes that she has a second heart and because she believes this she can accept a lie and protect it—Her wild clinging to this false trust is a result of her not wishing to discover that she has only one heart after all. . . . She guards her false trust in order not to fall into her single heart—The single heart is herself—it is suffering—it is God—it is nothing. . . ."

Now at the clinic at Málaga, blind, unable to move, most of the time unable to speak, she could no longer bear the burden of the sin. She accepted conversion to a God who, the nuns said, would take her sins upon Himself. And still she did not die.

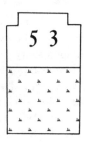

53

IN TANGIER PAUL WORKED TO FINISH *WITHOUT STOP-
ping*. Writing it was a painful process for him. In an autobiography there was
no escaping into another character as he did when he entered a fictional
world. Of Jane he said little in the book, a few words about their meeting,
about her work, about her illness. The book was criticized by reviewers for a
quality which they called detachment, yet there can hardly be an ending less
detached than the one he gave to the story of his life:

> I relish the idea that in the night all around me in my sleep, sorcery is
> burrowing its invisible tunnels in every direction, from thousands of
> senders to thousands of unsuspecting recipients. Spells are being cast,
> poison is running its course; souls are being dispossessed of parasitic
> pseudo-consciousnesses that lurk in the unguarded recesses of the
> mind. . . .
>
> Now, since I started this book, I stay in Tangier for months on end,
> choosing from among the vast number of fragments of memories
> unearthed those which can serve my purpose. The fragments are being
> used to reconstruct, piece by piece, a sequential skeleton, taking care
> not to force in any part that does not fit. As I see it, this precaution
> implies making the effort to reserve judgment and the resolve to give a
> minimum importance to personal attitudes. Writing an autobiography
> is an ungratifying occupation at best. It is a sort of journalism in which
> the report, rather than being an eyewitness account of the event, is
> instead only a memory of the last time it was recalled. . . . In my
> tale . . . there are no dramatic victories because there was no struggle. I
> hung on and waited. It seems to me that this must be what most people
> do. . . .
>
> The Moroccans claim that full participation in life demands the
> regular contemplation of death. I agree without reserve. Unfortunately
> I am unable to conceive of my own death without setting it in the far

more terrible *mise en scène* of old age. There I am without teeth, unable to move, wholly dependent upon someone whom I pay to take care of me and who at any moment may go out of the room and never return. . . .

" 'Goodbye,' says the dying man to the mirror they hold in front of him. 'We won't be seeing each other any more.' " When I quoted Valéry's epigram in *The Sheltering Sky*, it seemed a poignant bit of fantasy. Now, because I no longer imagine myself as an onlooker at the scene, but instead as the principal protagonist, it strikes me as repugnant. To make it right, the dying man would have to add two words to his little farewell, and they are: "Thank God!"

When he returned to Málaga he sat and waited at her bedside for some sign that Jane was aware. She had always said, "I am at the mercy of . . ." and now he had to sit beside her and see her at the mercy of what he could not know. It is as if he were required to be witness to a process being conducted behind an insuperable barrier. He had spent his life protecting himself against others, behind a barrier he himself had labeled "indifference," in order to be able to do the work he felt he must do. Yes, he had admitted he was selfish, but what was life for? "Someone who writes, who creates something—if he doesn't live for himself, how can he do that work?"

But now in Málaga he sat by her bedside and waited for some sign of recognition, sure that she knew he was there. They were bound together in the austere room, he who loved the night, she who cared for the day, he who refused to judge or be judged, she who felt herself always judged, he who insisted on the separation of life from work, she who could make no separation, she who had spoken to him of sin, he who had said, "But what do you mean? I know the words you're saying, but what do you mean?"—he whom she had once called her enemy.

In *The Sheltering Sky*, Kit had sat beside Port's bed, hating his illness, thinking he had stopped "being human." But Paul, sitting at Jane's bedside, waited for signs that it was not the "meaningless hegemony of the involuntary." He believed that she was aware of everything. When he saw the nuns act as if Jane didn't understand anything, he became very disturbed. He felt that it was they who did not understand her.

In June 1971 Jane's mother and stepfather arrived in Málaga. Claire had not seen Jane for almost three years and was stunned by the change in her. Claire herself was not well. She had had a heart attack and moving about was a great effort for her. She and Julian stayed in a hotel in Málaga for several weeks. She sat at Jane's bedside, waiting for a sign of recognition, each day. The last day of her stay, she stood by Jane's bed and cried out, "Look at me, Jane, look at me."

Jane did not respond.

Claire returned to the United States with Julian and died on July 13, 1971.

In June of that year Libby Holman had died. In her will she left a trust of $72,000 to Jane, the income to be used for her care while she was alive. At her death the trust was to revert to the estate.

IN MARCH 1977 I WENT TO MÁLAGA. THE CLÍNICA DE LOS ANGELES IS situated on a hill overlooking the city. Beyond the city is the Mediterranean. Across the sea, some ninety miles distant, is Morocco.

I was led through a sunlit entry hall, where two nuns in white habits were speaking to a group of patients, to the office of Dr. Ortiz. A man with a massive wrinkled face, his body crippled by an arthritic disease, Dr. Ortiz was at his desk. With him in the dark wood-paneled room were Lenore Werner and Sister Mercedes, a nun who had helped care for Jane.

They spoke of Jane's last days in the clinic:

Dr. Ortiz: "Señora Bowles came here with an attack of schizophrenia. Her life was very limited here. Her husband came from time to time to see her. He was very devoted. Her schizophrenia may have come from the stroke, but perhaps there was a predisposition. Her treatment here was that she was given drugs to avoid the hallucinations. It was more hallucinations from the ear, from thinking she was in a wall. These voices said things to her and made her afraid of people. She had confidence in the doctor and the sisters. She wanted them around her all the time so she would not be hurt."

Sister Mercedes: "Often the sisters sent Lenore to be with her because they could not be with her. She asked for Lenore all the time."

Lenore Werner: "We called her Juanita. She did suffer very much. When she first came here, she didn't speak very much, but then she got better and went to Tangier. The doctor said not to take her, but she wanted to go and her husband didn't want to go against her."

Dr. Ortiz: "When she came back here, she was much worse. At the end, we couldn't tell if she saw or not, her relationship to the exterior world was so limited."

Lenore Werner: "Later she lost her reason. At the last, there was nothing. She said nothing. She was like a baby."

Sister Mercedes: "It was very hard for her here at first. She was upset not to be able to drink. She wanted to drink sometimes. She smoked a lot. We had to be careful because sometimes she would let the lighted cigarette burn her finger."

Dr. Ortiz: "When she saw the sisters had such a love for her, then she wanted to join them in their prayers. The sisters were so glad. The conversion was not forced. The sisters were so kind and loving to her. It was like an admiration in her that she had to see how they were at peace and could love others. And she was very thankful after the conversion."

Sister Mercedes: "She asked for a long time to be a Catholic and at first the sisters would not agree. They always said, 'Better consult your husband.' And her husband said, 'Do whatever she wants.' So the sisters accepted and baptized her. In her calm moments she was very happy and satisfied about her conversion. She was sorry, she said, for having been in a 'field of existentialists.' She would say she was sorry to have belonged among those who did not believe in God. She thought she had had a good life, though now she was not very happy. All the patients liked her and the people who worked at the clinic. She needed that love.

"Once when her mother came she took her out for a walk. Her mother was very elegant. Jane said she herself was very rich. She said she had a sister."

Lenore Werner: "I don't remember her saying that. Earlier she talked about her writing. She said the book she liked the most was about a house burned in a fire, and she said it was going to pass into the movies. Later, she only wanted to talk English and I was the only one who could speak English. I only remember that she told me that she lived in an elegant apartment in Paris and was very happy with her husband. Generally she knew me, though sometimes she did not. Often she would call for me. She was very appreciative of others and what they did for her."

Sister Mercedes: "Often she spoke to herself and nobody knew what she said. Nobody understood. Sometimes she said something in Spanish against an Arab and about her leg. She said the Arab had left her leg in that way. We decided it was part of the hallucinations. She spoke of some drugs of the Arabs. She kept saying that. It was an obsession. Sometimes she was saying that because she came to Morocco from the U.S., that was why she was sick. She had many clear moments and she said she liked nature very much. We thought she meant the sky, the world. We were not sure. Sometimes she would get very bad, very upset, and then, after a while, she would become calm. She always rejected food. We had to persuade her to take it. At the end she could not speak or take care of herself at all."

They called it schizophrenia: she would have said she had fallen into "the single heart."

ON THE EVENING OF MAY 3, 1973, PAUL RECEIVED A TELEGRAM FROM the clinic, asking him to come to Málaga at once. The next day he took the seven o'clock ferry to Algeciras and arrived at Málaga about noon. At the clinic he found Jane unconscious. She had had another stroke on April 30. He stayed with her that afternoon and in the evening went back to the hotel. At nine o'clock the mother superior called him. Jane was dead.

Miriam Levy was in Málaga that day. She had come to Spain on vacation with her husband. She had not seen Jane since 1953, but had heard that she was ill in a hospital in Málaga. All day she went from hospital to hospital looking for Jane. And again the next day she tried to find her. "We kept looking and looking and we couldn't find her. But I felt I had to find her."

On the sixth of May she and her husband went to Algeciras and took the ferry to Tangier, hoping to locate Paul. When they arrived, they could not find his name in the phone book. They kept searching through the center of the city for someone who could help them. In the market they saw a man who was obviously an American: it was Boo Faulkner. He told Miriam that Paul had just returned from Málaga, and that Jane had died.

AFTERWORD

Jane is buried in the San Miguel cemetery in
Málaga in an unmarked grave. Since it is a Catholic cemetery, only stones
with crosses upon them are permitted. But Paul will not put a cross on Jane's
grave. He is not convinced that Jane truly converted. Besides, he adds, "As
far as I'm concerned she has no grave. I don't believe in cemeteries or graves.
For what? For mourning? For getting over it? You never get over it. It's
always with you. At least I don't, because it's disconnected me. I think I
lived vicariously largely and didn't know it. And when I had no one to live
through or for, I was disconnected from life."

He continues to live in the Inmeuble Itesa, where he and Jane had flats
one above the other. He lives a daily life almost ritualistic in its discipline,
going with his driver Abdelouahaid Boulaich each day to the market, to the
post office, returning home to see visitors for tea, then working late into the
night. In the years immediately following Jane's death, he worked on
translations, primarily of the works of Mohammed Mrabet and of Mohammed Choukri. Now he is once again working on his own fiction.

In 1975 he wrote a poem called "Next to Nothing."

> *At first there was mud, and the sound of breathing,*
> *and no one was sure of where we were.*
> *When we found out, it was much too late.*
> *Now nothing can happen save as it has to happen.*
> *And then I was alone, and it did not matter.*
> *Only because by that time nothing could matter. . . .*
>
> . . .
>
> *We thought there were other ways.*
> *The darkness would stay outside.*
> *We are not it, we said. It is not in us. . . .*

. . .

There was a time when life went along brighter lines.
We still drank the water from the lake,
and the bucket came up cold
and sweet with the smell of deep water.
The song was everywhere that year, an absurd refrain:
It's only that it seems so long, and isn't.
It's only that it seems so many years,
and perhaps it's one.
When the trees were there I cared that they were there,
and now they are gone.
On our way out we used the path that goes around the swamp.
When we started back the tide had risen.
There was another way, but it was far above and hard to get to.
And so we waited here, and everything is still the same.

. . .

There were many things I wanted to say to you
before you left, and now I shall never say them.
Though the light spills onto the balcony
making the same shadows in the same places,
only I can see it, only I can hear the wind
and it is much too loud.
The world seethes with words. Forgive me . . .

In late May 1973 Tennessee Williams was in New York in the office of his agent Bill Barnes. Audrey Wood, who is with the same firm, sent a note in to Tennessee. It was a letter to her from Paul, telling of Jane's death. Reading it, he became distraught. Then he wanted to know why there had been no mention of Jane's death in any American paper. He called Clive Barnes at *The New York Times* to say that they must run an obituary. Tennessee was unable to continue speaking, so Bill Barnes took over for him.

On May 31 the *Times* published an obituary that quoted John Ashbery's review of *The Collected Works*:

It is to be hoped that she will be recognized for what she is: one of the finest modern writers of fiction, in any language. At the same time it should be pointed out that she is not quite the sort of writer that her imposing list of Establishment admirers seem to suggest. Her work is unrelated to theirs, and in fact it stands alone in contemporary literature. . . .

Jane's work was reissued in 1978 as *My Sister's Hand in Mine*. Yet she remains a figure outside of the mainstream of contemporary American literature. It is true that there is something mysterious in her work, something unsettling in its originality, something separating in her odd sense of sin. Her preoccupations with sin and salvation have a curious resemblance to the paradoxical and disturbing thought of the medieval Jewish mystics, the Kabbalists. Yet she was no Kabbalist in the intensity of her passion for life as life, without reference to any other world beyond this world. ". . . don't you know me?" she wrote. "I am Bozoe Flanner—I am exiled from the earth and I love the earth."

Despite her oddness, despite her originality, she wrote finally of what is common to us all: of that place within ourselves where we are at one and the same time masculine and feminine, childlike and powerful, aged and just beginning, of that place where we go to death and we hold on to life.

CHRONOLOGY
AND
PUBLICATIONS

CHRONOLOGY
OF THE LIFE
OF JANE BOWLES

1917	Born February 22 in New York City, daughter of Sidney Auer and Claire Stajer Auer.
1927	Auer family moves to Woodmere, Long Island.
1930	Sidney Auer dies. Jane and her mother return to New York City.
1931	Jane attends Stoneleigh. Falls from a horse and breaks her leg.
1932–34	Treatment for tuberculosis of the knee in a sanatorium in Leysin, Switzerland.
1934	Returns to New York City to live.
1935	Operation performed to permanently stiffen the knee joint.
1935–36	Writes *Le Phaéton Hypocrite* (manuscript lost).
1937	Meets composer Paul Bowles. Travels to Mexico with Paul and Khristians Tonny and Tonny's wife, Marie Claire.
1938	Marries Paul Bowles. Honeymoon trip to Central America and Paris. Begins work on *Two Serious Ladies*.
1940	Goes to Mexico with Paul and Robert Faulkner. Meets Helvetia Perkins in Taxco.
1941	Lives on Middagh Street in Brooklyn with Paul. Returns to Mexico with him. Finishes *Two Serious Ladies*.
1942	Returns to U.S. with Helvetia Perkins.
1943	*Two Serious Ladies* published by Knopf.
1944	"A Guatemalan Idyll" published.
1945	"A Day in the Open" published. *A Quarreling Pair*, puppet play, performed.
1946	"Plain Pleasures" published.
1947	Paul's "A Distant Episode" published. First act of *In the Summer House* published. Paul goes to Morocco. He completes "Pages from Cold Point."
1948	Jane goes to Morocco. Meets Cherifa. Paul completes *The Sheltering Sky*. Jane completes "Camp Cataract."
1949	Jane completes "A Stick of Green Candy." "Camp Cataract" published.

The Sheltering Sky published in England. Jane in Paris with Cory, working on *Out in the World*.

1950 Paul's *The Delicate Prey and Other Stories* published.

1951 "East Side: North Africa" published. Jane returns to Tangier. *In the Summer House* produced at the Hedgerow Theater.

1952 Jane goes to New York. Paul's *Let It Come Down* published.

1953 *In the Summer House* produced in Ann Arbor, Michigan, and in New York.

1954 Jane returns to Tangier. She goes to Ceylon with Paul and Ahmed Yacoubi.

1955 Jane returns to Tangier. Paul's *The Spider's House* published.

1956 Jane transfers house to Cherifa. Cherifa moves into apartment with Jane. Paul goes to Ceylon.

1957 "A Stick of Green Candy" published. Jane suffers a stroke and goes to England for treatment.

1958 Jane and Paul go to Madeira. Jane goes to New York and is hospitalized in White Plains. She returns to Tangier with Paul.

1965 *Two Serious Ladies* published in England. Paul's *Up Above the World* published.

1966 *Plain Pleasures* published in England. *The Collected Works of Jane Bowles* published in U.S.

1967 Jane institutionalized in a psychiatric hospital in Málaga.

1968 Enters the Clínica de Los Angeles in Málaga.

1969 Returns to Tangier. After four months goes back to the Clínica de los Angeles.

1973 Dies May 4 at Clínica de los Angeles.

PUBLICATIONS
OF JANE BOWLES

Two Serious Ladies. Knopf 1943.

"A Guatemalan Idyll." *Cross Section 1944*. Edited by Edwin Seaver.

"A Day in the Open." *Cross Section 1945*. Edited by Edwin Seaver.

"Plain Pleasures." *Harper's Bazaar*. February 1946.

In the Summer House (Act I). *Harper's Bazaar*. April 1947.

"Camp Cataract." *Harper's Bazaar*. September 1949.

"East Side: North Africa." *Mademoiselle*. April 1951.

In the Summer House. *Best Plays of 1953–1954*. Edited by Louis Kronenberger. Dodd, Mead 1954.

"A Stick of Green Candy." *Vogue*. February 15, 1957.

Two Serious Ladies. London: Peter Owen 1965.

Plain Pleasures. London: Peter Owen 1966.

The Collected Works of Jane Bowles. Farrar, Straus and Giroux 1966.

Feminine Wiles. Black Sparrow Press 1976.

My Sister's Hand in Mine (an expanded edition of the *Collected Works*). Ecco Press 1978.

NOTES

NOTES

The following abbreviations are used:

JB   Jane Bowles

PB   Paul Bowles

DP   *The Delicate Prey and Other Stories*, Paul Bowles, Random House, 1950

FW   *Feminine Wiles*, Jane Bowles, Black Sparrow Press, 1976

MSHIM   *My Sister's Hand in Mine*, Jane Bowles, Ecco Press, 1978

WS   *Without Stopping*, Paul Bowles, G.P. Putnam's Sons, 1972

HRC   Humanities Research Center, University of Texas at Austin

MMLBU   Mugar Memorial Library, Boston University

MLYU-VTA   Music Library, Yale University, Virgil Thomson Archive

Note: In Jane Bowles's letters prior to 1957 occasional and inconsistent errors in spelling and misleading punctuation have been silently corrected. Errors in letters after April 1957 have not been changed. These later errors were connected to her illness and were of great concern to her. The letter on page 703, taken from previously published material, does not show these later errors.

(All letters not otherwise cited are used with permission.)

page   CHAPTER 1

7   To Mir: autograph album belonging to Miriam Levy.

8   "My cousin Jane: unpublished draft in possession of Robert Saltzer.

     CHAPTER 2

16   "I don't want: Martha Finley, *Elsie Dinsmore* (Chicago: M. A. Donahue, n.d.), p. 104.

16   "All you ever: Ibid., p. 107.

17   "The darling: Ibid., p. 263.

17   "It's a very little: Ibid., p. 281. (Italics in quoted text.)

page   CHAPTER 3
20   "Escapism is the big: notebook 23, HRC.

CHAPTER 4
25   "a fairly small: Elizabeth Bohning to author, August 2, 1977.
25   "I'm afraid: Elizabeth Bohning to author, February 13, 1978.
25   "rather withdrawn: Elizabeth Bohning to author, July 22, 1977.
25   When I was little: *FW*, p. 35.

CHAPTER 5
27   "I was neither: John Wakeman, ed., *World Authors 1950–1970* (New York: H. W. Wilson, 1975), p. 203.
29   Dear George: JB to George McMillan, undated.
31   "She seemed very: Miriam Levy to author, June 8, 1977.
32   "Instead of a belt: Wakeman, *World Authors*, p. 203.
33   I find myself: JB to Miriam Levy, undated.

CHAPTER 6
36   Dear Spivy: JB to Spivy LeVoe, January 29, 1937.
37   For Heaven's sake: JB to Miriam Levy, undated.
38   He came home: *WS*, pp. 38–39.
38   "I became: Ibid., p. 17.
39   "Nothing's so much: Ibid., p. 43.
39   "a registering consciousness: Ibid., pp. 52–53.
39   One evening: Ibid., p. 59.
40   Far down below: PB, "The Waterfall," *The Oracle* (May 1926), p. 41.
40   "It evokes more: PB, in *The Oracle* (November 1927), p. 22.
40   "This strange disease: a quote from Matthew Arnold's, "The Scholar Gypsy."
40   It was a pleasant: Paul Bowles, undated fragment, HRC.
41   knew at once: *WS*, pp. 77–78.

CHAPTER 7
43   "sweet and natural": notebook 38, HRC.
44   "Relationships with other: *WS*, p. 69.
45   Wish that you: PB to Virgil Thomson, undated, MLYU-VTA. (Translated from the French.)
46   It was nearing: notebook 26, HRC.
48   My darling: JB to Miriam Levy, undated.
48   My mother: John Wakeman, ed., *World Authors 1950–1970* (New York: H. W. Wilson, 1975), p. 203.

page	CHAPTER 8
49	"We must have: _WS_, p. 205.
50	"Jane and I: Ibid., p. 107.
50	"From fantasy: Ibid.
50	"I can still: David Diamond to author, June 15, 1977.
51	They got into: _MSHIM_, pp. 37–39.
52	"We got in touch: _WS_, p. 208.
53	"Its favorite word: PB, _Their Heads Are Green and Their Hands Are Blue_ (New York: Random House, 1963), p. 161.

	CHAPTER 9
56	In Central America: _WS_, p. 210.
57	Jane and I: Ibid., p. 211.
57	"Please let's not discuss: _MSHIM_, pp. 66–70.
58	"I hope his day: Ibid., p. 68.
58–59	Quotations from "Call at Corazon": _DP_, pp. 60–77.
59	"Once I got: _WS_, p. 211.
59	. . . at the age: Ibid., pp. 104–5.
60	She had started: unnumbered notebook.

	CHAPTER 10
62	We were now: _WS_, p. 213.
64	The investigator came: Ibid., p. 214.
64	"I knew what: Ibid., p. 215.

	CHAPTER 11
75	There was a: _MSHIM_, p. 13.
76	" 'Not this time: Ibid., p. 124.
76	"She even felt: Ibid., p. 129.
77	"I suspected: _WS_, p. 217.
77	Dear Mary Oliver: JB to Mary Oliver, undated, from the Katherine Cowen DeBaillou Collection, University of Georgia Libraries, Special Collection.
78	"quantity of alcohol: _WS_, p. 218.
79	. . . I am asking: JB to Charles Henri Ford, undated, HRC.
79	"Jane came several: _WS_, pp. 218–19.

	CHAPTER 12
81	. . . they were a: _WS_, p. 216.
81	I had hoped: Ibid., p. 222.
82	"As we sped: Ibid., p. 224.
82	"I don't have: _MSHIM_, p. 62.

83   I was for: *WS*, p. 225.

84   It was a: Ibid., pp. 226–27.

85   "If she slept: Ibid., p. 229.

86   They were staying: Tennessee Williams, *Memoirs* (Garden City, New York: Doubleday, 1975), p. 59.

CHAPTER 13

90   "strange, very tender: Gordon Sager, *Run Sheep Run* (New York: Vanguard Press, 1950), p. 70.

90   the feeling of: Ibid., p. 55.

91   "All her: Ibid., p. 64.

91   "I think the: Ibid., p. 65.

92   "I once was: *MSHIM*, p. 49.

94   Lincoln had made: *WS*, p. 233.

CHAPTER 14

96   The surface of: *WS*, p. 235.

96   "overlooking an abyss: Ibid., p. 236.

97   The old, accustomed: PB to Virgil Thomson, July 27, 1941, MLYU-VTA.

98   The hatred of: *WS*, p. 239.

CHAPTER 15

99   "going through many: *MSHIM*, p. 216.

99   "no better liked: Ibid., p. 8.

100   "when people believed: Ibid., p. 40.

100   "find a nest: Ibid.

100   "True enough: Ibid., p. 197.

100   "You used to: Ibid., p. 198.

101   "Certainly I am: Ibid., p. 201.

101   This latter possibility: Ibid.

101   "One must allow: Ibid., p. 154.

101   "Now," she said: Ibid., p. 71.

102   "an old dream: Ibid. p. 40 / 222 "things I have: Ibid.

102   "It's not for: Ibid., p. 6.

102   "It is not: Ibid., p. 124.

102   "I can't stand: Ibid., p. 191.

102   I do not: Ibid., pp. 110–11.

104   "All right: Ibid., p. 193.

105–06   All quotations from unnumbered notebook.

CHAPTER 16

108   "Now lie on: *MSHIM*, pp. 97–98.

110   "Farther from the Heart": retitled "Song of an Old Woman," lyrics by JB, music by PB, copyright 1946, G. Schirmer, ms. at HRC.
110   I have been ill: PB to Virgil Thomson, undated, MLYU-VTA.
112   Very early one: *WS*, p. 248.
113   We had never: Ibid., p. 251.
117–18 Quotations from *A Quarreling Pair*: *MSHIM*, pp. 414–19. (*A Quarreling Pair* was first performed in September 1945 with puppets by Kurt Seligman and music by PB.)

CHAPTER 17
119   I will write: notebook 38, HRC.
121   got hold of: *WS*, p. 257.

CHAPTER 18
127   The dangerous thing: notebook 27, HRC.
127   There is a: notebook 25, HRC.
127   Tommy falls in: unnumbered notebook in the possession of PB.
128   "of an extraordinary: *MSHIM*, p. 299.
128   "equally reserved: Ibid.
128   "Don't you think: Ibid., p. 301.
128   The tables were: Ibid., p. 312.
129   While she sat: notebook 27, HRC.
130   I waited where: Ibid.

CHAPTER 19
133   "a territory I: *WS*, p. 259.
133   ". . . Then you would: notebook 35, HRC.
133   the world was: *WS*, p. 262.
134   Little by little: *WS*, pp. 261–62.
134   Then she realized: *DP*, p. 162.
135   "Poets have ears: "The Jazz Ear," *View*, (April 1943), p. 28.
136   The room was: *WS*, p. 9.
136   The soldier watched: *DP*, pp. 306–7.
136   This dream was: *WS*, p. 274.
137   The morning of: *WS*, pp. 275–76.
138–39 Quotations from "Pages from Cold Point": *DP*, pp. 175–205.
139   Paul Bowles opened: Norman Mailer, *Advertisements for Myself* (New York: G. P. Putnam's, 1959), p. 468.

CHAPTER 20
141–42 Uncited quotations: JB to PB, undated letters, HRC.
142   His head ached: notebook 26, HRC.
146   "Don't my arguments: Ibid.

page   CHAPTER 21
148–52   All quotations: JB to PB, undated letters, HRC.

             CHAPTER 22
156   She had not: *WS*, p. 286.
156   After a half hour: Ibid., pp. 285–86.
157   I have been: PB to Peggy Glanville-Hicks, April 20, 1948.
158   "whenever I think: *In the Summer House, MSHIM*, p. 210.
158   My novel is: PB to Peggy Glanville-Hicks, May 10, 1948.
159   Dearest Bup: JB to PB, undated, HRC.

             CHAPTER 23
163   Dearest Bup: JB to PB, undated, HRC.
165   Dearest Bup: JB to PB, undated, HRC.

             CHAPTER 24
168–69   Quotations from "Camp Cataract": *MSHIM*, pp. 359–401.
170   Dearest Buppie: JB to PB, undated, HRC.
172   I have done: JB to PB, October 1, 1948, HRC.

             CHAPTER 25
174–77   Quotations from *The Sheltering Sky* are from the New Directions (New
             York, 1949) edition.
176   The structure and: *WS*, p. 278.

             CHAPTER 26
179   small, piquant: Tennessee Williams, foreword to *FW*, pp. 7–8.
180   "We arrived at: Tennessee Williams to Donald Windham, January 26,
             1949, in Donald Windham, ed., *Tennessee Williams' Letters to Donald
             Windham* (New York: Holt, Rinehart and Winston, 1977), p. 228.
180   "Morocco is: Ibid., p. 229.
180   Dearest Katharine and Natasha: JB to Katharine Hamill and Natasha von
             Hoershelman, undated. (A slightly altered version appears in *FW*, pp.
             63–4.)
182   When the rooms: JB to Katharine Hamill, undated.
182   Katharine dear: JB to Katharine Hamill, undated.
183   There were some: *WS*, p. 292.
183   "The summer proved: Ibid.
183–84   Quotations from "A Stick of Green Candy": *MSHIM*, pp. 420–31.

             CHAPTER 27
185   They had been: David Herbert, *Second Son* (London: Peter Owen, 1972),
             p. 123.

185 "an unpredictable marmoset: Ibid.

185 "tallish, fair: Ibid.

185 "They want to: *MSHIM*, p. 94.

186 I was not: *WS*, p. 293.

186 Do you know: Alice Toklas to W. G. and Mildred Rogers, November 7, 1949, in Edward Burns, ed., *Staying on Alone: Letters of Alice B. Toklas* (New York: Liveright, 1973), pp. 178–79.

187 I have never: JB to PB, undated.

187 I have miraculously: JB to PB, undated, in *FW*, p. 66.

188 . . . (the strain of: Ibid.

188 I had counted: JB to PB, undated.

188 "A help because: JB to PB, undated, in *FW*, p. 65.

189 My work went: Ibid.

189 The book, though: Ibid., pp. 68–69.

189 Yesterday the whole: JB to PB, undated.

190 I was wildly: Ibid.

190 So that will: Ibid.

191 Peggy took me: JB to PB, dated "Monday 13th" (1949).

191 This is not: JB to PB, undated, in *FW*, p. 67.

191 "no novel since: Alice Toklas to PB, February 22, 1950, in Burns, *Staying on Alone*, pp. 188–89.

191 I haven't seen: Ibid., p. 189.

CHAPTER 28

193 Dearest Paul: *MSHIM*, p. 445.

193 I want you: Ibid., p. 447.

194–96 All uncited quotations: notebook 23, HRC.

196 Automatically she: *MSHIM*, p. 449.

196 . . . the distinct: notebook 38, HRC.

CHAPTER 29

198 "Alice Toklas had: Wendell Wilcox to author, August 23, 1977.

200 "unbearable": Gore Vidal to author, January 14, 1977.

200 "I could never: Gore Vidal, "Selected Memories of the Glorious Bird and the Golden Age," *New York Review of Books* (February 5, 1976), p. 15.

200 "small room, where: Wendell Wilcox to author, August 23, 1977.

209 "Paul had the: Ibid.

209 "going on in: Alice Toklas to PB, July 12, 1950, HRC.

210 Jane Bowles's play: Alice Toklas to Samuel Steward, November 22, 1950, in Samuel M. Steward, ed., *Dear Sammy: Letters from Gertrude Stein and Alice B. Toklas* (Boston: Houghton Mifflin, 1977), p. 188.

210 "a very handsome: Wendell Wilcox to author, August 23, 1977.

210   When I reached: Jane Bowles, "East Side: North Africa," *Mademoiselle* (April 1951), p. 163.

211   pleasantly shabby: Truman Capote, introduction to *MSHIM*, p. vii.

211   "her spectacles: Ibid.

211   Jane is strange: Alice B. Toklas to Brion Gysin, February 26, 1952, in Edward Burns, ed., *Staying on Alone: Letters of Alice B. Toklas* (New York: Liveright, 1973), pp. 252–53.

CHAPTER 30

212   The memory this: PB to Peggy Glanville-Hicks, December 15, 1950.

212   Inside I am: PB to Peggy Glanville-Hicks, February 25, 1951.

213   This shocked me: *WS*, p. 307.

213   We nearly had: Ibid., pp. 308–9.

214   "Ahmed has been: PB to Peggy Glanville-Hicks, June 29, 1951.

215   She sees Tommy: notebook 35, HRC.

215   Theme of Andrew's life: Ibid.

215   "This is a book: notebook 36, HRC.

215   Agnes Leather can: notebook 35, HRC.

216   She could not: notebook 37, HRC.

216   "One night: PB to Peggy Glanville-Hicks, November 5, 1951.

216   "attacked by a: Ibid.

216   The show has: PB to Peggy Glanville-Hicks, December 12, 1951.

217   At the party: notebook 35, HRC.

217   Usually such unseasonable: Ibid.

218   "Her Siamese cat: PB to Peggy Glanville-Hicks, January 29, 1952.

CHAPTER 31

219   . . . [It] has more: Robert Gorham Davis, "A Relentless Drive Toward Doom," *The New York Times Book Review* (March 2, 1952), p. 1.

220   "Are you from: Paul Bowles, *Let It Come Down* (New York: Random House, 1952), p. 119.

220   I went to: *WS*, pp. 271–72.

221   "A whole generation: quoted in "Contributors," *Mademoiselle* (April 1951), p. 93.

224   Ahmed returned from: PB to Virgil Thomson, July 7, 1953, MLYU-VTA.

CHAPTER 32

227   a piece of: Telegram from Tennessee Williams to Mendelssohn Theater, to be used for publicity purposes. From the Michigan Historical Collection, Bentley Historical Library of the University of Michigan at Ann Arbor.

227   All the efforts: Harvey Taylor, *Detroit Times*, May 20, 1953.

227   The chief weakness: Harvey Taylor, *Detroit Times*, May 24, 1953.

227   *In the Summer House:* Russell McLaughlin, *Detroit News*, May 20, 1953.

228   "somewhere on the: *MSHIM*, p. 207.

228   "a beautiful: Ibid.

228   "You can't even: Ibid., p. 208.

229   "You were my: Ibid., p. 209.

229   "strangest feeling: Ibid., p. 210.

230   "conviction that his: *MSHIM*, p. 436.

232   It is going: Brooks Atkinson, *The New York Times*, December 30, 1953.

234   "sweet and natural": notebook 38, HRC.

234   Jane Bowles's play: Alice Toklas to James Merrill, February 22, 1954, in Edward Burns, ed., *Staying on Alone: Letters of Alice B. Toklas* (New York: Liveright, 1973), p. 298.

234   When I asked: Alice B. Toklas to Mercedes de Acosta, February 24, 1954: Ibid., p. 299.

235   "There's no point: *Vogue* (May 1, 1954), p. 137.

CHAPTER 33

237   The fear of becoming: reprinted in Walter Kerr, *Pieces of Eight* (New York: E. P. Dutton, 1968), p. 156.

238   She believes that: notebook 32, HRC.

238   The double heart: unnumbered notebook, in the possession of PB. Published in a slightly altered version as "Curls and a Quiet Country Face," *FW*, p. 70.

CHAPTER 34

240   Darling Natasha and Katharine: JB to Katharine Hamill and Natasha von Hoershelman, undated. Published in a shorter version in *FW*, p. 70.

CHAPTER 36

256   "The whole civilization: notebook 22, HRC. Published in a slightly shortened form as "The Iron Table," *MSHIM*, pp. 465–67.

CHAPTER 37

259   When we got: *WS*, p. 325.

260   "staid members of: Ibid., p. 326.

261   What she did: based on an interview with Dr. Thomas Gonda, Professor and Chairman of the Department of Psychiatry at Stanford University School of Medicine.

261   Paul Bowles had: Peggy Guggenheim, *Confessions of an Art Addict* (New York: Macmillan, 1960), pp. 151–52.

263   Three letters arrived: PB to JB, February 24, 1955, HRC.

page CHAPTER 38
264   Dearest Bupple: JB to PB, undated, in *FW*, pp. 76–80.
267   What a shame: PB to JB, April 25, 1955, HRC.

        CHAPTER 39
271   He says he: PB to JB, March 25, 1956, HRC.
271   I don't know: PB to JB, undated, HRC.
273   This plan, preposterous: notebook 39, HRC.
276   Beryl Jane fights: notebook 29, HRC.
276   "I'm asking you: Ibid.
276   Beryl Jane: Gabriel: *FW*, pp. 43–44.
276   Dear Bubble: notebook 23, HRC.
277   I have been: JB to PB, February 1, 1957.
279   Dear Paul: JB to PB, February 1957, in *FW*, pp. 81–82.
280   I should have: PB to JB, March 2, 1957, HRC.
280   I do think: Audrey Wood to JB, March 11, 1957. . . . I haven't started: PB to JB, April 6, 1957, HRC.

        CHAPTER 40
286   "that genius imp: Truman Capote, "Answered Prayers," *Esquire* (May 1976), p. 128.
287   woman is: Edward Westermarck, *Ritual and Belief in Morocco*, vol. 2 (London: Macmillan, 1926), p. 5.
287   uncleanness: Ibid., p. 3.
287   old women: Ibid., p. 7.
288   I cabled you: Libby Holman to JB, May 2, 1957, HRC.
289   The typed letter: Libby Holman to JB, June 1, 1957, HRC.
289   She has no: PB to Peggy Glanville-Hicks, July 11, 1957.
291   On the ship: PB to Virgil Thomson, August 31, 1957, MLYU-VTA.
292   It is much: PB to Peggy Glanville-Hicks, September 3, 1957.
293   To communicate at all: PB to Virgil Thomson, September 10, 1957, MLYU-VTA.
294   I am on my: PB to Virgil Thomson, October 2, 1957, MLYU-VTA.
295   "It seems that: Dr. I. E. J. McLauchlan to author, July 30, 1979.
296   "partially because the: *WS*, p. 339.
296   Jane was just: PB to Peggy Glanville-Hicks, February 17, 1958.
296   I'm trying to: PB to Peggy Glanville-Hicks, March 8, 1958.

        CHAPTER 41
297   I have only: notebook 25, HRC.
298   ". . . if she doesn't: *MSHIM*, p. 302.
298   To think of: notebook 25, HRC.

299   "In collective egos: Ibid.

299   "I was born: notebook 24, HRC.

299   " 'Your life is: Ibid.

299   I am going: notebook 25, HRC.

299   I'm trying to: PB to Peggy Glanville-Hicks, March 29, 1958.

CHAPTER 42

302   What you say: PB to Katharine Hamill, April 26, 1958.

303   No news from: PB to JB, May 2, 1958, HRC.

304   Dearest Paul: JB to PB, undated.

307   "quick-tongued fragile: Patricia Bosworth, *Montgomery Clift* (New York: Harcourt Brace Jovanovich, 1978), p. 222.

307   "although I shuddered: PB to JB, May 14, 1958, HRC.

309   Dear Paul: JB to PB, undated, HRC.

CHAPTER 43

312–14   Uncited quotations from "Compositions Written During Her Illness," Jane Bowles Miscellaneous File, HRC.

315   "My mother and: PB to JB, undated, HRC.

316   Dearest Jane: Helvetia Perkins to JB, January 19, 1958, HRC.

325   Dear Virgil: PB to Virgil Thomson, December 27, 1958, MLYU-VTA.

CHAPTER 44

328   "Jane's strategy was: unpublished diary of Lawrence Stewart.

332   Dearest Janie: Pamela Stevenson to JB, May 9, 1962.

332   Dearest Libby: JB to Libby Holman, undated, in *FW*, pp. 83–85.

CHAPTER 45

336   Jane and I: *WS*, pp. 346–47.

338   I think it: PB to Rena Bowles, March 8, 1962, HRC.

339   Jane never did: PB to Rena Bowles, April 3, 1962, HRC.

339   Our combined worlds: *WS*, pp. 351–52.

339   At cocktail parties: Tennessee Williams, *Memoirs* (Garden City, New York: Doubleday, 1975), p. 187.

340   Characteristically, you: PB to JB, December 5, 1962, HRC.

340   First, however: PB to JB, December 11, 1962, HRC.

CHAPTER 46

343   Dearest Ruth: JB to Ruth Fainlight, undated.

344   very expensive but: JB to Ruth Fainlight, undated.

345   I am sad: JB to Ruth Fainlight, undated.

347   "I've returned the: Alfred Chester to JB, undated.

348   "Our friendship with: Rex Henry to author, June 28, 1977.

349   "He wanted to: PB to Rena Bowles, September 27, 1963.

350   Jane: I can't tell you: undated tape.

CHAPTER 47

354   "My wife and I: Rex Henry to author, June 28, 1977.

358   I speak to: JB to Isabelle Gerofi, undated.

358   I have never: JB to Ruth Fainlight, undated.

CHAPTER 48

360–62   All quotations from unfinished play from unnumbered notebook.

362   purely pleasurable pastime: *WS*, pp. 356–57.

363   Underneath the jovial: Paul Bowles, *Up Above the World* (London: Peter Owen, 1967), p. 88.

363   In India, you: Ibid., pp. 96–97.

364   "that soon there: Ibid., p. 107.

364   "I have never: *FW*, p. 35.

364   We are both: JB to Lawrence Stewart, February 1965.

364   "a friend of: Ibid.

364   My father seems: PB to JB, April 12, 1965, HRC.

365   Thank you for: JB to Frances, undated draft.

366   I seem to have: JB to Frances, undated draft.

366   Her fanatical secrecy: JB to Libby Holman, May 14, 1965.

367   The day before: PB to Virgil Thomson, June 21, 1965, MLYU-VTA.

368   I am really: JB to Libby Holman, August 26, 1965.

370   The depression after: JB to Libby Holman, April 1, 1966.

371   "She was short: Montgomery Orr to author, August 25, 1977.

CHAPTER 49

372   "there was no: *WS*, p. 358.

372   "Very likely the: Ibid., p. 361.

373   I don't see: JB to Hal Vursell, undated fragment.

373   I hope you've: Dr. Yvonne Marillier-Roux to JB, July 25, 1966. (Translated from the French.)

373   I miss you: Martha Ruspoli to JB, July 25, 1966.

373   No news from: Martha Ruspoli to JB, August 3, 1966.

374   I have been: JB to PB, August 9, 1966, HRC.

375   I have been: JB to Gordon Sager, undated.

376   Jane my angel: Claire Fuhs to JB, September 3, 1966.

376   Darling Jane: Claire Fuhs to JB, September 10, 1966.

377   Jane my angel: Claire Fuhs to JB, September 17, 1966.

377   Jane darling: Claire Fuhs to JB, September 25, 1966.

378   Jane my Angel: Claire Fuhs to JB, September 28, 1966.
378   Dearest Bup: JB to PB, undated, HRC.
380   Your letter was: JB to PB, September 28, 1966.
381   I'm very frightened: JB to PB, undated.
381   Martha has been: JB to PB, October 11, 1966.
382   Dear Jane: Carson McCullers to JB, October 14, 1966.
382   Dearest Carson: JB to Carson McCullers, undated fragment.
382   Jane my angel: Claire Fuhs to JB, October 14, 1966.
383   Dearest Libby: JB to Libby Holman, undated.
384   "I literally only: PB to JB, October 31, 1966.
384   I wouldn't be: PB to Libby Holman, December 9, 1966, MMLBU.
385   Darling Frances: JB to Frances, undated.
385   Dear Janie: Hal Vursell to JB, December 16, 1966.
385   I am afraid: JB to PB, undated.
386   Jane darling: Claire Fuhs to JB, January 1, 1967.
387   From the psychic: Dr. Yvonne Marillier-Roux to PB, January 9, 1967.
       (Translated from the French.)
387   Dr. Roux writes: PB to Libby Holman, January 20, 1967, MMLBU.

       CHAPTER 50
389   Darling: Claire Fuhs to JB, February 22, 1967.
390   Jane darling: Claire Fuhs to JB, March 10, 1967.
390   Jane my Angel: Claire Fuhs to JB, March 16, 1967.
391   Jane darling: Claire Fuhs to JB, March 30, 1967.
391   She could be: PB to Virgil Thomson, April 27, 1967, MLYU-VTA.
391   "As reading was: David Herbert, *Second Son* (London: Peter Owen, 1972),
       p. 127.
392   Unfortunately I have: PB to Virgil Thomson, June 1, 1967, MLYU-
       VTA.
392   "inferiority complex: Sister María Candelas to author, June 26, 1977.
       (Translated from the Spanish.)
392   "not enough . . . to: PB to William S. Gray, May 26, 1967.
392   "I'd been waiting: Written statement by Isabelle Gerofi. (Translated from
       the French.)
393   "I was unpopular: Jane Howard, "A Talk in the Casbah," *Washington Post
       Book Week*, March 19, 1978.
394   Jane darling: Claire Fuhs to JB, September 3, 1967.
394   The maid was: Interview with PB by Michael Rodgers, *Rolling Stone*, May
       23, 1974.
395   I feel guilt: Howard, "A Talk in the Casbah."
396   Jane may have: PB to Libby Holman, September 9, 1967, MMLBU.
396   As Jane recovers: Ibid.

396   Jane darling: Claire Fuhs to JB, October 10, 1967.

397   Jane had another: PB to Oliver Evans, November 13, 1967, HRC.

397   I started to "write": John Wakeman, ed., *World Authors 1950–1970*, (New York: H. W. Wilson, 1975), pp. 202–3.

CHAPTER 51

400   Darling Paul: JB to PB, undated.

401   Jane darling: Claire Fuhs to JB, January 9, 1968.

402   Dear Paul: JB to PB, undated.

402   Dearest Paul: JB to PB, undated.

403   Jane my darling: Claire Fuhs to JB, April 10, 1968.

403   Jane my darling: Claire Fuhs to JB, April 20, 1968.

404   Señora Jane Bowles: Dr. Antonio de Linares Pezzi to author, September 27, 1978. (Translated from the Spanish.)

404   "We had a letter: Mrs. Hall to author, October 7, 1978.

CHAPTER 52

406   "The sojourn was: *WS*, p. 368.

406   As you know: PB to Isabelle Gerofi, October 22, 1968. (Translated from the French.)

406   The correspondence with: PB to Libby Holman, November 19, 1968, MMLBU.

407   Jane's mother is: PB to Isabelle Gerofi, November 28, 1968. (Translated from the French.)

409   Taking care of: PB to Lawrence Stewart, May 28, 1969.

409   Janie lay on: David Herbert, *Second Son* (London: Peter Owen, 1972), pp. 127–28.

410   I got back: PB to Libby Holman, June 11, 1970, MMLBU.

410   I won't be giving: Narayan Kamalakar to PB, June 5, 1970.

413   When I begin: JB, undated fragment.

413   Jane lies out: PB to Libby Holman, October 11, 1970, MMLBU.

CHAPTER 53

416   I relish the: *WS*, pp. 369–70.

417   "being human: Paul Bowles, *The Sheltering Sky* (New York: New Directions, 1949), p. 214.

418   "Señora Bowles: This interview was conducted in Spanish. Joaquín Andreas acted as translator.

INDEX